Winner's Dinners

Winner's Dinners

Michael Winner

Cartoons by the author

Robson Books

WINNIE AT GORDON RAMSAY

This edition published in Great Britain in 2000 by Robson Books, 10 Blenheim Court, Brewery Road, London N7 9NT

A member of the Chrysalis Group plc

This edition first published in Great Britain in 2000 by Robson Books
Text and illustrations copyright © Michael Winner 2000
The right of Michael Winner to be identified as author of this work has been asserted by him in accordance with the Copyright, Designs and Patents Act 1988
Edited by Norma Macmillan

British Library Cataloguing in Publication Data
A catalogue record for this title is available from the British Library

ISBN 1 86105 358 4

Publisher's Note
Although this is not a conventional guide book, we have included as many addresses and telephone numbers as possible to help the reader. However, these and other details may have changed since the author's visit.

Typeset by SX Composing DTP, Rayleigh, Essex
Printed and bound in Great Britain by Bell & Bain Ltd, Glasgow

C O N T E N T S

WINNER'S AWARDS

BEST RESTAURANT IN THE WORLD: Harry's Bar, Venice
BEST RESTAURANT AMBIENCE IN THE WORLD: Downstairs at Harry's Bar, Venice
BEST COOKING IN THE UK: Gordon Ramsay
BEST RESTAURANTS IN THE UK: The Ivy?/Assaggi/San Lorenzo
RESTAURANT WHERE YOU SEE THE MOST PLASTIC SURGERY: San Lorenzo
BEST HOTELS IN THE WORLD: La Réserve de Beaulieu/The Splendido, Portofino
BEST HOTELS IN LONDON: The Dorchester/Claridges
BEST HOTEL OUTSIDE LONDON: Chewton Glen
WORST HOTEL ANYWHERE: Cliveden
BEST HOTEL SERVICE: The Oriental Bangkok
WORST HOTEL SERVICE: Cliveden
BEST AND BRIGHTEST PERSON IN UK CATERING: Marco Pierre White
BEST HOTEL MANAGER IN THE UK: Peter Crome, Chewton Glen
BEST HOTEL MANAGER OUTSIDE THE UK: Maurizio Saccani, The Splendido, The
  Splendido Mare and Villa San Michele
BEST HOTEL SUITE IN THE WORLD: 224-5 Cipriani, Venice
BEST WAITRESS IN THE WORLD: Pauola Prian, Assaggi
BEST RESTAURANT GREETER: Colin Smith, Chez Moi/Pietro Fraccari, Assaggi
BEST RECEPTIONIST IN THE WORLD: Mati Conejero, Belvedere, Criterion etc.
BEST WINE WAITER IN THE WORLD: Jean-Louis Valla, La Réserve de Beaulieu
NICEST CHEF IN THE WORLD: Robert Reid, The Oak Room
BEST RESTAURANT NEAR MY HOUSE: The Belvedere
MOST DISAPPOINTING RESTAURANT IN THE UK: The Waterside Inn
BEST RESTAURANT NEAR LONDON FOR A DAY OUT: The French Horn at Sonning
BEST TEA IN THE WORLD: The Mount Nelson, Capetown
RUNNERS UP FOR TEA: Claridges and Ston Easton near Bath
WORST SERVICE IN A RESTAURANT: Jean Christophe Novelli, Clerkenwell

SECOND WORST SERVICE EVER: The Pont de la Tour

THIRD WORST SERVICE EVER: Nobu

BEST SERVICE I EVER HAD: When Claridges sent a portion of pommes soufflé round to the Dorchester Grill for me

BEST EGYPTIAN MANAGING A JAPANESE RESTAURANT: Mohammed Ibrahim at Hiroko, Kensington

BEST GUEST RELATIONS MANAGER IN THE WORLD: Fausto Allegri, Hotel Splendido, Portofino

WORST CONCIERGES I EVER MET: The Plaza Athenee, Paris

PHONIEST RESTAURANT LINE: 'Your main course will be with you in a minute, sir'

BEST HAMBURGER: Sticky Fingers, Kensington

BEST FISH RESTAURANT IN THE WORLD: Tétou in Golfe Juan

BEST RESTAURANT THAT NO-ONE KNOWS: La Testiere, Venice

BEST CHOPPED LIVER MAKER: Matthew Norman's Mum Suzanne

BEST ICE CREAM IN THE UK: Harbour Bar, Scarborough

BEST ICE CREAM OUTSIDE THE UK: Miki, Santa Margherita

BEST EXCURSION EVER: The Road to Mandalay, Burma (Now Myanmar)

BEST INDIAN RESTAURANT: Zaika, Fulham Road

BEST CHINESE CHEF IN THE UK: Kam Po But, Memories of China, Pimlico

BEST JELLY: The Mirabelle

BEST VIEW FROM A RESTAURANT TABLE: The Grill, Hôtel de Paris, Monaco and La Tour d'Argent in Paris

BEST PIZZA: Guy Pizzeria in Venice

BEST AMBIENCE: Colombe d'Or, St Paul de Vence and Wandie's in Soweto, South Africa

WORST AMBIENCE: Tamarind, Mayfair

WORST MEAL I'VE EVER EATEN: The Eurostar train

WORST MAITRE D: Fred Serol, The Mirabelle

BEST VALUE: The Patio, Shepherd's Bush

BEST SET MENU: Locanda Dell'Isola Comacino, Lake Como and La Chaumière, Eze

HOTEL I'VE MOST ENJOYED STAYING AT: The Sandy Lane, Barbados.

HOTEL I'VE LEAST ENJOYED STAYING AT: The Malmaison, Glasgow

HOTEL I GOT OUT OF QUICKEST: The Normandy, Deauville

MOST WOBBLY TABLE I EVER SAW: L'Ortolan, Berkshire, and the food wasn't much either.

BEST WAFFLE: The Beverly Hills Coffee Shop

LONGEST I'VE EVER WAITED FOR A MAIN COURSE: The Oriental at the Dorchester

BEST PUB MEAL: The Churchill Arms, Paxford

WORST PUB MEAL: The Gwynn Arms, Glyntawe, Wales

TACKIEST PUB: The Mason Arms, Southleigh

GREATEST RESTAURATEUR OF ALL TIME: The late Jimmy Marks of Wiltons

BEST SPAGHETTI WITH MEAT SAUCE: Made by Sophia Loren in St Lucia

BEST SPAGHETTI WITH MEAT BALLS: Scalini, Walton Street

GREATEST LOSS TO UK RESTAURANT LIFE: The departure of Chris Corbin and Jeremy King from The Ivy, Le Caprice and Sheekey's

BEST LINE ABOUT FOOD I EVER HEARD: 'Michael, why do the unit always laugh when I eat on the set? They're always stuffing themselves!' Orson Welles in 1967

MW: "I DON'T WANT TO FRAME
IT, I CAME TO EAT IT!"

F O R E W O R D

For this updated version of last year's hardback book, the publishers have asked me to write a new foreword. So I looked at the original foreword and thought, with surprising modesty, 'This is really very good. Why am I writing a new one!'

I suppose something happened in the last year. The most significant food thing was the departure of Jeremy King and Christopher Corbin from the Ivy, Le Caprice and Sheekey's, three restaurants which were the cornerstone of my eating out in London and which had achieved a success unparalleled in the history of British catering. So although I give the Ivy Best Restaurant again, I put a question mark by it. Because I've never known any restaurant stay as good after the owners left. On the other hand, Wiltons after the death of the great Jimmy Marks still kept a very high standard. In the meantime I, and many others, wait for the return of Mr C and Mr K.

What strikes me most about food in this country is my inability to find it as good as food abroad. I know we're meant to be the cooking capital of the world. I accept that people like Gordon Ramsay produce a standard of cuisine that is astonishingly high. But this is specialist cooking. This is major-night-out cooking. This is not what we want as a general diet. The greatest 'general diet' country is Italy. There food on the whole is so fresh and so simply presented and the basic ingredients seem to be of such quality that I think it wipes out English food by a very long way. It also lacks plate decoration. I cannot recall ever in Italy seeing a yellow sauce with a red squiggle in it. That does nothing whatsoever to improve the taste of the food. To me good presentation is the sight of extremely high quality meat, fish and veg sitting on a plate, each item clearly identifiable as what it is, and each an item that will shortly taste marvellous.

I'm sure the culinary world will express disdain that I put the very long lasting San Lorenzo in my top three restaurants in the country. But I do. I think on the whole the quality of their food is excellent and as an experience, going there is always a great pleasure. Massively enhanced by the presence of Mara and Lorenzo Berni who host the place so brilliantly. I was interested, recently, when a very major movie star who I know always loved the Ivy suggested we had dinner. 'Let's go to the Ivy' I said. 'No,' he said 'lets go somewhere else.' I think this indicates that the presence of senior people with great charm, and the knowledge that they are managing the restaurant and will turn up, is very important. Because this movie star had no bad experience of the Ivy. He just felt less attracted because Jeremy and Chris were not there.

I always like restaurants where the owner is on the premises and chipping in. At my best restaurant in the world, Harry's Bar in Venice, Arrigo Cipriani is invariably there with his wry smile and his ability to identify everyone to me and to have a bit of a chat about Venice. That is a major plus.

I view going to dinner as an evening out that must be overall enjoyable. It is not enjoyable if the food is superb but the atmosphere is cold and the service is charmless. It is not enjoyable if you cannot hear yourself talk over the din of other diners. It is not enjoyable if you are so close to the table next door that every time that you take a knife or fork of food you nudge the person on either side. I find the general lack of space in British restaurants appalling.

My worst restaurant experience remains the one that caused me to start writing Winner's Dinners in *The Sunday Times*. A dreadful meal at the Pont de la Tour where everything went wrong, followed by a rude letter from Terence Conran when I dared comment on it. I therefore started writing for *The Sunday Times* solely in order to get revenge on Terence Conran. I think that is a splendid reason. Revenge is a splendid reason for doing anything.

Nor does it do any good to go out and remain silent when things are wrong, fume about it, and go home and say how awful things were. It is far better to say at the time, very pleasantly and quietly, if something is really wrong.

The catering trade is laughingly called the hospitality industry. That's a joke. Any less hospitable industry would be hard to find. The frequent receptionist greeting 'Have you got a reservation?' typifies the arrogance of many restaurants. On the staff side of the Hilton Hotel Park

Lane reception desk there used to be a large sign facing the receptionist saying 'Smile'. How many times are you greeted in a restaurant with a smile? A smile to most restaurant employees is like a silver cross to a vampire.

Except when faced with really appalling service, and that appalling service is repeated again and again in the same meal, I sit very quietly. I am in no way the rumbustious character people imagine. Things were so dreadful at Cliveden, with filthy lipstick-stained glasses being passed off as 'orange juice residue.' The 'orange juice' later confirmed by a Daily Mail reporter as not being fresh and therefore not having any residue. At times like that I think one is entitled to get a little irritable especially when it's in one of the most over-priced hotels in the world. As well as being one of the worst. Bill Gates is a part owner. If he'd run Microsoft like they run Cliveden he'd be living in a bedsit in Paddington.

I remain of the view that English cooking has not improved at all from the golden period of the 1950s when food tasted like what it was meant to be, every vegetable and meat had not been over purified, chemicalised and messed about. Packaging and deep frozen were hardly known. There were a large variety of traditional English dishes available which are now considered too simplistic or common. I'm getting extremely fed up with what is laughingly called English Cuisine or Nouvelle English Cuisine. It's had a shelf life far too long for its inadequacy. It's definitely time we developed a new style of cooking and for that I think we should look back rather than forward. In this respect I'm interested that the great chef and restaurateur Marco Pierre White rang (as I was writing this) to tell me he intended to open Drones (probably opened by now) as a way of serving traditional English fare with a slightly modern touch.

I hope that those of you who buy this book will use it with confidence. Because unlike all other food critics I pay my own way everywhere. You are getting the views of a genuine punter. A few of the reviews may reflect times gone by but they are, I hope, interesting little stories of eating out. Where possible I have updated each entry if something new has happened in the restaurant.

Thanks for reading and God bless you.

HOME

WINNIE SNACKS AT HOME

SERVICE AT CLIVEDEN

I

L O N D O N

Greet Expectations

Someone I greatly admire (me) once wrote: "The ambience created by restaurant staff is vastly important. After all, you meet the staff before you meet the food. Sometimes a very long time indeed before you meet the food."

Contrary to myth and legend. I am extremely docile in restaurants. I thank everyone endlessly. I talk quietly. I'm a model of decorum. Only on very rare occasions do I become snappy. This happened recently at the **Mirabelle**. I'm a great admirer of the restaurant, but not of its general manager, Fred Serol.

I once telephoned to ask if I could have a certain table, to which Fred replied: "I'll do my best." I found this highly annoying. I didn't care if he did his worst. All I wanted was an answer. Do I get that particular table or not? If not, I'd happily go somewhere else. Eventually, I got it, but I was left feeling a great favour had been done.

So when I was asked to dinner there by the owner, Marco Pierre White, and his wife, Mati, I wasn't that keen. I received a surly "Good evening, Mr Winner" from Fred Serol; no mention of Miss Lid, who was with me. Then, as we entered the restaurant itself to wait for the table, a young, junior manager greeted me. He smiled warmly. "Good evening, Mr Winner," he said. "Nice to see you again." When I got to the table I decided silence was not golden. "Fred," I said, "you're a dreadful maitre d'. Your greetings are surly at best. I suggest you go to that young man there [I

3

pointed to the fellow who'd met me nicely] and learn how to greet people."

Later Marco and Mati joined us. I didn't mention this minor incident, but obviously Fred had told Marco because when he stood by the table later, Marco said: "So Winner had a go at you, Fred."

"I'll tell you something, Mr Serol, which may surprise you," I said. "You will not develop a serious illness if you smile. Nothing untoward will happen. You should try it sometime."

It's odd that Marco Pierre White so often employs non-charming restaurant managers. He had a man called Max at the **Oak Room** who could have depressed a £10m lottery winner with one glance. By contrast, Marco himself is the most charming of people. I've seen him work his restaurants many times, smiling at customers, being thoroughly pleasant. And Mati, whom I met when she was working at the **Canteen**, is the best receptionist in the world. Her smile lights up the place.

This set me to thinking of other meeters and greeters who know how to do it. One of my favourites is Colin Smith, the owner of **Chez Moi**. He won the Outstanding London Host Award from Carlton. "I can't believe it, Colin," I said. "You never say anything and when you do it's so quiet that nobody can hear it."

"I was a little surprised myself," said Colin with his half smile. He's terrific really. And there are lots of others. Fernando Peire, once a stalwart at **The Ivy**, but now at **Quo Vadis**, got my Best Maitre D' Award. He greets you with real warmth and interest. And Jimmy Lahoud's man at the **Belvedere**, Jean-Christophe Slowik, proves that not all Frenchmen are snooty. He's a delight.

Dougal Spratt at **Orsino's** is good; he has a nice diffident way of making you feel welcome. So do Michael, John and Simon at the **Dorchester Grill**. Mohamed Ibrahim, the Egyptian in charge of the Japanese **Hiroko** in Kensington, beams delightfully.

Raj Sharma, who was at **Zaika** and now wanders around hosting for the group, is superb. Jeremy King and Christopher Corbin know how to stroll through **Le Caprice, The Ivy** and **Sheekey's**, spreading happiness. And all their staff are first-rate.

Moving into the world of legendary greeters, I'd place Mara Berni at **San Lorenzo** very high on the list. Plus, the food there is excellent. Johnny Gold at **Tramp** is an Olympic gold medal greeter, so is Peter Crome at **Chewton Glen**. He always manages a deprecating, funny remark.

But my award for Greatest Greeter goes to Pietro Fraccari at **Assaggi**. He has that wondrous Italian quality that makes everyone feel special. They keep his partner, chef Nino Sassu, out of the restaurant a lot of the time now. Nino can get a little over-agitated by the customers. He once had the cheek to phone me at 8.12pm to check why I was late for an 8 o'clock table reservation. I arrived two minutes later. But Nino's wonderful as well. I admire him greatly. Just don't get on the wrong side of him.

In restaurants, on average, a bottle of wine costs two and half times the purchase price plus VAT. This has become a problem for me, because if I am to drink out what I enjoy at home, the price is ludicrous. So I seldom order wine in restaurants. However, I found the answer to my prayers: a Persian restaurant that serves no wine but invites you to bring your own. It is called **Alounak**, in Russell Gardens, near Olympia, and is run by the brothers Janzamini. I left it to them to decide what we ate, and a series of totally fresh, highly likable dishes appeared as well as newly baked naan bread. It was all pretty good. They also had the extreme good sense to give me, for two of us, a table for six. This is a place to which I shall occasionally return. I do have one serious criticism, however. The napkins are blue paper. Never mind, next time I shall bring both wine *and* some of my Ritz hotel serviettes.

Having lived in my manor since 1947, I keep a wary eye out for new arrivals. Down that end of Kensington High Street, shop and restaurant turnover is somewhat high. Here today, gone tomorrow. So I had noticed that the Al Basha, an Arab restaurant that had, seemingly, been there for ever, had transmogrified into rather a smart-looking, somewhat more downmarket restaurant called **ASK Pizza e Pasta**. It is extremely well designed, lot of space, comfortable, tiled floors, and was packed out. I give them multi marks for being prepared to put fried eggs on their pizzas – Orsino, which I like, won't do that.

Booking good

It is rare that I am pleasantly surprised. Upset, yes. Disappointed often. Appalled, not infrequently. To find a restaurant almost beyond criticism, practically unique. I was recommended an Italian restaurant above a pub in Notting Hill Gate by someone whose views of culinary matters I suspect. Why I even went I cannot imagine.

    Assaggi is in a street of pleasant Victorian houses with a pub, nicely lit, suddenly appearing on the left. That's if you're going south; if you're going north, it's on the right! There's no sign, so I entered the pub, wooden-modern but pleasant, quickly realising this was not it. Round the side there's a door under an arch. You go up stairs covered in rough matting, bright red walls, squares screwed onto them that could be decoration or could be modern art. This leads to a large room with a wooden floor, wooden tables, no cloths, wooden chairs, no padding, three high windows looking onto the street, tables well spaced, similar squares of "art" on the walls. Rather nice.

I was greeted most warmly by the owner, Pietro Fraccari, who had served me at Cecconi's. His partner Nino Sassu, the chef, also used to be at Cecconi's.

Assaggi provides quite the most marvellous food. I have recommended it effusively to many of my famous friends (yes, I do have famous friends!), but none of them has eaten there. This is because when they phone up, Pietro tells them he's full! When I go back I say: "Pietro, how can you turn away so-and-so?" He just shrugs and says : "There was no room."

This is largely because there are only 10 tables and 35 seats. Pietro only takes bookings for that number. He doesn't try to fill any table twice. If someone finishes early, or someone doesn't turn up, and you phone or drop by, then you might get in at the last minute. Otherwise it is not easy.

On a recent visit I started with *pane carasau*, which is crisp, almost poppadom-like bread, Parma ham, grilled vegetables in olive oil, then tortelloni with buffalo ricotta and a little tagliolini with sea urchins. Vanessa had brill with spinach, capers and lemon peel. My main course was prawns wrapped in pancetta. Pud for madam was figs in red wine with cinnamon and lemon peel, for me chocolate truffle cake with white chocolate ice cream. It was all historic, the cake being as good as I've ever eaten, even in Harry's Bar in Venice, which is my all-time favourite for everything.

Au Jardin des Gourmets in Greek Street, Soho, is not a garden nor is it for gourmets. It should tour catering establishments as an example of how not to run a restaurant. I enjoyed it, not for the food or the service, but because I was with two of the most entertaining and nice people I know, Marie Vine and her husband, Barry, who are film distributors (it's rare to find nice film distributors!). It says a great deal that during the lunch period on a working day in Soho there were only four other people in the place. On our table there were some large pats of butter and some sort of dip. Nobody offered us bread or anything to dip in the dip. I felt nobody was running the room at all. I had to beckon to get anybody to come at any time. Barry and I ordered cream of pumpkin soup flavoured with nutmeg. It arrived nicely presented in a sliced pumpkin with large serrated edges. It tasted of nothing in particular, and its temperature was between tepid and cold. My main course, fillet of plaice with candied aubergine and tomato, was also under par in the heat department and equally under par in the food department. Things rose a bit with the pud, a pretty good pear flan with dreary honey ice cream. When we left, the door closed behind us. It was locked. I was cast out for ever. Back in Greek Street, a strange lady, who told us she was known as Mad Mary and proud of it, asked me, "Are you married? Do you want a mistress?" That's the Soho I remember, full of delightful nutters.

Star turns

People I know are divided on **Aubergine** in Park Walk, Chelsea. Eighty per cent say "wonderful", the rest "dreary food, awful service". My friend Michael Caine wanted to go there, so I phoned. "This is Michael Winner speaking. I'd like to book a table next Wednesday for myself and Michael Caine and his wife."

"It will be a great honour to have Michael Caine here," said a man with a strong French accent. "What about me?" I replied. "Won't it be an honour to have me?" There was a pause. "It will be nice to have you as well," said the Frenchman dismissively. "What time would you like to come?" "Eight o'clock," I said. Another pause. "Could you make it 7.45?" said the Frenchman. "Look," I said, "if it's a great honour to have Michael Caine, do you think we should really ask him to come at a time he doesn't want?" "It will be all right at eight o"clock," said the Frenchman, "but 7.45 is better."

I put the phone down in stupefaction. "This is what eating out in London has come to," I said to myself. The customer is a pawn for the convenience of the restaurant. Ghastly beyond belief. We duly turned up at three minutes to eight, both Mr Caine and I being fastidiously punctual. It was Shakira's day to drive, and parking near Aubergine is impossible. She was gone for a full 15 minutes finding somewhere to leave the car; luckily I'd brought the chauffeur! We were joined by Roger Moore, having phoned first, of course, and then turned our attention to matters in hand. The room is inoffensive, some uninteresting paintings on the wall, no sense of style, but it's all right, it's just there.

For a starter I had langoustine soup, which was exceptional. Sarah had a tian of leeks and scallops, sauce champagne (that's how the menu put it!) She pronounced it good. My main course was pigeon pôche, purée of swede and wild mushroom ravioli, jus Madeira. As pigeon goes it was impeccable. Sarah had fillet of sea bass roasted with braised salsify, jus vanille. I didn't understand the menu at all, but she liked it greatly. We had a bit of free chicken soup to start with, and all of us voted the food thus far tiptop. I found the desserts a considerable let-down. The orange tart was heavy, the crème brûlée jus Granny Smith marginal, the millefeuille of vanille with red fruit okay at best.

We adjourned to the front bar area for a gossip and coffee. An enormous, tough-looking man in white, wearing a chef's hat, appeared. He turned out to be the owner, Gordon Ramsay from Scotland. I was glad I could say I genuinely liked his cooking. He kindly offered us the meal free. I should obviously go out with Michael Caine more often. But it was my turn to pay, so I said, "Thank you, no," much encouraged by Michael Caine, who said: "Let him pay, he's a millionaire, he won't notice it."

Overall I found the atmosphere in Aubergine rather tepid. No buzz, although our group was a delight. I prefer to see a bit of adrenalin flowing, as it does at The Canteen. I'm sure Aubergine will get a Michelin star when they next hand them out. Gordon will deserve it.

PS Gordon got his Michelin star shortly thereafter, then a second. Then stormed out to open his own place called, surprisingly! – Gordon Ramsay. I've been there too – see my review.

It's the real thing

Without Robert Summer and his wife, Susan Kasen Summer, I would never have become a food-life writer. Bob and Sue are marvellously eager-beaver New Yorkers who know far more about London restaurants than I do.

Bob and Sue take me to many London restaurants I would never have gone to, thinking they were largely for tourists. Thus I got to clear plates at Le Gavroche, waited endlessly for a main course at the Dorchester's Oriental Restaurant and had the most horrible meal at Le Pont de la Tour, where everything went wrong. When I wrote to Terence Conran, he snarled: "Thank you for your film script. We will investigate..." He's a wag, old Terry, isn't he? So when a *Sunday Times* editor said: "Have you got anything you'd care to write about?" I said: "Yes, I want revenge on Terence Conran. I'll say how awful his restaurant was." Thus my column started, based solely on an impeccable desire for retribution.

Bob and Sue recently took me to **The Avenue** in St James's, another place I would normally have stayed away from. Not because it's touristy, quite the contrary – it was full to overflowing with young semi-trendies, all enjoying themselves greatly and making a lot of noise in the process. It's a typical mid-1990s, cavernous, sheer-surfaced, minimalist room with hard chairs and a white tiled floor. Lights of various colours play on the walls. Bob had booked, so The Avenue didn't know it was getting me. When I saw the table offered for five people, they did. I pointed to something much larger. After a hurried whisper, we were allowed to sit there. Our other two people were Sue's daughter Wendy and her fiancé, Steve, who owns a popular Beverly Hills car wash. I sensed service would not be fast (boy, was I right!), so I ordered a Coca-Cola with a lot of ice and lemon in a voice that brooked no delay. I find if you knock back a few Coca-Colas, a wait for the food becomes more tolerable.

After Bob observed they had a list of only five red wines, the oldest being 1992, we got to order. I pointed out The Avenue was for young people who created a nice buzz, not the superwine-drinking crowd. The other wine problems: for some reason Bob didn't get any for a long time after everyone else. And when he'd finished his wine, Steve noted: "They don't refill." I was on my third Coca-Cola, so none of this bothered me at all! My first course eventually arrived: bruschetta of sardines with wilted dandelion leaves and pancetta. This was good, old-fashioned sardines on toast (which I always liked), with some horrid stringy things that I took to be the dandelion leaves. Bob observed he was eating "a real risotto".

My next course was vegetarian spring roll with chilli plum sauce. I decided not to eat it. I tried a couple of fried veggies and some champ potatoes, which were fine. Then we voted on the main course. Susan gave her veal chop 8 out of 10. Steve's guinea fowl also got an 8. Wendy brought us down to earth. She had the same as me and gave it a derisory 3, Bob had chicken confit. He said: "A bistro 7." He repeated the word "bistro". The puds were reasonable. My mascarpone ice cream, rhubarb compote, ginger syrup was adequate. People gave me bits of theirs, which I thought were much better.

The next day, I was deeply put out when I phoned to get the name of the young lady behind the bar I wanted to commend for doing her job with admirable charm. A woman put her hand over the phone and, talking to her, said of me: "I think he's safe." Me! safe?! I've never been so insulted in my life! Miss charm's name is Vanessa de Souza Lage. It really is! That's a giggle, isn't it?

In the Balans

In my ever-enthusiastic quest for fine-quality snack places, I listened intently when my neighbour, the lyricist Don Black, spoke of a new arrival in Kensington High Street called **Balans**. Don had been there and liked it.

I have a problem with Kensington High Street. I keep seeing it as it was when I moved there in 1947. Faded gentility, a place for the elderly. A home for those who couldn't afford Belgravia. Lovely little tea shops with waitresses in black uniforms, white lace tiaras and white aprons. Bebe Daniels and Ben Lyon, once big Hollywood movie stars, ran a sweet little antique shop. Later, it all became terribly flash and tarty. Now, it's very lively, massively open on Sundays, youthful, with its own reinvented energy. And large houses with real gardens and trees just a few feet from the High Street. Far better than overbuilt Belgravia.

Balans fits well into this ethos. It's part of a chain scattered around posh areas of London, from Knightsbridge through Soho to Chelsea. It's bright, with an art-deco feel to it, a bar, some leather armchairs facing banquettes in the midsection and elsewhere what appear to be tin chairs with brown seats for the less critical. "Paintings" consist of framed coloured water with bubbles floating up. A man called Andrew Gray was in charge. "Andrew Gray, like the footballer," he said, trying to be helpful. If there's a footballer called Andrew Gray, I've certainly never heard of him.

"We've got freshly squeezed orange juice, but we don't squeeze it ourselves," said Andrew, uttering classic words of twaddle. Freshly squeezed means squeezed extremely recently. Orange juice when squeezed degrades within a couple of hours. If there's a preservative added, that degrades it too. I am astonished by how many top-price hotels now fob guests off with second-rate, plastic-carton orange juice.

At Balans I opted for a frozen coffee, which was nice and milk shakey, the only problem being the unbelievably thin straws.

Balans is a very lively place with lots of specials on a blackboard. The service was quick. I received, fairly smartly, robust eggs benedict with bacon, two large servings. Miss Lid had blueberry pancakes with fruit salad.

"It's got a cheerful atmosphere," she said, eating her pancakes, which were thick and doughy but not heavy. I followed my iced coffee with a frozen mocha, a coffee and chocolate blend. I admired the Argos homestore opposite.

The difference between this and New York snack places, which I greatly like, is that there they offer so much more space. You get large booths for four or six people, often inhabited by only two. In Balans I'd chosen the poshest section, central and opposite the bar, which was just acceptable spacewise. The rest of the place was crammed. This is fine for the owner, but indelicate for me.

I tasted the kumquat-marmalade bread-and-butter pudding with crème anglaise. I'm not sure what it had to do with bread-and-butter pudding, but the kumquats and the crème anglaise saved it. It was pleasantly light.

As the Rolls pulled away, I phoned Don Black to tell him I'd followed his advice. "We went there last night," he said. "Shirley had a vegetable lasagne and I had spinach and bacon salad and a marvellous fruit salad." Don paused. "It was within our budget," he added. Balans is not the Ken High Street of old, more a much jazzed-up Richoux. It's the sort of place I'll go to about three times a year.

Good as Gold

I first visited the **Belvedere** in 1947. It was part of a bombed Jacobean mansion in what is now Holland Park, then privately owned by Lord Ilchester. Everything around belonged to him. In Melbury Road, bordering the park, each house was a masterpiece of Victorian architecture. Mine was designed by the famous architect Norman Shaw and built for the Victorian artist Sir Luke Fildes. When I moved in, the area was full of film directors: David Lean lived behind, Michael Powell was opposite. Now it's full of BMWs.

I'd clamber over the fence and play in the grounds of Holland House. It could easily have been restored. But this was after the war. We were going forward to a greater world. Victorian and other old buildings were demolished massively in the mid-1950s when building materials came off ration. Then Lord Ilchester died and his heirs started selling the land. Hideous blocks of flats sprouted. The Belvedere became a restaurant run by the J. Lyons group. It was a marvellous building, the interior beautifully done out with very comfortable chairs and the environment of a gentleman's club. The food was ghastly.

Ten years ago a Swiss friend of mine, Dieter Abt, bought it. Dieter knew nothing about restaurants. He totally redesigned the place, making changes to the windows and the entrance and carving up the main room. Only a non-genius could erect a wavy interior wall in front of historic windows looking on to a park. He achieved suburban denigration of a lovely Jacobean building. The food was no better. His company went into liquidation. Dieter was charged with fraud. I always said he was too stupid to be fraudulent. He rather liked that. He intended to have it brought up by the defence at his trial. In fact, the case against him collapsed in days.

John Gold and Bill Ofner, two heroes of British club life, then bought the lease from the liquidator. Johnny Gold should be made a lord for his services to London's social life. His Tramp discotheque remains "in" after 30 years. At the Belvedere he added a superb set of celebrity photo-portraits by Terry O'Neill. I wonder why mine was above the entrance to the toilets? Johnny attracted the glitterati, the food was good if not historic, but he was approaching the time when sensible people cash in and retire. So, some years ago, well before most people knew it, Johnny sold out to a Scots pub group, staying on to front the enterprise.

I could always find something nice to eat and a good atmosphere at the Belvedere when Johnny was fully in charge. When the Scots took over it was tarted up a bit; some horrific oil paintings were added. It looked even tackier. They brought in staff who were inefficient and rude. One of the worst meals I ever almost ate was some extraordinary deep-frozen rabbit thing preceded by a grotesque risotto. The rabbit was sent back. I never went in again.

Then, recently, a restaurateur with the wonderfully Runyonesque name of Jimmy Lahoud bought the Belvedere. He owns L'Escargot in Soho and the nearby Quo Vadis jointly with Marco Pierre White; he's a partner in the Mirabelle with Marco Pierre White and also in the recently opened Sugar Reef. The president of Lebanon, Emile Lahoud, is Jimmy's second cousin. His girlfriend Tessa Ferguson owns the Blue Room, an excellent coffee and sandwich place in Soho.

I dined with them recently at the Belvedere. It still looks awful, but Jimmy is closing it for two months, for improvements. The chef, Jeremy Hollingsworth, earned a Michelin star for Quo Vadis. He's spectacularly good. I've waited 52 years for someone like that. My house is only a few paces away. Properly run and redesigned, the Belvedere could be one of the greatest restaurants in London. Everything I've eaten there indicates it will be. From the foie gras to the tarte tatin of endives with sea scallops, the starters are superb. My main course, honey-glazed duck, was good; so, too, was roast chicken from Bresse. The fresh fruits in champagne jelly were unbeatable, the other desserts equally fine.

Jimmy plans to restore much of the period elegance, redecorate entirely, get permission to floodlight more of the adjacent park, and change the horrendous chairs. All excellent ideas. Only one thing worries me. He's taken on the decorator David Collins, who did the awful Claridge's bar and a host of other dreary, bland-looking restaurants in London. I'll just have to go there and eat with a blindfold.

I've been back to the now magnificently refurbished Belvedere, and it has definitely become one of the top restaurants in London. The food is superb and not expensive.

Marco Pierre White is now a partner in the Belvedere.

Charm counts for a lot. You couldn't call the food at **Biagio** in Charing Cross seriously excellent. But Bekim, from Yugoslavia, was such a jolly waiter it made up for the bland spaghetti (we couldn't decide if it was vongole or bolognese), the tired salami and mortadella, and the After Eight mints that were so frozen you could double them over and they still didn't snap. The strip lighting was particularly odd. It was heavily smeared in what looked like blood. Didn't really go with the endless hanging Chianti bottles. Nor did it complement the album of greatest hits signed by Diana Ross: "Biagio restaurant lovely, thanks for staying open."

It takes the biscuit

I have recently had the worst meal I've ever eaten, and not by a small margin. It happened at a restaurant I have previously admired, **Bibendum**, in Fulham Road. I've been going there since it first opened – I've taken Burt Lancaster, Lord Glenconner, Joanna Lumley, Oliver Stone and Brian DePalma (not all at once!) – and it's the place I normally recommend to visitors. Even though Simon Hopkinson, its founder-chef, left, I have found it just as good under his successor, Matthew Harris. So when I strolled in one Sunday evening with a film producer from Los Angeles and one of his workmates, I thought: "This'll be fine." Boy, was I wrong.

The first course passed uneventfully. Mind you, how eventful can three green salads and scrambled egg with tuna be? When we got to the main course, things plummeted. The two Americans had asked for medium to well done steaks. Not difficult, is it? I could – and frequently do – knock that up in my kitchen. I mean, you don't need to be an atom physicist to grill steaks, do you? They arrived so raw you could have drowned swimming in the blood. They had to be taken back, leaving chaos. Vegetables going off, a delay that was not short, some people ready to eat, some not. Eventually they returned. One okay, one still far short of medium to well done. We groaned and carried on.

Vanessa had started eating her sea bass as soon as it arrived. It was, she pronounced, cold. I tried it, and it was. The boiled potatoes with it were grossly undercooked. Horrid.

But the *pièce de resistance* was my persillade of tongue. Leathery, so hard it was difficult to cut and, as far as I could tell, not fresh. I picked away at it. Now why did I do that? Why did I not take it straight into the kitchen and say to the chef: "Taste this, it's totally revolting, isn't it?" Instead, like a wimp, I ate about a third of it, moaning internally as I did. But that dreadful desire to keep the evening moving along, not to make a scene (yes, even for Winner) prevented me letting my feelings be known.

After this horrible main course was cleared away, the desserts were fine. Except for my American producer's. He ordered cheese and biscuits. Now to serve cheese and biscuits you do not need an advanced degree in culinary art. All you need is some cheese and some biscuits and the strength to bring them to the table at more or less the same time. This was too much for the Bibendum waiter. He managed the cheese all right. Then he went and stood next to the biscuits sitting on a serving area nearby. He stood, and stood. My American friend, after a long wait because he was one of those quiet, far too polite Americans, said: "I did ask for biscuits." At that point my frustration boiled over, and I gave the waiter speech 24A. Biscuits appeared with total regularity after that.

This makes me recall those people who say to me: "It's no good you writing about food. You don't get the treatment everyone else does, you get special attention." Oh yes! Cold fish, uncooked potatoes, steaks all wrong, tongue that was to any sane person inedible and cheese served with no biscuits. That's *special*! I checked the next day. The normal chap, Matthew Harris, was off. A sous chef, named Athene O'Neill, was in charge. I have nothing else to say, except that Bibendum, being nice people, apologised profusely, knocked off the charge for the meal and offered my guests a free meal when they come back to England.

PS In spite of the above, Bibendum is usually excellent and I have returned many times.

One of the worst dinners I ever had in my life was in a basement called **Downstairs at 190** in Queen's Gate, SW7. The chef was Antony Worrall Thompson, and my host was a well-known movie star. Everything went wrong, from very slow food delivery to courses that were so heavy that if Worrall Thompson had been chef on the *Titanic* it would have sunk long before hitting the iceberg. I am prepared to accept that was an off-night, which we can all have, because Mr Worrall Thompson has flourished. He rarely cooks now, but is the "creative director" of his six restaurants, one of which is **Bistrot 190**. This is a jolly spot with a lively atmosphere, located just above my earlier disaster. When I went there, the first table I was offered was too small, and the second, ostensibly for four people, was so squashed that even with only two of us my head kept hitting some dried flower arrangement hanging from the wall. *Worrall Thompson is not associated with these places now.*

Table manna

It didn't go down too well when my location manager, Michael Harvey, asked for ice cream at **Bloom's** kosher restaurant at Golders Green Road. "In this place, not allowed anything with dairy," explained Leon, the waiter. "Don't mix ice cream with meat."

Leon's a Greek Cypriot who looks Jewish. "You even sound Jewish," I observed. "You've got to with the people here," said Leon. "After 32 years, I think I'm one of them." To demonstrate the international standing of the place, Leon pointed out a nearby waiter who was French and another who was Greek.

The restaurant itself is a marvellous time warp, reminiscent of New York delis and every bit as good. Over there, you have The Stage, the Little Carnegie (Woody Allen's favourite), the 2nd Avenue deli, Barnie

Greengrass and Sammy's Rumanian, to name a few. In London, since the original Bloom's in Whitechapel closed following a furore because they were found serving non-kosher meat, not much is left of the deli world. "It was all a mistake," said Leon. "The man accidentally delivered meat he had for himself. It closed when business fell off as the Jewish community diminished."

At Bloom's, and their rival Harry Morgan's in St John's Wood High Street, business always seems pretty good. Not that I'm a regular. I hadn't been to Bloom's for about 10 years; then, I'd found the latkes rather greasy and the mixed chicken soup with lokshen, kneidlach and kreplach poor. This time they were outstanding and the salt beef superb. If they did a Jewish Michelin Guide this would get three stars.

Shortly after we sat down on the chrome and brown-leather chairs – "Vinyl," pointed out my production designer, Crispian Sallis – Leon said: "Three mixed soups and then we'll discuss business." Off he went without a care for the main course. He returned to put some amazingly good, large pickled cucumbers on the table. "Believe you me, it's the best," opined Leon. "They do them here: cucumber, nutmeg, whole pepper, plenty garlic, kosher salt, concentrated vinegar, leave them in cold water for 24 hours. Crinkly cucumbers are much better."

I was considering a somewhat primitive mural of Jewish family life when Leon returned. Crispian ordered liver and onions, Mr Harvey had a Bloomburger and onions. I opted for salt beef, latkes and tzimmes – a particularly wonderful way of doing carrots with little dough balls thrown in. "Liver and onion's off," said Leon, so Crispian had the same as me.

They were all very impressed with the mixed soup. "The flavour is divine," said Crispian, eyeing with suspicion some matzos that had just been put on the table. Portions are so generous that we all left some soup, great as it was, and a fair amount of it slopped onto the table when Leon cleared the plates away. The cloths are not porous, so it sat there in blobs. Luckily, there was an enormous supply of paper napkins in a glass, so we set to work wiping it up.

"It's sort of melting," said Crispian of the salt beef, probably the best I've ever eaten. Leon gave Mr Harvey some salt beef with his Bloomburger. "I can't get through all this," said Crispian, looking at me. "I'm glad to see you can't, either."

We didn't actually want desserts, but Leon came with two enormous slices of lokshen pudding and two vast apple strudels. "Oh my God!" said Crispian, as Leon cut a third of both and gave them to Mr Harvey. Then he returned with a mound of white sugar on a plate and poured it over everything with a dessert spoon. It was all terrific.

"This bit, I can wrap it up for you, take it home," said Leon of the leftover salt beef for three and much of Mr Harvey's Bloomburger. "Why should we waste this beautiful beef?" he added, as he returned with a blue plastic bag. "I give you half a loaf of bread, I put the cucumbers in there and everything." "I shall enjoy this tonight with my friends," said Mr Harvey.

"Now I give you, compliments of the house, three black coffees to wash this down," said Leon, expansively. I'm so glad he did. At last I had something to complain about. I know you shouldn't look a gift horse in the mouth, but the coffee was awful.

Buffeted by change

When I came down from Cambridge I frequented a lovely little Indian restaurant in South Ken where I'd often see Alec Guinness knocking back a chicken tikka. That fell to the non-charms of a chain-pizza place. I moved on to the Bombay Palace, near Marble Arch, then the Shezan in Knightsbridge, the Kensington Tandoori and, finally, fashionable Chutney Mary in the King's Road, but I didn't rate any of them. So rather belatedly I entered the grand portals of the **Bombay Brasserie** off Gloucester Road. The room there is large, with well-spaced, comfortably sized tables and there is a pleasant greenhouse bit where they always seat me. It is run most efficiently by Adi Modi and Arun Harnal. Every Indian-type dish you have ever known is on the long menu, plus a few more, and – most importantly – they all taste delicious. There are even seven types of Indian bread. Desserts are never a speciality at Indian restaurants, but they produce an extraordinary thing called cobra coffee which is made, slowly, at your table. It includes scotch and kirsch, which are poured down a curling orange peel into a flambéed pan of coffee. The rim of the glass is coated with caramelised white sugar, and it's topped with whipped cream. Some sticky orangey substance lurks around too. It's terrific if you have the time.

One Sunday, I phoned the Bombay Brasserie. Arun Harnal, the manager, said: "We'll have your usual table ready." This turned out to be a foolish remark. I think restaurateurs have a duty to tell customers when things are not as they usually are. When I arrived at the Bombay Brasserie, my usual table was in exactly the same spot it had been for years. But the room around it was quite different.

Sunday at the Bombay Brasserie is now a cheap serve-yourself-lunch day. The buffet stretched in front of my table and people standing in line stared at me until they got to the end. Then they had a final stare before wafting off, waving their plates practically under my nostrils. "Why didn't you tell me Sunday is totally different from what I am used to?" I asked Mr Harnal. By now, I had walked out, and he was desperately trying to find my Bentley, which had been put somewhere by the adjacent hotel's doorman and had gone missing. I was not a happy bunny. "I don't know why you object," said Mr Harnal. "We've always been very good to you." Yeah, I thought, and I've been good to you. I've paid the bill on the dot. I've given you publicity. Now suddenly you're doing me a favour. I struck them off my list.

I went back to the Bombay Brasserie after they apologised nicely. Sadly, I found it changed for the worse. The food always had a relationship with the basic Indian food I ate when at Cambridge University. Back then, a chicken biryani with orangey sauce and yellow rice was quite delicious. At the Bombay Brasserie it was more refined. But this time the food had got far too clever. There was something odd about it. Worse still, the room was full of men. Table after table of business outings. A friend of mine said she went there and saw all these suburban male yuppies getting out of a bus. A great pity. I used to like the Bombay Brasserie.

"We must go to Southall," said my friend, gourmet and television writer Laurence Marks. "It's like little India, and there's the best Indian restaurant in England, **The Brilliant**." "Oh," I said, less than enthusiastically. But somehow or other on a Friday night there we were in the Ferrari on our way to Western Road, Southall. Not a place I plan to spend my holiday in. The Brilliant is a large, highly unattractive room with tables laid out in rows as if waiting for a major function. It is run by Kewal Anand and his younger brother Gulu, who is also the chef. We sat on nasty red chairs, eating very good rice, terrific jeera chicken with cumin seeds, pickled carrot and mango, prawns masala, karahi gosht lamb, mushrooms, peppers and kulcha bread, which nobody else makes! All excellent, but worth travelling to Hounslow for? Hmmm. It may be a bit chi-chi, but I'll stick to the Bombay Brasserie in South Ken.

Café Fish, in Panton Street, is the sort of place I would never go into. It is painted a bilious green with matching fake fishing nets draped over a bar, beside which sits a thumping pianist. But I found myself there with a very nice group of people, including my friend John Cleese. When I was served some excellent French bread on our tiny table I thought: "Maybe things will be all right." They were not. My fish soup tasted of no known ingredients. Had I been presented it in a competition I would have settled, uncomfortably, for tomato soup that was a bit off. My next course was worse: grilled sole that was hard, utterly lacking in succulence. I thought back to Soho in the 1950s, when I lunched daily at Wheeler's bar, sitting next to Francis Bacon and Clement Freud. Ah, the juicy soles there, the firm deep-fried scampi and other fish dishes. I looked around at the clientele, many of whom smiled at me most charmingly, and noted that nobody seemed particularly unhappy. There must be millions of people growing up today who have no idea of the real taste of food. They have come into a world so mass-fed with products chemicalised and factory-farmed that any similarity between these and the real thing remains only in the descriptions on the menu. I must report in fairness that Mr Cleese cleaned his plate with extraordinary thoroughness and looked around cheerfully for more. But then he comes from Weston-super-Mare, so what would you expect?

To show I possess the common touch par excellence, I visited the **Cafe Le Jardin** in Kensington High Street. This certainly doesn't have a garden – the outside chairs are inches away from the high street traffic fumes. I'm sorry to report that all was not well with my meal. I started with a vanilla milkshake that was memorably awful: watery and tasting of cardboard. There was then a very long wait indeed for the next course. As we left, my friend Nick Mead opined: "That's one of the most awful meals I've had in years. It tasted like it was all from a packet." He was about right. That's cafe society, UK version, for you.

To be fair, **Cafe Pasta** in Kensington High Street is not run for the likes of me. It was full of energised shoppers and secretaries, who probably thought the tagliatelle with fresh asparagus and cream was fine. I found it totally resistible. No taste, no texture, asparagus could have been anything, cream bland to the point of extinction. Rum and raisin ice cream was uninteresting, and I finished with a rather insipid cappuccino.

Caine and his able Canteen cuisine

When you find yourself searching the menu of a supposedly good restaurant, desperate for something you like, and ordering, again and again, the mixed grill – you know it's time to move on! Thus I departed from the squeaky chairs, the excessive noise and the erratic cooking at Kensington Place and sought pastures new. Why, I thought, could Kensington Place not be like The Canteen in Chelsea Harbour? Here is a restaurant which charges less but provides so much more.

If I had to nominate the most successful establishment in years, it would be **The Canteen**. Not only have I never had a bad meal there, I've never had a bad course, or even a bad item within a course! Why I put up with sending raw grouse, or salty duck, among other dishes, back to the kitchen at Kensington Place for so long, I cannot imagine. How is it that an actor, a supposedly hyped-up super-chef and the owner of the restaurant that failed in the same premises, can take on a new young chef and turn a space in one of the ugliest developments in England into a triumph? Obviously they know something the men at Kensington Place do not.

The first thing they know is to have a really inventive menu, that not only reads well on the card but tastes superb. Secondly, they sell it at absurdly low cost for the quality on offer – all 11 first courses at £6.50 each, 11 main courses at £10.50 and 10 desserts at £4.50. It's what Marco Pierre White, the Canteen's culinary Godfather, rightly described as "haute cuisine at affordable prices".

Thirdly, they have an extremely pleasant setting. When I first went to The Canteen I started to count how many types of light-fitting they had. I think I got to 12. None of them very attractive. Some have been changed, either way it doesn't matter. The old-fashioned, playing-card bench upholstery, the split levels, the view of the yacht basin, everything works. At Kensington Place, for more money, they don't even give you tablecloths or padded chairs. At The Canteen the place is laid out like a real eating room, not like a cafeteria with pretension.

And no-one should underestimate Michael Caine's contribution to his restaurants, all seven of them. He is not just a star who turns up for people to gawp at and go away feeling they've hob-nobbed with the glitterati. Having dinner with Michael in The Canteen is to see a man close to obsessed with getting things right. "We must make that corner more attractive", "Why have they put the thermostat right in the middle of that pillar?" and, to me, "Come on, Michael, let's go to the bar, we can re-sell the table then."

But the real star of The Canteen has to be Stephen Terry, the chef. I only learned recently that Stephen was brought up hearing about me and my exploits from his mother, who was my father's secretary. Even his pram was a gift from my dad. So I feel a personal pleasure at his success. He's a Marco Pierre White protégé, trained at Harvey's and various other well-starred establishments, and it shows. Anyone who can attract full houses every night to an out-of-the-way example of post-war Russian architectural mess, with the worst-designed, most irritating car park in London, has to be good.

In the early days, before Marco had to spend all his time at his new restaurant in Knightsbridge, there was the added attraction of seeing who he might ask to leave. On hearing his side of such well-reported events, I always thought he acted most properly. He can still be caught, looming in to keep an eye on things, around 11pm. Dad looking in to check on his baby. And with justifiable pride.

PS The Canteen in is now closed but Michael Caine is hoping to reopen it in the West End soon.

At his Caprice

Le Caprice has figured heavily in my life. When I came on to the "upper" end of the London scene in the mid-1950s, it was done out in red plush sofa-seating. A bobbing, smiling, small man named Mario Gallati (who had named it after his wife's bra) would greet evening-dressed celebrities after theatre and film first nights. Look to the left and you'd see Noël Coward, to the right Larry and Viv (Olivier and Leigh) and over there Rex Harrison and David Niven. It was all terribly "dahling" and posh.

The room was bigger than it is now, a large part of what was a seating area being the kitchens. The fashionable bit was on to Arlington Street, where the entrance door is today. A large alcove opposite was the place for racial minorities and nobodies. I qualified for both, but got seated in the best part because I was for a few weeks a theatrical agent, and an important, ageing, blonde lady in the same office took a shine to me and had me with her. I was an embryonic toy-boy, although nothing naughty ever took place, even if 40 years on is a bit late for a denial.

Later **Le Caprice** floundered, as the era when you wore evening dress for almost every night out vanished. In 1975 it became a tea shop! The next owner changed the red plush to brown and in 1981 it was taken over by Christopher Corbin and Jeremy King, who respectively managed Langan's and Joe Allen's. A lot of black leather and chrome entered, a sparse, minimalist chic, and the showbiz group began to return. It's now a noisy (unpleasantly so in the evenings), jolly and extremely well-run place, masterminded in the kitchens by Tim Hughes, who co-chef'd the Canteen when it first opened. The food is cheap and cheerful, a description the owners would probably object to, but it's very good. I remember when I first decided how much I liked eating there. I'd been having griddled foie gras in Kensington Place, then I had it at Le Caprice. This is a different world, I thought, much better. Since then Kensington Place has got even more past-it, but Le Caprice rolls on fresh as ever. The black wood chairs are rather chipped if you look closely, but other than that it retains a fresh appearance. The service is usually fine, although an occasional reminder that I'm an eccentric diner does no harm.

On a recent lunch the foie gras (they call it sautéed) was still as excellent, then I had Lincolnshire sausages with bubble and squeak and an onion gravy that was deliciously tacky. I finished with chocolate cookies ice-cream with butterscotch sauce! Marvellous!

After lunch I drove up Arlington Street to Piccadilly, where it's no right turn. Fifty thousand people marched in front of me in a March For Jesus. I had no option, as the centre was barriered, other than to turn left and join them, driving at walking pace. Thus I became the token Jew on the March for Jesus in, most suitably I thought, a Bentley – an old one, not a new, flashy thing. The police lining the route looked at me with interest, my car now fronted by two young girls waving streamers in moving, whirling circles. Were they available for premières, I wondered? Marchers galore shook my hand through the open window and a jolly nice lot they were! I was given masses of literature and a song book and joined in chanting: "Jesus is our battle cry. We want Jesus more and more." Well, when in Rome, I say. I was sorry to leave them at Hyde Park Corner, where they all waved goodbye and smiled. A nice after-lunch diversion.

All bets are now off with this restaurant now that Christopher Corbin and Jeremy King have left but we hope the standards will be maintained by the Belgo Group.

To call the **Carlton Tower** hotel in Cadogan Place, Knightsbridge, a mess gives new kindness to the meaning of the word. The Rib Room used to be fashionable in the 1960s – I once waited half an hour in the bar for Orson Welles while he waited in the upstairs bar for me – but on my last visit I had memorably one of the worst meals I have ever eaten. The set lunch, which costs more than The Dorchester or Claridge's, began with bread that was deeply uninteresting. Then I had chopped liver that was tired and Vanessa had pea soup that tasted of nothing. My main course was rib of beef with roast potato and Yorkshire pud. It was large but blank. Vanessa ate practically nothing of her main course. To end this fiasco I had coupe Robert, which was unexceptional strawberry ice cream with bits of fruit. Vanessa chose (from the à la carte) the Carlton Tower brownie with chocolate sauce. It was the *coup de grâce* – beyond-belief awful, and it must have been in the freezer for ever. It is quite astounding that in a London bursting with good restaurants, and in a very posh hotel on Sloane Street, a room can exist with such dire food. In all fairness (if I must!), the service was excellent: plates were whisked away as soon as we had finished eating, which was quite a skill because we had removed very little of the original food.
PS This has changed totally – due to me? I haven't seen the new version.

I first met Lawrence Leung in 1980. He was running movies for London's Chinese community and owned a small restaurant at the top of Earls Court Road called I Ching. I went there a lot. Mr Leung went on to even greater things, creating the Zen chain of restaurants. I recently met him at his newest acquisition, the very plush **Cassia Oriental** in Berkeley Square.

The place is very luxurious and spacious. It's on the first floor and in another incarnation was called China Jazz. The food is absolutely exceptional. And very cheap! Among the things we had were bahn tom, which is prawn in sweet potato cakes, and some spicy soup with squid, prawns, lemon grass and Thai herbs. The minced pork dumplings were super, the spring rolls very fresh. The inevitable duck, which came with round, fat pancakes, had fried squares of skin elegantly laid out around it. My dessert, called Indulgence, was bitter chocolate mousse, crème brûlée and orange crisp chocolate genoese. All fancy-sounding, but very good.

Enzo Cecconi has been running his place in Mayfair for nearly 20 years. It's a restaurant I used to go to a lot, but I hadn't been for a while. Led stupidly by fashion, I've been to newer places, but really they're not as good. Enzo used to be general manager of one of my favourite hotels, the Cipriani in Venice, so he knows a thing or two about Italian food. I had first a bellini, which are only really good at Harry's Bar in Venice and hideous everywhere else. **Cecconi's** did a rather fine one. Enzo recommended a lobster salad followed by *tagliolini verdi gratinati*, which I remembered as being exquisite. They were both very good, as were the raspberry tart and the millefeuille to follow. I finished with far too much espresso and then couldn't sleep.

Enzo has now given up. New owners will shortly re-open the restaurant.

Chez Moi in Kensington thankfully always stays the same, run by the world's most pleasant restaurateur, Colin Smith. It's a 1960s atmosphere, but chic in an old-fashioned way. You expect to see the young Princess Margaret at the next table. It is all very discreet, very comfortable. An absolutely marvellous place. They have a dessert called a Final d'Or. It's a pancake filled with Philadelphia cheese, yoghurt, almond liqueur from Portugal, and lemon and orange peel, with a maple syrup sauce around it. Sounds absolutely revolting, doesn't it? But it's one of my all-time favourites. A psychiatrist could make something of that.

Don't make waves

I never knew he was called Nico and if I had it would have made no difference. He was just an annoying young neighbour who'd married the beautiful girl upstairs, who lived with her mother. A girl I'd once tried, unsuccessfully, to seduce. When he had the impertinence to have children and took the greater liberty of leaving a pram blocking the elegant communal hall of the block I owned, it was solicitors at dawn. Thank goodness the nuisance didn't last. In 1965, the yuppie-led group left Cornwall Gardens, Kensington and calm returned.

Twenty-five years later, and before I started writing this column, I was taken, along with my friend Lord Parkinson, to **Chez Nico** at 90 Park Lane. Suddenly this bearded man started kissing me. Then his wife kissed me. Then two extremely beautiful daughters kissed me. That was very pleasant. It was all: "How lovely to see you again. We knew you'd come in sometime." I thought, "This is embarrassing, I'm being mistaken for somebody else."

It turned out mum was Dinah-Jane Zissu, now Ladenis, and Nico, who'd grown a beard, had become a self-taught, widely acclaimed chef. They were my old neighbours. The solicitors' letters were forgotten – although apparently not by Dinah-Jane's mum, who, I was told, still viewed me with a certain lack of warmth.

I was with Nico the night before he achieved his third, well-deserved Michelin star, eating a stunningly good grilled sea bass with basil purée and red-wine sauce. Nico's cooking is always very clean, precise, totally delicious and memorable. I find it unbelievable and grotesquely vicious that Michel Roux, a lower-rated chef down the road, should say, in an interview, of Nico's food "taste-wise it lacks". Nico rightly reflects on the togetherness of chefs in Europe as opposed to the pathetic bitchiness that goes on here.

Nico has calmed down from the days when customers were thrown out for daring to question his cuisine. I once heard him agree to provide mustard for a customer's Dover sole. "What do you expect?" he said. "They come from Claridge's". I was even privileged to be there one night when someone was throw out. "Don't mention it," said Nico. I have kept silent for years. It is an event I can no longer contain.

There is no better value in London than Nico's three-course set lunch at £25 including VAT, excluding service. I recently had some pithiviers of pheasant with smoked bacon and mushrooms preceded by velouté of cannellini beans with truffle oil and followed by a caramelised banana tart. Three-star Michelin cooking at 25 quid can't be bad. This was wonderful.

I felt somewhat guilty repaying Nico by imposing a film crew on him. Particularly as I totally misjudged how long it would take to shoot the restaurant scene in *Parting Shots*, which is partly based on experiences writing my restaurant-review column. Having taken up all of one Sunday, I needed another. Even I hadn't the nerve to demand a third, so we built part of the restaurant in a studio to avoid going back.

It's quite amusing directing restaurant staff in their own habitat. Jean-Luc Giguel, the restaurant manager, has all the chic gravitas you would expect of a seriously posh establishment. "Would you walk a little slower, Jean-Luc, and regard the reservations book with more disdain?" I asked. His glance in my direction could have given a nervously disposed diner a heart attack. Paul Rhodes, the superb chef, insisted that every plate of background food was hot and brilliantly prepared and laid out. More than was necessary, more than the camera could see. But try telling that to a perfectionist. They all loved the flamboyant portrayal of an over-the-top chef by Ken Kingsley. He throws out Chris Rea and Felicity Kendal, but gets his just deserts. Chris shoots him.

I did have to instruct Chris in the Winner napkin wave. I use it occasionally when I'm being ignored. "Slower Chris. Round the head and slowly." "Sorry," said Chris. "I've never done it before." The last time I had occasion to perform "the wave" was during a terrific meal at the Mirabelle. They forgot us somewhat when it came to ordering the dessert. I raised my hand in a measured manner and waved the napkin round my head. Two of my guests immediately raised their napkins and joined in. Thus was produced the first-ever triple napkin wave in the history of the world. It's achievements like that which make you proud to be British.

Nico Ladenis has now retired but the restaurant remains with the same chef, Paul Rhodes.

When I first visited **Chinon**, tucked away in backstreets south of Shepherd's Bush Green, it was ghastly. The hostess, Barbara Deane, who wore an old cardigan that looked like an Irene Handl cast-off, was extremely rude. The restaurant was gloomy, with food to match. The sauces were so heavy a lead weight would have bounced off them. Then I read that they had moved a few doors up the street, so, as they are near my house, I decided to give them another try. This shows that I am of a forgiving nature. Having been back a lot since, I can guarantee that things really improved, and Chinon has got better and better. Chef Jonathon Hayes at his best is unsurpassable. All the portions are very generous and on pleasing plates. And it has the best background music in the world, which may be because Jonathon was a musician. Barbara, though, is still sometimes brusque (readers go, get insulted and then write wonderful letters). I do have trouble with the seating arrangements, so dear Barbara (we're on almost intimate terms now) has to lug a very heavy marble-topped table from one side of the room to the other before I get there. Barbara does complain a bit about some of her customers, but not of me. I am a great fan.

Andrew and Madeleine Lloyd Webber asked me to join them at **The Chiswick**, not surprisingly in Chiswick. Andrew had been recording nearby. After playing me part of the fantastic rock score for his film, *Whistle Down the Wind*, we strolled over to view the simple-to-the-point-of-nonexistent decor at The Chiswick. But the food was tiptop. A ragout of snails with chorizo and chickpeas was memorable, but the beef tortillas and Mexican relishes surprised us a bit because the slices of steak were cold and we weren't sure if they were meant to be. Nevertheless, if you're in the area, go there.

I am always wary of going to places that are supposed to be chic. When people told me **Christopher's** in Covent Garden was "in", I stayed out. I did eventually go, however, with Miss Seagrove and the TV sex therapist, Dr Ruth Westheimer. Make what you will of *that*! The parsley soup was thick, my hamburger and bun extremely good, and the lime pie more like cheesecake, but edible nonetheless. Miss Seagrove and Dr Ruth enjoyed their grilled sole. The owner, called, unsurprisingly, Christopher, is the son of Lord Gilmour, a former cabinet minister. It is always nice to see the upper classes forced to labour.

Death wish

Ever since Vanessa found out she was in my will she's been trying to kill me. Knowing that everything in an English tea is fattening and a no-no, she nevertheless insists we have one.

One Sunday afternoon we decided to try **Claridge's**. My normal, dreadful clothing is tolerated in most places, but for safety I keep a pair of socks and a tie in all of my cars. I don't bother with the socks if I am going to Claridge's for lunch because nobody sees your ankles, as they're under the table, but for tea in the atrium lounge I donned my reserve socks and a Concorde tie. I thought the new doorman considerably lacked charm. But everybody else there was as polite as usual. We settled into a nice table facing marble pillars, gilt-topped, metal swags on the glass dining-room doors, thick floral carpets and a circular sofa with an enormous bowl of flowers in the middle.

The tea was prodigiously good. Unbelievably fresh little sandwiches, smoked salmon, cream cheese and cucumber, tongue and more. The scones, one pair with apples, one with raisins, were hot and of perfect texture, together with excellent jam and clotted cream. And the little cakes on one of those multi-tiered things had every item, from layered chocolate cake to strawberry tartlets, as good as you could possibly get. A real feast. The whole thing came to £32 inc VAT and service. I exited flourishing their nice little napkin with a yellow embroidered C on it. I told the excellent waiter I need it because the de-mister on the Bentley was a bit dodgy and it would be useful to wipe the windscreen with.

The restaurant at Claridge's is fantastic, like a vast 1930s ocean liner. The atmosphere is of another time and place. The service is first-rate to historic. Only once did it fail and thus it was here that I invented the Winner napkin-wave. The clientele is a wonderful mix. I have dined adjacent to or with Francis Bacon, Margaret Thatcher, Sophia Loren, Robert Mitchum and Jack Lemmon, as well as assorted geriatrics and the strangest of American families. The odd king is not an uncommon sight. Some people object to the formality of it all, but I am normally wearing no socks, and on one occasion my shirt was not tucked in and could not be buttoned at the neck because it didn't fit.

Far and away the greatest value in London is Sunday lunch at Claridge's for £26, including VAT and service. Please don't go there. I can't stand crowds. I started with grilled Pacific prawns with tomato that was blanched, peeled and baked with olive oil, garlic and herbs, and fennel braised with olive oil, Pernod, garlic and seasoning. This was a taste experience. You could have roast beef and Yorkshire pudding, a lesson in how to do them well; or their chicken pie, which is exceptional. I went off the set menu and had veal escalope Holstein with fried egg and anchovies – difficult to do, unavailable in most places, and superb. Then I had the best *pommes soufflés* I've ever eaten, deliciously crisp little "paper-bags" of potatoes, and a wonderfully smooth spinach purée. I grabbed a bit of Vanessa's specially roasted chicken – mmmm!

The desserts are masterful. They used to have two dessert trolleys, elegantly propelled by dark-suited waiters, one for fruit and one for cakes and mousses. Then they trimmed them down to one. I once was dining with Sir Hugh Wontner, then top man at Claridge's, at the Lord Mayor's house (Oh, how I used to get around!) and I complained bitterly. Sir Hugh reinstated the two trolleys, but he went and they've reduced them to one again. However, my strawberry millefeuille was mind-blowing; the tiramisù surprisingly magnificent and the petits fours delicious.

This place gets hardly any praise and it is extraordinary. Real food that looks and tastes like real food; that's rare. And on weekdays you get a

Hungarian string quartet playing in knee breeches. As long as Claridge's remains unchanged, one area of the world is incarcerated in quality.

I was eating some exceptional chocolate cookies and listening to the orchestra in the elegant lounge of Claridge's when their general manager, Christopher Cowdray, upset me. He didn't mean to. He thought he was giving me good news. "We're going to redecorate and refurnish this area," he said. He mentioned a designer who did homes rather than hotels and some figure in millions that would be spent. "Why, if I may ask," I said with uneasy calm, "are you doing that?" "Because it looks a bit worn," said Christopher. That hadn't occurred to me, but it could be true. So what? I like worn. I much prefer it to new, shiny, glossy. Certain hotels have particular charm because they are not super-recently done out. They look lived-in. Claridge's is one of them. I greatly approve of it as it is.

There is one important ingredient for an enjoyable meal that I never see in any write-up: the customers. I used to enjoy **Clarke's**, a Kensington establishment where Sally knocks out impeccable food in her see-through kitchen. When her set meals achieved media recognition, the jovial clientele changed to impeccably suited businessmen, mixed with over-expectant "special occasion" groups. It scared me away.

I don't understand how people hear of new restaurants so easily. I went to **Coast** in Albemarle Street, W1, a few days after it opened. It was packed. The chef is Stephen Terry, whom I'd supported at the Canteen. The place was indescribably noisy, decorated in a nihilistic style of non-decor, but the food was fine. Except for the dessert, which was a number of rock-hard chocolate balls. "Be careful," the waiter said, "they may shoot off the plate." They did. So why serve them?

Mogens and groans

There are places wild horses could not drag me back to. High on the list is **The Collection**, the fashionable restaurant in Brompton Road. It is just as well – they didn't want to let me in anyway! I telephoned at three in the afternoon. "This is Michael Winner, I'd like a table for two at 8.30 please." "We're full," said the girl. I repeated, patiently: "This is Michael Winner, could I please have a table for two at 8.30?" "Not a chance at that time," she said. Yet again I said: "Could I please have a table for two at 8.30?" "Is that your preferred time?" asked the girl. "Of course it is," I said with deadly quiet, "that's why I've mentioned it three times already." "We're very busy..." "Do you know who I am?" I asked the dread question. "No," she said. "I'm new here." "Well, could you please be so kind as to telephone Mogens Tholstrup [the owner] and tell him Michael Winner would like a table for two at 8.30." "Are you a friend of Mr Tholstrup's, Mr Withers?" asked the girl. "Winner," I said slowly "W-I-N-N-E-R. Now here's my phone number, please call me back." "There's no need if you're a friend of Mr Tholstrup's," said the girl. "You can come at 8.30."

An hour later, the phone rang. An immensely charming lady, Laura Anderson, said: "Welcome to The Collection, Mr Winner, we're looking forward to seeing you at 8.30." "No, you're not," I responded. "You didn't want to let me in." I've had trouble getting in there before. I was not one of Mogen's 500 nearest and dearest, so I was not asked to the opening night. I never go to restaurant openings, it's the principle! If I'd been Tamara Beckwith I'd have been high on the first-night list. If I'd been having an affair with Tamara Beckwith I'd have been higher. If I'd spent the night with Jack Nicholson at The Dorchester I'd have been the guest of honour. Being only a poor boy from you-know-where, I was out!

On the night of my dinner I was at a party near The Collection. A guest told me there was a man with a clipboard at the door and you could be held up for minutes while they checked you out. "A tenth of a second and I'm gone," I thought, as the Rolls drew up. Three people, one with clipboard, stood at the unsigned entrance. One was a young lady who showed us in. The room itself is immensely impressive. A great brick barn with steel supports and wooden floors, a long bar on the left with a lot of people drinking, tables on the ground floor and more on a large raised balcony. Very New York. I was shown to the balcony. Within seconds, I knew why I'd never return. It is terribly noisy: the people drinking below, some screaming/singing half-hidden by voice-noise, the animated diners upstairs. Result: you have great difficulty in talking even to someone close to you. I understand that's what it's all about today: big noisy restaurants where you are swept away (or in my case swept aside) by the cacophony and spirit of others enjoying themselves. But not for me.

The food was far less good than Mogen's other place a few yards away, Daphne's. There everything is pleasant. At The Collection we both left a lot of everything, from crispy duck with yaki soba noodles and plum sauce to noodle soup with shiitake, galangal and water chestnuts and spring roll. Even my dessert of ice nougat with chocolate was unfinished. A bit like airline food, I thought. Laura, the manageress, strode to and fro on long legs with a toothy grin, coping with aplomb. Strangely, I admired it all greatly. Mogens is the rich man's Terence Conran. He has great style. He has put his finger on what his public want and, like a finely crafted

Schwarzenegger movie, he is giving it to them. That it's not for me is totally irrelevant. Mogens himself appeared to greet us. "I told them not to let you in," he smiled. "You just can't get the staff these days, can you?" I replied. Vanessa wondered how all the people in the bar, without reservations and there only to drink, got past the clipboard führer at the door. "They say they're friends of Michael Winner's," said Mogens. When I got the bill, it was a rare moment. I had cash with me. I laid my notes on the table. Unfortunately, the bill was £113.50. I had £40. They had to send it on. Personally, I shall stick to the calm and charm of Daphne's. I wasn't asked to the opening of that either!

The pros and Connaught

I had one of the most awful meals of my life at **The Connaught** restaurant the other Sunday. At The Connaught! I hear people saying, you can't do that to The Connaught. Oh yes I can, even though I've had good experiences there before. The person I blame this time is Jean-Pierre Chevallier, the restaurant manager. I am always careful to the point of tedium when I book. I do not go to restaurants, I go to tables. So I rang a second time and discussed in detail where I would be seated, explaining, of course, I like a bit of space. "I've put you in a corner at a table normally for three people," said Mr Chevallier. On that basis, as far as I'm concerned a "contract" to be honoured, I got myself beautifully dressed in my best suit and tie and set out for The Connaught. When I got there my table was not in a corner at all! It seemed, at first, quite nice. It protruded out a bit, rather close to a service table, but with a good view of the restaurant and the door.

Then things went downhill. As the service table became more and more used it was indescribably over-bustling. The noise level was horrendous, not helped by the two very loud titled people behind me (I know they were titled because he kept referring to "Lady whatever") and a party in front with a man getting increasingly worse for drink. "May I tell you!" he kept repeating, and then: "They were all named after admirals of the fleet." You literally could not hear yourself speak. This was partly because the room is panelled, which bounces sound off, and is also overcrowded, with tables too close together.

The staff exuded: "We're at The Connaught and we're superior." When I asked for the tiny water glasses to be replaced with something larger so I could accommodate ice and lemon, the wine waiter gave a look saying it was highly impertinent of me to suggest a change in normal procedures. When Vanessa asked for a roast chicken, which she always gets at Claridge's, the waiter said, as if dealing with a total ignoramus: "A roast chicken will take an hour and 10 minutes." I later discovered

Claridge's puts one on the moment I book. "Why not have guinea fowl, it is very similar?" said the waiter. Now I may only be a poor boy from Willesden, but I don't need some snotty waiter at The Connaught telling me guinea fowl is very similar to chicken, because it isn't.

Eventually Vanessa settled on a poussin. "Bread sauce and gravy?" asked the waiter. "Yes please," she replied. And then when he'd finished taking the order, she asked him most sweetly: "Could I have some stuffing?" This threw the waiter into a tantrum of arrogance. "Stuffing *and* bread sauce," he said, like the bus from Scunthorpe had arrived. "Yes," I said icily. "Madame would like bread sauce and stuffing." Now, why put some young kid down? If she wants *ice cream* and bread sauce just smile and say: "Of course, Madame." I see nothing wrong with having bread sauce and stuffing at all. They're different textures. I shall now have them every time I order chicken or poussin, and God help the waiter who tries to sniff at me about it.

As for the food: the bread, two types, brown and white only, they don't serve it, you take it from the basket; dreary. My first course of various pâtés, pompously named "prélude gourmand Connaught", was acceptable but uninteresting. Vanessa's *feuilleté d'oeufs brouillés aux truffes de Périgord* bland to the point of extinction. A similar dish at Claridge's the following week was excellent. My roast beef was fine, the Yorkshire pudding the best ever, but the *pommes purée* soggy and crude. Vanessa left most of the poussin, but thought her carrots excellent. My two things from the dessert trolley I remember thinking at the time I would never remember. Vanessa's sherry trifle was totally historic, as in great. Overall when you add the noise and the service, a ghastly experience. And very overpriced at £37.22 inc coffee. And they don't even give you petits fours!

Hospital case

What I only go through. How I suffer. Unbelievable really. I'm referring to the food at the multi-million-pound refitted Lanesborough Hotel. It is grotesque, so awful as to be almost indescribable (though I shall try) and an absolute disgrace. The owners, if anyone knows who the owners are of these strange places, should call a board meeting at once and fire themselves. And, believe me, what I've written so far is kind.

It all started when Mrs Hylda Gilbert, a close friend and wife of the film director Lewis Gilbert, rang me. "Take me to lunch at **The Lanesborough**," she suggested. "It's the most beautiful room." "How's the food?" I asked. There was a pause. "Average," she replied. Now, I don't totally trust Hylda on rooms. She once told me the lobby of the Carlton Tower was the most beautiful room in the world. But when she said "average", I knew the food would be dodgy.

Nothing venture, nothing gain. So Vanessa and I picked up Mrs G and set off for Sunday lunch at The Lanesborough. The building, on the site of the old St George's Hospital at Hyde Park Corner, is severe Georgian. It looks from the outside like a home for the mentally unstable. Once you get in things perk up a bit. The Georgian lobby/corridor is classy, although I don't know why they've got one of those awful gas imitation coal fires. If Claridge's can have a real fire, why can't they?

The Conservatory is the name of the only restaurant in The Lanesborough. It is indeed a nice room. Rather camp, done out in Georgian chinoiserie with a lot of pink, models of mandarins, various Chinese lanterns and two enormous urns with palm trees and assorted plants in them. The ceiling is glass and high, the tables are well apart, the chairs are comfortable, the crockery is good with blackberry decoration. There is pleasant music from a real-live pianist and double-bass player on a little platform. If only they served food as well.

Guessing things would be in need of help I went totally mad and ordered a bottle of Château Lafite-Rothschild 1961 for £499. Before you think how utterly decadent, I drink very little but tend to spend a lot when I do.

I ordered Chinese duck cakes with oriental aioli to start. It might match the decor, I thought. This turned out to be no more than duck hamburger, with no sauce to help it. It was bland and dreary. Vanessa had asparagus soup. I tasted it, or rather non-tasted it. The flavour was nil, and it wasn't very hot either. Mrs G had smoked salmon. The service was fine – the room is run by John Davey, a great pro whom I knew at Bibendum and The Belfry.

For a main course I ordered a kedgeree of salmon and haddock with curry butter. It came with rice and, for some odd reason, boiled egg slices! It was totally uneatable. It is very rare I leave a main course. I pig out and then complain. This was so drab and tasteless I just nibbled a bit and gave up. Vanessa's chicken was dry and horrid, but the corn fritters with it were good. Mrs G had roast beef and Yorkshire pudding. She picked at a nasty-looking piece of overdone beef and from time to time pulled a face and looked round at the decor. At the end she left half of it; Vanessa left most of her chicken.

Dessert was cappuccino brûlée for me and Mrs G; thick and horrible is the best I could say. Vanessa had apple pudding and honey ice cream. I tasted it. Rather like it came from a packet, I thought.

At that point the manager came over. "The chef would like to know when your write-up will appear," he said. "No he wouldn't," I replied. "The food is disgusting. I shall say so in no uncertain terms."

As I left a bevy of people in dress suits bowed a bit and said, "How was it, Mr Winner?" "Lovely room, awful food," I muttered without pausing. They deducted everything except two set lunches at £23 each and the expensive wine from my bill as a gesture of regret. The next weekend a friend of mine went and his meal was so terrible they gave him two meals free. This, however, is not the point of a restaurant. After all, this is on one of the most expensive sites in London. If other London hotels can get in excellent chefs, why can't The Lanesborough? "When they shut the hospital they should've kept the chef," I said to myself as I left.

The only Criterion

When Marco Pierre White told me he was taking over the Criterion, a restaurant in Piccadilly Circus, I said: "Ridiculous! You can't park, you have to walk through those night-time oddities that hang around Eros to get there..." Needless to say, Marco ignored my advice, opened up, and has done splendidly .

After deciding that the Rolls and chauffeur should wait on a taxi rank at the north-eastern end of Lower Regent Street, I walked the few paces to the **Criterion Brasserie**, safe in body and spirit, as it was lunchtime and not raining.

People always say the Criterion is such a lovely room. I think it looks like a Victorian gents' toilet. That still places it well above the visual standard of most new restaurants. They all seem to be decorated by the same man, whose name I forget, who obviously got the job lot of yellow paint from the Dulux catalogue and has been splashing it about ever since.

The clientele of the Criterion looked to me like the public you see on quiz shows. The menu bears a large cartoon of Marco, with his favourite slogan: "To know how to eat well, one must first know how to wait." As far from the Winner philosophy as you can get. Marco said: "You never have to wait here." "I'm waiting for my Coca-Cola," I said. "They're doing the sliced lemon for you," said Marco. "They got the ruler out, that's why we're waiting," said his beautiful girlfriend, Mati. She works at the Criterion in the evenings. That's a good reason for going there.

We got only one set menu between four people. Vanessa ordered the cabbage broth. "I didn't like it last time I had it," advised Marco. "What do you mean, you didn't like it? You own the place!" I said. Marco recommended some special skate from the à la carte, but I decided to have fried skate from the set menu. I took Marco's advice and had ballottine of salmon to start. It was very good. The bread was awful.

I surveyed the room. Various upper-class shoppers had arrived with carrier bags. "I'm normally at the Ivy for Saturday lunch," I said.

Marco looked as if that was something on which he wished to have no opinion. "They do corned beef hash," he finally remarked. I nodded. "We're thinking of having that at the Mirabelle, but we can't because it's not right for us, is it?" "Well, you come from a slum in Leeds, Marco, so you're very posh," I said. "But I'm just an ordinary person and we liked corned beef hash." Marco found that amusing.

Vanessa didn't like her soup. "It's Paul Gaylor's recipe, it's not one of my recipes," said Marco. Then he started piling the used plates up and put the knives and forks on top. Didn't look to me like a man who enjoyed waiting.

Vanessa found her main-course haddock very good. My fried skate was dodgy, but I'd been given a side order of chicken consommé with brioche dumplings. That was lovely. Then I finished with two jellies – red fruit and Sauternes jelly – and I had a bit of treacle tart. All superb.

I'm not surprised Marco made it work, really. And if you're addicted to gold mosaic ceilings and Victorian Arab decor, you could even find it wondrous.

The **Daphne's** in Draycott Avenue, SW3, that I knew in the 1960s had been opened by a robust theatrical agent called Daphne Rye, and was a hang-out for showbiz types. Now owned by two revoltingly lovely young people (Mogens and Paola Tholstrup), I had heard Daphne's now was full of Sloane-type lethargics (the staff) and rowdy diners. I wasn't endeared to it when I rang up and said "Is that Daphne's?" and a lady said "Mmmm". Still I persevered. When we turned up for lunch we were shown to a corner table in the back, almost-garden patio. It was very Los Angeles, with plants creeping up white walls. There were four different types of bread, all good. I started with fried calamari and Ms Seagrove with zucchini fritters, both excellent and well presented. I found my main course of the "special" risotto with chilli, tomato and prawns with a lobster sauce uninteresting. But to be fair, I have never found risotto interesting except once when it was served to me by Rocco and Alya Forte – then it was unbelievably good. Ms Seagrove generously swapped, giving me her most tasty and perfectly cooked spaghetti with fresh plum tomatoes and basil. For dessert I ordered crostata with apples, which turned out to be a superb apple tart with vanilla ice cream. There was a tiny dip when it took far too long to give me back my credit card. I usually walk out of restaurants without even asking for the bill, saying "Send it to me" as I sail by. I must remember always to leave my credit card at home. It's far simpler.

A good grilling

I was at The Dorchester because, when dad was alive, we used to alternate Sunday lunch between home, Claridge's, **The Dorchester Grill** and the Savoy Grill. I thought I'd check out The Dorchester after the addition of all that gold leaf. I had lunch there once with the lovely Ruby Wax when filming her show. But she was so hyper, much worse than me, I couldn't really judge it. "Where's the food?" she kept saying, when even I didn't expect to see it so soon.

Thus, in the calm of my own life, I sauntered into the room, which has not changed at all. Spanish-lunatic, with tapestries and strange red directors' chairs in leather. It still looks good. The bread trolley was remarkable. About 20 loaves on it, rolls and wheat in a floral display. I had Stilton cheese bread and Vanessa walnut. Both good, mine better. The dress code was lax to nil. There were people in T-shirts, no jackets, jeans, sneakers, all in this very elegant and immaculately serviced room. The assistant manager, John Wade, looked after me; he's definitely a great pro.

Next to us, two tables were laid for a party of 23. "When are they coming?" I asked John nervously. "Not until 3pm," he said. "It's Jesse Jackson." I decided to compare The Dorchester, amazing value at £24.50 all-in for three courses, with Claridge's, which is first rate at £29 for the same. Vanessa's smoked salmon was as good. I had Lancashire black pudding and diced apple served on mashed potatoes with a spinach cream sauce, not on the set menu but fine. The roast beef and Yorkshire pudding was not quite as good as Claridge's. My chair was less comfortable, but the room had a good buzz. Vanessa's chicken breast had a bone sticking out, which frightened her and had to be removed. She thought it far less good than Claridge's. But the spinach was better. Vanessa's sherry trifle had too many blackcurrants dominating the flavour. I had a tiptop two-tone cream chocolate thing.

The Jesse Jackson group hadn't arrived and we were on coffee. The petits fours were historic, far better than Claridge's, except they don't leave them on the table, which isn't surprising. Fudge, white truffle, soft green mint in chocolate, all to drool over. Then at 2.45 the party could be seen gathering outside. When they came in I thought: "Jesse's aged a bit!" A white-haired man with a stick led a distinguished group of well-dressed black people. Inexplicably, a man in soldier's uniform flash-photographed him on the way in, sitting down and at the table. I decided it wasn't Jesse Jackson at all. "That's what they said when they booked him in from the Cumberland," said John as I was leaving. "Looks more like leaders of an African state," I observed. "They're speaking American," said John. I later found out it was the Rev Dr Bennett W Smith Sr, president of the Progressive National Baptist Convention Inc!

For years, driving through George Street, Marylebone, I have admired the clean, white façade and the myriad hanging baskets of geraniums that make the exterior of **Durrants Hotel** so attractive. As we were filming at the Wallace Collection, Durrants was the nearest place for lunch. Sadly, it illustrated the old saying: "You can't judge a book by its cover." The dining room was pseudo, and the food of a type that I thought had disappeared from London decades ago. I started with mozzarella and tomato, difficult to mess up, but Durrants succeeded. It was soggy and of no known taste. I turned to the trolley: slices were cut from a little piece of pork that were tasteless and spoke of the deep freeze. A couple of bits of crackling were given separately; they lacked oomph. The vegetables were overcooked and boring. For dessert I chose some sort of pastry with cream and strawberries. I have pigged my way through many of the worst puddings ever. I left most of this. At least the service was excellent.

I made a reservation some time ago at **The Fifth Floor Restaurant** at Harvey Nichols, went up there and was so appalled by the snotty, aren't-we-wonderful approach of the two girls on the desk that I fled without eating. Bravely, I returned with an American couple, he being terribly important at Sony Music. A tall, dark girl at the desk gave us a look as if a smile to her was like sunlight to a vampire, but another lady rushed us to the table before I could run for the lift. The room, which was crowded, is grey and looks like a canteen, but the chairs are extraordinarily comfortable. The menu is large and can't make up its mind whether it's in English or French. Words of both languages mix uneasily. I chose for my first course Henry's black bean soup – called that, I was told, after the chef's first name. Since it's the only dish he put his name to I had some hopes, but it was dark brown and desperately uninteresting. My American lady companion had grilled clams in garlic butter; I ate one, bland and of dreary texture. She agreed. My main course, described as "Bury black pudding, potato, apple and bacon galette, mustard sauce and onion rings", was horrific. The black pudding was tasteless, difficult to get out of a tough sausage skin and oddly textured. The potato etc galette was soggy and tasted rather nasty. The onion rings were limp. In fact, the whole course was limp. Personally, I don't see any point in eating in a clothes shop. I mean, you wouldn't buy suits at the Caprice, would you? I'm sorry to say my first impressions were right. The Fifth Floor may be fashionable, but it's absolutely awful.

The greatest hole in what is laughingly known as the hospitality industry is the lack of cafes, snack bars, superior sit-down delicatessen joints. Call them what you will, I mean places where you can order simple stuff without feeling you're in for all the formality and trauma of a main meal. New York is full of them, Paris has them by the score. In England, I can

think of none, except for **Fortnum's Fountain** restaurant on the ground floor of
Fortnum & Mason. This remains delightfully old-fashioned. I found the last manager
insufferable, so I stopped going. But now there is a nice new manager, Sunil Sood. The
Fountain was once renowned for its Mont Blanc, a historic dessert of meringues with a
chestnut filling. They don't make it any more, but the Welsh rarebit is very good. I had two
slices with grilled tomatoes and fried eggs. I'd asked for the bacon crisp, but it came soggy,
as I feared it would. When I was last in they did exceptionally good waffles, but that's
another thing no longer on offer. When the waitress came with the bill, she asked: "Is this
your first time in the Fountain restaurant?" "I've been coming here since 1942," I replied.
She was Kirsten, from Boston, so you can excuse anything. "It was a pleasure meeting both
of you," she said cheerily as we left.

I have always considered afternoon tea one of the great achievements of British culture. At
Fortnum & Mason's St James's Restaurant they do it brilliantly. They have
Gentleman's Relish, lovely scones and, a sight not often seen these days, the English toasted
teacake. Crumpets, too. The pastries are not as good as they were in the old days, but
what is?

   On another day, I arrived with Vanessa at 1pm for lunch. We were dealt with, and I
mean that in the best possible way, by a wonderful old (sorry, ma'am) Irish waitress,
Frances McNamara, whom I've known for a long time – she's been there for 17½ years.
She is exemplary. What a mover! We both had cold cucumber and mint soup. It was good.
I then had Lady MacLean's beef stroganoff. I've no idea who Lady MacLean is, but she
knows absolutely nothing about beef stroganoff. It was revolting. Tough, tasteless beef, a
horrid sharp sauce. I won't go on or I'll get upset. I went on to bread and butter pudding. It
wasn't awful, but it was well on the way. The event was not saved by some excellent
choccy mints in silver paper.

You could not call the **Four Seasons** restaurant at The Inn on the Park in Park Lane an
elegant room. I am hard pressed to know what to call it other than a place I do not wish to
sit in again. (The whole hotel is a lesson in how not to decorate.) Vanessa ordered a
chicken freshly cooked, so they bunged one on. Thinking I'd get bored waiting, they kindly
gave us both an extra starter to follow their good, hot walnut bread. I had tartare of diced
trout and Vanessa had queen scallops with polenta. Both were fine. Then came the real
first course: baby squid, salmon and langoustine kebab with wild roquette. I could see why
the young chef, Jean-Christophe Novelli, had a Michelin star. The main course took us
downhill. Vanessa actively hated her chicken and the stuffing. I had beef from the trolley,
not roast but a fillet, that was pleasant, but the *pommes gratin* were unexciting to say the

least and the roast potatoes weren't good. I don't know why so many posh restaurants can't roast a potato. Housewives know the skin has to be crispy hardish and the inside soft. But then Jean-Christophe redeemed himself with the dessert – a truly terrific steamed chocolate pud with chocolate sauce inside it and a delicious home-made vanilla ice cream. Definitely one of the best desserts ever. The petits fours were a variety of chocolates, all right but not historic, and some brandy snaps. Personally, I like a big display! Icing-caked gooseberries, tiny cakes, that sort of thing, but outside of Claridge's and The Dorchester, where are they?

On another visit, in the tea area – I will not call it a room – a harpist played the Mrs Robinson theme from *The Graduate*. The other guests looked as if they were bored, just passing through, and had nothing better to do. Mr Howard Moss took our order. He produced fresh sandwiches, but odd – grilled tuna and vegetables, Stilton and port, and pesto-marinated lamb are not classical English fare. "I can get you the Devonshire tea sandwiches, if you prefer," said Mr Moss. The menu should tell you what they are – nice, normal egg and tomato, smoked salmon etc – so happy tea-ers know there is a choice. The cakes were not so hot. The teacake was particularly odd. I would rate the tea good minus, the setting ghastly minus minus. They should definitely have a serious redecoration at the Inn On.

Olympian appetite

My dad's office was a period house in Addison Bridge Place, a small cul-de-sac south of the railway bridge that leads you to Olympia. On the corner was **Frank's Sandwich Bar**, run, not unsurprisingly, by Frank, second name Cura, together with his son Frank Jr and a thin man with brilliantined black, sleek hair, Ronnie Oddi. Opposite was a small garage where dad bought my first car, a black Austin A35 with bright red seats. I have not been back to that spot since – oh, probably 1960. It's quite near my house, so I recently walked there for lunch to see if Frank's was still very good.

It used to be the original ticket entrance to Olympia station. It's still very 1950s. A few cracks have appeared in the large painted sign outside. They've added a couple of white plastic tables with matching chairs; otherwise it remains a time warp. I ordered a bacon, egg and sausage toasted sandwich from a young man who turned out to be Frank Jr's son Paul. Frank Sr has passed away, so Frank Jr is now called Frank and he's still there. The thin, sleek black-haired chap, Ronnie Oddi, is still there, too, only he's put on a bit of weight, lost most of his hair and what remains isn't black.

But the sandwich was terrific. So were the accompanying cups of tea, served in nice china cups with saucers and proper spoons. The place was packed with regulars who obviously know a good thing when they eat it, many of them taxi drivers, which I always take as a good sign. Dad always used to have a cream-cheese sandwich brought to his office. The garage my first car came from is now called Boot Tree Ltd and looks very posh. Frank's Sandwich Bar is the sort of place most people pass by. But if you're at Olympia, or just feel like dropping in, I think you'll find it excellent of its kind. It was nice to be back.

People often say, "You must get special attention when you turn up." To which I reply, "I certainly hope so." My reception at **Frederick's** in Islington proved that not always is any particular effort made. "Do you have a reservation?" said a surly girl at the door. I stayed silent. "What's your name?" she persisted. I told her. "Table 52," she called out, as if a train was to be shunted into a loading bay. We were shown through into a gloomy room with glass walls and ceiling. Once settled, after a long delay, our drinks order was taken. And then came the food. There is a wonderful line in the play *Kean* when Edmund Kean has to see an audition by an aspiring actress. "Was I awful?" she asks. "My dear, you were worse than awful, you were quite good." Thus was the food at Frederick's. The crudités were tired. My soup was bland but not nasty; Vanessa's hot asparagus wasn't hot. My liver and onions were okay but fairly tasteless; Vanessa's dover sole was a bit rubbery. I ordered an apple tart and if I'd been blindfolded I'd have had difficulty saying what it was. The service was slow to awful, and the restaurant manager crept about looking as if a smile to him would be like a silver cross to a vampire.

Goolies, a bar and restaurant in nearby Abingdon Road, Kensington, is owned by Mike Gooley, the chairman of Trailfinders. Mike was in the SAS for eight years and looks like it. I expected him to come crashing through the plate-glass window on the end of a rope, pausing only to slit the throat of the head waiter. Goolies is a pleasant, narrow bar with tables on one side you can eat at and a raised level with more tables. For a starter I had white crab cake with apple sauce. It was a very pleasing crab cake. Extremely large. My main course was roast rump of kangaroo, roast sweet potatoes and beetroot pesto. The kangaroo was all right, a bit chewy. It's not going on my regular eating list. Goolies is a nice local hang-out with rather good food, but I think a sparse bar-type place should go back to basics. Fish and chips. Hamburgers. Irish stew. Lancashire hotpot. Hot dogs. Where can you get a good hot dog today? And waffles – they're a thing of the past. Forget trying to be posh. There are already too many restaurants drowning in plate decoration. Good fresh ingredients and simplicity are the best. I'd be a regular then – not necessarily something desirable.

Ramsay's Treat

I am not a regular at **Gordon Ramsay**. I dined at his old restaurant, Aubergine, in May 1994 before Gordon had a Michelin star, and only visited him again recently. A gap of five-and-a-half years. Previously, I'd liked the food, found the desserts highly iffy and predicted, accurately, that he'd get a star next time the guide came out. Gordon then got a second star and become famous for being in a state of high excitement in his kitchen, even reverting to what is laughingly known as bad language. I squirmed when a lot of extremely untalented chefs ganged up on him, making ludicrous pronouncements about how he was letting down the catering industry and how youngsters would not wish to join for fear of being knocked about by our Gord in one of his temper fits.

Having lived my life among movie stars, bouts of perfection-induced hysteria are nothing new. My dearest friend in show business, Burt Lancaster, once held me over a cliff in Mexico, threatening to kill me. He shook me to and fro, assuring me I'd be dropped 2,000ft below. His language made Gordon at his worst seem prim. That night Burt graciously served me and the girlfriend a delicious barbecued lamb in the garden of his Durango villa. I see nothing wrong in chefs getting over-excited. A restaurant kitchen must be the most difficult place to work in: hot, rushing out food of impeccable quality, trying to keep up standards, horrifically long hours. At least Gordon is always in his kitchen. The young people, who looked extremely unbruised when I met them, have the advantage of working with one of the greats at close quarters. Even if, at times, the quarters may be uncomfortably close.

I've met Gordon quite a bit since my first visit, dined with him and his mentor, Marco Pierre White, and spoken to him on the phone. I always found him exceptionally well mannered, charming and of exemplary character. So when I rang at short notice and said: "Can I come tonight, Gordon, please?" he was predictably affable and said: "Yes," even though there's usually a five-week waiting list.

Things did not start perfectly. I was shown a table far too small for my requirements, so I moved to a bigger one. The first food arrival was the bread, which was memorably one of the most awful rolls I've ever eaten. I kept returning to it throughout the meal, because I couldn't believe it was so dreadful.

To say that hereafter things started to look up is an understatement. I suggested a quick three-course bash so I could get out and leave the table clear for customers who had undoubtedly booked it. The maître d', Jean-Claude Breton, responded: "Do you want the chef to do a little surprise for you?" That was the best offer I was likely to get, so I said: "Yes, please."

There followed a number of courses defined by the extreme delicacy of their taste and composition. It was as good a meal as I've ever eaten in my life. I'll name the dishes but it's the quality that counts. There was a freebie starter of baby spring roll stuffed with duck confit and deep-fried fillet of monkfish. Then a small, exquisite pumpkin soup, followed by ravioli of langoustine with a light lobster vinaigrette and other bits and pieces, a combination of flavours I shall long remember. Then a salad of sea scallops and new potatoes. My main course was pigeon de bresse in a consommé de ceps with truffle herbs and hot foie gras. Pigeon may sound plebeian, but this was a gourmet delight. A granita of pineapple to clear the palate preceded desserts that had strikingly improved since my last Ramsay visit. There was an orange soufflé, a thin orange tart, three different sorbets, a hot chocolate fondant, ice cream, a pistachio soufflé, little cornets with crème fraîche and passion fruit – all utterly memorable.

Only two downers, other than the bread, which I mention in case you think Gordon and I have started a serious liaison. The mint tea that finished the meal was utterly revolting. Overstewed, not a trace of fresh mint anywhere, just tea bags. And the wine waiter, Thierry Berson, who had done a great job, produced lovely wines and also helped to serve, made a really silly error. When I said: "No, thank you," to dessert wine, he said sarcastically: "You're better on Coca-Cola." It was an impertinent remark, chipping otherwise unblemished service. But, overall, Gordon Ramsay is a great culinary experience in a relaxed atmosphere. Certainly, in my view, a three-Michelin-star meal.

"Go to **The Greenhouse** in Mayfair," people said to me. I went. I wish I hadn't. At the end of their Sunday lunch I reckoned I hadn't eaten food like that since I was last on British Rail. It's a very posh place with far too much glossy cream paint inside. The poached egg salad with sauté potatoes and black pudding I shall spend a long time trying to forget. The deep-fried plaice was bland to the point of non-existence, and only became interesting when my guest, Dorrit Moussaieff, the international jeweller, tried to dab it with a tissue to take the excess grease off. Her roast beef looked good, but lacked any known taste, and the so-called chocolate steamed pudding was grossly inferior chocolate gateau with a watery sauce. The regular chef, Gary Rhodes, was off. I think the dishwasher stood in.

Fearlessly I trod through the gleaming, bronzed entrance of the Cafe Royal and into the marble lobby that leads to eight floors of conference and banqueting rooms, together with assorted bars and restaurants, housing at peak well over 3,000 people! "Oh dear," I thought. Is this the place where Oscar Wilde held court, where Beardsley, Beerbohm and

Shaw argued literary matters and gossiped? When you enter the **Grill Room**, you realise that it is. It is quite simply one of the best rooms in London: ornate, rococo, mirrored, beautifully preserved. Its gilded nudes hold garlands, its ceiling is painted with foliated panels showing almost naked ladies dancing a chiffon striptease while cherubs and doves cavort. Subtle it isn't. But it has all the marvellous, thrusting vulgarity of the supposedly prudish Victorian era.

Marco Pierre White and his girlfriend, Mati Conajero, invited me to dine with them at the **Halkin Hotel Restaurant** in Belgravia because he admires the Italian chef, Stefano Cavallini. I am now fatter and wiser: never let the chef choose what you will have to eat, unless you're close to total starvation. They are so determined to show how much they can do and how good they are at it that you end up with far too many rich courses. Even someone as brazen as I did not have the heart to say "Enough! Good as it is, take it away!" From the starter of warm mussels in sour cream and caviare, through the best pea soup I've ever had, through a risotto of sea bass cooked with red wine sauce, through roasted kidneys, through chocolate soufflé with brown bread ice cream, to petits fours and coffee – and all this on a Sunday night after a large roast at home for lunch! It was beautifully done, but much too much, even for a pig like me!

Lionel Blair, starring with style at the King's Head Theatre (a cause I donate to), said the Turkish restaurant next door was excellent. He'd even seen Ralph Fiennes there. I tried a Turkish place across the road, the **Harbour Restaurant**. They produced some rather good lamb and a salad with roast potatoes and a mezze for Miss Lid plus soft drinks and water – all within six minutes of our entering. The owner, Volkan Altinok, said he and his brother had been there three years. Their father had opened Britain's first kebab restaurant in the Holloway Road. "It was very popular with Irish people," he explained.

Georgian On My Mind

A friend, the impresario Michael White, had suggested **Harrods' Georgian Restaurant** for lunch. I was met by Nigel Moore, the general manager of the Georgian, who came to escort me. "There are 21 outlets where you can eat in Harrods," he said. I'd never been to any of them.

The Georgian Restaurant is spacious and elegant with pink chairs. Conversation is easy. All the tables are large enough, even for me. There's a vast buffet; you can also order from a menu. We went to the buffet. I was behind a customer who took every single shrimp, picked it up with the tongs, inspected it and put it back. I impatiently grabbed some with my fingers, did likewise with mussels and bits of lobster, proceeding to the gravadlax and smoked salmon. A slight refrigeration feel about it all, but highly pleasant. They kindly wheeled out the chef, Tim Powell, who took over at the Canteen after the bust-up between Michael Caine and Marco Pierre White. A few moments later, Emad Estafanous, who was in charge of all the restaurants, came along to see if I was happy. He pointed out the pink "free loo" slips, one for each customer, which save a pound if you visit Harrods' "luxury bathrooms".

Then Michael Neuner, the general food and beverage manager, senior to those who'd already visited, turned up. "It's like eating with the Maharajah of Hendon," observed Mr White, regarding the felicitations from so many executives. "It always happens when I eat out," I said. "Staff who haven't been seen in the restaurant for 100 years are dragged out to greet me."

"It's a good moment to go to the buffet," said Michael. "There's only two old ladies in front of us." The buffet sported beef on the bone before it had been officially legalised, roast veal and lamb, veggies and a good array of gravy and accoutrements. I thought the food excellent. I like buffets. I don't have to rely on waiters to let me down.

We went back for desserts and the pastry chef was introduced, a girl called Tanya Addison. "The mousse is white chocolate; can I explain anything?" she asked. "Not really," I replied, "I never know what I'm eating anyway." I had four desserts, all extremely pleasing. Then, just as no more executives could possibly come over, I looked up. There – sailing majestically between tables – was the superboss himself, Mohamed al-Fayed. Mr Fayed was the height of graciousness and hostlike charm. He insisted that we be his guests, which I attempted to stop. In the end I gave £100 for the staff, which was well over the price of our meal. A man came with a book on the history of Harrods and some chocolates. "Mr Fayed would like a card with your home number," he said. I had no card, so I wrote on one of the pink lavatory tokens.

Michael White was outraged. "I could have used that!" he protested. "Well, you're too late," I replied, handing it to Mohamed's emissary. Michael hastily pocketed the other voucher. "I'll use it tomorrow," he said.

Hot tip for fish lovers

Personally I find everything and everybody north of Hyde Park highly suspect. Until you get to St Albans that is, and I'm not sure about them either. But I do like **Harry Morgan's** Jewish restaurant in St John's Wood

High Street. I remember one delightful Saturday lunch there with my ex, Miss Seagrove. We were at right angles to a Jewish couple two tables away. The man sat in front of his lockshen soup, his eyes riveted on the movement of his spoon from bowl to mouth. His wife looked around.

"Look," she said, her eyes alighting on me, and nudging her husband. "It's him!" "Who?" muttered the husband in between mouthfuls of soup. "Y'know, that director, the director, Winner. It's Winner." Her husband seemed deeply unimpressed. He kept working at the soup without even a glance. The woman had a go at her soup. Then she turned again to us and back to her husband. "He's with the shiksa," she said. At this point I must explain to those who do not know that "shiksa" is a Yiddish word for a gentile woman, and fairly derogatory. It can also be used as "the shiksa", meaning the maid or domestic. The husband remained totally disinterested, shiksa or no shiksa. His wife continued to scrutinise Miss Seagrove. "You know," she said, nudging her husband, "the actress, you know her name." Since the husband's eyes remained on the soup, he was unable to provide much help in identification. The wife gave up and returned to her meal. Miss Seagrove and I carried on with ours.

After that I didn't visit Harry Morgan's for quite a while. But I was seduced back by my friends John Gold and Terry O'Neill. Johnny and Terry are an unlikely couple to lunch regularly on Saturday at Harry Morgan's – or Herschel's as they call it in honour of the owner, Herschel Havakuk, an Israeli. Terry is a nice Roman Catholic from somewhere in Ireland and Johnny, Jewish, is the owner of Tramp discotheque, the Belvedere Restaurant in Holland Park and a few more. He is always putting money on the horses, following magnificent inside tips which, in my experience with him, are a near-total disaster.

One recent Saturday lunch we assembled at 1 o'clock on the red imitation leather banquettes, in front of the shiny tables, and ordered variously salt beef, gefilta fish, chopped herring, mixed chicken noodle, kneidlach and kreplach soup, some latkes, and a display of pickled cucumbers. All of this is totally delicious. In fact I have never had anything at Herschel's that was not delicious except for one Saturday when I asked for hot fried fish and he obviously didn't have any, and warmed up some cold fried fish and it tasted ghastly.

This particular morning we were surrounded by the usual Damon Runyonesque characters. As Johnny studied the racing form, one of them, called Monty Marks, offered up a tip. Johnny phoned his bookmaker and asked me what I wanted. I shook. I have joined Johnny on his top tips at the Belvedere and Herschel's and I don't think I've ever won. So keen is Johnny that I should join his money-making schemes that he actually opened an account for me with a bookmaker, something it took me 57 years to achieve. After all, my mother lost £6m at the Cannes Casino, so I gave already. Wearily, I looked at the "selections". I don't remember the name of the horse, but I do know it was Monty's tip, which, I guessed, had to be better than Johnny's. Having placed our bets, Johnny then listened to the race on the phone from the bookie's. When it was over, amazing and miraculous, I had won! My, or rather Monty's horse had come home for a change without a clear view of the rear of eight other horses and jockeys. I was so excited I ordered an apple strudel. Then I left Herschel's £300 richer!

The next time I was in, Monty was nowhere to be seen. As I knocked back some chopped liver, Johnny looked up from the paper. "Carranita for the 2.10 at Doncaster," he said. I pretended not to hear. It's the best thing, I assure you.

At Harry Morgan the fish is usually superb. For the first time ever, the batter tasted hard and greasy, as if the oil was not fresh. Also, the chicken soup with noodles was poor when it's usually historic. I only go to Harry Morgan about once a year, but a regular fan told me he'd recently been very disappointed with them.

PS The food's still good, but they've rearranged it so it all seems to be communal tables, like a synagogue social club. Too much for me. I order takeaways.

The **Hilton National London Olympia** is the sort of hotel for people I never meet. I walked there for lunch the other day. I was seeking adventure. You go up gold escalators past a bizarre chandelier of chrome and strip lights to the first-floor dining room. Strangely, I thought it all worked rather well. The dining room is large, bright, big windows, very comfortably furnished and with good-sized tables not set too close. We decided to go for the buffet, £11.95 inc coffee and mints! It looked all right. A cold table and hot tureens of lamb, turkey, chicken and what have you. I took a bit of this and that. The lamb was surprisingly good. I grabbed a lot of apple sauce and mint. The roast potatoes were noticeably better than The Ritz or the Four Seasons. My guest, Michael Guest, a film producer, had the scampi, which were okay plus. The veg were particularly fresh, tasty and crisp. Unbelievably, I found myself viewing things as almost excellent. We then had ice cream, a mousse (both good), an excellent red jelly with fruit and cream (I *like* jelly), plus fairly feeble meringue cake and weak apple and berry tart. Still, for the money, it was good value.

Kimono my place

All Japanese restaurants look the same to me. They have a sparse, slightly wooden feel, with white walls and little china bowls. The one I go to most is the **Hiroko** in the London Kensington Hilton. I made a reservation and wandered in the other evening. The manager appeared; he's the one in evening dress as opposed to the girls in national costume with little rolled up silk back-packs. "Yes?" said the manager, "I've booked," I volunteered. "How many are you?" he asked. I looked around in case Vanessa had skipped to a more handsome escort. "Two," I said.

The manager indicated a table for two on my left. "Er, I'd like to sit there," I said pointing on my right to a large booth for four, or even six. It had one of those little metal triangular, stand-up "Reserved" signs on it. "It's reserved," said the manager, "one of our regulars. Party of four." This annoyed me. I did something I have never knowingly done before, but which people who parody this column claim I do all the time. I drew myself up to my full 5ft 9½in. "Do you know who I am?" I asked with as much pomposity as I could muster. The manager was thrown completely. He looked absolutely bemused. "No," he said.

This was a problem. If I had to tell him who I was, how could it possibly have any effect? What should I say? "I'm a famous international film director and restaurant critic"? Obviously to him I wasn't famous at all. Oh dear. We stood facing each other in the space between one lot of tables and another. Desperately grasping for any reason why he should know who I was, the manager finally broke the silence. "Have you been here before?" he asked. That was my chance! I was unleashed! "Yes," I said firmly. "Many times, long before you arrived and always," I spun round to face the large booth, " I sit at that table!" Either the brilliance of my response did it, or perhaps it was because the manager had got fed up with standing staring at me. Either way, he whipped the reserved sign off the booth and let us sit down.

After that little adventure, the meal was rather tame. I am always reminded, when ordering in oriental restaurants, of the joke about the American pilot shot down in Vietnam who is sentenced to death. "This is your last dinner," they say on his final evening alive. They bring him a solitary bowl of rice. "But just a minute," says the American, "You said I could have anything I liked." "Ah, yes," say his captors. "If there were six of you, you could have had the sweet and sour chicken, the prawn crackers, the Peking duck... But as you're only one...". Thus I studied my menu at Hiroko, gave up and settled for the set dinner. The tempura was excellent, bits of fried fish all succulent with a light batter. The soup was good, too. But the main course, strips of beef you cooked yourself in boiling water, was less exciting and the veg, which you also dunked, okay but no more. There was a second soup at this stage, which was quite ghastly. And the tea with the dessert was a bit iffy. On the whole, an acceptable meal. "But," I thought to myself, "next time I order a lot of tempura, and not much else."

As I left I noticed a millionaire friend of mine with a party of four at a rather small table. I wondered if he was the person who had booked the booth where I'd been. If he was, quite honestly I didn't care.

The **Holland Park Cafeteria** has its admirers. The singer Van Morrison has been seen there, as has Joanna Lumley and many other glitterati. I have lived a few paces away for 25 years of the caff's life, but had never set foot in it (it is self-service and I get irritated with my serving abilities). It was time to give it a try. There is a display of robust rolls with ham, cheese and lettuce, a variety of biscuits and cakes, and a menu of hot dishes. I chose spaghetti bolognese; my co-luncher, a young screenwriter, Nicholas Mead, ordered baked potato with chilli con carne. Both were fine. But I was slightly put off by pigeons landing like vultures on every vacated table to eat the leftovers, and children screaming and running about before their parents hauled them away.

A Kind of Hush

I rarely read restaurant reviews, but I saw some for **Hush**, the Mayfair place opened recently by Roger Moore's son, Geoffrey, and one of my former lawyers, Jamie Barber. Even critics who are normally bland or relentlessly kind went bananas with their invective. A lot of it seemed to be, rather unreasonably, because the two young men who own it had never been in the restaurant business before. So what? Everyone has to start somewhere.

I had my moan before I got there. I found it impossible to locate. It's in an alley leading to a mews off Bond Street. I've heard of exclusive, but hidden is ridiculous. As a result of my complaints a sign was put in Lancashire Court saying "Hush". The last time I looked it was on another building altogether with no arrow to show the direction one should take. Anyway, I found it, eventually, and thought it exceptionally pleasant. Downstairs, it's lively, canteen-like, with no tablecloths. Upstairs, it's grey, elegant and with a long bar. "Isn't this the most comfortable bar stool you ever sat on?" asked Roger Moore with paternal pride. I'm not the best person to judge bar stools. I don't go to bars. It seemed perfectly all right, but not a stool I'd write home about.

I chose "Hushed" – a delightful drink consisting of "Svensk vodka, tichenne butterscotch, schnapps and cinnamon cream". "I'll only have one," I volunteered. "You certainly won't have two, because I won't buy you another," said Rog. I noticed lunch was expensive. The set menu upstairs is £32 for three courses, excluding vegetables, coffee and 12.5% for service. That makes a normal meal for one £46.69. As opposed to three courses, including everything, at Claridge's or the Dorchester, for £29.50. Geoffrey Moore came over. "Are you going to take an order, Geoffrey?" I said. "You haven't got a pad." "He's not taking the order, he's the owner," said Roger.

Unlike some serious food critics, I liked what I ate. I had salmon fish cake with crème fraîche and chilli sauce, then sea bass on spinach. Kristina, Rog's lady friend, chose moules. I nicked some. They were superb. I then started on Kristina's soup-like sauce, which was not a south-of-France taste, but excellent. Rog, the proud father, showed me his celeriac and foie gras soup and said: "Doesn't it look pretty?" Desserts took a very long time, so I watched Lulu doing some interview in the bar. When they arrived, the chocolate pud was okay, the apple crumble very fine indeed.

The waiter offered two types of espresso: "One is rossa blend, which is smooth and subtle, the other's paradiso, which is more robust, it gives you more of a lift." I should have ordered both, swilled them around in my mouth, spat them out all over the place and given you a definitive view of the tastes. But I ordered paradiso and it was charming.

Hush is definitely good, but I think the menu could be more inventive. More different. I'm getting bored with British nouvelle cuisine. If I see another piece of grilled fish on a bed of spinach I shall vomit. Hush is in central London and it looks jolly. They should pinch some of the Ivy menu ideas. There, they try more unusual things and they're terrific.

Il Portico is a terrific local eating place in Kensington High Street. It is time-warped in the 1960s, but the food has stayed fresh and pleasant. It's uncomfortable, very family run by Pino Chiavarini and his wife, and I'm a terrible nuisance there! I am only prepared to sit in one of the booths and then I insist the next one is kept empty. Despite this, we all remain good friends. I have visited it on and off since 1969, usually for *al dente* spaghetti with tomato sauce, but there is a varied menu and the service couldn't be better.

Prior to a theatre visit to *Fosse* (very good) one Saturday night, I decided to grace the **Intercontinental Hotel Coffee House Restaurant**. I arrived at 5.43pm. Kim, from South Korea, in a green blazer, greeted me most charmingly and said the buffet would be up until 6pm, but we could order from the à la carte. She said it would take 10 minutes to squeeze two fresh orange juices. I checked what was on display: a very fresh-looking fruit salad, desserts and some light and dark fudge in a bowl. I like fudge; it was good. Biljana from Macedonia, in a striped waistcoat, took our order. After that, food appeared all over the place. Miss Lid tried sushi from the buffet and said it was marvellous. I grabbed everything as the waitresses carried it in. "What's that?" I'd call out and it would be brought over for me to taste. Cubes of sauté potatoes, stir-fried lamb and prawns in Thai curry sauce (got a bit of that on the tablecloth), carrots, clear chicken soup, egg and dumpling soup, confit of duck legs and then the ordered course of roast maize-fed chicken with bubble and squeak and shallot and white wine chicken jus. I finished with some very nice chocolate-chip cookies.

The food ranged from good to acceptable. The main problem is the room itself, which is stuck in an ugly part of the 1970s: sort of fake Georgian with prints of jockeys. I think a coffee shop should have more snacky things, be open all day, which this isn't, and not worry about tablecloths and flowers in little pots. The hotel PR is obviously aware of this, because she wrote to me: "The current décor is rather old-fashioned and we hope to completely update it."

When I later wandered into their posh restaurant, Le Soufflé, the manager said they'd had tarting-up plans for ever, but nobody ever did anything. Bass plc bought the place two years ago. They should definitely spend a few bob. It all looks dowdy. The lobby was full of French doctors wearing signs and here for a conference. My film people were much more interesting.

Ivy league

I hate it when people ask me, "What's the best restaurant in London?" Best for what? The best restaurant on any particular day depends where you feel like eating, and what sort of food you fancy. If someone were to ask me "What restaurant do you most enjoy being in?" I would answer, **The Ivy** in West Street. I have been going there for more than 40 years.

In the 1950s it was owned by Bernard Walsh, who founded and ran the Wheeler's restaurants when they were superb (which they certainly aren't now). Bernard was a wonderful old character. He had two beautiful daughters, one of whom, Carol, worked in the kitchen at The Ivy. It was Carol whom we would ogle during her time at Wheeler's in Soho. She had the most wonderful bosom. Francis Bacon, Lucian Freud and I, and others, sat at the bar just to see them. Carol later married a Jewish chap, Ronnie Emmanuel, who was selling toilet rolls from a barrow outside in Old Compton Street. She and Ronnie now run the marvellous French Horn at Sonning with their two grown-up children.

One night, Bernard Walsh came to The Ivy very drunk, Carol told me, found her in the kitchen and said, "Do you want to take over The Ivy?" "No," said Carol. "It's too big for me." "I'll sell it then," said Bernard. And he did – to an Italian, Joe Melatini, who ran it successfully for many years. Other stories have it that Bernard Walsh lost it in a card game to Joe Melatini.

It was always a haunt of the theatrical crowd, along with Le Caprice, which in the 1950s was its rival but is now owned by the same people, Jeremy King and Christopher Corbin. They are rare creatures in the restaurant world: they are gentlemen. They acquired The Ivy in 1990 after it had been owned by a number of people, including Charles Forte and Lady Grade. It had gone downhill, as had Le Caprice. Jeremy and Christopher pushed them both up to be the great successes they are today.

The Ivy looks pretty much like it always did: low ceilings, stained-glass diamond-shaped leaded windows and only a hint of the theatrical greats who used to eat there. Old photos displayed on the walls show Frederic March, Jack Buchanan, Marion Davies, Vivien Leigh, even Churchill and others. "Inherited memorabilia?" I asked Christopher. "No, it's by Peter Blake", he said. "He collects old photos, he made a collage for us."

The Ivy has an absolutely enormous menu, everything from shepherd's pie to grilled rabbit with rosemary and salmon fish cakes. It all looks like food, not ponced-about plate decoration. It tastes good, too. Another thing I greatly like is that they invariably offer jelly. The other day they had two jellies, an elderflower one on the à la carte and a raspberry one on the set menu. I ordered them both. They also do extremely good blinis with the caviare. After lunch one day Christopher came to my table and asked what I had eaten. "I had a double portion of caviare followed by corned beef hash with two fried eggs on top," I replied. "That's what The Ivy is all about," said Christopher.

The weekend three-course set lunch is an amazingly cheap £14.50. They add £1.50 if you don't eat it in the bar. Only £1.50 for the right to sit in the dining room and see me! That's another amazing bargain.

I've been part of London's restaurant scene for a great many years. Places and people come and go. Nobody has equalled the achievements of Christopher Corbin and Jeremy King. They created three restaurants. The Ivy, Le Caprice and J Sheekey, all of unparalleled quality and ambience.

As important as their food is the skill with which they select clientele. You know that Ivy regulars, many of them working in what is laughingly known as "The Arts", will always find a place, even if other people have to wait for weeks. The resulting atmosphere is perpetually pleasing. It's unheard of for any business to remain the same after the founding bosses leave. Particularly restaurants, which lean so heavily on the personal charm and presence of the owners. I hope their three places hold on until Jeremy and Christopher start again somewhere else. If you want backing, fellas, call me. And thank you for giving so much pleasure.

All bets are now off with this restaurant now that Christopher Corbin and Jeremy King have left but we hope the standards will be maintained by the Belgo Group.

A look west, and a flight out

In 1969 Julie Hodgess, famous for designing Biba's, the 1960s rocket-up-and-down clothes superstore, went into the restaurant business. She opened **Julie's** in Holland Park, or rather what estate agents have now named Clarendon Cross. After a couple of years she threw in the towel, and the place has since been owned by the property people who had the head lease, Timothy and Cathy Herring.

I used to go to Julie's a lot in the early days. In their large back room with a table not unlike that used by King Arthur I would entertain the likes of Burt Lancaster, Marlon Brando, Robert Ryan, Ryan O'Neal and other luminaries of the cinema. Although the food was a bit ropey, they all liked it because of its atmosphere. It had a 1960s charm, inventive but safe, twee but delightfully odd. I went back recently and it had changed hardly at all. While the area had poshed up no end, with the suspect Orsino's opening opposite, Julie's remained a time-warp of dark cellar-rooms, tunnels, a sort of greenhouse white place and, of course, the old back room.

Even the food had moved up a notch. It is pleasant without reaching any serious culinary standards. My wild mushrooms in a pastry basket had very good pastry, my companion (there's a word I hate!) had aubergine and sour cream mousse with toasted pumpkin seeds. And liked it. My beef stroganoff was pretty revolting, old and tired beef strips in indifferent wild rice; the lady chose better with salmon baked in puff pastry with fennel and dill. The butterscotch crêpes with cream cheese and ginger could generously be described as adequate. But the overall feel of the evening was rather endearing. No-one wants major meals every time they go out, it would be too exhausting. Ambience and charm make up for a lot. I do wonder, though, about all those diners sitting in a corridor leading from the bar to the back room and the greenhouse area. I've decided that any restaurant that can sell seats in a passageway must have some secret of success.

Kai Mayfair is one of my favourite Chinese restaurants, even though the decor is too posh by far. It lacks the chummy slapdash I like in most Chinese places. Oddly, waitresses are dressed in sailor-suits, as if auditioning for *The Pirates of Penzance*. When I go there's a lot of moving about before a table is placed in a corner that I can accept. The owner, Bernard Yeoh, did a big sell on the chef, which isn't really necessary because the food is wonderful. Bit of Chinese shaoshing hot wine there, very sweet with crystal sugar to add to it, bit of fresh prawn crackers there, a Chinese croissant filled with minced prawns, flaming pork in silver foil with onions…all things I find impossible to order. Just let them sort it out for you, I say, as a major restaurant expert. The meal ends with a bit of total nonsense. In comes a large bowl belching masses of swirling steamy-mist, like the dungeons in *Phantom of the Opera*. A major presentation! Inside were two of the dreariest little mint chocs I've ever eaten. Never mind, I adored the sea spice lobster.

Kartouche is in a particularly dreary part of the Fulham Road. The person who dragged me there (I'd certainly have never gone on my own) assured me it was the new "in" place. That's enough to scare anyone off. Actually it was full of people who looked like they'd been contestants on a TV quiz show. The maitre d's attention was transfixed on anything but the customers: the walls, the floor, the street outside, all these he found fascinating. My smoked haddock and poached egg was madly salty. Vanessa had Rinktum Ditty (*really*) – American-style Welsh rarebit. This was just grilled cheese on a roll. She said that was salty, too. For a main course I had the roast of the day, which was belly of pork (fatty and horrible) with soggy roast potatoes and some greens I didn't dare try. The famous restaurateur who had recommended the place left 99% of his hamburger and later told the owner he liked his meat to taste of meat, which it didn't. The waiter told me the dessert of coffee truffle cake was addictive. It wasn't. There was no style or plan to the food, no concept, no good ideas, no fine ingredients, no good cooking. Nor was it that cheap. The noise was horrific, and this on a day when it was not full and the glass hinged shutters to the street were open. If it's ever full, which it doesn't deserve to be, take earplugs and learn sign language.

Kaspia is buried away in an ultra-posh mews in Mayfair. You walk through its shop selling caviar and vodka to get to the restaurant. It is classily decorated with old china in cabinets and, as well as caviar, they do a just-all-right borscht and, at the cheaper price-level, fish cakes. Michael Caine took me there first and the place was empty. When I went back the service was unbelievably surly. Again it was empty and the waiter grudgingly showed me to a revolting, tiny table. "The reason there's nobody here," I said with great charm, "is because when it's empty you show people to lousy tables." Then I sat where I wanted. There's a new manager now and probably a different waiter, because the other evening it was crowded.

At **Kensington Place**, on a day things had come to a halt, I ended up serving the entire restaurant with bread. I was so keen to get some for myself, I got up, took the basket from the serving area and then helped Alan Yentob, who was sitting some distance away. At that everyone called out for "service", so I did the whole room.
PS I think Kensington Place became careless and dreary. I stopped going after I ordered the mixed grill three times in a row because I couldn't find anything more interesting.

La Brasserie in the Brompton Road was recommended to me by my neighbour, lyricist supreme Don Black. It is very French, pleasingly decorated with glass-bowl lamps hanging on chains. The two-course set lunch is £14 – £19.50 if you add the Brittany prune flan with cream, which I did, and it was excellent. Vanessa had Caesar salad followed by haddock. I had buckwheat pancake filled with eggs and gruyère cheese, then braised rabbit with cider and prunes. Whoops! I've just realised I had prunes twice – must have been a subconscious desire to get my visit to Cliveden out of my system.

La Gaffe in Hampstead is a bit of a find. It has great individuality and atmosphere. The owner, Bernardo Stella, looks like what you imagine old Hampstead was: artists and writers, somewhat bohemian.

Getting on famously

I'm not a regular at **Langan's**. I know it's very chic an' all that, but somehow it's passed me by. Where it scores miraculously is at private parties in the rather strange Venetian room upstairs with its mural by Patrick Proctor. The catering is exemplary. Stars stand in line dutifully to pick up really excellent smoked salmon, shrimp, boiled salmon, roast beef, sausages and mash to die for, goujons of sole. Very well done and fresh, with superb canapés and desserts. I only once saw someone, an actress well known for not much, crash the queue at one of these glittering events, I thought: "What a cow!" But, like everyone else, I said nothing.

Downstairs in the large painting-filled room with fans overhead I have had some strange meals. Once I took O J Simpson and his late wife, Nicole, very good friends of mine both, after we'd been to see *Cats*. That was a nice evening. Another time I was with Judy Mazel, who wrote *The Beverly Hills Diet*, a book devoted to eating pineapples, which produced great medical angst and gave people mouth ulcers. Sometimes I've liked things, sometimes I haven't. But with or without me, it is one of the enduring successes of London and that is to be much commended.

My friend Michael Caine recently asked me there to lunch with him and Shakira. We had a lovely table by the window (well, if you're with the owner you're hardly likely to be by the men's toilet, are you?) and the service was attentive to perfection. Michael directed me to the melon and the roast free-range chicken, thyme and parsley stuffing, bacon and bread sauce. They were both extremely fine. "People think good chicken's easy," said Michael. "Well, I can tell them it isn't." I nodded agreeably. Shakira had a plate of vegetables, which accounts in part for her glowing youthfulness. "The best I've eaten anywhere in the world," she said slowly enough for me to write it down. But they did look terrific. An enormously rich American lady, rather nice, too, had a spinach soufflé. "One of our biggest sellers," obliged Michael.

For a dessert, Shakira suggested we share a treacle tart with custard. I liked that. I took the bigger half. Richard Shepherd, the co-owner, came and sat with us. He looks healthily fat, if that's possible. I always think restaurant owners should be fat. If they're not it means they don't like their own food enough to eat it. Marco's got fat, I thought to myself, and Nico's fat. Mosimann could put on a bit... Those are the sorts of things I muse on from time to time.

All right Coq?

I have always been an admirer, though not a fan, of Langan's in Mayfair. I appreciate its professionalism, its continued popularity. I like the room, the staff, the party catering upstairs, but I've never been crazy about the food. One of my most awful nights was when I took Charles Bronson and his dear late wife, Jill Ireland, there. Peter Langan, bless him, joined the table and spat at us, the tablecloth and anything else in sight for nearly three hours. I was all for asking him to leave, drunk as he was. But Jill had decided to save him from the evils of alcohol, so Charlie and I put up with it as graciously as two Scorpios are able to. After that, other than when Michael Caine gave a dinner, I seldom went back.

So when my friend Bill Tennant, the highly superior movie executive, suggested we go to **Langan's Coq d'Or** in Brompton Road for lunch, I was not enthusiastic. Although on the phone I'd been told only assistant managers were on duty, when I arrived the excellently familiar Peter Malva, now grandly titled group manager, was there to greet me. The room itself is extremely attractive. Sort of fake 1900 with nice brass hanging lights from the George V in Paris, pleasing oil paintings, photos of regulars to the "old" Langan's, which of course don't include me, pink and yellow flowers and one odd thing – layers of paper cloths on top of a real tablecloth on the tables.

The room was pretty empty, but one of my favourite MPs, Tony Banks, was at one table, and the always delightfully up-and-jolly Tara Palmer-Tomkinson appeared at another with the UK boss of TAG Heuer watches, Neil Duckworth. He'd paid a great deal at a charity auction to be in one of my films, ending up in *Parting Shots* at a pub in Fulham with a parrot and Joanna Lumley. He acquitted himself superbly. Apparently that nice-looking brunette lady ahead on my right, lunching with a gossip columnist, was Tara's sister, Santa. A table away sat a baroness from Brussels whom I like, but whose name I forget. A pleasing group.

I noted they had Langan's bangers and mash with white onion sauce on the menu. They're always very good. Bill ordered crab and ginger dumplings to start. I nicked some when they arrived; they were most pleasing. I asked for gravadlax with mustard sauce.

"That's adventurous," said Bill, meaning it wasn't. Safe it may have been, but it was first-rate.

The bread was all right, not over-exciting. Bill declared his main course, grilled tuna, to be superb. I rated it good. I'd decided to forego the sausages for beef bourguignonne: it lacked that extra something.

By now the paper tablecloths were becoming a real bore. They kept rising every time I brought my arms up with my cutlery. Peter Malva explained they were meant to give a brasserie look. I ended up eating my apple strudel dessert with one hand, while holding the paper cloth down with the other. This is something new in my vast experience, and not necessarily a plus.

I thought the strudel presentable. Bill didn't like his lemon cheesecake. "Try it," he said. "There's no hint of cheese." Indeed it was a very light lemon mousse on a pastrylike base. As I prefer lemon mousse to cheesecake, I had no complaints.

I'd rate this a pleasant meal in very nice surroundings. I even made a note of the table number of my corner setting, which means I'd be happy to go back. Peter pointed to the other corner. "That's Lord Archer's table," he said, as if his restaurant had thus achieved the apex of distinction. I found that totally bizarre.

I must admit a great liking for Polish cooking. I don't think it's because my mother was born in Poland as, sadly, she never cooked the local dishes. I do recall with great pleasure a few trips to a very strange building in King Street, Hammersmith, which looks like a seedy government office. In fact it houses the Polish Social and Cultural Association and a Polish restaurant open to the public called **Lowizanka**. It has quite extraordinarily good food at very low prices – so cheap that I ordered three main courses just to have the pleasure of tasting each. Unfortunately the waitress was extremely snooty about it as she tried, with difficulty, to fit them all on the table.

Novelli wears off

Having had nice times at Novelli W8, both with food and service, I was pleased when a newspaper editor asked me to dine at the posh part of Jean-Christophe Novelli's group, **Maison Novelli** in Clerkenwell. The food was excellent, the room okay, but not as nice as W8. Everything else was a nightmare.

I arrived at Clerkenwell, a place I can live without, alighted from the Rolls and entered the door to a small hall that is Maison Novelli. A brusque lady said: "Do you have a reservation?" Not hello, not a smile, not a greeting, just the question. That always annoys me.

I remained silent and climbed the stairs to the first-floor dining area. On the way up, another woman faced me. She had obviously been to the same charm school as the first one. "Are you with someone?" she asked, presumably not meaning Vanessa, who was with me, but someone of enough stature to permit me to enter and eat.

I arrived in the restaurant to be met by a formal-looking man, Giusseppe Vurchio, the front-of-house manager. He seemed to be in charge. "I have just had a depressing welcome," I said, never one to keep quiet. "You can read about it!" Then I sat down to hear a horror story from my host. His group of three had arrived to be shown a dreadful, small table in the middle of the room. He informed Mr Vurchio I was his guest and would certainly not sit there. "Why?" asked Mr Vurchio! He then ungraciously moved them somewhere better. The proffered table was all right for three people, just okay for four; for five it would have been "How many students can we get into the phone box?" It was later used by three customers. The place was never more than half full. When we left, Vanessa said: "It was like they didn't want people in the restaurant." They were well on their way to success.

I found all this odd because three days earlier, I had told Jean-Christophe we would be there that night and he had them give us some muscat and champagne with his compliments. The service was poor to dreadful. The food was lovely, but it was all incredibly slow. They should send Eric Chatroux, their maitre d' from W8, to sort this lot out; he's tiptop.

The wine service was particularly odd. I was host for the wine, the editor for the food. I ordered the best available. The white, Puligny Montrachet, was decanted and poured. As I don't drink much, it took me a while to realise there had been no effort made to refill our glasses. We had now eaten our first course. The wine waiter came over and said: "Shall I serve the red wine?" "We haven't finished the white, have we?" I questioned. "No," he said. "Would you pour the white then, please," I asked. The wine waiter walked away!

After a short wait, I said to my host: "Am I going mad? Did I ask him to pour the white wine?" "You did," said the editor. His deputy reached for the ice bucket. Seeing this, a member of staff, not the wine waiter, took over and poured. At least half the decanter had been left waiting. Were they hoping to drink it in the kitchen? I neither knew nor cared. It was ridiculous. When I got my wine bill, the two bottles came to £293.82. This included a "suggested gratuity" of £38.32!

I have a silly habit of not looking at bills at the time. When I get home I sometimes read them. I have no objection to a 15% gratuity being added. I usually pay more, but I do think it's steep for opening and serving two bottles of wine. I recall once Marco Pierre White graciously repaid me by way of donation to charity the far larger gratuity on a wine bill at The Restaurant. When it comes to wine, if it's a really large figure, a 5% gratuity is generous.

When we left, Signor Vurchio came down and handed his card to me through the car window. "I haven't been with Jean-Christophe long," he said. "I hope you'll be back." To quote George Bernard Shaw: not bloody likely! *The staff have now changed. I've not been back.*

Because the Michelin Guide gave the **Malabar** in Notting Hill Gate a red M, which means it merits your attention, I attended. Very ordinary. Heavy naan bread, cloying sticky samosas, and only fair murg makhni and accompanying fried pumpkin, and sliced banana cooked with ginger and spices. It read better than it tasted. Not awful, but I wonder if the Michelin-Guide man had had a drink too many or was just feeling generous.

Remember me

At last I have a serious claim to fame. I have founded a restaurant. Were it not for me, **Memories of China Kensington**, a small but beautifully formed restaurant on the western approaches of Kensington High Street, would not exist. For years the space was an Italian place, Al Gallo d'Oro, run by a nice chap named Renato. I spent many hours there, sometimes in the company of famous persons such as Peter Falk, Burt Lancaster, even Frankie Howerd. My table was halfway up on the left with a china cockerel featured on an adjacent shelf. The food went from okay to oh dear to diabolical.

Restaurant life changed, but not at Al Gallo d'Oro. On the few occasions I went in later years, Renato would crow over how wonderful his offerings were as we ate dried-up ham, ageing smoked salmon and much worse besides. "Get a decent chef in," I'd plead with Renato when I saw him walking past the Odeon Kensington on his way home or to his restaurant, according to the hour.

Finally Renato made a life-changing decision. With customers dwindling, he asked me to come and give a comprehensive, written report on yet another chef and what he was offering. It was six pages, single-spaced, of the worst review I have ever given anything. I destroyed it all, from the food to the service to the individual waitresses to the presentation. You name it, I killed it. I concluded that as Renato seemed totally out of touch with restaurant life in the 1990s, the best thing he could do would be to sell up. A few weeks later he rang. "Can you find me a buyer?" he asked.

Quick as an overweight flash I rang my friend Claudio Pulze. Signor Pulze is not a household name, but he is the man not far behind a great many of London's best restaurants. He has the Michelin two-star Aubergine, the excellent L'Oranger in St James's and the Canteen at Chelsea Harbour (with my pal Mike), one Michelin star each, Memories of China in Ebury Street and the appallingly run Zafferano in Knightsbridge. Claudio hot-footed it round to Renato's and, before you say spaghetti bolognese, it had changed hands and reopened as Memories of China Kensington.

This was particularly nice for me as it is within walking distance of my house. Thus Al Gallo was transformed from its Italian origins by the addition of some white paint, some red stick-ons with Chinese writing and a few other minor decorations. They kept the 1960s Italian chairs. Claudio, whatever other considerable skills he has, will not win the award for Most Money Spent on Restaurant Transformation 1997. That is for sure.

What matters is that he brought over Kam Po But, the brilliant chef from Shanghai and Ebury Street, a first-rate team of presenters headed by Guiliano Movio, and voilà!, marvellous food, cheap at the low price, and very pleasant, too. I went recently with my old friend from the days when debs were debs, the Hon Camilla Jessel. We had a superb lunch. Scallops in some slightly hot sauce, a white fish with fried seaweed, crispy duck of outstanding standard, some nicely fried thin strips of meat with rice and veg, all topped off by Häagen-Dazs chocolate, vanilla and pink-with-blobs-on ice cream accompanying superb toffee apples and toffee bananas.

That was a good meal! Although it's only been open a few weeks, we Holland Parkers have discovered it big. It's already turning people away every evening. I have changed my table to one in the bay, the ex-cockerelly spot being a bit too near other people. In the lobby there are photos of the late sagacious and charming Ken Lo, who discovered the trade name with Paul McCartney and other luminaries. They should put me up there, really. On second thoughts, no. It might frighten the customers.

I was pleasantly surprised with **Michel's Brasserie** in Chiswick, where I went a couple of times with the marvellous Diana Rigg. It's sort of French with Caribbean music playing. The soup came within seconds. Being highly expert, I can't remember what it was. "Delicious," said Diana. It was a nice, dark-yellow colour. We had nouvelle duck, sliced up, which Diana liked greatly. I gave the lemon cheesecake very high marks indeed. Robbie Hamilton, the waitress from Adelaide, said it was made there by Tim Butler, the chef. As long as he stays, it's worth a visit.

Waffle mistake

Marco Pierre White is highly talented and amusing. He's also nutty, Machiavellian, mercurial, utterly childish, irrational and dangerous. All qualities I greatly admire. It was Michael Caine who first took me to some narrow, suburban restaurant where Marco knocked up sensational food that took for ever to arrive. Some time later, Mr C transposed Marco's fortunes from diminished to substantial by ferrying him across the river. Marco now acknowledges this graciously.

The **Mirabelle** is a great achievement of which Marco is rightly proud. After clumsy decor by David Collins, Marco charged in, added a wonderful, twirling glass disco ball from the Hôtel de Paris, relaid the floor in attractive, warm panelling, got cheerful pictures and nice sculptures, and created details that make it genuinely elegant. Large white bowls of Maureen tulips from France abound in the alcoves. At a recent lunch they didn't have crisps in the bar, but excellent fried calamari turned up, then home-made chipolatas wrapped in ventreche bacon. These were an epic taste experience.

We sat at a large table in the window. I started with the best kipper I've ever eaten. And in the middle of Mayfair on a Sunday! Marco ordered Château Lafite 1982 and Mouton-Rothschild 1970 – extremely serious wines. "Wash your mouth out after the kipper," he instructed, "otherwise you won't taste them properly."

Vanessa adored her main course of smoked haddock with bubble and squeak, but my corned beef hash was odd. There was hardly any corned beef and the hash brown potatoes were so overcooked and tough I had difficulty cutting them with my knife.

The waffle that followed was a total disaster. Marco may be a three-star Michelin chef, the toast of London, a rightly acclaimed celebrity, a food expert supreme, but when it comes to waffles he knows zilch. These were white and rubbery, no taste, no texture, just ghastly.

"They're French," responded Marco glumly when I proffered my view.

The French are famous for many things. The waffle is not one of them. You could write all Marco knows about waffles on the head of a pin and still have room for the collected works of Jackie Collins. I'm an expert. Waffles are best eaten in America, specifically at the coffee shop of the Beverly Hills Hotel. There Gary produced the finest waffles in the history of the world. He has departed, but passed on the secret to Julio Herrarte. Marco should fly him over.

Waffles are made from a batter and have to be "cooked" immediately. The Beverly Hills base is a malted pancake waffle mix from Carbons of Los Angeles. Julio adds eggs, milk, melted butter and a little vanilla. The vanilla, he assures me, is the secret. This is poured straight into the griddle and out comes a lovely, golden brown, slightly crisp, totally historic taste sensation. No French are involved at all and thank God for that.

You add maple syrup so it soaks through and, if you like, more melted butter or cream or ice cream. Marco ordered jam and whipped cream to go with his. It shows even someone of extraordinary culinary talent can have an Achilles heel. I'm sure Marco's extremely pleased I've offered advice that could turn the "Mirabelle Waffle" from ghastly to great. Beyond that the whole place is terrific. Even Jeremy King of the Ivy was there. If you can get in, go!

Eating out is quite a hazard, really. I was served with what looked like a nut and bolt in my pasta at **Mosimann's** in Belgravia. When I complained, the head waiter said: "It came from the kitchen – we're doing some building." "I didn't think it came from Harrods," I replied. We got four free champagne cocktails for that, but since we'd finished our main course, they seemed a bit inappropriate.

Let Them Eat Cake

In my never-ending search for good snack places, I listen intently to my neighbour, lyricist supreme Don Black. Mr Black is to me what canaries were to coal miners. In days gone by, the canary would be carried down the mine in a cage. If it died, there were dangerous levels of gas, so work was called off, at least temporarily. Don Black is the canary of Kensington High Street. He wafts into various restaurants that I wouldn't dare enter. If, on his return, he is capable of speech, I deduce that the place is safe and investigate.

I was particularly interested when Don spoke of **The Muffin Man** in Wright's Lane, close to Barkers department store. I've always liked tea places. London used to be full of them. Gunter's in Curzon Street was particularly posh. I visited The Muffin Man prior to a theatrical outing. Nowadays, I prefer to eat before the play and then go home to enjoy hot chocolate and Marmite on buttered toast. Does this imply senility? The full title of the place is The Muffin Man and the Kensington Gift and Craft Centre. I can't imagine why. It looks like a Cambridge cafe: simple, with wooden chairs and glass-topped tables. I was reminded of The Copper Kettle in King's Parade, which has a wonderful view of King's College and in my day was run by two little old ladies serving marvellous teas. Now it's drastically downmarket, for tourists only.

The Muffin Man sported a large display of cakes. The waitress assured me they were all home-made, although only some had "home-made" written by them on the menu. Georgina ordered carrot passion cake with Earl Grey tea. I decided on two buttered crumpets with jam, a lemon cake and tea. The menu boasted items such as Muffin Man rarebit with cheese and ale, cheese and apple salad, and chicken in a mild curry dressing with apricots and avocado. "It's very cheap for home-made," said Georgina after scrutiny.

The boss brought our stuff over. He's from Jordan and used to have a big Arab nightclub in Earls Court. He announced, "I like catering," and told us his name was George Salman. Then his Polish wife, Elizabeth, joined him. She makes the lemon tea bread cake in her kitchen at home and her husband makes the Queen Mother's cake on the premises.

I said: "Bring over the cakes. I'm an official taster." Then I said: "I don't think this is Earl Grey tea." Georgina responded: "It's not, but it's very pleasant anyway." I ordered a cheese and apple salad as well.

The waitress asked, "Don't you like the cakes?" because I'd left most of them. "I'm only tasting a little bit of each," I explained. "I'm an official taster, that's my job. I never finish anything. I just taste." This seemed to satisfy her.

My cheese and apple salad never turned up. The waitress looked confused and said she'd forgotten it. Then she came back and announced: "We've run out of apples." When we went to have the photo taken, a mass of smoke suddenly poured from the kitchen. George rushed in. His toasted chicken sandwich had caught fire. My meal was compliments of the house, so I gave him £20 for the staff. I thought: "The waitress will reckon that, if she gets £20 for forgetting the cheese and apple salad, she might get £100 if she forgets an entire meal." George said: "Tell them why I burnt the sandwich." I said: "Because you were talking to me, George." He said: "Yes."

Show Trials

I'm well known as an angel. Both in the sense of being personally angelic and as an investor in – and occasional presenter of – theatrical productions. My theatre-going experiences stretch back to the Academy Award-winning actor Paul Muni starring brilliantly in *Death of a Salesman* at the Phoenix Theatre in the 1950s; Tyrone Guthrie's spectacular productions at the Old Vic; and Laurence Olivier with Vivien Leigh alternating *Antony and Cleopatra* with *Caesar and Cleopatra* at the St James's Theatre. There, I once saw my grey-haired, teetotal and supposedly eminent headmaster with a blonde and a large gin during the interval.

The chance of getting any money back after investing in West End plays is minimal, unless Maggie Smith is starring. This does not deter me. Those of you with long memories will treasure my presentation of Paul Scofield in *The Tempest* at the Wyndham's Theatre, which miraculously made a profit. Other shows I produced were less fortunate.

I spend quite a lot of time at the National Theatre. Their **Mezzanine Restaurant** looks like a school canteen, with illustrated figure on a band around the walls. I once ate some awful sausages there with the impresarios Michael Codron and Sir Cameron Mackintosh. Later Michael Codron said they'd improved. So I gave it a try. The restaurant manager, Giuseppe Fortis, is exceptionally pleasant. He has been there 21 years. You feel no dramatic change has taken place during that period.

On a recent visit I had roasted peppers with goat's cheese (adequate) and steak baguettes for both of us. Nobody asked how we wanted them cooked, but we got one medium rare and one medium, which was okay. My only complaint was that they didn't have Coca-Cola, only Pepsi.

In the interval, I got Coke in the VIP room, which is excellently hosted by Nick Huggins. As I entered the elevator to return to the play, two middle-aged ladies got in. "You're famous, aren't you?" said one of them.

"I was last week. This week I'm a has-been," I replied.

She persisted. "No, you're famous."

"Not any more," I said.

"Are you a chef?" she asked.

"I'm nobody," I admitted.

The lady suddenly got it. "I know, you're BBC2, aren't you?" Mercifully, the lift doors opened and I was able to leave.

On a return visit to the Mezzanine Restaurant, I had fish cakes, which were all right, and an orange sorbet. Miss Lid had pasta in the shape of teensie-weensy bow ties. The tomato sauce was pleasant. I'm a great admirer of the National Theatre. The restaurant isn't appalling or anything, but it would be nice if the catering was upped to near the level of their productions. I'm sure Trevor Nunn will want to spend personal time achieving this.

I think the **National Theatre** does a terrific job. Not only are the productions invariably excellent, but they've managed to take an awful building, which looks like an unfinished car park, and jolly it up no end with musicians, exhibitions, bookshops, stalls and three places serving food and drink. I've only eaten once in the main restaurant, the Terrace Cafe, and it was dire beyond belief. I am told it has improved, but I'm not about to find out. The other two are cafeterias, both rather good.

As I frequently arrive early, being punctilious to a fault, it is then that I grab a snack from the Lyttleton buffet. Often I am put off by the queue. But I have invented a way to get to the front without offending people. A lady with two children was at the cash desk with her tray, just about to pay. I went up to her. "Excuse me," I said. "You have won tonight's prize. I am going to pay for your food. You can have anything else that you want, and I'll have a coffee and a piece of carrot cake." Thus I got served without delay, for £7.50 extra. Perhaps I should wait until someone comes along with just a lemonade – but that would spoil the fun.

No thanks, Nobu

Attached to the Metropolitan, a new hotel in Park Lane, is the "in" Japanese restaurant, **Nobu**. It is an enormous success. I have read nothing but praise for it. I spent, without doubt, the most awful evening of my life there. It was horrific. Ghastly beyond belief. A total nightmare. And, believe me, that's being kind.

The room itself is like a corridor. Even Nobu's admirers admit the tables are small and too close together. I was led, arrogantly, to a table I wouldn't sit at. The assistant manager (the place is full of assistants –

nobody seems to be in charge) stood at the table. I remained some distance away. Eventually, and grudgingly, I was shown to a corner table, not larger but better positioned.

A young lady, later revealed as Kelly from Cheshire, said "Would you like something to drink?" Vanessa said she'd like mineral water, whereupon Kelly walked off. "Excuse me," I said, halting her in mid-flight. "There are two people at this table. I would like...."

Thereafter things went downhill – steeply. I asked Kelly if we could see the wine waiter. "I do everything," she announced. She slopped wine on the table, then poured water onto it and Vanessa without so much as a "Sorry".

The menu is vastly confusing to ordinary folk. Vanessa said she didn't eat meat or shellfish, ordered one item, baked aubergine, and we left the rest to Kelly. "I don't think they're very welcoming," I said as she left. "I don't think they want you here at all," Vanessa replied. "You're not chic enough."

We were then given 12 – yes 12 – courses before dessert, which we didn't have anyway. The first was a little starter of beans that you shelled yourself. Perfectly pleasant.

A long wait. A man in a white V-necked sweater, no shirt, blue jeans, was kissing a large group opposite. Some interesting-looking Japanese people sat next to us. "They're talking about you using a spoon and fork," said Vanessa. "That's all right," I replied, "I"m talking about their hairstyles."

The second course was immensely hot sauce on pieces of white fish. Vanessa couldn't eat it. I tried it. It was full of chilli, the sort of thing you should ask if people like before offering it.

Then came the baked aubergine. Okay, not spectacular. Fourth course was sashimi salad with a lot of raw fish. I quite liked that. Vanessa hated it, pulled a face and drank some water to get rid of the taste. The room was wearing me down. Overcrowded, overactive, it reminded me of the 1948 movie *The Snake Pit*, where poor Olivia de Havilland was trapped in a lunatic asylum.

Fifth course was very garlic-laden squid pasta. Kelly kept trying to make me use my dirty fork for every course. I declined. The sixth course was marinated cod in a leaf. This was the best offering. We were getting overstuffed. These courses are not small.

By the seventh course, Vanessa had a small dorade fish, complete with fins, tail, head, and set in a slight wriggle. It looked like an ornament. She found it uneatable. I had rock-shrimp tempura. No cutlery arrived, so I started eating with my fingers. Vanessa went to the ladies' room. Kelly came and took her napkin from the banquette, folded it into a design and put it back on the table.

There followed, in very slow succession, vegetables steaming on a plate, then two chicken dishes. "But I asked for no meat," said Vanessa. Kelly looked as if this was highly impertinent.

The 10th course was a vegetable tempura, the 11th was soup. I am a pig, but by now even I couldn't face any more. The worst was yet to come. A large bowl arrived. Six bits of sushi, eight bits of fish, two enormous black rolls and some other stuff. "I think she's taking the mickey," said Vanessa. "It's not a main course: sushi is always served last," said Kelly haughtily.

I may only be a poor boy from Willesden, but I don't need some snotty girl telling me it's "in" to serve a plate of food that would satisfy three people as a main dish 2½ hours after dinner has started.

"Do you want anything else?" asked Kelly. "I'd like to go," I replied. I'd also like to be lobotomised, so the evening in Nobu is removed from my memory. That isn't likely. I'll just have to live with it.

Ark angel

I first wrote about food in a letter to the editor of the Ronay guide complaining about the Ark, a gloomy restaurant in Kensington Court, which revealed one of the most memorable sights ever: chicken in some grossly congealed sauce, so awful I still have nightmares about it. "How dare you include this dump in your guide," I wrote (or similar words), the exact text of my missive being lost to mankind).

The editor of the guide telephoned me. "Confidentially," he said, "we're not putting the Ark in our next edition."

The Ark carried on for a number of years, then sank. I read that Jean-Christophe Novelli, a nice chap I'd met when he cooked at the Four Seasons on Park Lane, was to take over the premises. I always worry about people who use three names. Two is quite enough. Would you think more of me if I called myself Michael Robert Winner? Of course not. Chefs, particularly, seem addicted to the extra-name syndrome. It must be something to do with the atmosphere in the kitchen.

A colour photo of JCN duly appeared in an ad in my local freebie magazine. He had a lock of dark hair carefully placed to fall over the left side of his forehead. He referred to himself as a "critically acclaimed chef". I gave him 6½ out of 10 for my Sunday lunch at the Four Seasons: "Marked down because of the room; cooking worth more." I decided to telephone **Novelli W8**.

A girl said: "Jean-Christophe is taking photographs. He will call you back." I took that to mean he was being photographed, doubtless with aides in attendance to make sure the lock of hair fell attractively. After a while, JCN returned my call. I welcomed him to my manor and asked if I could come to dinner that night.

"We are overbooked, I will have to call you back," said Jean-Christophe.

"You are the boss now," I said, "not an employee. Bosses can do anything."

Jean-Christophe thought about that for a moment and said: "All right, what time?"

"Between 7.45pm and 8pm," I replied.

I greatly believe that customers should turn up at the time for which they booked. On the rare occasions I find that difficult, I telephone. The establishment is usually surprised at my courtesy. Everyone seems surprised when I behave well, which is almost always.

We set out early, parked in Kensington Court and walked to the pedestrian bit that joins up with Kensington High Street, then to the exact location of my congealed chicken disaster. But what was this? No Novelli where the Ark had been. I was near panic.

At some place – I knew not where – Jean-Christophe Novelli was pacing up and down, confronted by hordes of apoplectic customers he had turned away for MW, and cursing in perfect French the day he had taken my call. I got through to directory inquiries on the car phone, found out it was the other ex-Ark, the one nearby, in Palace Gardens Terrace, where M Novelli reigned. When I arrived, only two minutes late, Jean-Christophe was nowhere to be seen. I imagined somewhere a line of photographers waiting patiently to encapsulate him and that lock of dark hair. Ah, such is fame.

Eric Chatroux, the maitre d', showed us an excellent position. We faced an endless row of tables with people sitting opposite each other – so many, I assumed there was a mirror and I was seeing them doubled up. This was not so. The room is long, thin and most attractive. Purple is the prime shade. It is on the paintwork, on the menus – and a man two seats away wore a shirt that matched it perfectly.

The bread was dull and tedious, but everything else was very good indeed. This is a cheerful, inexpensive bistro, with real taste to the food. I started with home-smoked stuffed goose neck, gizzard and mixed leaves. It sounded surgical, but tasted great. Vanessa, who is even more critical than I, pronounced her pan-fried celeriac and potatoes, goat's cheese and mozzarella terrine "very good".

My main course, poached rabbit leg *à la ficelle*, stuffed piperade risotto and pepper juice, was a delicious casserole and the accompanying veggies undercooked to perfection. Desserts were equally up to standard.

How the turgid Kensington Place a few yards away keeps going against this stylish competition, I cannot imagine. Their place is noisily cavernous. Novelli looks like a hut – probably because it is a hut.

Jean-Christophe even turned up to greet me and see me out, perhaps grateful I was going. I went back another night – it was just as good. Now if he could move it to the bottom of my road, life would be even better.

PS I have been disappointed on recent visits.

The **Oak Room** in the Meridien Hotel, Piccadilly, is large, high-ceilinged and overbright at lunchtime, although I'm told it's more romantic in the evening. I thought it a pity that only 14 people had turned up for lunch, because the food was outstanding. There was an attractive set menu at £29.50 excluding service, but Marco took over and a series of exquisite dishes rained down on me. Seafood marinière with caramelised squid, a sort of soup. Then grilled Cornish blue lobster, then terrine of fresh duck foie gras, then some oysters, then a main course of pig's head with mash, with various types of pork, which was always my favourite. Even I, glutton of all time, found this a bit much. But I managed to wolf down my caramelised pineapple with ice cream and some petits fours and coffee. With a half bottle of Mouton Rothschild 1986, the bill for two, including a 10% tip, was £496.

I had dressed in a black jacket and an old silk kipper tie for the occasion. Marco, unkempt as ever, sat back and looked me up and down. "It's good luck for you we don't have a dress code or you wouldn't get in," he observed. "Nor would you, Marco," I said. I was rather pleased with that little riposte.

I go to **Orsino's** in Holland Park quite a lot – even though, as at Orso's, which is owned by the same group, they won't put an egg on my pizza. It's an okay place, pleasantly decorated and with large tables. The food is cheap, cheerful and rather likeable. But the service on a bad day can be so slow you'd think the entire kitchen staff were on holiday in Skegness.

Orso's is a subterranean place in Covent Garden with adequate, quasi-Italian food and excellent service. On one visit I had a bit of a drama trying to persuade them to serve me an egg to go on the establishment's rather dry pizza. And this despite them serving eggs on my pizza for 10 years. I only succeeded by entering the kitchen and smiling at the chef. When I phoned Orso's boss, Richard Polo, the next day to ask why there was a problem, he said he didn't want to discuss it. This man was obviously frightened by a chicken at an early age. I suppose that's as good a reason as any to go into catering.

Miss Caroline Langrishe, actress of beauty and taste, told me she went to all the "in" places, such as Bluebird and the Oxo Tower. "If you phone, they say you can't have a table for six weeks," she said. "But if you turn up and say have you got a table, they'll look and say, you can have that one over there." "That may only work if you're blonde and beautiful," I suggested. I have telephoned the **Oxo Tower** twice to make a reservation. All I got was classical music. It went on for ever. No human voice did I hear. This is ridiculous – if I want a concert, I'll visit the Albert Hall. I may only be a poor boy from Willesden, but why should I put up with that? I'd rather go somewhere less chic where they answer the phone. Thank goodness I no longer aspire to be trendy. It makes life so much easier.

Taste of Fame

My dining table looks Georgian, as do the 10 chairs. In truth they're very good Victorian copies. You can easily get 12 people round it. And at a pinch, 14. None of this matters as I never have dinner parties anyway, because I worry too much about the guests. Should I produce the Latour 61, or fob them off with the Lafite 82, which sells in most restaurants for a mere £1,200 per bottle excluding service, even though some time ago it cost me 80 quid?

I gave my last dinner party in May 1992 for Arnold Schwarzenegger on his first visit to England for many years. It was a grand affair, but illustrates why I find these events so exhausting. Half an hour before Arnold was due to arrive, my friend Robert Earl rang from the Halkin hotel. "Arnold likes pear schnapps," he announced. Pear schnapps is not readily available in Holland Park at 7pm, but to my immense credit we found some and had it taxied in. Arnold then spilt it on the polished table top. He was greatly worried about this. I was totally unconcerned. I take my friend Diana Rigg's view that being too immaculate is nouveau riche. A little "distressing", as they call it in the antiques trade, is all for the good. "If anyone did this to me," said Arnold, surveying the stain, "They would be banned from Beverly Hills society."

I have a photo of myself making a speech of welcome to Arnold. At the table, guests include his wife Maria Shriver, John Birt, Bob Geldof and Lew Grade. Arnold's response was very witty, he said: "Michael Winner is more than a good friend to me. He is a complete stranger." This was true at the time, although we've since buddied up.

Recently, I was partially responsible for a larger dinner party, a function. The Directors' Guild of Great Britain, a trade union of which I am the longest-serving founder-council member, was to honour Stanley Kubrick with its Lifetime Achievements Award. It was my idea. His wife

Christiane – I'd known them both for 30 years – wrote: "I remember Stanley being flattered to receive the Lifetime Achievement Award, though with horrible foresight, he added, 'This is a bell-tolling award!'" Thus it sadly turned out to be. But it was a moving and excellent tribute. I chose the **Park Lane Hotel** – their art deco ballroom and balconied cocktail area are particularly attractive.

After worrying about the menu and the seating, I worried about whether guests would turn up. Particularly as I'd done a deal with *OK!* magazine – well, a trade union needs all the cash it can get – and they listed certain people as essential. My table was as nice a group as you could muster. I took the delightful Miss Cherie Lunghi, recently returned from foreign parts. On my right was Miss Joanna Lumley with her husband Stephen, very smart in a red jacket and looking like a musician, which is just as well as he is one. A conductor, anyway. Then there was the flavour of the month, red-haired and very lovely Patsy Palmer, Sir Peter Ustinov and his daughter and, on the other side, Maureen Lipman and her husband, the writer Jack Rosenthal.

Dinner menus are always a bit of a joke, especially as, at any function for more than 300 people, you know it isn't going to be great. But I thought the Park Lane Hotel did well. Their Italian antipasto of roast artichokes, grilled vegetables, mozzarella, olive bread and rocket salad might not have won first prize in Siena, but for a catered event it was excellent. The inevitable chicken, in this case supreme of chicken (is any menu chick not supreme?), with a tarragon mousse and a wild mushroom cake, was rather good. The dessert was memorable, chocolate *millefeuille* with orange sorbet. Coffee or tea was accompanied by dark, white and milk chocolate truffles. Alexander Walker, who produced an excellent piece about Stanley on page two of the menu, wrote of our design: "It is quite the most elegant example of its kind I have seen." Even though he had to be somewhere else.

Sir Peter Ustinov made the best speech I've ever heard. His impersonation of everyone from Charles Laughton to Laurence Olivier to John Gavin at the script read-through of *Spartacus* was historically hilarious. He presented our trophy to Christiane Kubrick after her daughter Anya had spoken most movingly. The *Evening Standard* described my compering as "brilliant" – so I should have been happy. But it is exhausting organising dinners for any size of group. I shall now retire to be, as before, the host with the least. It's a role I delight in.

Patio is in the most unremarkable street, close to the southern end of the Shepherd's Bush Shopping Market – which I used to own in my days as a landlord. It's comfortable, old-fashioned and Polish. It has a spick and span look with white tablecloths, and the customers were like I used to see in Hampstead: intellectuals, quiet, nice-looking. Ewa Michalik and her husband Kaz, who own it, have the air of well-turned-out eastern Europeans who really care. The food demonstrates this. I had herrings with sour cream, red borscht and a sausage called cabamos for starters; then veal à la cracova, a rump of veal with a wine-cream sauce. For dessert I had nice fluffy cheesecake and a pancake filled with vanilla and rum. The bill for three, including vodka, was £34.70 ex service. Incredible. I asked Ewa when she last put the prices up. She thought carefully and said, "Seven years ago". "Don't you think it's time to strike out again?" I ventured. Ewa said, "I'm afraid of the competition", adding something about pizza parlours.

A Feud is Born

The feuds in chef-world make show-business bitchiness pale into insignificance. Even if I cared it would be difficult keeping up with who's talking to who. For many years Gordon Ramsey worked with Marco Pierre White at Harvey's in Wandsworth. Then Michael Caine brought Marco into town to The Canteen and Gordon went to the Aubergine. For reasons I will not reveal, they fell out. For some time now they've been friends again (the civilised world breathed a sigh of relief!) and it was Marco who suggested we visit **Petrus**, a restaurant in St James's owned by Gordon where the talented Marcus Waring is cooking. Gordon also joined us.

He and Marco were once the bad boys of chefdom. Tantrums, expletives, even minor violence were supposedly the norm. I find them both thoroughly well behaved. Although I did see Marco on heat recently. I was with him and his wife Mati, the Best Restaurant Receptionist in the World, at Marco's Mirabelle restaurant. Tim and Tina Zagat, who edit a famous restaurant guide, came to the table to greet me. I'd met them very briefly five years ago on a boat. Zagat readers had just voted Gordon Ramsey's own restaurant best in the country. Tim turned to shake hands with Marco who refused and said with considerable clarity he didn't want the Zagats in his restaurant. Apparently they'd published some rude things about Marco's establishments. The manager was despatched to escort Tim and Nina to the street. I remained. The meal was splendid. Another restaurant feud was born.

Petrus resembles an art gallery selling 17th century Dutch paintings that serves coffee on the side. It's narrow and exhibits large reproductions of Flemish still lifes of oysters and fruit. "Cauliflower soup," I dictated into my tape, "is our freebie starter." "Crème du Barry," corrected Marco. "That's the classical name for cauliflower soup." Either way it tasted great. It came in one of those tiny bowls. "I hate drinking with teaspoons," said Marco drinking from the bowl. He looked around. "Very nice clientele," he observed. I found them rather dull. Business types.

My starter was marinated foie gras, apple and artichoke salad, creamed vinaigrette. The main course – which took forever to arrive – was pork belly rolled tight, sliced, cooked in sherry and vinegar sauce, served with aubergine purée. From these ponced up descriptions you'll deduce it's a serious place. It's also very good. Somewhere along the line we got another freebie, of red mullet.

Marco started his main course at once, saying "It's rude to wait if you've got hot food". I agree. It's ridiculous. If the waiter's preparing food for one of your party, why should everyone else wait, their food getting cold, until the last person is served? Pitch in, I say. I'm glad Marco approves.

On the dessert menu it read: "Please allow a minimum of twenty minutes for the preparation of your dessert". In that case, I thought, why didn't they give us the menu twenty minutes ahead of time, not ten minutes after we finished the main course. There's a limit on how long I want to look at fake Dutch oil paintings and other diners in suits. The desserts were truly memorable – from a freebie treacle tart to pistachio soufflé, crème brûlée, and iced coconut cream with candied coconut and warm chocolate sauce.

The wine waiter took Marco's glass when it still had some Petrus in it. He rightly asked for it back. Marco waved his empty plate about the second he'd finished his pud and a waiter took it. I asked for mine to be cleared and the waiter took that. Mario's wife Mati was left sitting in front of her dirty plate. The service needs tightening up, but Petrus is a nice place.

Taking the cure

I don't want to be "in". Being in is one step away from being "out". When I hear recession is coming, I think: "Good, then all those dreadful, ephemeral 'in' restaurants can collapse. The sound of falling catastrophes will be music to my ears." I could give you a list of restaurants I'd be delighted to see go down. And their owners with them. I'm sure I will live to enjoy the spectre of it all. So when a very famous chef (hereinafter referred to as VFC) suggested we had dinner at **Pharmacy**, the newish place in Notting Hill Gate, I said to myself, "I can't think of anything worse." This restaurant is so chic, they have a special phone number for the superchic to use so they don't have to get ear contamination from being listened to on the same phone as the less chic.

In case there is anyone who doesn't know, Pharmacy faces the busy through road from Bayswater to Shepherd's Bush. It's done out by Damien Hirst, he of the half-cow school of art. On being driven past it from time to time, I noted it was an Addams family version of Disneyland chemist's shop. I like theme restaurants. In the 1950s, I was very fond of El Cubano, a Mexican-style, glossy-table-topped place in Knightsbridge, full of exotic birds in cages, which served an excellent chilli con carne at any hour of the day. The exotic birds bred so speedily they had to open a second, similar place up the road. We understood they were closed because the kitchens were filthy. Doubtless lining them up with many of today's posh places.

Pharmacy's shelves of supposed chemist products (a jar of Rimactane caught my eye) were quite inoffensive. The downstairs bar seemed a perfectly decent place for a snack. I was greeted by Ruth Mayer. She's nice, very pretty. I knew her from the River Café. She led us up to the first-floor dining room. I must admit it looked very good: plastic-covered panels with butterflies in them, airy, spacious, interesting. I was sat obscenely close to a molecular sculpture which probably came from a school for retarded car dealers. Imagine my surprise when told it was terribly important and some art expert had bought 11 of them at £150,000 each. Believe that if you wish.

The bread was unspeakable. Like rock. It was Sunday, when frequently the bread isn't fresh – but really! I ordered foie gras cooked on sel with shaved fennel, then pavé of cod Grenobloise. "Good choice, you'll like that," said the general manager. My foie gras was pretty good. The same horrid bread was with it, but toasted, so marginally better. The dressing on the fennel was rather tart. The VFC pointed out that I had sliced pear as well. Vanessa greatly liked her goat's cheese salad.

The chairs were very comfortable. Robbie Williams, formerly of Take That!, walked by from right to left wearing a hat. Mr Robert Earl, emperor of themed restaurants, was at the next table. I was told the female toilet was identified by a round circle with a cross, the male one by a round circle with an arrow.

I liked my cod very much. Vanessa had sea bass. I don't remember her complaining, so it must have been good. "Look," I said, "there's slices of grapefruit with my fish." "It's lemon," said the VFC contemptuously. I don't care. Lemon, grapefruit – it's all citrus fruit to me. The chips were disappointing. For pudding, the apple crumble was off. The lemon tart had a too-solid pastry base, but the orange sorbet was the best ever.

It was all very trendy. Surprisingly, I found myself enjoying it. I even checked the number of a couple of tables I'd ask for on my return. Pharmacy has a lady chef, Sonja Lee. She's half Norwegian and half Korean. I meant to ask her if, being Nordic, she ever did herring. I like herring. You don't see prawn cocktail or fried scampi much, either; I like those, too. The VFC, sitting beside me, was apoplectic when I said I really missed sole Capri, which they used to do at Wheeler's when it was in its prime. That is sole with chutney and bananas. I think there is getting to be a certain sameness about nouvelle British cuisine. Back to basics, I say. But if you want to be part of Cool Britannia, you could do very much worse than earn your badge at Pharmacy. I'd heard good and bad of it. I side with the goodies.

There are restaurants you pass, year after year, but which you never enter. So I was pleased when the actress Kathleen Breck invited me to lunch at **Poissonnerie de l'Avenue**, Chelsea, a restaurant I have ignored all my life. Kathleen was the lead in my film *West 11* in 1962. She went on to better things – she quit acting, found a handsome and rich husband (the famous screenwriter Allan Scott) and settled down to a delightful life. When I entered the premises I thought they looked extraordinarily dull. I had impressed upon Miss Breck the importance of having a large table well enough away from other diners. Kathleen had done well. At the next table Mary Quant turned up, so it was a really 1960s reunion! The food was remarkably good. I had langoustines, Kathleen had field mushrooms with polenta. We both had the grilled sole. The carrot purée was so exceptional I ordered seconds – something I have never done before with carrots! I was obviously impressed because, two days later, I suggested Vanessa went there for dinner with me. This time I started with some smallish fried sardines – good, not spectacular – followed by the best salmon fishcakes I have ever eaten. Again, I ordered a second portion of the carrot purée. I finished with *oeufs à la neige*, which were okay.

Excellent as it is, I am not going to put the Poissonnerie on my regular list because of its ambience. I wish they'd open up near me in Kensington with brighter decor. Don't get me wrong. I like old-fashioned. You can't get more old-fashioned than Wilton's. But there you see Mrs Thatcher. Oddly, I've always considered that a plus!

River disaster

The least enjoyable restaurant evening of my life was at Sir Terence Conran's **Le Pont De La Tour**. I was the guest of an American music supremo; Chris Wright, the chairman of Chrysalis Records, was with us. An evening of tepid food, of unremarkable quality, and poor service was rounded off with a remarkable performance by one of the most unrepentant managers I have ever come across. One guest wasn't served until everyone else had virtually finished a course. My fish came without any vegetables; it tasted old and tired. We'd ordered coffee and after a while I saw two young waiters staring in confusion at a tray with cups on it. I suspected they couldn't work out which was decaffeinated and which wasn't. After a while, I looked again. They were still staring. Eventually they took a chance and served it. "This coffee's cold," murmured my quiet American host. I shot up.

The manager, resplendent in evening dress, was way down the restaurant. I walked over. He saw me coming and headed for the cash-desk. "Excuse me," I said. He seemed to ignore me. That was a mistake. "Excuse me," I said again, a bit louder. He kept walking. "Excuse me!" I yelled. When I yell you can hear it 60 miles away. He turned. "We're having a terrible time at our table," I said with venom. "I suggest you come and deal with it."

He followed me back. I pointed out that the coffee was cold and asked could he get some more. Things were not going well and one guest mentioned my fish. This clearly upset the manager. "What was that?" "It's not important," I said. "Let's just have some hot coffee." But that was a forlorn hope; the manager wanted to know "what was wrong" there and then. Oh dear, I thought. I told him my fish had been solid and unfresh. He protested at length about how fresh everything was. Always. Inevitably.

The wife of our host, trying to calm things, said how nice the place usually was, what famous rock stars she'd brought, but how tonight we'd all thought there had been a collapse of service and quality.

"I shall go to the kitchen and discuss this," said the manager, walking off with all the neurosis of Basil Fawlty. He returned with a delivery note. "That proves the fish was fresh this morning," he said. "Ah well, perhaps it was overcooked," I said.

The manager stormed off again, returning to whisper in my ear: "The chef was very satisfied with your fish." "Well, he didn't have to eat it," I replied.

I wrote to Sir Terence, detailing how a distressing meal had been turned into a remarkably unpleasant evening by the quite extraordinary antics of his manager. Unlike other restaurateurs I've written to, Sir Terence replied sarcastically: "Thank you for your film script, I shall certainly investigate the situation." I did not hear from him further.

I went to **Quo Vadis** with Marco Pierre White and his extremely pretty, beautifully behaved and highly charming nine-year-old daughter, Letticia. It's another Marco eatery, with The Ivy's marvellous ex-manager, Fernando Pere, in charge. I'd been once before and found the food iffy. This time it was excellent. Marco ordered Chateau Margaux 1961, one of the great wines. "It's the year daddy was born," he said, offering some to Letticia. She sipped it, pulled a face of total disgust and stuck her tongue out. If this girl thinks Margaux '61 is awful, some man's in for a very interesting time.

Worth waiting for

On Tuesday of last week Marco Pierre White, the council-house lad from Leeds, completed his journey to London's West End with the opening of his new restaurant at the Hyde Park Hotel. It is grossly unfair to comment on the first occasion he decided to serve in his new abode; but this will not hold me back.

My first impression was absolutely horrible. You enter through a tired, chipped, miserable lobby that leads to the Hyde Park banqueting rooms. I was faced by an unprepossessing carpet leading up the stairs, a sign saying "Gentlemen's Cloakroom and Hairdressing Salon", some plastic sheeting and an odd smell.

Not having any directions I started to climb the seedy carpet. In fact, Marco's restaurant, unsignposted, is through some doors on the left of the lobby. The room is spacious and cool, with floodlit flowers and ivy through the windows which look on to Knightsbridge.

My host was Marco's partner, Michael Caine, and Marco himself appeared briefly, very harassed, then vanished behind a screen near our table and back into the kitchen. From time to time throughout the evening, his voice could be heard in a frenzy of excitement.

I had put myself into a mind-set in which things were bound to be slow, there could be no napkin-waving, banging on the table, or jumping up to admonish the head waiter. That was just as well, because it was two and a quarter hours before the main course arrived.

I knew things were touch and go when our waiter dropped a bread roll down Michael Caine's back, showering white flour over him. Then another waiter dropped Mrs Caine's champagne glass, breaking it, and my bread was thrown in front of me on to the plate, nearly bouncing off. The waiter returned and greeted us with "Good afternoon" at nine o'clock in the evening. Michael Caine, a man of high professional standards, flashed a glance memorable to behold.

I was beginning to wish I'd stayed at home and watched the spin-dryer, when some hot vichyssoise with oyster and caviare was delivered. One taste of that and I knew Marco was on brilliant form. Then came a vinaigrette of leeks and langoustines with caviare, which could not have been better. I tried a bit of everyone else's portions, which were equally impressive.

There followed a long delay, during which I mulled over the fact that were I in charge I would probably fire every waiter in the place and start again. This was broken by the arrival of my pot roast pork with spices and cuvée of vegetables with *pommes persillées*. It was as good a main course as I have ever eaten, and I had the sense to be born to extremely rich parents, who kept me gloriously fed from childhood. Once again I nicked a bit from everyone else's plate and the extraordinary culinary standard was maintained.

Marco's desserts have always been legendary. I had a *pyramide* which I will not attempt to describe, but which was to die for. Mr Caine had a selection of chocolate items, each one more delicious than the other. I know, because I nicked his plate after he'd had only a tiny mouthful.

I ventured into the kitchen, where Marco's language flowed unabated. But he had to be congratulated. (He was at the time screaming about Nigel Dempster's tarte tatin). Later, and calmer, when he showed me out to my car, we stood under the blue awning with "**Marco Pierre White The Restaurant**" on it and chatted about the "theatre" of that night.

It had been deliciously memorable, and when he gets the service sorted out it will be historic.

PS This restaurant has now gone – Marco went to the Oak Room at the Meridien, Piccadilly, but no longer cooks! He supervises!.

Richoux in Mayfair is an all-day dining place, with "Victorian" waitresses in full theatrical gear, most of whom seem to be oriental. My mother used to give them hell in Grosvenor House, where she stayed for long periods, walk to Richoux, cause trouble there and then go back to resume duties at Grosvenor House. She was a game girl, God bless her. Even if she did lose £6m in the Cannes Casino and nick antiques, jade and furniture, left to me to sell off to pay the bill. Anyway, Richoux has a wide menu but it also does the usual scones, cakes and a variety of teas. It's all perfectly adequate and a cutesy setting.

Cross my palm...

The Ritz Hotel, Piccadilly, should be ashamed of itself. I refer not to the establishment in general, which has many fine attributes. I mean the overcrowded, crammed-up, ludicrously small tables in the **Palm Court**, where they serve tea. It resembles a Balham car dealer determined to stuff every possible vehicle onto his lot. Or a contest to see how many students can pile into a Mini. With the Ritz, it's how many people and tables can be forced into a Palm Court. The tables are so small that to pass the cream and jam from one person to another involves moving everything in sight to accommodate this. It is like an intelligence test. Anyone who achieves it, deserves senior membership of Mensa.

I decided at the last minute to take Sunday tea at the **Ritz**. It is something I have never done. I understand people from out of town book a long way ahead, so I was happy to be accepted (why not?) and offered space. At that point, I had not seen the space! A tie is necessary, so I dug out one of my old wide, kipper ties which are now all the rage. I see half-naked men in my Versace catalogue wearing these knotted so they only come halfway down your chest.

Vanessa declined to have her new sports car parked by the Ritz doorman, so she parked it by the Caprice and we walked up. The doorman paid little attention to my entry. At the last moment, he nodded. I think on entering the Ritz the doorman should acknowledge you with a movement of hand to cap, in my case more. I passed into the attractive lobby – at least people inside greeted me – then to the Palm Court. It's a raised bit on the left. A pianist was playing "Unforgettable", doubtless referring to the room arrangement. A young man said: "Afternoon tea?" What did he think I'd come for? An enema? "What do you mean, afternoon tea?" I said sharply. "I made a reservation." I was shown to a table, just big enough to put things on. There is a set menu – sandwiches, cakes, scones – for £18.50 per person, including service and VAT. We ordered Earl Grey. A few moments later the Palm Court manager, a nice chap named Darren Yeap (pronounced "Yup"), said: "Two people are leaving by the statue, would you rather go there?" "Is the table the same size?" I asked. "It's a bit smaller," said Darren. I stayed put, but, after a short time, got aggravated by the activity at the service bar behind me, so we moved to the "statue" table. The statue was of a gilded lady looking up at two cherubs blowing through seashells. The room is delightfully kitsch. The table was so small I could not believe it.

The tea arrived. Strainer, not tea bags. A three-tier rack, with sandwiches on the bottom. "There's smoked salmon, cucumber and anchovy, egg mayonnaise with mustard cress, smoked turkey and sweet mustard, and cottage cheese with carrot and hazelnuts," intoned the waiter. They were all superb. So much so that, after the cakes and the scones, I went back, fully stuffed, and finished them off.

The cakes were only marginally below historic; I've never had better scones. But the throng of people made it look like a cheap restaurant. It invaded my enjoyment of the food. Opposite me was a nice family of four, father in dark suit, wife with aunt/mother-in-law/granny in floral dresses, and young boy playing with toys. Pa got the bill. He looked at it for a long time, laughed to himself, his eyes still riveted to the bill, gazed longer and finally put down his credit card. I asked if Vanessa could take a photo of his four-year-old Jack, sitting beside me. The family were delighted: "We'd love that," "He doesn't like being photographed," muttered father, Michael. This became abundantly clear. Jack threw a tantrum greater than any I have seen on a movie set. His father and the ladies tried, without success, to pacify him. After, he cried for 30 seconds, then gurgled with laughter as he looked back at me from dad's arms.

An interesting afternoon. If I was a resident of the Ritz paying highly for my accommodation and had to have tea with this excessive number of visiting firemen in over-crowded conditions, I would give the manager a speech on Sunday that would be ringing in his ears on Thursday. As I was only a tourist myself, I politely made my views known to Mr Yeap-Yup and wandered out. This time the doorman saluted like mad. Must have realised who I was.

A Curate's Egg for Lunch

I phoned **The Ritz** in Piccadilly. "Can the lady wear designer jeans?" I asked Yves Deret, one of two assistant restaurant managers. "Yes," he replied. "So designer jeans are all right?" "Yes," he repeated. "Do I need a tie?" "Yes," he said. So I took an old Turnbull & Asser kipper silk tie from my museum collection and set off for Sunday Lunch, accompanied by Miss Lid.

No Ritz doorman opened the Bentley door, because he wasn't there. "Saving on staff, are you?" I announced cheerfully to the concierge as I entered the lobby. "Doorman's fired, is he?"

I was told: "There's only one and he's gone to the gents."

"God help us all if he has diarrhoea," I thought. "The customers would never be dealt with."

I went into the dining room. It's certainly busier than it was before Giles Shepard – nicest and best-dressed man in the world and Ritz supremo for four years – took over. He's spruced the place up no end. I considered the comparative value of the southwest corner table as opposed to the southeast one. I chose the southeast through force of habit; I've sat there before. It has a better view of the entrance and is closer to the kitchens in case I need waiter assistance. The set lunch is £34. Quite a bit more than Claridge's and the Dorchester at £29.50. The other diners looked as if they were on special outings, always a bit off-putting.

I ordered Coca-Cola and Miss Lid asked for fresh orange juice with no ice. The Coke came warm. I didn't ask for no ice. I requested that M Deret bring me a bowl of ice and some still mineral water. A small glass with five ice cubes in it appeared. We ordered. When M Deret came again, I pointed out that I'd asked for a bowl of ice, not a small glass. This is, after all, a supposedly high-class place. They should know the difference. Everywhere else does. After sitting for a very long time without the waiter appearing and with no wine waiter in sight, I asked specifically for him. When he came, Stephane assured me that he normally goes to guests of his own accord. I suppose I'm insignificant. I must learn to live with that. I told him I had asked M Deret for mineral water but never got any. Stephane promptly brought some. It was Ashe Park, which I don't like. "Is this all you have?" I asked. It turned out they had Evian. Why wasn't I offered it? Stephane took the glasses away and brought Evian. A Thermos bowl of ice appeared.

This is all exceptionally sloppy for a beautiful, high-priced dining room in a top-class hotel. "If you need anything else, please call me," said Stephane. I felt like saying: "Well, you're unlikely to come of your own accord, so we'll have to."

Miss Lid had a timbale of lobster, crab and langoustine amoureux. It was an okay fish pâté. They didn't offer her any toast, only me. I had potted smoke salmon, trout and brown shrimps with pickled baby vegetables. I prefer simple potted shrimps, but I hadn't ordered them. I noticed a 13-amp plug in the marble skirting board with a white device attached sporting a flashing red light. It was labelled Pest Control. "That's for people like you," said Miss Lid. A wit if ever there was one.

Luckily, she thought her main course of linguini of smoked salmon and asparagus with caviar cream was exceptionally fine. My roast beef was superb, the veg tasty and well cooked. I liked the Yorkshire pudding, but it was odd: crisp on the outside, runny inside. I'd been told the chef, Giles Thompson, was not on duty. But after the meal he appeared. He admitted: "Your Yorkshire pudding should have developed more." He revealed he'd had my favourite pommes soufflées ready in the kitchen. Excellent, but why didn't someone tell me? Giles, a nice chap from Halifax, explained he worked from 8.30am to 10 at night with an hour off in the afternoon. His food was very good in general and I'm not saying that out of sympathy for his hours of labour. I finished with a vanilla soufflé that was impeccable. Miss Lid pronounced her pear ice cream and chocolate slice totally superb.

As I left, M Deret moaned about my being in jeans. I object to this as I'd checked with him and visited in jeans many times before. The doorman, now potty-trained, said: "Wonderful condition." "Me?" I asked. "No, the car," he replied. It was that sort of a day.

Head of the river

From time to time, not too often, thank goodness, friends phone and say: "Can you get me into this (or that) restaurant? They're full." So far I am batting 100% in success. But when a long-time employee's mother-in-law recently came from Los Angeles and wanted to relive memories at the **River Café** and had been told there was no table, I thought "Oh!"

I'd only been to the River Café once and hated it. A lot of overhyped twaddle set in an industrial area that should be reserved for works outings and demolition crews. The food was equally dreary. That was some years ago, so maybe they'd forgotten my pained expression and my non-return. I phoned and spoke to the boss, a Mr Richard Leslie. Of course there'd be a table for my friends! What a sensible man, I thought. He deserves promotion. I must go along and see him.

So I rang some weeks later and asked for Mr Leslie, but he'd left! A Mr Giles Boden was the new chap in charge. "He's in a staff meeting," said the lady on the phone. "Well, when he's finished perhaps he could be so kind as to call me back," I said somewhat icily. Although why Mr Boden should interrupt a staff meeting to speak to me I agree is not self-evident.

Anyway, Mr B called and I booked for that very night. The River Café was once ever-so-chic, but as new Italian places have sprung up like truffles, it's not so talked about now. I parked carefully outside a lovely Edwardian terraced house and a nice blonde lady inside waved at me through the window and smiled. Then we walked into the ghastly compound that is the River Café. A small area was jam-packed with cars, but a polite car-chap said: "Can you give me your keys, Mr Winner? We'd like to bring your Bentley in here, the neighbours don't like us." "That lady liked me," I said, "she smiled and waved." "Yes, she's the only one," responded the doorman. "Well, since I've parked in allied territory, I'll stay there," I remarked as I wafted towards the restaurant.

Mr Boden had suggested an outside table would be best. Having done that, he then sensibly took the night off. A pleasant, dark-haired lady showed me the chosen spot on a paved area overlooking a modest lawn. "It's depressing," I said. "Why?" she asked. "Because there's that very large group next to it," I replied. I wandered into the restaurant itself to look for something more suitable. I noticed it had considerably brightened up. A bar now extended down the longest end of the room and behind it people were bustling. It's sort of high-tech cheerful, if those two words can possibly cohabit. The waitresses wore long aprons, but as they walked by, their backs revealed the tiniest of mini-skirts. They were very pretty. Even the diners looked all right. I picked a table that was just good enough. A view of the gardens, but, as Vanessa pointed out, they should plant some bushes to hide the car area. I suggest they start now.

The menu was in squiggle script I could hardly read. The bread was appalling. The olive oil tasted like varnish. The salt and pepper were in little open bowls, inviting people to take them with their fingers. And who knows where the fingers might have been! This will be a total nightmare, I said to myself, trying to figure out which of the passing miniskirted waitresses had the longest legs. Then things improved dramatically. My first course of *rotolo*, fresh pasta roll of spinach, marjoram, chanterelles and ricotta, was very, and I mean very, good. The calves' liver with pancetta (I thought it was crisp bacon), red chicory, mint and casteluccio lentils was equally fine.

The desert was totally historic. It was almond and plum tart, but light, fantastic pastry, good filling. "Who made that?" I asked, pointing to my empty plate. The dark-haired lady-boss paled. "Why?" she said nervously. "Is the person here?" I continued. "With her hair scraped back, at the bar," she pointed. I got up. A frisson of tension was evident throughout the room. I walked over to the counter. "Did you do the almond and plum tart?" I asked the lady with her hair in a red carnation clip. "Yes," she muttered, inwardly seeking somewhere to hide. "Totally brilliant," I said smiling and shaking her hand. "Congratulations." You could feel the sigh of relief echoing from the strange waving-metal ceiling to the straw chairs.

I don't know why people think I always knock things. I am kindness itself occasionally.

Halcyon days, at last

In 1987 I put a number of major American stars I was employing into the newly opened Halcyon Hotel, a massively tarted up row of Victorian houses near my residence in Holland Park. As a result I got a 40% discount in their restaurant. So awful was the food and service that I closed the account, but not before sending them a letter saying how sad it was that a good hotel had such a ghastly restaurant. Among the politer things I wrote was that the staff would be better off at the Berni Inn, Slough, the food was horrible and the head waiter declined to interrupt a long personal call on the phone because something as inconvenient as customers turned up.

A few years later I went there again and things had not improved. An American lady was now running the room. She walked up and down eating with her mouth open. I was served the worst dish I have ever tasted, supposedly warm duck salad, which was dried up, tough bits of duck, almost certainly from the day before, and some limp leaves.

When I was told they now had a new young chef who was very good I naturally viewed the news with total doubt. So I went to the pompously renamed **Room at The Halcyon** looking for trouble and it was soon available. It started when an extremely surly man answered the phone to take my booking. When I said I'd like to come between eight and eight-thirty, he said "Would you come at 8.30." I did as told and was greeted by a restaurant with only four tables occupied. So why couldn't I have come earlier? At the desk where I had previously encountered rude restaurant managers there was no one at all. I greeted some friends sitting nearby, and eventually a smartly dressed young lady turned up. "Ah," I said. "There is someone in charge." She ignored that pretty well and showed me to a disgusting corner harbouring the sort of tiny table where you face your guest and the next people are too close by far.

"Not for me," I said and turned to go. "It's the second-best table," said the manageress desperately. "Simon Gray's at our best one, he comes in every night." Indeed the excellent playwright was in the other corner at a nice round table, and deservedly too. On the way out I passed a round table I found acceptable. "How about this?" The manageress breathed a sigh of relief and Mrs Lagoudakos, my receptionist and a former Miss Great Britain, and I settled down. It is almost with regret I have to report that from then on things improved greatly.

There is a lengthy menu with a three-course set dinner at a bargain £17 per person, excluding service. I settled for that. Mrs Lagoudakos comes from the Wirral so she rightly likes to take advantage of a night out. She chose everything à la carte.

Some very good oysters in cheese sauce came as the starter-freebie, followed by, for me, some langoustine cream soup which was very good but not hot. Mrs L had langoustines with fresh noodles and a ginger and spring onion butter. I nicked some and could not complain. The delay that followed before the main course was a bit too much. I had rabbit confit with noodles and mustard sauce, done as well as you could hope for. Mrs L had brochette of salmon on a bed of cabbage cooked in sesame oil, ginger and chilli, served with crispy wonton and plum purée. At first she thought there were too many flavours, but at the end she decided it was all terrific. By now even the manageress was improving, being charming and efficiently attentive.

The desserts – blueberry delice on the set menu, banana pancake with butterscotch sauce and vanilla ice cream on the other – were close to historic. I had no option but to call for the 24-year-old chef, Martin Hadden, and congratulate him. Pity, really. I was hoping to murder the place for all the rotten times they'd given me in the past.

In 1999, Martin Hadden left, and a new chef, Toby Hill, arrived. I visited.

Martin Best, a tall man, who had worked in Casinos, greeted me. I noticed they'd stopped serving Evian water and served a vile concoction with their own name on it. They'd also added piped music, which I persuaded Mr Best to turn off. At 8.09pm we were served bread, but no butter. Mrs Lagoudakos, my former Miss United Kingdom receptionist, was about to tuck in. "No, let's see if they notice we've no butter," I said. This did not please Mrs L, who hadn't eaten all day. Mr Best visited a number of times to take the order, pour water, collect menus. He didn't notice the absence of butter.

We got red mullet and saffron soup as the freebie starter. And two canapés. Mrs L took one and said it was awful, so I didn't eat mine. The soup was okay. Then we were served another tiny cup of soup, which was announced as saffron. "Don't be silly," I said, "we've had that, take it away." They then decided it was pumpkin soup, now being reheated.

By now, Mr Best had come to the table eight times and not noticed that we had no butter. Mrs Lagoudakos said: "Look, those people by the kitchen have got butter. They came after us!" At 8.36pm, 40 minutes after we arrived, the first course came. And there were only 10 people there. Endless French waiters kept asking: "Is everything all right?", "Did you like this... or that?"

My mosaique (sic) of foie gras and canard confit roulette of duck tasted of very little. Mrs L was shocked to find iced tomato sorbet clinging to her hot scallops. When the loquacious French waiter took my plate, he left a side plate with a brioche on and a napkin around it and crumbs all over the table.

The main course arrived after an hour. Mrs L said of her lamb: "It's not very tasty. It's like lamb with a bit of Bisto gravy." I took some. Nowhere near the quality of the lamb that the Oak Room chef serves me for lunch at home or that I buy from R Allen of Mount Street. My salmon was not the best, but perfectly cooked. Served on an unoriginal bed of spinach. Nothing had the flair or flavour of Martin Hadden's reign.

The staff were all pompous. Mr Best came to the table for the 12th time, to pour water. When he left, Mrs Lagoudakos said: "I would have liked my roll." As the rolls were about to be taken away, I called Mr Best and told him what I thought of a butterless table that nobody had even noticed.

Mrs Lagoudakos ordered cheese. I've never seen such a tiny portion in my life. I got a pre-dessert crème brûlée. Mrs Lagoudakos's cheese had been set aside, but she got no crème brûlée. "It's not as if I'm tucking into cheese," she said. When it came, she demolished it all on one biscuit. Later, the deputy restaurant manager, Tracelee Ireland, asked:

"How was your cheese?" Mrs L nodded noncommittally. "You should have said 'small'," I remarked. My orange tart took for ever. All they had to do was slice it and put it on a plate. It was a meaningless soufflé on pastry. It certainly didn't taste of orange.

The Halcyon now has yet another new boss. Its public-relations doyen, Alan Crompton-Batt, wrote about my visit: "I would be grateful if you could let me have your comments with a view to us taking the necessary action."

Here they are: 1) fire the chef; 2) fire the restaurant manager; 3) fire his deputy and the waiters; 4) carpet the place – it's a stone-floored basement, clinical enough already; 5) get rid of those awful paintings they sell, which change regularly, each lot worse than the one before; 6) any time you want advice, Alan, just call.

Meals on wheels

I'm a dab hand in the kitchen. I can knock up scrambled eggs and royal beluga caviare as expertly as Marco, Nico or Groucho – Marx, not Club. Take four eggs, add much milk, energise with an electric whisk, get butter sizzling in a frying pan. When the eggs are peak-frothy, bung them into the pan and stir with a wooden spoon until they reach your preferred texture. Then slop them on a plate, add 100g of royal beluga, preferably from W G White, prepare some Earl Grey tea and voilà! – a masterpiece. My adorable friend Ava Gardner told me that was how Frank Sinatra did his scrambled eggs, although I created my way separately.

I was about to produce this gem, then thought: "Not caviare again." I remembered a booklet that came unsolicited, advertising restaurants from which food was delivered. I'd never done this. Facing an evening with my favourite person – me – I decided to give us both a treat from **Room Service Deliveries**. I selected Havana, a restaurant in Mayfair. You order by numbers, so I carefully marked those pertaining to food I wanted. I telephoned at six minutes to seven. I was asked to hold on. When I was allowed to order, I learnt Havana wasn't with them any more. Nor were my next two restaurant choices. My book was out of date.

We settled on **Luna Nuova** in Covent Garden. I ordered No 117, sardines on a mixed tomato, black olive and red onion salad with oregano dressing. But that was off. So was the poached veal, so was the stuffed breast of guinea fowl. I settled for No 326, char-grilled veal escalope and tomato salad with basil dressing, plus 605, char-grilled bananas with toffee sauce. I threw in five other things to ensure I had lots to judge. I put the phone down from giving my order at 7.02pm plus 30 seconds.

I laid out my cockerel mats from Fortnum & Mason; it wasn't a special enough event to use the super-posh mats I made as a hobby. I put some plates in the warmer, arranged my "nicked" hotel restaurant and airline cutlery and watched a television programme about how to light cities. It was now over an hour from my order and I wished I'd done baked beans on toast.

Then at precisely 8.10pm, the bell rang. At the door was a man in evening dress, slightly diminished by a zip-up outer coat, carrying large plastic hampers with "Room Service" written on them. "We recommend the pizzas from Luna Nuova," he said as he laid my goodies on a kitchen surface. I opened a cardboard box: there was a garlic pizza "Have it while it's hot," advised my delivery chap, Michael Bell. I took some: it was cold, rubbery, awful.

After he left I went straight for the veal escalope. In tipping it onto the plate some went on the floor. I was over-excited. So much so I'd forgotten to open one of my half-bottles of Pétrus 1981. The veal came with potatoes and beans. It was no gastronomic thrill, but it wasn't bad. I had great difficulty opening the stuff in plastic containers. It included antipasti, a lot of very poor salami, some ham, cheese and tomato. I cut the corners of the packets off with scissors to get at the interior. Little bits of plastic flew onto the floor. I'd set up my Leica Summarit camera on a tripod and using Ilford HP5 black-and-white film at two metres (I know you like technical details) I took a number of photos of myself throughout this unique, if tragicomic, experience.

The cold stuff was pretty dire. The char-grilled banana looked absolutely dreadful. It had its skin on, which had gone blotchy. It was like someone with a serious disease. But the banana came out of it quite easily as it was sliced down the middle. I was very pleasantly surprised with the sauce and banana quality. It was after I'd eaten as much as I could stand that I saw the bill: "Driver gratuities are appreciated as a reward for efficient service." Oh well, Mr Bell had the pleasure of meeting me: that would have to suffice.

I pushed 75% of what I'd bought down the waste disposal and clogged it up. I had to bring out a metal pole with two prongs and fight to get it going again. The kitchen looked horrid with so many plastic containers around. Acting like an ordinary member of the public is ridiculous. It's back to caviare for me next time. And the time after that. And for ever.

Why Berni's in

It's the done thing to knock London's most fashionable restaurant, **San Lorenzo** in Knightsbridge. "Terrible food", "full of pseuds", "arrogant service". All I can say is, if it's that awful, how come it's always full and has been for 22 years? They must be doing something right! I've always been a little wary of it. All those paparazzi outside, too many celebs inside, everybody so desperately chic and determined to prove it. *"The"* meeting place. Eric Clapton here, Lauren Bacall there. A lot of "darling" and kissing and exaggerated movements of greeting; smiles just a bit too wide to be sincere. And at one lunchtime recently some gems of over-the-top "in" crowd dialogue, all accurately recorded in my humble squiggles.

"How's Irving Lazar?" "He's been dead for two years." "I tried out the new 230 Mercedes, you can walk faster." "I've got this gorgeous flat in New York, it's been empty for 10 years. I stay in hotels." But enough of this cafe society clap-trap, what about the food? I thought it was most acceptable. In fact better. We started with a Rossini prosecco – fresh raspberry juice and sparkling wine – very nice. Then I had one of the best soups I've ever eaten, *pasta fresca con fagioli*, or bean soup to country folk like me. The grilled sea bass was okay plus, and the dessert of *zabaione con lamponi* (raspberries) as good as even I could wish for. Vanessa liked all her stuff, too!

Atmosphere-wise it's one of the most pleasant dining rooms anywhere. Light and bright, and lots of plants and arches to other rooms. A wave to one of my favourites, Louisa Moore and her family, a nod to somebody terribly important in property (people in property should never get more than a nod) and a "hello" to a famous movie star.

All this is an incredible credit to Mara and Lorenzo Berni, who started in small premises here in 1963 and grew because, quite simply, people liked it and them. Mara does not look the chic restaurant owner. If you didn't notice the confident and lovely smile you might think she was the cleaning lady. Lorenzo could be the maintenance man. He was, in fact, a captain's steward on a ship. But, my gosh, how hard they try. Mara can work a room better than anybody in London (except possibly John Gold at Tramp) and both have lasted forever because they know what they're doing. I have decided San Lorenzo is somewhere I must go more often. I can always stroll down the street and get there quicker than the idiot in the 230 Mercedes.

Stomping at the Savoy

I had an awful Sunday lunch at the Savoy recently. When I was a kid my parents used to rotate lunch on Sunday between Claridge's, The Dorchester and the Savoy Grill. Business has dropped so much, the Savoy Grill no longer opens on Sundays at all! You're stuck with the main, supposedly river-view restaurant. I stopped going to the Grill some years ago. I'd had ghastly lunch service, the veg all wrong, slow, a total mess. I told the head waiter on the way out. In a broad, loud, cockney accent his reply was: "Give over, guv! Give us a bleeding chance!". This sort of dialogue in the posh confines of the **Savoy** so shook me I never returned until Vanessa's birthday party last year when, you may remember, after I had left the restaurant, they threatened to incarcerate her while they decided if I (who had booked and been there) was likely to pay the bill! The general manager of the Savoy, Duncan Palmer, later behaved like a true gent. He sent personal letters of apology and a Savoy bathrobe to every guest (and me) and some flowers as well to Vanessa.

I doubt if the new Granada owners will finance him to have a serious "re-do" of the **River Restaurant**, but hopefully the Sultan of Brunei or some other nice man with an eye for quality will take over and permit it, because it's a big disaster. First of all, Steve Yildiz, the assistant manager, led me to the worst table anyone has tried to palm off on me in living memory. It was tiny and boxed in a corner, with a large group the other side. It would have been inadequate for Snow White and the Seven Dwarfs if six dwarfs and Snow White were dining elsewhere. As Mr Yildiz walked there to pull out a chair, I turned and went in another direction. "Are you crazy?" I asked, "Showing me that!" "It's the best table in the room," said Mr. Yildiz, either ignorant or shameless. I looked around and picked a larger table by a pillar. Even that wasn't my usual table-for-four size.

The place was about a third full of people who all looked like middle-class day-trippers. We ordered two buck's fizz. I noticed Mr Yildiz didn't ask if we wanted mineral water. Much later, Vanessa said: "They should have been here with the wine list by now." "Don't rush," I said, "Let them hang themselves." Eventually the wine list arrived. We were given special freebies of langoustine in filo pastry with a mango sauce. It was the only really good thing we ate. My seafood ravioli starter was pink tasteless stuff in pasta. Bland to the point of extinction. Vanessa liked her melon, but I tasted it and thought it far from the best.

By now the room itself was wearying me. It all looked tired, no unity of style, pillars like this here, like that there. Unbelievably horrid sunken lights in the ceiling, the sort that were fashionable in the early 1970s for offices. All needs gutting, I thought. The size of the table was beginning to irritate me greatly. "Look," I said to Mr Yildiz, as the main course came. "We're having to move the ashtray to make room." "Well, you don't smoke," he said, smiling as if he had made a real funny. The beef on the trolley was near the end of its life. Only a little bit stuck up from the bone. It may have been all right when it started, but now it was well past its best.

"Why didn't you get some more in?" I asked Mr Y. "There weren't enough people to warrant it," he said. The sort of answer you'd expect in a caff in Balham. And, earlier, when I'd asked him to have the kitchen make fresh Yorkshire pudding for me, as they do happily at all other good hotels, Mr Yildiz's expression was as if I'd asked for a free magnum of 1961 Petrus. Reluctantly, they did some newly made Yorkshire and it was pretty good. The beef was, at best, adequate, the carrots so tough they were raw heated. The roast potatoes were soggy.

The dessert trolley looked all right and my chocolate mousse cake was not at all bad. Vanessa's strawberry millefeuille was okay but soggy. The petits fours were ghastly beyond belief. Why, I thought, should they get them from a different supplier to Claridge's in the same group? Theirs are great.

The Good Fellas

I exclude anyone who is Italian from my general displeasure with hospitality in the catering industry. The Italians are natural experts at being genuinely charming hosts. They make you feel at ease and wanted, unlike many English restaurant employees who make you feel edgy and unwanted. This bonhomie, if I may mix languages, is never more evident than at **Scalini**, a popular place in Knightsbridge. I've always considered it too noisy for one of delicate disposition, but I risked it one Saturday lunch. I was greeted by a jovial man with a large moustache, Valerio Calzolari. Then I met another senior person, Michel Lengui. "Valerio is the owner, more or less," he said when I tried to establish the pecking order. "I'm the deputy manager." I walked round a bit, finally settling for the table Valerio originally suggested, in the corner of the main room. It's all very bright and cheerful. Above us was an oil painting entitled *Spring in Provence* by Janine Mackinlay, priced at £275. That seemed about right.

Papardelle with prosciutto, peas and meatballs was the speciality of the day. Miss Lid and I opted for that. A nice selection of focaccia, Parmesan squares and bruschetta was speedily plonked on the table. I admired a fine view of the police station opposite. Then Michel brought "English calamari, they're the best in the world, from the south coast, Portland Bill." I thought Portland Bill was in Scotland. He put some pork spare ribs on the same plate. Everything so far was superb.

We'd come early as I was due in Brent Cross shopping centre to do a book signing. But it soon filled up. A lot of buongiornos and "Good afternoon and welcome" from Valerio, followed by "The toilet's on the first floor".

"They certainly need these fans," I said to Miss Lid. "It's boiling hot." "It's not boiling hot, it's cold," she replied. "Then why are those children sitting without jackets, in just shirts?" I asked perceptively. "Because they're fat enough to be warm," said Miss Lid, as I watched a very good-looking Dover sole served to the table opposite.

It made me seek my main course. "He's taking hours to put it on the table because of you," said Valerio, indicating a man at the serving table. "He's trying to be French. Italian food should be thrown on the plate." It was a good, flat, robust pasta. Nice sauce. A Barolo Bersano wine was produced. Before I could form an opinion, Miss Lid observed a man lighting a cigar at the next table. "Where's the gun? Do they serve guns here?" she asked menacingly.

They did a particularly thorough job of crumbing down (clearing the mess off the tablecloth) and then put a new tablecloth on top anyway. The dessert trolley bumped its way through the crowded restaurant. Apple flan, fruit flan, a strawberry cheesecake, sacher torte, tiramisu. By 17 minutes to 2 things were slowing down. Miss Lid chose an apple pie hours ago, I thought. All they've got to do is cut it and bring it.

"They're putting it in the oven," said Valerio. "I didn't ask for it to go in the oven," I huffed. I started to wax poetic. "They've decided, for no reason at all, to put this apple pie in the oven," I dictated into my tape, thinking of thousands of north Londoners waiting at W H Smith, devastated at my late arrival. When the dessert came, I thought the chocolate cake was good, the apple pie with raisins better. And I had to admit that they were quite right to heat it.

Valerio arrived and said to Miss Lid: "Here's your cappuccino." "She didn't order a cappuccino," I thought angrily. Valerio then tipped it all over her. But it wasn't real coffee, it was a plastic fake. Good gag that. I like a bit of knockabout comedy.

At **Scotts** in Mount Street, Mayfair, the wine waiter appeared with admirable promptness and brought two buck's fizz very quickly. He recommended the Barossa Valley Shiraz 1994. Not harmful is the best I could say. Vanessa started with a salad of warm English goat's cheese marinated with apple in a sage dressing. She pronounced it excellent. I had Mr Scotts game pie of wild rabbit and boar, which wasn't. It would have been all right in a pub: no particular taste, the crust rubbery. Our main courses were pretty dire. I had Cornish cod deep-fried with chips and mushy peas. The mushy peas were the best ever, the chips all right, the cod tired with no freshness of taste. I left most of it. Vanessa thought the lemon butter sauce with her sea bass sickly sweet. Desserts were disappointing too. The staff, however, were all very nice indeed.

At **Sheekey's**, near Leicester Square, the food is totally superb, beautifully cooked, a wonderful menu, all seafood and puddings. The service is as good as you could get in the history of the world. The general manager, Robert Holland, came from The Ivy; he was always first-rate. I had a delicious meal, and I shall return, but there is a problem for us space-lovers. Sheekey's is not so much a restaurant as four separate corridors with tables and chairs. Plus a "crush bar" so narrow that if you put a couple of people in it, you could define "crush" for ever. I had as large a table for two as you can get, but it was still so dinky that when a waiter brought the main course and the veg plates I was in a panic. "Let's take away the bread basket…" Nevertheless, I'm sure Sheekey's will be a success. I certainly hope so.

All bets are now off with this restaurant now that Christopher Corbin and Jeremy King have left but we hope the standards will be maintained by the Belgo Group.

Dusty reception

I ran my finger along the leather-topped Regency table in the lobby of the **Sheraton Park Tower**. It was black with dust. I tried the desk top in the nearby alcove-room. Black again. I wandered towards the restaurant, occasionally fingering surfaces; all were grubby. But in their **Restaurant 101**, although it's a strange and dowdy room, no dust at all! Not even on the mouldings on the wall panels. This is potentially one of the great spaces in London. It looks directly at pavement level onto Knightsbridge. It's large, it's light and at the moment it's awful.

Tacky-looking carpets, a large stain near my chair; curtains in a different mix to colour and design; and old, soiled chairs, marvellously comfortable, but in a faded blue pattern that doesn't match anything else. This could be used as a lesson in how not to decorate. I surveyed the menu. Mine was clean. Vanessa's was dirty. "We're ready to order," I told the waiter. He had no pad. "I usually do it by memory," he said. I've had many messed-up meals that way, so I asked him to write it down. "The pommes frites," I asked, "are they made here?" "Oh yes," said the waiter. "You mean they come into your kitchen as potatoes, a member of the staff takes them, cuts them by hand and then they're fried and served as chips?" "Absolutely," said the waiter.

Three types of bread appeared, not very good but with olive oil served too, so good marks for that. My starter was a salad niçoise, unlike any I'd ever seen. Eight full potatoes stared at me, enough to make anybody queasy, then some large slabs of tuna, which were good, some lettuce, a couple of beans, some small eggs and olives. Anchovies and a large number of other key ingredients were missing. I asked the restaurant manager, Frank Tyler, what he had against anchovies. "We slightly change most of the dishes," he volunteered. "For the worse," I thought. My main course, duck, was okay, but meaningless; the square, cut-up potatoes served with it were very underdone; the rest of the veg well cooked but with no taste. The "home-made" chips looked odd to me. I called Mr Tyler over. "Are those chips cut and made in your kitchen?" I asked. "I don't know," he replied. "Please find out," I said. Mr Tyler came back sheepish. "They're frozen," he admitted. "Then why did your waiter assure me they were hand-done on the premises?" Mr Tyler looked uncomfortable. They featured on my bill even though I left them uneaten, £2.19 including service and VAT. Vanessa's fish cakes were good, but the whole thing, as she rightly observed, tasted of hotel food. No style or shape, just grey. No wonder the elderly couple nearby said the place had gone downhill for the last six years. "Why are you here then?" I asked. "We're local, it's convenient," was the answer. Mr Tyler has been brought in "to lift things from the embers", he explained. He'll have to be an Olympic gold medal weight-lifter for that. He recommended the orange sponge pudding; it had no excitement, the sauce was indifferent.

They should bring in an outsider, like Forte brought in Nico and Marco to liven up hotel spaces that were sitting dull and placid. With the management of this place they'll never get it right on their own. Back in the lobby I wetted my hankie a bit and ran it along the same desk top. I showed the blackened area to the receptionist. "Can I keep the handkerchief?" she said. A manager-type came over. "Did you have a good lunch, Mr Winner?" he asked. "Come here," I said, leading him to the centre table. I rubbed my hankie over a bit and showed him the black. "It's the flowers," he explained, with a straight face. Obviously the Sheraton's small bowl of flowers came from a planet where dust-ridden plants scatter everywhere.

PS Since I wrote this I've checked and dusting is now happening – an example of my improving things for everyone. The restaurant has been renamed one-o-one and tarted up.

My friend Roger Moore was feeling like a bit of Japanese, so he suggested **Shogun**, buried behind the Britannia Hotel in Mayfair. This was once terribly fashionable, largely with people in the music business. I had been there with a rock star, but so long ago I had no real memory of it. Shogun is entered through a small door in what looks like the back of an ill-designed council block. You descend into a cellar of indeterminate style, reminiscent of French existentialism in the 1950s. Edith Piaf could have sung there, or Juliette Gréco. With a bit more cigarette smoke and a few people in blue and white horizontal sweaters, it would have been a perfect place for Gene Kelly in one of those magical MGM musicals. In fact, it was full of Japanese – I suppose a good sign. We waited a very long time for a waitress to pay us any attention. I've never mastered chopsticks, or had any interest in them, as they impede the progress of food to the gullet, so I asked for a spoon and fork for my sushi. I then had tempura fish with tempura sauce. Excellent. Rog had chicken teriyaki with soya beans. He liked that. Vanessa had salmon grilled with sake sauce, and uttered rare words of praise: "Lovely meal." Rog looked round the room. "You look good in this light," he said to me. "But then, anyone looks good in this light, even Darth Vader, sitting behind you." He indicated a squat figure of a Japanese warrior in armour lodged by the wall.

"How can you judge a restaurant properly?" people ask me. "When you go in everyone does their best; you get special attention." Oh yes? Then how come I was served these dreadful, burnt fish cakes at **Snows on the Green**? My host, someone terribly important at Polygram, couldn't believe it. "I can understand me getting burnt food," he said, "but *you*?! It's like they're taking the mickey!" I sawed away at the hardened edges of my lunch and then gave up. Snows had been recommended to me by various celebrities. It's a cafe-like place on a hideous main road near Shepherd's Bush, very noisy, no tablecloths. In the cause of learning how common folk live, I was having the set lunch. I had started with linguine with pesto that was so uninteresting I left most of it. Then came the fish cakes with spinach and chips, and then the worst pear and almond tart I have ever eaten. The pastry was heavy, the taste like mass catering at its worst, the texture clogging.

Soho so good

I don't like Laurence Isaacson. He's the boss of the Chez Gérard group, a megalomaniac company that keeps buying up individually owned places, whereupon they usually get worse. I've never known any personally owned restaurant that sells up and doesn't slide. It's only a question of how much. This is not why I dislike Mr Isaacson. It's because he once asked me to a restaurant opening and then insulted me in the press before my arrival. That was tacky. If you don't like me, don't invite me; if you do, you're a host, so shut up. His name came into play when I entered **Soho Soho**, a restaurant, surprisingly, in Soho. I asked the girl at the desk, Collette Dudman: "Who owns the place?" "Laurence Isaacson, he's very rich," she said. "Yes," I replied. "I met him on the beach in Barbados." "That must have been a dreadful sight," said Collette, I assume referring to Mr Isaacson's fat. "It was a toss-up, dear, as to which was worse, him or me," I responded.

We were shown upstairs to a nice bright room with views onto Frith Street and the pavement drinkers outside the Dog and Duck, "we" being myself and Dennis Michael, who is managing director of a very posh PR company. I remember him as a lad when he worked for Rank on my early acerbic comedies. The third man in the group hadn't arrived, probably because Dennis gave him the wrong address. I'd just been having my hands set in plaster for a pavement plaque in Leicester Square. We were a bit early, but Peter Edwards, a brilliant portrait painter who has had many works bought by the National Portrait Gallery, found us anyway, which was clever as he lives in Oswestry.

The main people who attended us at Soho Soho were two of the most charming and efficient restaurant employees I've ever met. The receptionist was a South African girl, Freda van der Merwe. She would grace any establishment and deserves greater things. Not that Soho Soho is bad. I rather liked it. Our smiley waitress was Joanna Fiedorowicz from Poland. "Are you an illegal immigrant?" I asked. She said no. And who am I to argue? I also liked Collette, who had the grand title of hospitality manager.

The food was pretty good: not what I'm used to, but creditable. Dennis greatly liked his mushroom soup. Peter thought his salt-cod starter "nice". "How nice, Peter?" I asked. "Well, it's salt cod. Salt cod is salt cod. How nice can salt cod get?" he answered wisely. He later found his duck underdone. "I should have asked for it well done," he said, when I pointed out that semi-raw duck was all the rage in high society. Dennis thought his tuna "wonderful" and kept pointing at it and repeating his praise to ensure I got the point. He considered his lemon tart "one of the best I've ever tasted". I tried it. It was okay.

My salmon mousse, pan-fried sea bass and apple crumble with ice cream were perfectly acceptable. I was going to add "for a cheap restaurant" but I did something I seldom do. I checked the bill. Food and coffee alone for three including service was £33 per person. This compares unfavourably to superb three-course set lunches at The Dorchester Grill (£29.50 including coffee and service) and at Claridge's (£29).

Occasionally I lunch in the chairman's suite at Sotheby's, but when Henry Wyndham, their immeasurably affable European chairman, asked me this time, he said: "Would you rather we eat in our café?" "Much rather," I said. I prefer a bit of bustle. **Sotheby's Café** is adjacent to the corridor as you enter the building, so there's a lot of lobby activity.

. I went in the Sunday before our date and faxed Henry a Winner-drawn plan showing the exact table I wished to sit at. We were due to meet at 1pm. After a bit of chitchat, with Henry mentioning very fashionable names, he said: "Let's order. I always have the lobster club sandwich. It's legendary." And, in case I didn't get the drift, he added: "It's incredibly good." So we all asked for it. It was invented by Sotheby's former chairman, the American Alfred Taubman, and comes in a brioche. I was looking forward to it.

At exactly 1.03pm the waiter returned. "We have no lobster sandwiches left," he announced. "What a dump!" I thought. "They have a tiny menu and before lunch has even started for most people, they've run out of the best thing."

Then the restaurant manager, Ken Hall, appeared and said: "For you, we're not out of them." He told us they're so popular that people order their lobster club sandwiches in advance. I suggest that anyone planning to eat at Sotheby's Café phones Ken six months ahead and orders the lobster sandwich. It's ridiculous.

My chilled spinach soup with yoghurt was fine. The lobster sandwich was, indeed, deliciously special. I felt sorry for diners who couldn't get one. Hugo had changed to quail and I tried a bit. Perfectly pleasant.

The situation of the café is particularly interesting with bulky men in overalls walking past carrying furniture. "I like the stuff coming in," said Henry Wyndham. "Means we've got something to sell. Something to look forward to." At one point three small tables, a commode and four large pots went in right to left. Henry was practically orgasmic.

For dessert I had baked vanilla cheesecake with fresh apricots. That was excellent. Henry had toffee-apple ice cream on shortbread. He said he loved it, but then "he would, wouldn't he", as Mandy Rice-Davies once brilliantly remarked.

It was an extremely amusing and pleasing lunch. Afterwards, we admired a Degas bronze of a dancer. It later sold for £8m. If people say to me, "You're rich." I say, "No, I'm not." When I can afford knick-knacks like the Degas, I will be.

Sound bites

I was outraged when my vegetarian ex-girlfriend, Jenny Seagrove, received a gold card to get her ahead of the queue at the Hard Rock Café – and I didn't. A bit later, I was on the beach at the Sandy Lane Hotel, Barbados, when someone told me the man on a nearby sunbed was the proprietor. I walked over. "Do you own the Hard Rock Café?" I asked. Thus disturbed, Robert Earl announced to those in earshot: "You see? He hasn't said a word to me for years; now he thinks I own the Hard Rock, he talks to me."

"I only came to complain, Robert," I said. Mr Earl promised to send me a queue-barging card. Strolling past a week later, I murmured: "Do you do bathrobes?" "I'll have two sent at once," Robert said. Thus love blossomed to the point where Mr Earl co-financed and was producer of my film *Dirty Weekend*. He even got all his money back. Then he went on to greater things, rushing up the *Sunday Times*' richest-ever list, opening Planet Hollywoods all over and heaven knows what else.

His latest enterprise is **Sound Republic** in Leicester Square. Robert, bravely, thought I should go and give my views. Although it's not my usual type of dining room – large and bedecked with videos of rock concerts and music, which, mercifully, is not ear-splitting – I had considerable confidence in it all. This was because the "concept chef" is Tom Dimarzo, who had opened London's Vong restaurant quite superbly. The last time I parked the Phantom Rolls in the Leicester Square area, damage was done, so Robert sent a black-tinted-windowed "people carrier", and bulky security men met it to walk me through the crowds to the entrance.

Two big ramps lead you down to a subterranean area. I understand these will have photos of rock stars travelling on rope pulleys, but they hadn't reached their destination when I went. Down below, the tables were large and well spaced apart. The booths were very big and comfortable. There is a stage which on my visit remained unused.

"I'm going to tell you the components," said Robert, helpfully. "An 800-capacity live venue that we'll open in October, a 400-seat restaurant, an outside terrace restaurant and a TV studio that MTV broadcasts from daily." I waited for further information. But Robert was temporarily exhausted. It seemed as good a time as any to bring on the food.

Robert came to and ordered all nine starters. Before you say pan-fried pork dumplings, £4.95, Tom Dimarzo joined us. I had been sorry when he fell out with Vong, but he's found a good home with Robert and will travel the world opening Sound Republics. Please do not think that friendship influences my opinion: all the starters were excellent. Not Nico Ladenis excellent, not Marco Pierre White excellent, but very tasty, the sort of food I'd be quite happy to eat on a daily basis.

I don't know how many main courses we had, but the table was full. I homed in on bacon, egg, "fresh-cut" chips and tomato. Superb. I grabbed some grilled steak ramen, prawn fried rice, an incredible mushroom risotto and probably a lot more, too – by now, I was getting food-confused. Not that I failed to recognise the historic sticky toffee pudding, with two layers of toffee contained in the light sponge and a lot more around. The apple and blackberry crumble with crème anglaise would have passed muster in a two-star Michelin place, and the home-made ice cream sampler included a memorable banana ice cream. The Spice Girls were in concert on the TV screen, replaced by Tori Amos and then Noel Gallagher.

The only thing I hated to death was the rock concert simulation that occurs every 40 minutes; then all the lights go down and the noise level increases. But luckily it's very short. "Baby Face is our creative director," said Robert, as if I was meant to know who that was.

Square Meal

I'd heard a lot about **The Square** in Bruton Street, Mayfair. Some good, some bad. It has two Michelin stars. I always thought it too posh for a poor boy from Willesden, so I didn't go. My friend the impresario Michael White and I usually lunch at Wiltons. "I've got two very pretty girls who want to meet you," said Michael. "We'll go to The Square."

Twenty minutes before our rendezvous I was in my 1966 Rolls Phantom V, being driven in stately fashion, when I suddenly thought: "I bet the table will be no good." I rang Michael White, but he'd left. "Who booked the table?" I asked an office assistant. "Mason Rose," was the reply. "Who on earth are they?" I asked. "They book tables," said the assistant. "The chance of my staying more than two minutes is remote," I said – and rang off.

I arrived three minutes late, which is rare. I'm normally early. Mr White sat with two nice-looking blondes at a good corner table with a view of the room and people who entered. One of the ladies was Tanya Rose, the Rose of Mason Rose that books tables. "We don't book tables, we book hotels," said Tanya indignantly, hearing me dictate this into the tape. "Tables, hotels, all the same to me," I replied. "We've got a very good list," said Tanya. "Chewton Glen, Parrot Clay..." "They get you upgrades and better rooms," interrupted Michael. The other girl worked with Tanya. Her name was Lavinia.

The room was quite pleasant, café-like with bizarre paintings resembling hawks gone wrong. The freebie soup arrived. Tanya and Lavinia guessed it was mushroom, Michael White said crab; I said with him – some sort of fish. "It's a langoustine bisque," we were told. Very nice. Then we got fish cakes. "This can't be the right fork," said Michael, waving a normal-size fork in the air. I was already eating happily with the same fork. It just shows how sophisticated Michael White is, I thought. My bread was dreary. But, tasting everyone else's, theirs was better. The fish cake was highly enjoyable.

I remarked that the service was very slow. "The reason it's slow," said Michael, "is because you ordered pigeon and it has to be specially cooked. You have to think about these things. You have to ring in advance to book the pigeon." What a load of codswallop, I thought. But as Mr White is the finest of people, I said nothing.

A lady manager I'd beckoned over assured me: "The food's coming now." I've heard that before and waited another 20 minutes. But it did come pretty soon. It was, again, very pleasant. Not massively mucked about and overdecorated, which I'd read some food writer say of The Square. Not the two-star Michelin quality of Gordon Ramsay, that's for sure. But I greatly liked it.

For "pre-dessert" – wonderful word that – we got cinnamon *beigne*, which to simple folk like me is a cinnamon doughnut. This was totally top-of-the-line historic. I ate mine. Then I nicked Tanya's. Then I ate Michael's. They were so delicious that I asked to take some with me. Thus, I left with six doughnuts in a see-through plastic bag. I gave one to my PA, Margaret, and ate the rest myself. Beside that, my main dessert of apple-and-raisin strudel with vanilla and spices was fine, but nothing special.

It was a most pleasing meal, company-wise and food-wise. I'd definitely go back.

Sticky Fingers, just off Kensington High Street, is near my house, but I had seldom been there because on an early visit the music was far too loud and I had a hot dog that was revolting. I returned when the owner, Bill Perks (better known as Wyman), told me he'd told them to lower the music level. I found that the food had perked up no end as well. The potato skins with cheese, bacon and sour cream were a delight, and Vanessa's vegetable chilli was excellent. For the main course I had to try the hot dog again, but I also ordered a hamburger as it is a sort of hamburger joint. Both were superb. Vanessa ordered a strawberry milkshake and I sipped a bit. Totally historic. The best milkshake I've ever had, and I used to be a milkshake freak. Just the right texture, a nice light pink colour, exceptional taste. We ordered another. For dessert I had chocolate iced yoghurt, which the menu said had "no fat, no cholesterol". If it's true it's the most delicious thing ever to be so kind to heart and waistline. All in all it's a terrific place, with good service. It delivers exactly what you'd expect and does it very well. I have only two complaints. Firstly, the menu card was filthy, full of old smears and slimy things. Secondly, and far more serious, why did I not get my free balloons, colouring book and stickers?

Sugar daddy

It was Deidre's idea to go to the Sugar Club. She's Nadia's PA. She knows the chef. **The Sugar Club** is in All Saints Road, which used to be rough, but with the gentrification of Notting Hill creeping further north, is now the "in" thing. Gosh, if they went a couple of miles on they'd hit Willesden, birthplace of me. On reflection, nothing could make that fashionable.

If I had my own way, which tragically, I don't, I'd shoot 99.9% of public relations people. One of the few left alive would be Nadia Stancioff, the grand PR lady for the Orient Express group of hotels and restaurants. She's quite something, Nadia: regal, witty, warm, wrote a book on her friend Maria Callas, been around, brilliant at dealing with Winner. She's as classy as the Orient Express group. When she leaves in May they're going to have an impossible task replacing her. I can think of no other PR person I'd wish to have dinner with.

Notting Hill is in my blood. My grandfather, whose naturalisation papers were personally signed by Winston Churchill when he finally took them out in 1901, had a clothes store in Portobello Road, the hub of his mini shop empire. My dad was born there, within spitting distance of the Sugar Club. If you're a champion spitter, that is.

The SC is bistro-like with a long bar on the ground floor, posher in the basement. I was put in a ground-floor corner facing the room with a view of people entering. I like that. An efficient and charming manager, Fred Martell from Cuba, looked after us. He proudly told me they did the first-class catering for Air New Zealand.

Our three starters were extraordinarily good. They made up for the horrible bread: not warm, tough, rubbery, beyond belief. My kangaroo salad had very tender bits of tasty kangaroo and some nice, spicy sauce that I mopped up with the bread. Vanessa used the word "excellent" for her salad of green beans, marcona almonds, balsamic roast onions, watercress and avocado. Except, as she was eating it, the waiter took her plate away and replaced it with another. They'd forgotten the avocado. Nadia chose the grilled scallops with sweet-chilli sauce and crème fraîche. So far, a triumph.

The decor is somewhat minimalist. Nadia said the walls reminded her of a faded Rorschach test, where they do patterns and you have to say what they represent. Then she said: "What do they do with old napkins on aeroplanes?" This is not a subject I am expert on. "They always give you new ones; the material has never been washed. What do they do with the unused salt, pepper and chocolates? Do you think they give them to the poor? Do they send them to Namibia or something?" I thought it unlikely.

I noticed they had a Sugar Club cookbook. Everyone has a cook-book. There will soon be a British Telecom cookbook, a Dixons cookbook and, to beat them all, a British Rail cookbook, published posthumously.

The main courses were okay, but let the high standard down a tiny bit. I'd chosen pan-fried red emperor with macadamia nut crust, spicy carrot and anchovy salad and herb couscous. I think they'd run out of anchovies. Red emperor is an Australian fish, which, with their Air New Zealand connections, was apparently flown there in seconds. It didn't taste of anything much. It looked like a white hamburger. Nadia liked her duck. Vanessa said her Savoy cabbage, truffle and Parmesan risotto cake with green beans and wild mushroom was okay, then upped it to good. They gave us some mustard mash – their way of doing potatoes. This I found memorable. The chocolate mousse cake with whipped cream was heavy; I mean that as a compliment.

The place is owned by Miss Vivienne Hayman and her partner, Ashley Sumner. He was off that evening. Miss Hayman was jolly. She used to work at the BBC on Janet Street-Porter's *Dance Energy* programme. The chef, Peter Gordon, came up to say hello. He looked like a serial killer, but had nice manners.

Out of the tall windows you could see yellow streetlights illuminating the pillared Victorian stucco of the houses, and a very ugly modernish building called the Notting Hill Training Centre. It's one door away from the Bicycle Workshop. Years ago, I dated an American actress who'd been in *Playboy*. She had me wait disapprovingly outside a house nearby while she bought cocaine. What more can I tell you?

Sweet Spot

I once watched a documentary about the opening of the restaurant **Sugar Reef**. It featured the co-owner, who was the strangest thing I've ever seen on TV, or indeed anywhere else. Every other word began with "f". He bullied, screamed, showed off and generally ran amok, making pronouncements of unparalleled absurdity. The restaurant itself looked ghastly beyond belief. There was a pink waterfall that never seemed to work, horrid décor and an opening night where the usual ragbag of non-celebrities appeared, to the horror man's apparent delight. Lurking in the background was my friend Jimmy Lahoud, a partner in the venture, who wisely said nothing. I thought: "At least I'll never have to meet that monster or go to his appalling restaurant."

I told Marco Pierre White of this at his wedding. "You're wrong, Michael. The man's Mark Fuller. There he is," said Marco, pointing to a nearby table. "He's a very nice family man."

I didn't meet Mr Fuller then, although I did some weeks later, when Robert Earl of Planet Hollywood fame asked me to join him and Marco at Sugar Reef. It's a large place seating 320 diners, has lots of bars and is licensed for 1,000 people. It's in Great Windmill Street, Soho, close to where a wondrous café called the Nosh Bar used to be. I was most charmingly greeted by a reformed, highly pleasant Mark Fuller, not a swearword in sight, and met by a wall of noise. Hundreds of people, mostly quite pretty girls, sat on rattan chairs having a good old Friday night out. "There can't be anyone left in Essex," I thought.

Mark led us to a round corner table away from the worst noise blast, where he'd considerately arranged for ice cubes and lemon slices to be ready for me. It was still an acoustic nightmare.

Some rolls appeared, which were hot and tasted fine. The menu offered chargrilled lobsters at £23, but, ever frugal, I ordered American breakfast waffle, ham and eggs (£6.90), followed by prime fillet burger with home-made barbecue relish (£10.50). "Can you cope?" asked Georgina. "With ordering?" I asked. "With the noise," she responded. I had to. It was either that or leave. Anyway, I liked all the young people enjoying themselves.

"I'm an expert on waffles," I explained to Robert Earl when he asked what I'd ordered. "You're a big waffler," he replied. My waffle was excellent. Very light, magical taste and texture, crisp on top. It was quarter-size, which was fine for a starter. The egg was good; the ham was good. If they served this around Kensington, I'd have it every day.

I wondered how they got such a small waffle. "They have a small waffle pan," said Marco, who was beautifully dressed in a blue pinstriped suit, blue shirt and red tie. Marco knows a prodigious amount about food, but nothing about waffles. I remember the terrible ones he served at the Mirabelle, which have now, mercifully, been removed from the menu. The waffle pan was brought to our table. It was very large and produced two waffles. I suppose they must cut one down when it comes out. "Where do you get your waffle mix from?" I asked the man with the machine. "They buy it in a packet," volunteered Marco. "I find the American Carbons mix far and away the best." The girl who makes the waffles appeared. She said Sugar Reef made its own waffle mix of egg yolk, sugar, flour – then egg whites to give it white colour. My hamburger was superb; so was the bun, the cucumber, the tomato, the relish and the onion.

An entertainer arrived and said: "May I show you some magic?"

"Can you make him disappear?" asked Robert Earl, pointing at me. He's a wag, isn't he?

Everything was going so well, I was truly sorry dessert was a disaster. It took forever to arrive. I asked some snotty manageress where it was and she said, "It's coming straight away," which it wasn't. Then everyone had the wrong choice placed in front of them. I got someone else's apricot strudel, which was awful. My own coconut parfait was acceptable, but it was all a dreadful mess and put me in a bad mood. I speedily recovered because I'm a wonderful person. "You've got to be kind," said Marco. Boy, did he have a wrong number.

Suntory, a Japanese restaurant in St James's, was once very chic. All the guides go on about how expensive it is. What then were that group of charming, giggling but cheaply dressed students doing at a centre table? Or were they millionaires in disguise? The room looked like the corner of an airport lounge in need of modernisation. Perfectly pleasant, soulless, not chic, but far more nicely proportioned than the hideous, corridor-like Nobu. After some excellent soup, I enjoyed all of my tempura of prawns, turbot, squid and more, as well as a second main course of boiled eel with sweet soy sauce. The eel came in a black bowl looking like sliced roast duck. Vanessa liked her selection of white fish. The Japanese have odd ideas about desserts. Everything seems to have red bean in it. I selected three: green-tea ice cream, jelly without fruit salad and some red bean hot jam stuff. The red-jam stuff tasted like soup and had little balls of mochi in it. The jelly was red and green, with a blob of red bean in the middle. It's much crisper than English jelly. I'd have preferred it moulded as a rabbit.

Tamarind in Mayfair is a disaster. It is the most ghastly room I have ever seen. Golders Green minimalism would be a kind way to describe it. A works canteen with horrid gold pillars in the middle, no sign of humanity and 1950s-type office chairs with over-curved hard backs which kept bashing my arms. Things did not improve when I was told they only had spicy poppadoms, the ones that look like they've got mumps. I much prefer the old-fashioned large potato-crisp-appearance type. We waited for ever for our main course, and this at lunch time with only five other tables occupied. After looking at the room for 50 minutes, and having great difficulty in getting any service from anyone, by the time the food came I was ready to kill. It wasn't as good as my favourite Indian, the Bombay Brasserie, where the service is immaculate and in pleasant surroundings. If Tamarind survives it'll be a miracle. I wouldn't move a millimetre to give it the kiss of life.

Waiter! Waiter!

I'm delighted that Pierre Koffmann at **La Tante Claire** recently got his third Michelin Guide star. He wouldn't have got it for service the night I was in. I did think the food was terrific, even if Miss Seagrove found her duck somewhat awful. We were a party of six, as they say in the trade, and the service had been sloppy. The bread arrived at the end of the first course, the plates sat uncleared. That always annoys me, but I was a guest: I said nothing. Eventually a waiter took three plates away. My host, a quiet American who was something terribly important at Sony Music, murmured: "I see they have a strange habit here, they only clear half the table."

My left arm shot upwards to beckon a waiter. He gave me a look that said: "At La Tante Claire you don't call us, we call you." "Excuse me," I tried another waiter. He ignored me too. I got up, lifted the knife and fork from one of the plates, put that plate down a bit noisily on top of another plate, crashed the knives and forks on top and walked calmly through the restaurant. All eyes were upon me. A silence descended.

I was heading towards the kitchen door. I'll tell Pierre things are a bit dodgy out there tonight, I thought. Then I thought, just my luck; as I get to the kitchen door it'll swing outwards, straight into me, I'll drop the plates and my gesture will end in fiasco. I veered right, through an arch, to plonk the dirty plates on the bar. A waiter was already taking the remaining plate from the table when I walked back. For the rest of the evening the service was immaculate.

There are a number of good ways to get attention in restaurants when waiters ignore you. A fairly crude one – which I'm not averse to using – is to smack the table-top loudly and shout: "Ere!" Another, as a waiter sails by, is to call out: "Middle." There's something about the word "middle" that spins them around. The best method, which I use a great deal, is to raise my napkin in the air, arm outstretched above the head, and wave it around slowly. That always gets them.

PS Pierre Koffman is now at the Berkeley Hotel. The premises are now Gordon Ramsay's restaurant.

Teatro in Shaftesbury Avenue is another of those ever-so-chics that seem to open every day. It is not for actors, even though an actress is one of the owners. It's very grand and seriously designed. You go up metallic stairs to a rather dark members' lounge. The restaurant is fairly minimalist, inhabited by uninteresting people. Except for us. I started with duck foie gras served over poached rhubarb. It was extremely good. Then I had roast breast of squab glazed with fresh dates served with root vegetables. I had great difficulty finding any vegetables. It was a bit tough, not bad, nice gravy, but they'd failed to give me any mashed potatoes, so Michael Grade's sister Anita Land, sitting next to me, gave me some of hers. Robert Earl was eating rack of lamb. "They do it like that at Marks & Spencer," Anita said. I wouldn't know. They all seemed to like their food very much. I thought the service was slow. I noticed many tables had only men sitting at them. Cellular phones have to be left at reception – an idea that should be widely adopted.

My favourite radio station, Melody, plays the records I used to seduce girls to when I had the energy: Frank Sinatra, Nat King Cole and so on. They have recently been accompanied by commercials for the restaurant named **The Tenth** at The Royal Garden Hotel in Kensington. This is, if you believe what you hear, inhabited by, in order of appearance, a Posh Woman talking about walking her dog, a Gruff Man who didn't care, a Business Type, a rich American conferring with her effeminate Interior Decorator, and an Upper Class Man and Girl talking as if they were in a Noël Coward play. Unfortunately, on the day I went for lunch, none of these people was present. Just a few bored-looking businessmen. By the end of the meal I'd have paid anything to have the Noël Coward touring version and the gay decorator there to liven things up. The room has one thing going for it and it isn't the food. It has a wonderful view across Hyde Park and Kensington Gardens. With scenery like that, it could be something big. However, although the food isn't awful, it isn't worth going up 10 floors for.

In a business where bad will exceeds all, the expectation of failure was never more gleefully anticipated than when Marco Pierre White announced the **Titanic**. Fellow restaurateurs and chefs rubbed their hands at the thought of Marco's downfall. But, to many people's immense disappointment, Titanic has been a great success. When I went I was pleasantly surprised. The Titanic is a wonderful room, full of old-world charm. Very buzzy. An enormous bar area, then dining on two sides of a central, oval bar and at the back a lounge, visible to plebs like me, for the stars – all of whom where off-duty that night. The food was very nice. My fried calamari were excellent. The hamburger, which Marco assured me was the best in the world, was a bit overdone, but the bun was superb. The sticky toffee pudding was not historic, but pleasant. Marco took my bread plate away with the bread on it and when I complained he said: "It's the same bread we have at the Criterion and the Mirabelle, and you don't like it anyway." He added: "The less we give you, the more chance of success we have." I thought that was very funny. The wines were beyond belief. I forget what year the Mouton Rothschild was, but the Chateau d'Yquem was 1921. I had a very jolly time indeed. The paying customers seemed to enjoy it, too.

When I went to an excellent Knightsbridge Italian place, **Toto**, I was greeted by the dreaded words: "Who are you with?" As I was on my own at the time, this seemed a fairly pointless remark. "Nobody," I said. The door official repeated his question. "Roger Moore," I replied. "It's that table in the corner," I was told gracelessly. A short time later, Roger himself arrived, fuming. He, too, had been asked who he was with. "I'm Roger Moore," he responded. The man thought for a moment. "Ah, you're with Roger Moore," he said. "That's his table in the corner." This is not what I call a grand start to an evening. I shall not go there again until I am assured there is a sympathetic greeter on the premises.

Tramp's Gold

I could not be described as a devotee of **Tramp**, the discotheque that remains endlessly in fashion, but I have had some marvellous times there, the greatest being the night I was dining with Robert Mitchum in Claridge's, and we saw Jack Lemmon at another table. We all got together for coffee and Jack said to me: "Can you get us into Tramp?"

"Of course," I said. "They know me well, I've been a member since 1970!"

So I presented myself at the desk, flanked by Jack and Bob. The two receptionists looked up ferociously. "Michael Winner," I announced. "He's not here," said a receptionist, quick as a flash.

"Come on, Bob," I said, "Follow me," and we walked off down the stairs into the smoke-filled, dusty atmosphere. Jack Lemmon had been drinking a bit. Jack is the best drunk ever. Nothing malicious comes out; he's just unbelievably funny. The comedy performance he put on, his eyes swivelling as each new girl came in dressed in less than the one before, is a great treasure that I hold in my memory. Bob Mitchum had just come out of the Betty Ford clinic, so he sat, very sober – a wonderful, benign presence.

A few years ago, Tramp was bought by some Scots group headed by a very nice chap called Kevin Doyle. Johnny stays as employed boss of the club, which is just as well because it's his extraordinary charm and talent that have made it what it is. Originally, the premises were a posh restaurant with a gypsy orchestra, owned by my good friend Bill Offner and his partner, the American comedian Al Burnett. Bill, bless him, died before the new management started their huge renovation, which is just as well because seeing what they were spending would have killed him.

When Johnny and Bill ran Tramp, they had a board meeting to decide whether to splash out and hoover the carpet; they looked at the cost of a woman to do it for a few hours and voted against.

The place has been spruced up but, cleverly, looks much the same. The 17th-century oak panelling in the main room is seriously historic. It has been cleaned, so the carvings can be admired if you go in early and persuade them to turn on the lights. This is now possible because, rightly proud of their new kitchens, they open for dinner at 8pm. There are more than 6,000 members. I went along with a few of them – Mr M Caine and his wife, Mr T O'Neill and his friend Laraine – and we joined Mr and Mrs Gold at Johnny's famous table. I've always liked the food at Tramp. Limited, but very good for what it was. The old favourites – sausage and mash, excellent smoked salmon, prawns, steak – remains. But a rather classy menu has been added. I had duck salad to start, expecting some ponced-about, cut-up bits of leftovers warmed up with some shredded lettuce. I got a superb breast of duck, quite enough for a main course, sitting on salad. Miss Lid greatly enjoyed her asparagus with hollandaise sauce, and then risotto of Mediterranean vegetables with parmesan. I had a steak followed by vanilla cream. "Is it bought in?" I asked. "It's Wall's," I was told as a joke. It was definitely home-made, though it tasted like Wall's. Which is fine. I like Wall's ice cream.

The **Village Bistro** in Highgate holds a Winner world record. When I went there, of the four people on my table three got the wrong main course. That takes some doing. It's a tiny, twee, but nice little place. If you go there, I advise you to order something you absolutely hate, because you won't get it and, who knows, you may like what they bring.

Vong, in the Berkeley Hotel at Hyde Park Corner, is an absolutely terrific place, serving a unique mix of Asian-influenced European food. Or is it the other way round? Either way, it's miles from the becoming-tiresomely-uniform taste of new English restaurants. I dropped in to Vong one evening without booking, something I seldom do. They found me a table, although I later heard it was the new "in" place and you had to book well ahead. I had lobster and daikon roll, rosemary ginger dip, then spiced cod and curried artichokes. A warm Valrhona chocolate cake with caramel sesame ice cream ended a meal consisting of taste sensations that took me by storm!

Vong is decorated like a posh cafe – too many hard surfaces for sound-deadening, but pleasant to look at. As the place got full, the noise became horrific. The restaurant has one of those large glass windows showing the American chef, Tom Dimarzo, at work. He first came here as a rock musician to play the Hammersmith Odeon in 1976! He's not only a very good chef (to put it mildly), but he's jolly. You can't imagine his place running with staff blood as on the television show with a hidden camera in the kitchens because (a) he's so pleasant and (b) there's that glass window to the restaurant that would reveal everything. *Tom Dimarzo's left; it's still good.*

On the first tea

I do not know Mr Elliott Bernerd. I've never set eyes on him. I met his ex-wife at La Réserve de Beaulieu once; she was very cheerful. His daughter, whom I also haven't met, moved into one of four terraced houses whose gardens run down to my back garden wall. I normally object to every planning application in my conservation area, acting as local snoop for The Kensington Society, an excellent organisation that tries to protect what is left of Old Kensington. But when Elliott's daughter and her hubby applied to make a terrace out of a flat roof, I was unusually noncombative, although I thought of writing to them saying that, in my opinion, more than four people with drinks and cocktail canapés constituted an environmental hazard.

I mention this because I recently took tea at the **Westbury Hotel** in Mayfair, which Mr Bernerd's company, Chelsfield, bought a while ago. Mr Bernerd is delightfully acquisitive. When he bought Wentworth Golf Club – now famed for its temporary proximity to General Pinochet – a friend of mine, very British and plummy of voice, worked for Mr B. He went to see them as an advance guard. "Is this a very exclusive club?" he asked. "Well," said Wentworth's representative, "we try to be. We don't like to have too many Jews." "This is your unlucky day then," said my friend. "You've just been bought by one." I"ve heard him tell this story with great relish many times, and smiled in recollection as I walked under the Westbury's tacky sign in what looked like yellow stick-on lettering saying Bar Lounge with the word Polo in larger letters underneath.

We sat in the corner of a light, wood-panelled, low-ceilinged room. "Not a place of beauty," I dictated. I ordered two full afternoon teas at £12 each. I'd chosen an armchair, which I kept falling back into. I prefer upright chairs. Very prompt and charming service. "Good cup of tea," said Vanessa, adding of a smoked salmon sandwich: "That was horrible, it tasted old." The scones were cold, but other than that very good. The sandwiches were acceptable; it seemed as if they'd been in the fridge. An iced tartlet cake was passable, a meringue chocolate cake okay. I liked the flapjack. "Er, tastes like it's gone wrong," said Vanessa, "too sweet." "I liked that," I persisted.

I took a stroll through the narrow bar full of lively people, into a cold marble lobby and then to what I remembered as a very pleasing dining room. It had apparently been "cut up" and reduced to a nasty oblong box by Forte, the previous owners. Quite unsuitable for what should be a classy hotel a few yards from Bond Street in one of the best locations in London.

This place is supervised by Willy Bauer, who was managing director of the Savoy. He's no fool. He should give it a jolly good shake-up, posh it up a bit. I have fond memories of the Westbury. I used to put some of my movie stars there. I wouldn't now. Mr Bernerd also bought the Westbury in New York. He turned that into apartments. He must have made a few bob. Why not spend it on the London hotel? It's pleasantly serviceable, but for a man who's chairman of the South Bank Centre, the purifier of that horrid concrete jungle, he should realise "charity" begins at home.

I was making a commerical in Wandsworth, directing one of my favourite people: me. **Willie Gunn** was recommended for a quick lunch as we had to be back – both of us, actor and director – within the hour. I expected nothing. The restaurant itself was pleasant. Plain, wooden floors, tables spaced well apart. It started remarkably well – my goat's cheese soufflé came like a small upside-down pot, nicely crisp on the outside. Vanessa's eggs benedict were on a particularly excellent muffin: very fresh, not soggy. Perhaps this would turn out to be a real find. My main course was braised oxtail, flageolet beans and mash. It alone could convince anyone that banning meat on the bone was a terrific idea. It was stringy and tasteless. Vanessa had ravioli; she left most of it. She liked her pot of chocolate for dessert. I hated my steamed apricot pudding with crème anglaise. But I give Willie Gunn high marks for the charm of its owners, Giles Cunliffe and Duncan Turner.

Tie rant

How often do you see Irish stew or Lancashire hotpot or shepherd's pie on pretentious menus? What about a jolly good sausage and mash? There was one place that did all this and more with total brilliance. This was **Wilton's** in St James's, under the autocratic rule of Jimmy Marks, my favourite restaurateur of all time. Cockney, grey-suited, rolling through the old-money booths as if he were on a ship at sea. Marks knew about fresh. Fresh is a much over-used word. What does it really mean? How fresh does something have to be, to be fresh? In my view, fresh fish is fish that came in that morning from the seaside and was caught the night before. Marks used to sell his fish at the end of the day to a nearby restaurant rather than keep it in the fridge overnight. Wilton's is now run by the Savoy Group. It's still excellent, but not a patch on what it was when Marks ruled the roost.

Marks also had exceptionally good taste in people. He was very attached to me. I was allowed to eat in the bar if the place was full, at a little round table. Now that is permitted on all the bar tables, to keep the money rolling in. "Michael can do anything he likes," old Marks used to say before he sadly died in 1976. I, alone, was allowed in without a tie. But recently the restaurant manager, Robin Gundry, said to my Mr Fraser when he made a booking for me: "Could you please ask Mr Winner to wear a tie?" I was outraged. I phoned up. "Who," I said icily, "told you to make this ridiculous request?" "Our chairman, Rupert Hambro," said Mr Gundry. "He wants everyone to wear a tie." Being a good boy, I donned one for my next visit, but I wrote to Mr Hambro to give my views. I pointed out I had been going to Wilton's for more than 50 years and that I was sure, up in heaven, Jimmy Marks was shouting: "Michael doesn't have to wear a tie!" I asked for his angelic wishes to be considered.

Mr Hambro wrote back pointing out I must have been nine years old when I started visiting Wilton's (I was), which made me the oldest customer. He wrote: "Jimmy Marks was much loved by us all, and the stories about him are legend. The only story I have the greatest difficulty confirming is that he ever went to heaven – but obviously you have greater connections in that direction than we all have." (I do.) He finished by saying that my letter had prompted a somewhat unexpected and most out-of-character reaction. "We have commissioned a Wilton's tie, which we shall offer to our favourite customers. You shall be the first to receive one." I don't want to look a gift tie in the mouth, but that letter was written in August, and I'm still waiting four months later!

Their tie-manufacturing speed is clearly slower than their restaurant service, which has always been exemplary. Under Marks you could get a three-course meal and coffee, effortlessly served and of magnificent quality, in half an hour. You sit at Wilton's among cabinet ministers and heavyweight chiefs of industry. I recently took Peter Wood, the brilliant creator of Direct Line Insurance. He's saved me £5,500 a year on my car insurance! He said when he came in that nobody greeted him and he had to find my table on his own. Now come on, chaps, Marks would never have let that happen. If I put on a tie, surely you can see my guest is directed to it!

The **Windmill Whole Food Restaurant** in the Fulham Road is not everyone's idea of haute cuisine. It is near bus stops and other unsavoury sights. Inside, it is pleasant in a frugal way. The place is excellently run by a nice-looking young couple, Gillian and James Cooper, Gillian quick to point out that she is the owner and James is an artist. Indeed, his paintings are on the walls. I tried leek, potato and spring onion strudel with a Dijon mustard cream sauce and roasted potato fans for my main course. That and my first course of deep-fried mozzarella and fruit were both very pleasant. My rhubarb crumble was somewhere between school and Claridge's. Vanessa totally loved it all, but I'm not booking for New Year's Eve.

When I visited Portobello Road one Saturday, I went into a restaurant called the **Wine Factory**, a narrow buzzy place offering Lurex-bright pictures of ships and castles for sale. "The restaurant's full," I said, looking round. "Who can I pay to leave?" I was introduced to Dee Bliss, the manageress. "Tell that man," I said, pointing to a couple sitting next to my friend Didier Milinaire, "that if he leaves in five minutes his meal is free." "You can't do that to people," said Dee. "I do it all the time," I replied (a slight exaggeration, although it usually works). This man looked ferocious, so I decided to wait. Didier offered us a piece of his garlic bread as we squashed in beside him, his girlfriend Lesley Burton and their two friends. Then, thank God, the man at the table I was waiting for left. I ordered a four seasons pizza. First I was given grilled vegetables with what had been described as a hot chilli sauce. It was so strong that, after one mouthful, I was dying. I gulped water. The pizza was pretty good and my hot toffee cake perfectly pleasant.

All Things Spice

A little choice on the Indian restaurant scene is desirable. So when Marco Pierre White invited me to **Yatra**, in Dover Street, Mayfair, I thought: "Good, another Indian place for my list." We entered a bar overfull of screaming people. I pushed through nervously to a strange room. One half had diners sitting close to floor level: the other half, where I sat, had normal-height tables with black tablecloths. A very charming man, Sonu P Lalvani, opened Yatra. He'd never run restaurants before. He told me Yatra is a Sanskrit word meaning sacred pilgrimage or spiritual journey. All I can say is that it was a very heavily booked pilgrimage in the bar. So much so that I told Sonu I couldn't sit and listen to that din. So he kindly sent them down to the basement, which apparently was not yet completed.

My napkin was served on a red cushion. Mati, Marco's wife, suggested this was in case you had too much to drink. If your head dropped toward the table, the cushion softened your fall. It was so bright that Marco asked for the lights to be turned down.

Sonu recommended a starter of chicken mince flavoured with galangal and kaffir lime, and moulded on a crab claw. I took one bite of it, choked, and my eyes watered. I coughed and they rushed extra water to me. I couldn't speak it was so spicy. "I've got water, I'm half-dead, but I'm all right!" I gasped when able to mutter. Marco grabbed the plate and started eating my food. "Delicious," he said. Unfortunately, he gave me, in return, his grilled fruits and vegetable salad, which I found appalling. Miss Lid pointed out my starter only had one pepper-like mark by it on the menu. "Some of them had three peppers," she explained. If anyone lives after a three-pepper marked item, I'd like to hear about it. But I did drink a milk shake-type thing called a mango lassi. That was exceptionally pleasant. Miss Lid started with a Yatra salad, which is a grilled Parmesan tower with tiger prawns. She said nothing, which is rare.

The waitress, Daisy, dressed in a sari, came from Maida Vale. She'd previously worked in Queen's Park, but the place went into receivership. I'm not sure if this is vital information, but I pass it on to you anyway.

My main course was a mixed grill of tandoori prawns, chicken, lamb and "everything else", I dictated. It could have fed a family of six. It was what I'd call "glumpy". Plodding. Not terrible, not worth coming back for. Miss Lid had chicken with coconut sauce and rice pancake.

My dessert was called Khekachelo's passion. It was mango-based. Daisy said it was like a cheesecake. It had no good texture or taste. Sonu explained it was made by a very young man. That is no excuse. Miss Lid's dessert looked like runny yoghurt with nuts in it. Having finished,she said: "It was good. All that I chose was good." But as she often says what she chooses is good and, according to her, she always chooses the best, this did not weigh very heavily with me. "My dessert was a yellow colour, so it probably had the yolk of egg in it," she added helpfully.

I was not pleased with Yatra and this distresses me, because Sonu and his wife, Liah, are lovely people. They've gone from supplying catering equipment into the quagmire of restaurant ownership. I hope they do very well. I shall revisit in a year's time. If they're still open.

Zafferano is a comfortable restaurant in Knightsbridge, co-owned by the chef, Giorgio Locatelli, and an Italian entrepreneur named Claudio Pulze. There I have eaten, again and again, some of the best Italian food in London. Indeed, none is better. Signor Locatelli manages to get real and delightful taste into everything, be it malfatti (ravioli filled with mashed baby potatoes and mint) or lamb sweetbreads in sweet and sour sauce, or a saffron brioche with apples, candied fruit and ice cream. Sadly I have struck it from my list. Enzo Cassini, the maitre d', was okay in the relaxed atmosphere of Château Eza in the south of France, but here, well I won't tell you what's gone on, but it's shambolic to say the least. I never like to go into a room that isn't well managed and Zafferano isn't. A friend of mine asked why his was the only table without bread, and witty Enzo said: "We're sending out to Marks & Spencer for it!"

There's a saying: when one door closes, another opens. A few days after another disappointing meal at the Bombay Brasserie, my friend Claudio Pulze told me of his new Indian restaurant on the Fulham Road, called Zaika. When I eventually got to Zaika, I found it to be, quite simply, a staggeringly good "Indian". Every bowl of everything is marvellously and individually prepared.

The chef, a partner in the concern, is Vineet Bhatia. He'd had rave reviews in Hammersmith and moved upmarket. In fact, **Zaika** is rather trendy. In spite of that, I've returned again and again. The first time I went, the chefs did what they tend to do with me, insist I try almost everything on the menu. I had four starters, five main courses, one vegetable dish, two "accompaniments" and two desserts. They were all brilliant, but even I could only pick at some of the copper bowls. More recently, I had a Zaika platter of salmon kebab, chicken patties and minced duck roll; a tava machli, which is pan-fried swordfish marinated in crushed fennel, koh-e-roganjosh, a classic Kashmiri dish of cooked lamb shanks in a rich onion and tomato sauce flavoured with fenugreek; chicken tikka... I could go on. For desserts, a chocolate samosa and a pista kulfi Indian ice cream.

The room is pleasant, with mirrors adapted from old Indian windows hanging on the walls. The greatest sign of Zaika's superb quality is that the most beautiful Indian in the world, Shakira Caine, asked me to dinner there with her husband, who is an old friend and a famous actor, and Johnny Gold of Tramp, with his wife Jan, who is also Indian. In fact, there is always a lot of Indian customers in the restaurant. They doubtless know what they're eating. As Clark Gable said at the end of *Gone With the Wind*: "I don't give a damn." It tastes good. I stuff it down. That's the fun of going out.

I check and recheck places on your behalf – little remains constant. So I'm happy to report that Zaika is still superb.

One of my favourite people, Miss Helen Zahavi, the writer of *Dirty Weekend* and a great admirer of the excellent film of the same name, asked me to take her to **Zamoyski** in Hampstead. I was somewhat apprehensive about this, particularly when I saw the place, next to a supermarket, with heavy wooden windows and a bunker-like appearance. But the menu looked interesting – Polish dishes with real Polish names and an English description – and the prices were unbelievably low! We both had some honey vodka and things became rosier. By the time I'd eaten the first course I knew it was a real find. I hate to recommend real finds because they get crowded beyond belief, but Zamoyski is absolutely terrific. My *borszcz Ukrainski* (beetroot soup) was tiptop, and the sweet marinated herrings coated in onions, apples and sultanas was totally exquisite. The main courses, some sort of blini and lamb for me and *kaczka* (a form of roast duck) for Helen, were quite superb. By now a genuinely talented violinist and guitarist were playing, anything from show tunes to Russian-Polish folk music. Helen finished with a *semifreddo* for dessert and I had a *szarlotka*. They were both near-historic. You'll have to go there to find out what they were in English! The bill, including two vodkas, three courses for Helen, four for me, plus coffee and mineral water, was £32.80 ex service! A bargain.

After the first night of Fame, John Gold and I gave up waiting for food at the party and I called **Zen Central** in Mayfair from the Rolls. I knew from the way they took the reservation they had no idea who I was. This was confirmed when we got to the restaurant and the manager went forward to greet John Gold saying, "Good evening, Mr Winner". After that it was all downhill. The waiter took a long and complicated order, refused to write it down, and said: "I'll remember." Those are words that fill me with fear. But he did bring all the right stuff, except when I ate I wished he'd got it wrong and brought something else. Everything, but everything, tasted tired. Seaweed, spring rolls, Peking duck, you name it, it slept.

Fishy Business

I'm a simple soul. I only want to have fun. I go to restaurants solely in the hope of having a nice time, good food, pleasant service, interesting atmosphere. I never go because I have to be somewhere for this column. I tell you only about places I voluntarily attend in my private life and where I pay full whack – and frequently more. Surprisingly, many restaurants absolutely refuse to give me a bill. This costs me a fortune because, not wanting anything for nothing, I feel obliged to leave cash gratuities for far more than the meal would have cost.

One totally adorable lady restaurateur keeps declining to give me a bill. When I left £100 on the table she rushed in, took it and gave it back to me. So, after the next lunch, I had to go to Barkers and buy something I didn't want just to acquire a box to use for a present. Then I took an expensive silver period ornament from my house, wrapped it, and dispatched the driver to her restaurant with it. The next time I went in, I begged the lady to give me a bill. "If you were at my house you wouldn't pay," she said endearingly. "This is my house."

"Please Mrs X," I said, "you'll end up with everything I own: the paintings, my television sets, the three-piece suite. I beg of you – let me pay!" I simply cannot afford all this hospitality. It will bankrupt me.

All this has absolutely nothing to do with the **Zia Teresa** in Hans Road, opposite the west side of Harrods. I've been going there on and off for over 40 years. It still looks like the archetypal Italian restaurant of the mid-1950s. Wrought-iron chandeliers with coloured bulbs, hanging copper pots, a bar, wooden banquettes, the walls full of postcards, which may or may not have been sent by satisfied customers. I went mostly in the late 1950s and early 1960s. Taking a trip down memory lane, I recently attended with Mrs Lagoudakos, whom you may recall is my chief receptionist and an ex-Miss United Kingdom. Mrs Lagoudakos hails from the Wirral, so on the few occasions I am munificent enough to take her out, she looks forward to eating well. On this occasion she was disappointed. The Zia Teresa was never posh; it's part of the Spaghetti House group. But it used to be robust, cheerful and with very pleasant food. I started by asking for one of my favourites: spaghetti with meatballs. Eugene Torretti, the manager, said: "We don't do them any more." "Why not?" I asked. "People stopped ordering them," said Eugene. Well, I thought, they didn't stop ordering them at Scalini. I've had marvellous versions of them round the corner in Walton Street.

We were recommended asparagus. It was very thin, tasteless and coated with melted cheese. The finger bowls were optimistic. You'd have had to prise the asparagus from the cheese and it was so stringy it would have flopped over if you tried to pick it up. My breadcrumbed veal was tough and of no taste. The tomato sauce with the spaghetti was just a pasty mush with a strange, tangy flavour. The *coup de grâce* was Mrs Lagoudakos's Dover sole, which smelled strongly of fish. Fish should not smell of fish. This usually means it's not fresh. It was sent back. Mr Torretti returned and said: "It's the smell of the grill not the fish," which struck me as a very odd excuse. If true, who wants a smelly grill whiff on fish anyway?

Everything was a disaster, except for a cheerful waitress called Irene Rodriguez.

WINNIE HELPS HIMSELF!

2

UK & IRELAND

ENGLAND

At a cafe-looking basement in Bath called, quite descriptively, the **Hole in the Wall**, I had some excellent food. From the three-course lunch menu at £11.50, I chose sweet pea soup, which was country-delicious, and pan-fried Cornish haddock with fresh samphire – soft and lovely, with a real taste. My dessert of iced armagnac prune and hazelnut ice cream was disappointing, but Vanessa's cinnamon biscuit of rhubarb and apple with elderflower custard was historic. Overall, wonderful food and unbelievable value.

Hunstrete House near Bath is "an 18th-century manor hourse set in 92 acres of deerpark, woodland and exquisite gardens", none of which I could see because it was night. The service was a delight, very friendly and together. The gem of the evening was a bottle of Haut Brion 1961 at £275 inc VAT. *What?!* I hear you say! Well, the same bottle is £790 inc VAT and service at Chez Nico, and I recently bought some in auction for £391.12 a bottle. So £275 is a gift. "Could you wrap a dozen up for me?" I asked the wine waiter. But they didn't.

I had seen **Flitwick Manor**, a country hotel in Bedfordshire, in a guide book. It being a sunny day and, as it was only an hour away off the M1, I thought I'd have a go. I phoned up. "Do you serve tea?" I asked Mrs Sonia Banks, the manageress. "If guests want tea, we do it," she said. "Suppose I want tea and I'm not a guest?" I asked. "We'll start baking," said Mrs B. Later, we arrived on a gravel terrace overlooking fields and a 600-year-old cedar of Lebanon. The sandwiches were not a good start. A lot of them, not terrible, just failing in spectacular. Then came the cakes. Enough for a party of 12. Shortbread, chocolate biscuit (amazing looking with choccy cream oozing out from a "sandwich"), strawberry feuilleté, fruit cake, banana strudel, profiteroles, scones, a large bowl of cream, home-made strawberry jam. The ginger cake was masterful; scones tiptip. I attempted, in the cause of duty, to try everything, but even I was defeated. I don't know how the Flitwick chef, Duncan Poyser, does proper meals, but his tea ranks with the greats.

Sitting pretty

At last Bray in Berkshire has a good restaurant. I certainly don't count the Waterside Inn as one. So much did I consider Bray a gastronomic disaster that when people recommended the **Fat Duck** in the high street I thought, no. One Sunday I succumbed. I rang up to hear that the owner-chef, Heston Blumenthal, had injured his foot and wasn't there. No point going without the boss to complain to.

I phoned a few weeks later. "We are absolutely full," said Mr Blumenthal. "I'll take your number in case we get a cancellation." "Tell me," I said, "on any given Sunday, do you ever not get a cancellation or a no-show?" "Very seldom," said Heston. "Then I'm coming at quarter past one, table for two. Worst that can happen is we have to find some funny place for me to eat. See you." I like doing that. It puts all the responsibility onto the restaurateur. They always rise to the occasion. Heston was no exception. When we arrived at the inn-type room, he had a nice corner table for us.

The trouble was the chair. Nasty, spindly, 1960s wrought-iron gone wrong, with a very tiny, cushioned seat. This is impossible, I thought, eyeing two old-fashioned wooden chairs at the table in front. I informed Nigel, who seemed to be in charge, that I might ask to change. This worried Vanessa. "Those wooden chairs don't have a cushion," she said. I sat in agony for a few more minutes, then got up and started the switch myself. "If that table has one wooden and one metal chair, the world will not explode," I said to Nigel. "Not at all," he replied, as he helped me, although a bit later a second metal chair was brought to match the other one I'd just put at the table opposite.

It's a serious menu. You can tell they mean business because of all the posh French words. The bread was ghastly: cold, nasty texture. Augurs ill, I thought. I started with lasagne of langoustines, pig's trotter and truffles. Excellent, memorable. Vanessa had escabèche of mackerel, carrots and saffron. She hated it. Too fleshy. Didn't worry me: I ate her portion. Then I had fillet of venison, gateau of potato with époisses, confit of chestnut and shallots, sauce poivrade. I have no idea what all that meant, but it was definitely good.

Just as well, because Vanessa hated her main course, too, so she ate my chestnuts. She almost had roast-pepper-marinated monkfish, tarte pissaladière, sauce barigoule. "You don't want to taste all these flavours," she said. "You want to taste the fish, because that's what you ordered. I could have had tofu with all these sauces and wouldn't have known the difference." I ate a lot of hers. Seemed fine to me, but she likes simple cooking and I eat anything.

It all took a long time to arrive. I watched every plate going across the room in case it was mine. We got there at 1.15pm and the main course arrived at 2.40pm. Even for a Sunday, that's a bit slow for me. My dessert spoon came from the Yuri Geller collection. It was very bent. Since everything took so long anyway, I ordered chocolate coulant with ice cream (please allow 25 minutes). Nigel said it was an Italian meringue mixed with sweet pastry. It's put inside a cake mould, frozen ganache of chocolate is forced into the centre, then it's covered and baked in the oven.

Poor Heston in the kitchen had reported to him my cries of "How many more minutes!" and "Isn't it ready yet?" "If you take it out too soon, it collapses," he told me later. It was one of the great chocolate puddings of all time. Even Vanessa liked it; she nicked as much as she could. She also enjoyed her apple crumble, so the meal ended on a high note.

Heston, a nice young man if ever there was one, turned up. He thinks the family came from Latvia years ago; he thinks there was some interbreeding, cousins marrying cousins; he's absolutely certain he once worked in his father's office-leasing business as credit controller. His culinary experience seemed limited. He met Marco Pierre White while working briefly at Le Manoir and then did a couple of weeks in the Canteen. Whatever – it did him proud. He made good.

I told him about my chair problem. "It's a pity, because we've got one of those metal chairs that was specially made for my father. He's 28st," said Heston. "Where is it?" I asked, "Upstairs," said Heston. "We'll bring it down if you come again." That's an incentive if ever there was one.

On my next visit I enjoyed one of the best lunches I've ever eaten. I noted that the guests were posher than when last I came. And Michelin has given it a star. What's particularly good about Heston Blumenthal's cooking is that he takes British nouvelle cuisine, which is getting very tired, and does new, inventive and tasty things with it.

You know you're in a classy place when the waiter cuts the butter from an enormous slab. It's goat's-milk butter, and the bread is made with potato flour. I have no idea what that means, but they both tasted terrific.

The food sounds overelaborate and it was a bit that way on my previous visit. Good, but experimentally fussy. Now, it's cleaner and more refined. I started with crab feuillantine with roast foie gras, marinated salmon, crystallised seaweed and oyster vinaigrette. A bore to read, absurd to say, but brilliant to eat. Miss Lid had lasagne of langoustine, pig's trotter and truffles.

My main course was pastilla of Anjou pigeon with cherries, roast breast with spiced nuts and Manjari chocolate, and watercress velouté. Like pigeon with millefeuille next to it. A very good fun dish. Miss Lid had piquillo peppers stuffed with truffled brandade, roast red mullet with borlotti beans and olive oil from Mausanne. All this food detail is like end-of-the-movie credits that go on for more than five minutes, naming even the secretary who was in for one day by mistake and walked out.

The Fat Duck staff cleared the plates with amazing speed, which I like. Perhaps they were trying to get rid of me, as, with my usual insouciance, I'd booked only an hour before arrival.

For dessert, Miss Lid had kouign amann tarte tatin Tahitian with vanilla ice cream. I chose millefeuille of pain d'épices ice cream, with pineapple and chilli jelly, and fleur de sel. I asked for extra jelly. Petits fours were crystallised red-pepper juice, like a thin biscuit. "The most delicious apple pie I've ever tasted," said Miss Lid, reducing the ponced-up description to reality. "It's the most wonderful meal I've ever had, all three courses," she added.

"You've eaten like a real pig," I muttered graciously.

"You can't see it on me, but you can see it on you," Miss Lid responded. Girls can be so cruel.

I had a superb meal in the private room at the **Waterside Inn** for Nico Ladenis's 60th birthday, but on my next visit, oh dear. In order of horrible: dreary bread, a canapé of duck rillettes that would have been at home on British Airways and a bellini that tasted of soap and wasn't cold (and then I had to face the empty, dirty glasses for ever until a waiter took one away, leaving the other for ages more). The table was so small the plate of the person opposite (very famous, but I won't give you the name) nearly touched mine. The freebie starter – tomato bavarois, cucumber and tapenade croutonne – was bland and the sauce tasted of mass-produced ketchup. My first course of salmon was okay, no more, and Vanessa's of eggs in a sauce and pastry was actively nasty, the pastry being soggy and tasteless. My kidneys main course was all right, but my guests had duck which was chewy and had skin like rubber. The dessert, *millefeuille de nougatine au melon de cavaillon glace* *vanille*, was just unbelievable! Soggy, over-ripe, odd-tasting melon, between layers of tasteless crisp brown stuff. In order to have the honour of eating this rubbish I had been instructed not to wear jeans. I didn't, but faced fellow diners in jeans, with denim shirts and without jackets. This is one of only two 3-star Michelin restaurants in England, and the menu says "Discover the delights of these exceptional dishes" (always suspect). What is Michel Roux's excuse for serving this quality of food?

I think a host is very important, someone you feel connected to. A place alone is not enough. I am drawn to these ruminations recalling John Guy, a small, intensely jolly Australian who owns **Hollington House** near Newbury, Berkshire. Like its proprietor, it is delightful and cheerfully odd. It was built in 1904, in styles ranging from gothic to Tudor through Victorian to American luxurious. I was put in supposedly the best suite, called Eliot-Cohen. My toilet bowl was so positioned that if you stood in front of it guests arriving in the drive below had a perfect view of you through high, leaded windows, as did other guests walking in the grounds. I stay at Hollington House when visiting Andrew Lloyd Webber, so usually only have tea and breakfast. Tea on the terrace facing a stunning English country view is amazingly good – banana cake, very light home-made scones, chocolate éclairs, jam rolls (which are very rare), sandwiches and a first-rate fruit cake. One one occasion we had lunch. I had chicken sausage and beans – very nice. Vanessa loved her poached salmon and veg. The apple and custard crumble tart was very good. John's wife is named Penny, which made me think: "I bet John gets fed up with people saying of his wife 'A Penny for the Guy'."

In a restaurant, it's no good the food being wonderful if you're squashed up in some tiny space closer to the people on either side of you than to your own companion opposite, so I always note the number of the table I like (all restaurants give their tables numbers). If I don't get it, I go somewhere else. I'm very seldom prepared to sit at a table meant for two people, even if we are only two. This makes it dangerous to go anywhere new. I sometimes walk out within seconds if shown a small table. But I think the worst is when the restaurant instucts you *when* to turn up. Miss Seagrove and I decided to try out **L'Ortolan** at Shinfield in Berkshire, having read good things of its chef John Burton-Race. I was asked to arrive at 12.15 or 2pm. I chose 2pm, got there 15 minutes early and was shown to a corner, where both the table and the chairs wobbled on an uneven floor. The view was part garden and part parked cars. The food wasn't much better, and I remained unconsoled when Mrs Burton-Race explained that I was at the wrong table because I'd arrived early – particularly as the table which had been meant for me had people who stayed until 2.45.

Tales of the riverbank

Restaurant guides are grossly perverse. I complained to the editor of the Ronay guide once that he didn't even list the **French Horn** at Sonning, Berkshire. He told me later that he'd sent an inspector there specially to re-check it – and still left it out! I think it is excellent. What it lacks is pretension. The food actually looks like food and not like plate decoration. The place itself is set on the river, at the edge of a lovely village. Lawns of some size slope down to the water, where swans dither about as swans are apt to do. The house itself is a large, converted 1850s grand dwelling, with some rooms for hire.

It is run by Carol Walsh, whose father founded Wheeler's in the good old days, and by her Portuguese husband, Ronnie Emmanuel, whom she met when he sold toilet rolls from a barrow. I have taken some of the greatest Hollywood stars there (all right, I won't list them, or someone will say I'm name-dropping) and they all loved it. Personally, I'm happy to see a roast duck that looks like a roast duck, not little slivers of what could be steak, set among a bed of tiddly whatevers. Crevettes thermidore and smoked salmon may not have endless blended sauces to boost them, but if they're good they can be exceptional. The whole place has a 1950s feel to it. The staff are discreet and efficient, there's a lot of space, so you're not eating with some stranger at the next table, and the river views are spectacular.

You have the feeling that it is all deeply professional. The wine list goes from plonk up to a 1945 First Growth Château Margaux at £2,000, but it's a snip really because that includes VAT and service. The only time I was a tiny bit let down was when I took Peter Falk there (see, I can't help name-dropping) and went mad and ordered some old wine for £400 which was a bit musty. And that's being kind.

I cruised into Beaconsfield like the shark in *Jaws* looking for its next victim. It was getting near lunchtime. Then I spotted **Gilbey's** in Old Amersham, Buckinghamshire. Old house, little flagstoned couryard in the sun with wrought-iron tables and chairs. This was to be *it!* The bread was excellent. Vanessa had sweet pepper and tomato soup, good but certainly not hot. I had spinach and dolcelatte tart with a fresh herb salsa. Pleasant, if unremarkable. Main course for me was grilled cod fillet served on a pancake filled with radicchio leaves, with a goat's cheese and basil salsa. The basil salsa turned out to be exactly the same green gunge as the herb salsa in my first course. Otherwise, it was pretty good. I was not unhappy. I also had an uninterrupted view of the A404, which I do not remember having seen before. "The chef recommends a crème brûlée and the lemon tart," said Miss Charlotte Gilbey, who served us. We had them both, and they were good to excellent.

Stephen Spooner, the young chef, was dragged out. "What did you think? he asked nervously. "Fine, a few quibbles," I said. "What quibbles?" "Soup was cold," I muttered. He asked no more.

The brochure for the **Bell Inn** at Aston Clinton, Buckinghamshire, says that the Bell helped to pioneer the country-house hotel concept. True, except industrialisation has taken over and it now sits on the A41 amid dreary suburbia. It's a listed 17th-century coaching house with the inevitable modern annexe. I liked the down-at-heel atmosphere and the desperately non-chic clientele. The three-course lunch is £19.50. Vanessa said her freebie starter of salmon mousse was delicious. She was equally enthusiastic about her hot cream of cauliflower soup with Arran mustard. My first course was an enormous portion of crisp confit of duck set on *lentilles du Puy*, crisp potato and light poultry jus. I liked it. I thought the roast beef was poor, and even though they did fresh Yorkshire pud for me – I insist on that everywhere, never have it off the trolley – it wasn't great. The bread-and-butter pudding was better. The Bell used to have a Michelin star. Now it's in genteel decline, and other, more ponced-up locations have taken over. But there's something very comfortable and well worn about it. I think you should support the Bell.
   This has now changed hands and is serving less exclusive fare.

Hello, Mr Chips

The Cyber Cafe in Dunstable was closed down. The Mouth Chinese Restaurant had its lips firmly shut. Nothing going on there. It was a grim winter day and past my lunchtime. We Scorpios like everything just so. Lunch at one, dinner at eight. If you're planning to drop in for a meal, always risky, stay away from the A5. I decided to cut my losses and turned off down one of those little white roads, too small to have identifying numbers on a road map. They're invariably the best. It was 1.30pm when we got to Great Brickhill in Buckinghamshire. **The Old Red Lion Inn** looked quaint. Signs announced the British Institute of Innkeeping and Andrew John McCollin landlord.

   Inside there were photos of Joanna Lumley, Jeremy Beadle, David Jason and Mick Jagger. This was clearly a glitterati area where two very glum customers sat at a table with a red check cloth. On the wall there was an identity poster of birds. I sat at the bar and surveyed the menu. "Is this all frozen or is it ...?" I started. "Combination thereof," replied the gentleman behind the bar, later revealed to be Andrew McCollin. I ordered a "Lion's Feast: two rashers of bacon, sausage, tomato, burger, two eggs, mushrooms, baked beans and chips. £6.25". It was as adventurous as anything else on the menu. Vanessa ordered a ploughman's lunch. "The atmosphere's bizarre," she whispered.

In the "public bar'" the other side of the counter, we could see a few men, very quiet, slightly menacing. "Come on, let's look in there," I said. Vanessa shook her head firmly in the negative. So I went alone.

The second bar had a sign on it: The Den. There was a TV – on. A real fire – not on. A nice view from the back window over a garden and some excellent countryside. A single slot machine. "What's Great Brickhill famous for?" I said quietly to anyone who cared to answer. "Barry McGuigan," replied a man in a blue sweater and a Levi's hat. Apparently, he lived next to the pub and Barry McGuigan used to live next to him. "He's into cabaret now, Barry McGuigan," volunteered a bald man. I was beginning to warm to this lot. They told me Barry used to drive in a motor-racing team for a local man. "MG Metros souped up to hell," said someone else. I definitely liked this group. It was a quiet Saturday afternoon, gloomy weather, and they were assembled for a drink and a chat. In those circumstances intruders have to move in slowly.

I went back to the other side. "They're nice people, come on," I said to Vanessa. She joined me. In came my robust plate of food. Very basic, very British. Perfectly all right. The chips were very chunky.

"Home-made?" I asked. "Not home-made, just excellent," said Mr McCollin. Apparently, they're by Brake Brothers. They had the light texture of bought-in chips, but they were quite good. "Bread's warm, it's nice," said Vanessa. More people came in. Bit of laughter. A white horse went by outside, right to left, ridden by someone with a black protective hat.

I thought it was a particularly relaxed, very English, understated atmosphere. I poured tomato ketchup on my fry-up. I enjoyed it. "Who are the big shots round here?" I asked, looking at old photos of the village on the wall. "Family called Duncombe," I was told. "My mother used to be their secretary. They've still got the big house," another man said. "There was a pub up the road, the Duncombe Arms," volunteered someone else. "It's shut now, it's houses," said the bald man. "Do the Duncombes join in everything?" I asked. I find this sort of local stuff very interesting. "No. He's about 90. Used to have two old gun dogs. He's on the parish council," said the man in the hat.

They started asking for autographs, quietly. "Not every Saturday we get celebrities in." A very well-mannered lot. Friendly, not pushy. One of them, with suitably long, artistic hair, had written a screenplay that had been optioned. "I'm not giving up the day job," he said. We shook hands and left. I thought it had been exceptionally pleasant.

My Cliveden hell

I was dining at Chequers with the prime minister, so I phoned **Cliveden**, which is also in Buckinghamshire. "Are you nearby?" I asked. "Yes," they said. This was untrue, but by the time I'd checked the map, I thought: "I'll stay there anyway." We arrived at four o'clock and were offered tea, sandwiches, scones and cakes. We sat in the main hall and watched a coach party walking through wearing nametags. Cliveden is for ever full of tourists and day-trippers. A group gathered to look at the fireplace, and a lady said: "Forgive me, we're butting into your tea." It's like eating in the lobby of Olympia exhibition hall. The tea arrived minus sandwiches, scones or cakes. "They come later," said the waiter. With English tea you should get everything at the same time, so I asked him to take it away until they were ready for normal service. That took another 10 minutes.

An elegant man came up. "Mr Winner," he said, "forgive me for intruding. You're not going to write about this aeroplane food, are you?" "Are you staying here?" I asked. "No, I've just had lunch. For an aeroplane it wouldn't be too bad." He left. Then his wife appeared. "Do you agree with him?" She said cheerfully, "He's a pain, but the food was terrible."

The tea eventually arrived. The bread stuck to the top of your mouth – most unpleasant. Vanessa found the smoked salmon odd. The scones were cold. After I'd eaten most of one they brought some hot ones. The small chocolate éclair was very good.

The bedroom door had a handwritten card with our names on in a brass holder. That's absurd. Suppose I didn't want people to know I was there? Or which room I was in? Confidentiality obviously means nothing to the management at Cliveden, as was further revealed when they later issued a newspaper with a five-page, highly inaccurate memo written by the general manager, Ross Stevenson, about my every move.

The hotel executive accompanying us said: "I'd like to explain your room to you." "What on earth is he talking about?" I thought. "It's a room. It's got a bed, two small armchairs and it's £450 a night, which is outrageous. What else do I need to know?" The assistant opened the television-cabinet doors. "Here are two videos about the hotel," he announced. "Why should I watch a video of the hotel?" I asked. "I'm here, I can see it for myself." Instead of pestering guests about videos they should tell them where the hairdryer is. When needed the next day, it was lurking under some bedding in a cupboard.

The view would have been pleasing were the grounds not full of families sitting on sheets, kids rolling down slopes, back-packers, locals, tourists. It was like Legoland on a bad day. This is National Trust property, open to all. Exclusive it isn't.

After dinner, the doorman said: "I'll park your car at the back." "Why?" I asked. "Because of the loose stones," he replied. "If cars drive quickly by, they throw them up and might do damage." "That's nice," I thought. What about all the other people parked in front? If you're at Cliveden and acquire chipped paintwork, you now know why. Back in the room we ordered hot milk. It came in tall glasses – impossible to hold because they were so hot. Why not serve hot liquid in something with handles?

At breakfast there was a delay while someone brought cups. "Hot!" the man eventually announced triumphantly. What phoney nonsense. Who needs hot cups for tea and coffee? They're not worth waiting for. The toast was unbelievable. It was a French white roll sliced thickly and cut in half. It had seen, possibly, a small amount of heat. It was nothing like toast as the world knows it. I turned to a sickly, sticky croissant-type thing. It was revolting. Vanessa was trying to eat her melon with the teaspoon that came for her tea. "They didn't bring any cutlery for the melon. Or a spoon for my muesli," she said. I rang down and made my displeasure known. The service at Cliveden, if you can call it that, is unctuous, overbearing and utterly incompetent.

At lunch we sat by the window. All you could see were the bottoms of day-trippers leaning on the balcony looking at the grounds. We ordered two bucks fizzes and I opened the wine list. This was beyond human belief. It said: "Half-bottles, page 31." But there was no page 31. Then I looked and realised page 28 is followed by page 31, then you have page 30 and then page 33. Page 32 is after page 33.

The set lunch is an astronomical £45 per person for the usual three courses. At Claridge's and The Dorchester it's £29 and these are marvellously run hotels. It's £14.50 at The Ivy and Marco Pierre White's Mirabelle. In all these places the quality of food and service is superb: vastly superior to Cliveden and a fraction of the price.

The bucks fizz arrived. Vanessa looked at the glasses. "They're filthy," she said. They were smeared with lipstick and washing-up grime. "Take them away. You wouldn't expect this in a transport caff," I said to John Rogers, the assistant dining-room manager. He left and came back with new glasses. No apology. Just a sneer. "I think it came from the orange juice, sir," he said, referring to the dirt.

I've been dining in great hotels (which Cliveden certainly isn't) for well over 50 years. I can tell lipstick and smear-dirt from orange juice. If it was orange juice, why didn't Mr Rogers show it to us before taking the glasses away? It was just a typically inept response from a hotel parading as having class when it has none. Compared to Chewton Glen in New Milton or Ston Easton Park near Bath, or Inverlochy Castle at Fort William

– all beautifully run places that I visit with pleasure – Cliveden is just a bad joke. I walked out. "You knew it was terrible from when we went before," said Vanessa as we drove off. "I don't know why we stayed for lunch anyway. It's only for tourists." She's right.

Knowing they were in for trouble, the hotel banned me. That's like being told I'm not welcome at the ladies' toilet in Middlesborough railway station. I wasn't going there, either.

It took me two weeks, and I had to write twice, before Cliveden even sent my bill. Then they didn't charge me for some key items. How dare they? Only friends can buy me food or drink.

When you think back, you often see a pattern where one was not visible before. Once I actually finished a lunch at Cliveden, Vanessa commented that her sea bass didn't taste fresh. Today, reading other guests' comments, "not fresh" seems a habit at Cliveden.

Then the general manager wrote to me trying to excuse it, saying: "The fish is Cornish. Cornish sea bass provides a meatier taste than that of its Mediterranean counterpart, which may explain Miss Perry's concern."

That sounded odd. I sought opinions from top chefs at Nico Ladenis's restaurant, at Claridge's and at Wilton's. All said Cliveden was talking nonsense. Sea bass was the same all over.

As Cliveden's came from Cornwall, according to them noted for its meatier-tasting sea bass, I spoke to Mr de Rozarieux, a leading light of the Cornish Fish Producers' Organisation. He said the only sea bass he'd heard of that tasted different were cheap, farmed French and Spanish imports. He, too, opined there was no way sea bass taste varied according to where it was caught. "Unless it's from Sellafield," he added. Touch of Cornish humour there.

So it seems at Cliveden the customer is always wrong. It's not dirt, it's residue from orange juice. It's not old sea bass, it's from Cornwall – so that explains everything. It's a pathetic attempt at flimflam. Because of them I'm attacked in Scotland. Deputy general manager Jörg Böckeler produced a ludicrous report on my every movement – I must see if I can get a copy under the Freedom of Information act. Cliveden's managing director, John Tham, refuses to give me one. The report said that when I got tea without cakes, scones or sandwiches, I remarked: "Are we in Scotland?" Mr Böckeler is German. Maybe my remarks suffered in translation.

Another week on: I can't resist giving you a quote from John Tham. It's so unbelievable. It came in one of the sarcastic, silly letters he sent me. In it he sums up his view of the excellence (that's a laugh) and the ethos of Cliveden. He writes: "We are ladies and gentlemen serving ladies and gentlemen." Can you believe it? How naff can you get? Per-lease, pass the sick bag.

Gowned and out

Why on earth should anyone buy a Cambridge University master of arts gown with a white-lined hood? Thus I mused while unwrapping the one I'd ordered from Ede & Ravenscroft of Trumpington Street, Cambridge. Perhaps I'd wear it to greet dinner guests. Unlikely: I've only given three dinner parties in the past 27 years. It rested on the sofa in my study until – knock me down with a feather – a few days later I received an invitation from the master and fellows of **Downing College, Cambridge**, inviting me to their commemoration feast. "Dress black tie, gowns with scarlet decoration may be worn" was hand-written on the bottom. Gown or no gown, this was not for me.

Invitations usually get put on the left of my desk. There they lie, soon covered with further ephemera, forgotten and unanswered. I wrote to Professor David King MA, ScD, FRS, Master, pointing out he really didn't want me. "I ask to see the seating plan, know exactly who is on the table, be told who's placed either side of me and opposite, have the right to make changes. All this is far too much for a man of your stature, so I'll say thank you no, and hope to meet another time." Professor King graciously replied that I was seated on his right-hand side, he would send me a top table plan and a thumbnail sketch of everyone on it, and let me do as I wished. Now it became: how to get the helicopter in? I liked the idea of returning, for the first time since I came down in 1955, in some style and with a bit of noise. Mrs Professor King told my copter man that we could land on the college lawn; others had done so before. But this was not to be. Apparently the "others" were royalty. Royal flights are okay; plebs like me, decreed the Civil Aviation Authority, had to land on a nearby rugby pitch. And I thought we lived in a democracy.

There was more trouble. I was doing a BBC television show just before the 20-minute flight from Battersea. So I took my evening dress and other paraphernalia into the lavatory of the heliport for a quick change. It was unimportant I'd forgotten cuff links. But my evening-dress trousers were not on the hanger. Oh well, I would appear immaculately dressed from the waist up. Below, there would be the considerable contrast of a pair of jeans. Nobody cared, even though I took the trouble to point out in my speech that this was not a protest, but an error, for which I apologised.

To describe any meal in a Cambridge dining hall as a "feast" would, I thought, require a stretch of normal meaning. But my Cambridge dictionary called it "a meal with very good food or a large meal for many people". Since there were 140 guests and a six-course menu in which the word "dessert" strangely meant cheese and biscuits, I suppose we qualified. I was particularly pleased that by the end of our correspondence the master was signing himself "Dave". Most unlike my dour tutor, Mr Norman, who referred to me, in student days, as "Winner", and endlessly told me I spent far too much time watching films and working on the university newspaper. But then my headmaster at school lectured me on how the Warner Bros gangster movies, now cinemathèque classics, would result in my growing up disturbed. Sit down the reader who said, "He was right".

Fronted by an ornate, silver bowl "from the Long Range Rifle Club", we started with *terrine de légumes*: fair to middling. Went on to *filet de bar grillé au safran*: very good indeed, first-rate sauce. Then a sorbet; I like sorbets. Thus to the main course, *suprème de faisan châtelaine*. Perfectly acceptable, but a bit dry. The carrots were historic. At this point I realised I was the only one at the table who was eating. Many others had not been served. I think it's essential to commence while the food is hot, regardless. I turned to the master. "Start, David, because I'm the only one," I said. "Right," said Dave, and started eating. College masters have certainly improved since my day. The only time I met Sir Lionel Whitby, Downing's boss in 1954, was when he hauled me up for taking the porter's bicycle and leaving it at the Varsity newspaper office. Sir Lionel sent me down for two weeks. Yah boo, Sir L. I've got the best seat in the house. I'm about to reply on behalf of the guests. I even scoffed the *poire macaron au coulis de fraises*. That's more than you ever gave me.

I almost stayed at the **Garden House**, a Moat House hotel, when I was in Cambridge to deliver a lecture. We were shown to a nice room with a view of the river with some cows on the other side, and had some hearty tomato, cheese and Branston pickle sandwiches. Later we partook of tea and biscuits in the lounge, where the pianist played 'The Sun Has Got His Hat On', before we decided to drive back that night anyway. The Garden House isn't a superposh hotel, but it was fine.

Carry on campus

My "lecture" is entitled My Life in the Movies and Other Places. It wasn't called that when I first gave it at the National Film Theatre in 1970. It's evolved in performances all over the place, from the American Film Institutes in Los Angeles and Washington to Oxford, Cambridge and Dublin. You name it, I've talked on it.

When I first spoke at Cambridge, for the film society, my host was an undergrad who did well – David Hare. A few weeks ago, it was Nishi Dholakia, the tall, elegant senior officer of the Cambridge Union Society. Mr Dholakia later wrote me a nice letter saying my visit had been "phenomenally successful", adding: "I am told the union has not seen an audience as sizeable as yours since Ronald Reagan came to visit in 1990." There's a moral there, though I can't be bothered to find it. Mr Dholakia also said: "I have little doubt that the meal I had at **Midsummer House** will be the best meal I will have during my time at Cambridge. If only more speakers took us to meals at the best restaurants."

Ignoring the fact that most speakers are probably mean bastards, I was extremely surprised to find a good eating place in Cambridge. There certainly weren't any when I was up reading law and economics at Downing. There was a strange diner with plastic table tops run by a nice Cypriot a few yards from the college gate and a goodish Indian restaurant near Magdalene where George Webb, who owned the Rex cinema, Leslie Halliwell, his manager, and I plotted to have Marlon Brando's banned movie *The Wild One* shown in Cambridge by getting permission from the council. We did. And people came from all over the country. A very young Jackie Collins even turned up to have a cup of tea in my rooms before going to see it.

The management of Midsummer House had written to me many times asking me to visit. It was once owned by Hans Schweitzer, who is still chef at the totally torn-down Sandy Lane Hotel. Midsummer House had been closed for four weeks; it was reopening the night I booked my party in for a 6.30pm dinner. They even had a new chef, Daniel Clifford, from Leeds. None of that promising.

The building is extremely attractive. It looks like an old rectory, facing Midsummer Common at the front and the River Cam at the rear. Knocking back a nice freebie starter vichyssoise were Vanessa and me – and, from the Union, Nishi, Peter Rutland, director of recruitment, Alex Slater, president, and Jodie Ginsberg, their red-headed press officer, who told us she wanted to be a foreign correspondent for BBC TV. All our starters looked the same. They were square, except for Jodie's, which was round. Some were duck and some were vegetable. I thought they were okay.

"My main course chicken is excellent," I dictated into my tape, and then plonked it on the president's bread plate. Jodie said of the chef: "He likes shredding things. This is my second thing that's shredded, whatever it is." She prodded her food. "I had the starter and that had shredded stuff as well. I'm not a big fan of shredded stuff." "I'd rather gathered that, Jodie," I said.

Vanessa had ordered sea bass. She liked it, saying: "I deliberately didn't eat bread because I expected the sea bass to have a selection of vegetables with it including carbohydrate, which would have been potato or rice, to make a balanced meal." She got a few little squares of vegetable as decoration, none of which was carbohydrate. "If there's not a full vegetable selection, you should be told," said Vanessa firmly. I think she's right. But we all decided the food was good. And even though it took for ever, my chocolate fondant was exceptional. The right lightness of sponge and a superb hot chocolate sauce interior.

Beau Gidleigh

What I like about Devon is that it's not the home counties. You feel you really are somewhere else. You can drive for miles and not see very much. In fact, a great deal of the time you can see nothing at all, except high hedgerows that tower over the one-track lanes. Set in the heart of it all is **Gidleigh Park**, a deservedly famous hotel with a Michelin two-star restaurant. I'd been wanting to visit for a while. When a gap appeared in their regular bookings, I got one room for £460 a night, including full breakfast and dinner. It was a nice room, but the one next door was better because it had a balcony. I was able to check this out as they don't give you keys at Gidleigh Park, on the assumption that everyone is unbelievably honest. Even in Devon this strikes me as optimistic.

The hotel is a fake Tudor 1920s Surrey-style mansion. There's a stream outside and it's all pleasantly well worn, with weeds (or were they flowers?) peeping out between cracks in the paving stones. Cat's hair is spread over the armchairs. This upset Georgina because she got her black trouser suit messed up. A couple from New York tried to strike up a conversation, but I decided against it. I was in shock when the owner of the hotel, a neat, professional American, Paul Henderson, explained it was the legendary jazz pianist George Shearing and his wife. I'd loved to have heard a few tales from him.

We started with a superb Devon tea. Best scones ever, great clotted cream, wonderful home-made jam, historic biscuits and pleasant sandwiches that were overfilled. The banana cake was poor, the chocolate cake just good. You sit on a lovely terrace overlooking the view.

The general manager, Catherine Endacott, is totally devoted. She walks quickly, with purpose. The hotel is obviously her life. "We don't reserve seats in the dining room," she advised. "That's all right, Catherine," I said. "I'll go now and leave a bar of soap and an old shoe on the table to show it's occupied." "Don't worry," said Catherine. "I'll fix it." I pointed helpfully to the table I wanted fixed.

The room literature advised that she and the chef, Michael Caines, owned the hotel. "Catherine's not a proprietor and Caines isn't either," said Paul later. "But it's in your guest book," I said. "I didn't proofread it," said Paul. Shortly thereafter I met Michael Caines. "Why are you giving me a left-handed handshake?" I asked rather tartly. "Because I lost my right arm in a car accident last year," he explained. That shut me up. They certainly did a wonderful matching job on the false arm.

There are two small dining rooms at Gidleigh. The guests talk in hushed whispers. The service is efficient but impersonal. I missed someone greeting and checking up on things, like Peter Crome does at Chewton Glen. This lack of human touch may have been because Mrs Henderson (the owner's wife) was laid up with a bad leg and the restaurant manager was on holiday.

Paul's much into wine. Georgina doesn't drink, so I only bought half a bottle. As I'm used to exceptionally good wines, many places let me carry my home-bought halves with me. A Pétrus here, a Château Latour there. Paul suggested an Italian Gaja Barbaresco 1988 at £52.50. "That's what it would fetch at auction," he told me. I checked with Christie's, where Tony Thompson told me it fetches £40 a bottle, plus commission and VAT. I make that £24 a half-bottle. Still a 220% mark-up is less than usual.

The food was good; not up to the Michelin two-star level of Gordon Ramsay, but commendable. We had lobster fricassée. The lobster was less tasty than the one from Highcliffe that I ate recently at Chewton Glenn; the sauce was okay. Georgina disagreed. "It was a superb dish," she announced firmly.

I didn't understand why, on my last breakfast, they cut up my overcooked kipper and laid the slices on top of each other. Massively inferior to the morning before.

One night, a group at the next table included a worse-for-drink English couple. The man, noticing me, kept saying very loudly: "So I wrote my restaurant review." His wife hissed: "Be quiet!" They then talked and laughed so raucously that, when the waiters came with our first course, I'd already risen. "Follow me, folks," I said, and walked to the adjacent dining room. Even there, I heard this shrill British couple through the walls.

"They weren't guests," said Paul afterwards.

"Good," I said. "I won't have to eat out in future."

I'm not sure whether Paul considered that a plus or a minus.

Hallsands, on the Devon coast, consists of a bay, a sandy beach, cliffs topped with rolling fields and, at one end, a cabin offering ice cream and cold drinks. High on the far cliff is the **Hallsands Hotel** – a cross between Anthony Perkins's place in *Psycho* and a run-down turn-of-the-century English house. I climbed many steps, arriving at a side terrace with two wooden tables and benches overlooking the beach. I sat down and admired the view. There was a large lunch menu, from which I selected a crab roll and Georgina chose cod and chips. "Do you make your own chips?" I asked, assuming they were bought in, as they are in many posh London restaurants. "We make them here," said Carol Light, the owner. "You mean you take a potato in your kitchen, cut it up and fry it?" I persisted. "Yes," said Carol.

The food arrived. My crab roll was excellent. There was white and brown crabmeat, very fresh, very tasty. The roll itself was long and white and of a type of bread I'd never seen before. But it was excellent. The shredded lettuce and tomato were first rate, too. Georgina's fish was exquisite: cooked to perfection and with a superb batter, which she meticulously peeled off. I ate bits of it. It was as good as you could hope for. The chips were the best I've ever eaten. She also had some very nice cucumber.

Oscar's, at the Royal Bath hotel in Bournemouth, is a corridor-like restaurant overlooking trees and the road outside. It features a photo of Oscar Wilde, who supposedly used to go there. Wilde would have had a seizure at the sight of the wallpaper. It was one of the most awful meals I have ever eaten. Don't tell me food is getting better in England. No French or Italian hotel in a place the size of Bournemouth would dare offer anything like it. Vanessa's cream of broccoli soup was so sweet even I found it impossible to take. She left most of it. I had tough, stringy Parma ham and mushy figs. A small white loaf was unexceptional in the extreme. I went on to grey mullet presented with a roast-tomato confit. It did not taste fresh – too long in the deepfreeze or fridge. Vanessa had cod fillet and potato mash with parsley and lemon sauce. Dull to awful. To finish, a millefeuille of chocolate filled with fresh cream and strawberries – beyond belief horrid. But the staff were all very pleasant, and it wasn't their fault that the food was dreary.

Ads to the pleasure

Peter and Nita Hauser star in an Ariel TV ad at their hotel **Stock Hill House**, in Dorset. A lot of tablecloths fly about, gleaming – and at the end they hold hands romantically. I asked Nita what they got for it. "Nothing," she said. "Nothing?" I asked incredulously as I stood near some enormous, carved 19th-century Indian horses in the hall. "What did you say when they suggested the advert?" I said. "Why not?" replied Nita. "You should've said, 'How much?'" I responded. They were offered a year's free supply of Ariel (which hasn't turned up yet) and a free liquidiser which also hasn't arrived. If a TV commercial company knocks on your door, ask at least £20,000 and creep down to £10,000 if you have to!

It was not the TV ad which brought me to Stock Hill House. Vanessa wanted a weekend in the country, so I picked it at random from the Ronay Guide because it was in an area I didn't know. The guide said: "Arrive in time for afternoon tea which is splendid." I did and it wasn't. The tablecloths may have been spotless, but my spoon was all sticky. I put my finger in the teacup (I'm very practical in these things) before the milk went in, ran it up and down the spoon and cleaned it with my paper napkin. The actual tea was excellent, but all we got with it was a swiss roll, a chocolate cake and an apricot tart, and they were unexceptional.

The accommodation was a bit off, too. I'd asked for a suite; in future I must remember to ask for a view, suite or not. We got a strangely furnished, comfortable suite, a bit away from the Victorian house, with tiny windows and outside views of asphalt yards and cars. It was like living in a car park. Ronay describes this as "the sumptuous Robin's Nest suite". It had chintz curtains one side and striped the other, one of the hundreds of animalia, a Chinese dog, on the floor and a very well-stocked bathroom.

The service at Stock Hill is unbeatable. We asked for an iron and Vanessa's dress was ironed for her in five minutes. I asked for a razor and three came over in seconds. The Hausers – he from Austria, she from Walthamstow – are as nice a couple as you could meet. They certainly care.

Thankfully, the food at dinner perked up no end. The canapés were beautifully done. My mango and chicken balontine starter was three large pieces of chicken with mango in the middle, all right but too much. The cream of lovage and sweetwater crayfish soup was historic. We'd seen the crayfish moving in a bucket a short time before. The main course of Aga-roasted duckling breast in cassis and blackcurrants was good, far better than Kensington Place and equal to Le Caprice, but this sliced duck nonsense is a bit suspect, I always think. The vegetables, all home-grown, were tip-top. The next morning Peter showed me round the herb and vegetable garden (not at its best this year through lack of rain), and then he called out and dozens of his chickens jumped on to perches to cluck back! So there's always fresh eggs.

The following day lunch offered supreme of chicken filled with sweetwater crayfish. I don't know why, but that seemed odd to me. The food in general is charmingly robust.

The place is typical of the massively over-decorated style that pervades English, privately owned, small hotels. According to your taste, it's either delightfully eccentric or totally bizarre. The Hausers are avid collectors and the place is awash with carved animals, bronzes, an absolute mishmash of different period and coffee tables, furniture and mirrors, all interesting, but certainly not "antiques of the highest standard", as the

Ronay says. But then Ronay is as erratic a book as you can get.

It was a very pleasant stay and, yes, I can recommend Stock Hill House. The most magical moments were after dinner. I suddenly heard the sound of a zither. An Austrian record, I thought. But no, there in the lobby Peter was plucking expertly at a 100-year-old zither while two Japanese children watched enchanted.

At my request he played *The Third Man* theme, my favourite film and my favourite film music. Exceptionally well performed too. Now, there's not many hotels where you get that!

Sizzling good

We'd decided to forego a posh dinner at Chewton Glen and take our chances. Vanessa had requested a brief walk by the sea. Now, we proceeded along the coast, but the only inn that served food on that stretch stopped at 8.30pm and that was the time. So I cruised down the main drag to Highcliffe, Dorset.

"There's something!" I exclaimed, jamming my foot on the brake. There was a screech of tyres behind. Two young men in a Jeep yelled something deeply unpleasant. "Entirely my fault," I said. "I'm so sorry, I'm a terrible driver." I say that a great deal, so I'm rather good at it. Then I continued down the street.

There it was: Erties Fish and Chips. Large gold letters standing out from a bright red background with four lights extending over them. Next door was a Methodist church. "No Parking. Private Property" it said of the area in front. I pulled into a gap labelled "Reserved for Organist".

We walked into Erties. A stand-up wooden sign in old-fashioned lettering read "Wait here to be seated". A waitress showed us a table for two; I sat at one for eight. The large, plastic-covered menu confused me. A blackboard announced **Bertie's** evening specials (the B was missing outside): tuna steak or rock, £5.75, lemon sole, halibut steak, skate wing, large haddock with chips, £5.95. I was baffled. "Is the owner in?" I asked the waitress. "Yes, Rob's upstairs," she told me. "What's he doing there?" I asked. "Watching the telly," she replied. Seemed a pity to disturb him, so I walked into the kitchen.

A chef opened metal drawers revealing frozen cod. "That's not on the board," I said.

"Outside, the catch of the day's the special stuff; cod's a regular thing," the chef explained. "Anyway, it's all frozen, except the skate."

It was a tough choice: beef and onion pie, steak and kidney pasties for £1.20, black-pudding fritters 40p, fish cake burgers 99p.

"Do you make them here?" I yelled. "Yes," said the chef.

"I'll have one and some cod, chips and mushy peas."

Vanessa ordered the rock. My Coca-Cola came with lots of ice. I guessed it was from a large container, not a tin or bottle – we experts can tell. I was right.

My cod had that too-long frozen taste, but Vanessa's rock was first-rate. We both had two enormous pieces, enough for a group. The chips were superb, made on the premises. "We get through two and a half tons of potatoes a week," obliged the chef. The mushy peas were good too.

I had trouble pouring the vinegar. "It helps if you take the top off," said Vanessa.

I'd made a mistake with the fish cake burger – I'd said yes to mayonnaise, which wiped out the taste – but when I got a bit on its own, it was fine.

I went to another kitchen to examine a syrup sponge, melancholy in a refrigerator. I ordered it together with some New Forest ice cream. It arrived microwave hot. I only ate the syrupy bits on the outside of the sponge and the ice cream. I liked it, but Vanessa said it tasted of spray cream that comes out of a tin. She's much fussier than me. We rounded it off with cups of Assam and Kenyan Ty-Phoo tea.

The stand-up sign had been turned around to read "Restaurant Now Closed".

"They're mopping the floors," I dictated into my recorder.

"Do you mind us doing that?" asked a waitress, hearing me.

"Not at all," I said. Then, for no reason, "Does Rob the boss have a wife?"

"Yes," said the waitress. "She's gone away."

"Permanently?" I asked

"To see her daughter in Majorca," was the reply.

None of my business, really. We Scorpios are just unbelievably nosy.

PS The ownership has changed, but it's still excellent.

Frederick the great

I can think of no restaurant in the history of my life that I less wanted to go to than **Frederick's**, which is situated in Highcliffe, Dorset. When staying at the nearby and excellent Chewton Glen, I'd often driven past in my search for an evening meal and always thought that Frederick's looked gloomy and uninviting. It is next to the Craft Wool Shop and Tapper Funeral Services, fronted by a board announcing the Ken Dodd Happiness Show. I passed it by yet again on a recent visit as we looked for somewhere else. After wandering here and there and finding nothing remotely interesting, we sadly agreed that, this time, Frederick's it would have to be.

It was Saturday night and there were only two other couples in the place. It had a desolate air, not saved by the sound of Frank Sinatra singing 'Chicago'. "We're a bit quiet tonight," said a tall, gangly man in dark trousers and a white, short-sleeved shirt, who turned out to be called John. "Not any more you're not," I said, sitting down at a table with a blue tablecloth and matching blue candle. The chintz lamp shades matched the curtains.

John produced a small selection menu – quite clever; better than trying to do too much – and informed us this was his first restaurant venture. "I used to work for the Home Office. I came under the Official Secrets Act," he told me subversively. It turned out he used to be a TV licence inspector. I didn't like to go into it too deeply. Maybe he was looking for Chinese spies at the same time. John assured me that the lemon sole was fresh and the only one left. I started with roes on toast. "You won't get those anywhere else," said John. "You will at Sheekey's," I said boastfully.

I studied the other two couples. They were rather nice. Elderly, quietly dressed, but they'd taken some trouble. Quietly spoken, too. I pointed out my candle wasn't lit. "That's nerves, that is," said John.

The roes on toast were excellent. Vanessa's melon and grape cocktail was good. My sole with duchess potatoes, sauté potatoes, red cabbage and string beans were memorable. The veg were cooked perfectly. Vanessa had a vegetarian peanut and lentil layer with veg. That was superb. This was really all rather excellent. The service was a bit slow, but the menu warned us that Sylvia was cooking in the kitchen, adding: "You may have to wait 20 to 30 minutes for your meal." I'd hate to be there when it's full, I thought. It was also quite fun calling "John!" from time to time. He was definitely a bit deaf, bless him. "Were you calling me?" he'd ask. I don't know who else he thinks I was calling.

"What about the desserts? Are they bought in, John, or made on the premises?" I asked. "We only buy in the 'eye of the storm'", explained John. "Sylvia makes an excellent bakewell tart and mince pies." "I'll have 'em both," I said expansively. They were not excellent – they were totally historic. Very fresh, good home baking. I was only sorry I'd missed the apricot and pear crumble. They'd run out of that. Sadly, I was too full to try the toffee pudding made with pecan nuts. The whole meal was real, old-fashioned, personal cooking. Overpresented it wasn't; very tasty it was.

Sylvia came out of hiding to take the applause. She and John used to live in Chingford, Essex. Sylvia made the desserts in Chasney's, a local place there. They'd been in Highcliffe for four years. "Done well?" I asked. "Not too bad. It's a quiet area here, but gradually people are getting to know us." "Four years, that's gradual," I agreed.

I thought it was all terrific. "That was a find," said Vanessa as we walked into the street and past a notice board saying "Get your dog wormed", with a picture of dogs waiting in the surgery. "You just don't get that sort of thing in London," she added. She was right.

We'd turned down Sunday lunch at Chewton Glen – beignets of cod cooked in beer batter, roast striploin Black Aberdeen Angus served with Yorkshire pudding, and much more – and had walked to Highcliffe on the sweeping Christchurch Bay. On the fringe of the car park were two stalls, one for ice cream and the other offering sausage sandwiches, hot dogs, fried-egg sandwiches and the like. 'I'll have a jumbo frankfurter hot dog," I said. "With or without onions?" asked **Linda Attrell** from her caravan-type booth. "With," I replied. I filled it with tomato ketchup. It was a nice hot dog. Not as good as Nathan's in New York, but very serviceable. I then had a sausage sandwich – two bits of white bread with two pork sausages sliced in between. I filled that with mustard. That completed, I chose a whippy soft ice cream. Tacky, no real quality, but a splendid experience.

Buckland Manor is one of those highly rated Gloucestershire hotels in lovely old stone with a row of ancient-tiled roofs and an adjacent church. My suite was chintzed out very well and had a bathroom in varied wood veneers reminiscent of the fantasy notion of a grand ocean liner. The view to the massive flower gardens and countryside beyond is spectacular. The food was plain, but not bad really. Poached pasta parcels of Scottish langoustine, rolled fillets of Dover sole filled with Cornish crab, that sort of thing. At breakfast, they let someone nick my space, which was a bit off. We all moved tables and chairs about madly until the other end of the room was Winner-organised. The "fresh" kippers I was told about puzzled me. I mean, you don't see many herrings swimming around Gloucestershire on a Sunday morning, do you? I asked how long they'd been sitting in the kitchen and the head girl said she'd ask the chef. She never came back with an answer, and I couldn't be bothered to make a fuss.

So far, so good

"This man's a total schmock," I thought. "Why's he taking me 30 minutes each way, in driving winter rain, from Burford to Paxford, to go to some pub for lunch? A pub is a pub: who cares?" Thus, with a certain lack of generosity, I considered my friend Richard Hanlon as we went through end-of-the-world weather along tiny Gloucestershire roads. His idiocy was compounded by the fact that I'd driven to Burford in these appalling conditions from Le Manoir aux Quat'Saisons and would have to drive back to London. Adding to car time in these circumstances was ridiculous.

I'd cooed about how nice Richard's cottage in Burford was (well, it is). I'd been the perfect guest... Oh, there it is, the **Churchill Arms**. Typical country pub. Village probably very pretty on a sunny day. I ducked through searing wind to enter the building. White plaster walls, old beams, some books on a shelf above the bar. "Big deal," I thought, "I've come all this way to see books above a bar." At least they'd reserved a window table for us (great view of the rain) close to a log fire. They don't usually keep tables.

I like to eat lunch dead on one o'clock. It was 2.15pm, so I went to the blackboard. Someone was removing faggots from the menu and chalking up duck breast. "That's odd," I thought. "Home-made chips, £1.50, are described as a starter." We ordered and I went to sit down. A gale of cold air blew in from somewhere. "It could be because the window's open," said Richard as I complained. He closed it.

My parsnip soup arrived pretty quickly. The bread was good, with unwrapped butter in nice pats on the table. I tasted the soup. Suddenly, things started to look up. This was utterly delicious and memorable. I know I loved it because half of it ended up on my shirt. Richard was having brawn with red leek and pepper. He described it as "jelly with naughty bits". It came with a yoghurt tartare. I grabbed some; it was staggeringly tasty. Somewhere, lurking in this pub, was a very expert chef. "It's Sonya," said Richard. "She's from Barbados. She and her husband, Leo, also run the Marsh Goose in Moreton-in-Marsh and the Hare and Hounds in Chedworth."

My main course of braised pork arrived with home-made chips. It was one of the finest main courses I've ever eaten. I'm not clever enough to describe why it was so good, but I hope you've noted the name of this pub, so you can try it for yourself.

"Sonya does the best sticky toffee pudding in the world," said Richard. I'd now decided he was a genius for finding this place. Well worth the drive. "I'll have it," I said. There are certain tastes that live with you for life. Sonya's sticky toffee pudding is one of them. To describe it as incredible would be an insult. It is in some pudding stratosphere I have seldom, if ever, encountered. The sauce with it was light, the pud itself just the right consistency. "It's got dates in it," said Richard.

Sonya Kidney, a cheerful black lady, appeared after the meal. Her parents emigrated to England in 1963. She met her husband, Leo, while working at the Feathers in Woodstock. His second name is Brooke-Little. His father is Clarenceaux King of Arms. He is apparently responsible for granting new coats of arms in England south of some river. Before that, he was north of the river.

Sonya spoke of working with Leo in the kitchen. "I expect to say: 'Will you do that?' not 'Can you do that?' and he says, 'Not at the moment'." "There is some disharmony in the kitchen," I dictated into my recorder.

The Churchill Arms is my amazing tip for the new year. Get out your maps, find Paxford and go from there. In case you think I'm overreacting, when I returned home one of the posh Saturday papers, in association with a food guide, listed the best 50 places to eat in Britain. Sonya was on it. Most of the places were rubbish. She deserved it.

A weekend in parfait harmony

After the excitement of Sir Clement Freud's 70th birthday party on the train to Worcester race course last weekend and thereafter at the races, where I lost a few hundred pounds, I repaired in my own car to **The Lords of The Manor** in Upper Slaughter, Gloucestershire, leaving the other guests, becoming increasingly merry, to go back to Paddington. The hotel is a 17th-century rectory with endless additions, in Cotswold stone and done up inside in an acceptably twee style, in which chintz figures heavily. Not only were the curtains chintz and the modern brass four-poster bed heavy with chintz, but the bath had a chintz pelmet on top and a chintz curtain at one side. I wondered if you could curtain yourself off while bathing, but it appeared the chintz there was purely decorative.

One window overlooked the wondrous sight of English country-side, rolling hills and a lake, the other had an uninterrupted view of my Ferrari. I have been waiting years for a TV or print journalist to ask me, "What was your greatest mistake in life?" to which I would reply, "Buying a Ferrari." But nobody's asked me.

The restaurant at "Lords of…" gets one star in the Michelin, but nothing in the Ronay. It's somewhere between the two. The room is pleasant and inhabited by young French waiters talking in an accent so thick I could hardly understand them. But they're ever so chic, and far be it from me to complain. My *soupe de poisson* was surprisingly good for land-locked Gloucestershire and would have been better if I'd dared add the garlic, but for the sake of my guest Sarah, a beautiful and posh English actress, I did not.

We both greatly enjoyed the freebie pre-starter. It was parfait of foie gras infused with lemon thyme, buttered brioche and an apple and grape cardamom chutney! My main course was assiette of pork, which suffered by comparison to a similar dish I ate recently at Marco Pierre White's, but you can't expect Marco to be in the Cotswolds as well, can you? Sarah thought her cod baked with mustard with tagliatelle and basil sauce okay, but not more. For dessert, I ordered one orange sorbet between us. It came, surprisingly, on an unbelievably delicious rich chocolate slice. So we ate it anyway.

The next day, breakfast was a bit of a hoot. I asked for fresh orange juice. "Is it squeezed by human hand from oranges here on the premises?" I enquired. The waiter reeled a bit, and said defensively, "It can be". Another waiter then brought the menu, which announced "A choice of freshly squeezed orange, apple and grapefruit juice".

"Ah," I said to Sarah, "I bet they're not doing fresh orange juice for everyone." Surely enough, when ours came it was of a completely different colour and texture to everyone else's! The menu said "oak-smoked kippers and haddock", so I ordered them. A few moments later the waiter came back and said, "No kippers". But it was a pleasant meal anyway and so was dinner, and the staff were exceptional. All in all, it's a smashing place.

My introduction to the **Wyck Hill House** was poor. It was raining. I opened the boot of the Ferrari. The porter stood inside in the warm hall watching through a glass-panelled door. I went moderately bananas. "Dare I say," I announced in a loud voice, "that the purpose of being a porter is to help the guests, not stand idly by." Thus the fellow was inspired to action. Our room was pleasant but odd, saved by a wonderful view of sweeping Gloucestershire countryside, and some very comfortable chairs and a sofa. The bathroom was appallingly small. The public rooms have a nice, not-done-up feel about them. Service at lunch was leisurely – it took 40 minutes for the first course to arrive. Vanessa's cream of asparagus soup was good, but coldish, and her chicken was all right. My roast beef and Yorkshire was okay at best. The wine waiter poured the Château Beychevelle without offering it for tasting, dropping blobs of it on the table as he did so. My chocolate brownies were sickly sweet and didn't taste of chocolate. Wyck Hill House is nice, but erratic. I've stayed in better country hotels, but this place is certainly not offensive.

Lord Montagu of Beaulieu recommended I visit the **Thatched Cottage** in Brockenhurst, Hampshire. Rambling roses up the wall, baskets brimful to overflowing with flowers. We arrived at 12.40pm, announced by the shouts of a driver enraged that I had turned into the parking area without signalling. "That's a man in a hurry," said Robert Matysik, a member of the family that owns the place. "I'm such a terrible driver, I'm used to it," I responded cheerfully. We wandered into the restaurant, all very twee and olde worlde. I turned my attention to the open-plan kitchen, where a basket of small sausage rolls attracted my eye. I took one. This was definitely the best sausage roll I have ever eaten. It was made of New Forest venison, still warm from the oven. I grabbed another. Then we sat down to eat.

There were three home-made breads on offer – not very good and none of them warm. Definitely a minus. An iced blueberry soup was served as a freebie starter with my old friend the venison sausage roll, except now the roll was cold and not the better for it. I had excellent smoked venison for a first course. My main course of lamb wrapped in a rösti of potato, leek and garlic was only fair. The dessert shot things up the scale again. My cup of cappuccino came with a handle of meringue and whipped cream on top. I had two more at the table and three with coffee in the lounge.

I seldom "drop in". I tend to plan. But recently, wending (I am very good at wending) down tiny country roads, I came upon the village of Longstock in Hampshire. Thatched cottages, flowers, an old red phone box and there, coming up on the left, a lovely little pub called **The Peat Spade Inn**. Ivy-covered, nice inn sign – some old twit with a wooden pole with peat on the end – and a Les Routiers sign. It was one o'clock. Ah, lunch, I thought. I parked outside. The second I got in, I reckoned this could be a mistake. No bustle, no happy yokels, no clatter of jolly drinkers. I decided to stay with it anyway. We ordered, and then waited. This is something I am not good at. Forty minutes after we'd entered, bread and butter appeared. It was home-made, and all right. There were 18 customers altogether and a singular lack of food. No good waving my red paper napkin about, I thought, nobody here to see it. Finally, at seven minutes to two, I rose, put £50 on the table and walked slowly out. The waitress appeared at the door. "Your food's nearly ready," she said. "Never mind," I replied as graciously as I could. "Give the change to a local charity." They wrote to me, apologising for the delay, and told me the change, £42.50, would go to the Macmillan nurses who run a hospice for cancer patients. I'm glad a minor benefit accrued to a good cause from my little trip.

In London I am deeply conservative. I retain a list of 37 restaurants with the owners, the maitre d's, the best tables and the phone numbers. I seldom go anywhere else. On my little trips, I make rare journeys into the unknown. I cruised through Lymington, Hampshire. We'd travelled a bit and it was getting cold, so **Peelers Bistro** would have to be it. Wooden floors, wooden chairs, painted beams, pink walls, candles and an overpowering air of quiet, good behaviour. I'll soon put a stop to that, I thought. I sauntered, unannounced, into the kitchen. The chef, Duncan Angus, looked concerned. He assured me, most charmingly, that his fish was very fresh indeed. In the dining room I chose supreme of turbot served with white wine and prawn sauce, £17.95 excluding service. With service, that's £20 for a main course. Not cheap. To start I got some mushy, overripe melon. Vanessa had gazpacho, which was "fine". There followed a very long wait indeed for the main course, possibly a world record. My turbot has a pink sauce in front and a yellow sauce at the back. It was perfectly pleasant. Vanessa pronounced her tomato salad and goat's cheese "very good" – and she's not easy to please.

The restaurant in Gordleton Mill, a hotel in Lymington, Hampshire, is called **Provence**. I found this odd. But I was pleased with my welcome from Melanie Philbey, fiancée of the patron, Toby Hill. Melanie led us over a wooden bridge, stretching across a millpond with waterlilies, to a setting of extreme beauty. We basked in the sun on nice wrought-iron chairs (not plastic, thank goodness), enjoying a half bottle of Château Margaux 1966 at £210 plus service. (I like that.) Eventually, we entered the stone-floored dining room. Very pleasant. I had the set menu at £19.50, commencing with a freebie starter of chilled tomato consommé. There were three different types of bread – all warm, all extremely good. I thought my main course of roast breast of guinea fowl with morels, *pommes fondantes*, foie gras and thyme jus somewhat overrich. The cheeses we ate were delicious. To finish, I had a crème brûlée, which was too sickly, even for me. The service was highly efficient. With our coffee they gave us absolutely exceptional vanilla truffles. I pigged out on them disgracefully. They have adapted the water mill to take seven bedrooms, which are decorated a bit like a motel but pleasant.

Proof of the pudding

The price of the helicopter from Battersea to **Chewton Glen** near Bournemouth had gone up. £246 for the round trip. Philip Amadeus said he'd been losing money. If tradesmen want to make a profit they should charge other people more, not me. We Scorpios are renowned for loyalty, so I bit the bullet and employed him anyway. I'd not been to Chewton Glen for two years. It's probably the best country hotel in Great Britain, if not the most beautiful of buildings. It can't make up its mind if it's a row of houses, a Georgian façade gone wrong or a modern annexe. But inside it's very elegant in a wonderfully camp style. Riding boots and binoculars are carefully left around. An interior Disneyland of *Country Life* rampant. The log fire is real.

On this trip the superb managing director, Peter Crome, actually deigned to give me a first-class suite. On other occasions I'd been put in a standard issue thing, too small and too square. This one had a roof terrace, shape and character. When you sat on the toilet you could see everyone eating in the gardens below. They could see you as well. If that didn't put them off their food, what would?

The hairdryer wasn't in the bathroom, but hidden in a cupboard. You had to bend down and fit it into a 13-amp plug in an inconvenient place. Otherwise it was all excellent. Peter himself was on morning room service when I rang. Just as well, because on my last visit there was confusion.

When I came downstairs, he declared: "I've decided you are my nemesis." I wasn't totally sure what that meant, so I looked it up. "Retributive justice, an agent of downfall," it said. I think he got it right. Peter was once an actor. I could imagine him cheering up the cast after a disastrous opening night.

The food was always reasonable, but on this visit it was much better. Apparently the sous chef, Luke Matthews, was heading the operation in the kitchen. Other than the rented Mercedes from Budget, which was filthy and with the tank nearly a quarter empty, everything was as near perfect as you could hope for. I sat down for Sunday lunch reckoning Chewton Glen was running 10 out of 10. Then disaster struck.

It came in the form of Patrick Floret-Miguet, the head waiter, who took our order. Vanessa asked for local asparagus and smoked haddock. I chose the roast beef. "Could you please," I asked charmingly, "make sure I get fresh Yorkshire pudding, not the stuff that's sitting about degrading itself on the trolley?" M Floret-Miguet sniffed. "I don't think that will be possible," he said firmly. A Winner-trigger switched over inside me. "Why not?" I asked, still nicely, but hiding displeasure. "They manage to make fresh Yorkshire pudding for me at Claridge's, the Dorchester, indeed everywhere I go. Why should it be difficult here? Why not ask in the kitchen?" M Floret-Miguet sneered; he spoke as if to a gross inferior. "Well, sir," he said, "if you're prepared to wait a long time, we can make it specially." "It doesn't take a long time anywhere else," I replied. I later checked with Marco Pierre White. He said it should take at most 20 minutes. Less if the batter was ready, which it would have been, because they'd be resupplying the beef trolley as the Yorkshire ran out.

Peter Crome appeared, smiling, unaware of the incident. "This is what happens when you leave me alone," I explained. He rushed off to the kitchen and spoke to Mr Matthews. "There's no problem at all," he said on his return. After that, things went well. Vanessa declared her asparagus the best she'd had for a long time. She used the word "delicious" twice about her fish. The beef was very good. The Yorkshire pudding was absolutely superb, maybe the best I've ever eaten. The chocolate tart was pleasant but a little bit sickly and without the clear chocolate taste that I'm used to in Assaggi. It was all perfection minus one.

On a previous visit I had felt obliged to make a few observations concerning the blini that accompanied the caviar. Stodgy and too thick. "It's like a muffin," said Vanessa. It completely outweighed the delicacy of the sevruga. I had railed against the blini before. Why, I thought, when I'm kind enough to make a helpful suggestion, do they not act on it? Why are these awful things still being presented? There was also a boo-boo concerning the caviare. It was offered in 30g jars. A stingy amount. I ordered two for each of us. Quite honestly, 100g is a proper caviare portion, but 60g would do. Instead of bringing two separate 30g jars like they do at The Ivy (where blinis are thin and nice), they brought two heaped-up 30g jars, which they assured me included the contents of the other jars scooped out on top. This is equivalent to delivering a fine, vintage wine already decanted and saying, "We threw the bottle away."

On my first visit to Chewton Glen I found the bread ghastly! The film producer Dino De Laurentiis said to me that you could judge a restaurant by its bread. If that was so, Chewton Glen was dead in the water. It was doughy, chewy, tasteless. But things improved. My double-baked Emmental soufflé served with a fondue sauce was totally historic. My friend J Cleese, ex of Weston-super-Mare, also found it exceptional. For my main course, I had braised pork cheeks and lobster flavoured with ginger and lemon grass garnished with young vegetables. It was a sort of Irish stew and the odd mix of lobster and pork worked wonderfully. Other than Vanessa's vegetarian courgettes filled with this and that, which she found pleasant but unexceptional, all the food was very good indeed. This included desserts such as compote of rhubarb and strawberries served with fresh ginger ice cream and an excellent meringue.

To be an annual arbiter of the nation's tastebuds is a heavy responsibility. Hotels and restaurants change with remarkable speed. So I thought it wise to check the quality, or diminishment of it, at Chewton Glen. It's over a year since I passed through their doorway, so the helicopter was summoned.
    I was saddened to discover that they'd fallen into the appalling habit of serving tea alone, without sandwiches and cakes. These came later and after a reminder. All should arrive together. A nearby group included a man with a rubber fish on a display board. He walked round the lounge gleefully squeezing the fish, which made loud "singing" noises. I appreciate quiet. This was gross and tacky. When I mentioned it to Peter Crome he looked pained. "I thought it was quite amusing," he said. I found this particularly odd because that evening Peter came to me after dinner to report that guests had commented I was wearing jeans. "I told them I only look at Mr Winner's face," Peter said. This means Chewton Glen guests accept a man with a singing, rubber fish in the lounge but don't appreciate my beautifully

pressed Versace jeans. Visitors to Chewton Glen are particularly pleasant people, but they're certainly not elegant. "Look at those awful crumpled, beige, cheap cotton trousers," I said to Peter indicating a man nearby. "And what about those shoes! They must be from a car boot sale!"

I thought I was rather natty. Beautiful light blue jeans, a dark blue Briony blazer, a Turnbull & Asser white shirt, my hand-made Bally black suede shoes and a very fine Patek Philipe watch. I certainly wasn't the worst dressed man in the dining room.

"I wear these clothes in Claridges, The Dorchester, and similarly elegant places!" I continued, warming to the subject. "I've worn jeans here for years." "I never noticed," Peter responded. "Does it mention jeans in the hotel rule book?" I asked. It did. Buried away it said, regarding dinner, "No Denim." "Denim, Peter, does not require a capital D," I pointed out.

Let it not be thought Chewton Glen is less than superb. Their Emmental double baked cheese soufflé was one of the best things I've ever eaten. The local lobster from Christchurch was likewise historic in taste and texture. At a later lunch the asparagus was great and the roast beef the best I've had in England. The freshly made-for-me Yorkshire pudding was also unbeatable. I'm glad an overtly pompous head-waiter, who'd previously refused to order new Yorkshire pud for me, had gone. "You frightened him away," said Peter. It's nice to know I'm of service as I progress through life.

There were eleven desserts on the set menu. My caramelised pineapple and marzipan cake topped with home-made rum and raisin ice cream was fine but read better than it tasted. I had a half bottle of Haut Brion 1988 for £225 including service. Chris Davis, who sells to restaurants and me, offered the same half at £52.50. So that's a truly whopping – well over 400 per cent – mark up!

I remain firmly of the view that Chewton Glen is a beautifully run hotel. Even though I waited an hour and a half for an urgent fax one morning and for an hour of that time it was sitting untouched in the fax machine!

After an evening out I returned to their lounge. "I can't believe it!" I thought. "There's a really elegant group." I got up to peer at four people from a different planet to everyone else. It was this newspaper's A A Gill with his exquisitely dressed, beautiful accomplice Nicola Formby and with them film producer Eric Fellner and model girlfriend Laura Bailey. Joyous greetings followed. Peter should pay them to sit around every night. They didn't mind my Versace jeans! Poor old Mr Crome. Can you imagine – A A Gill and me turning up on the same night. There's a co-incidence he can do without!

Nomansland is not a first world war no-go area, it's a village on the edge of the New Forest. The **Restaurant and Bistro Les Mirabelles**, next to the Nomansland Methodist church, was recommended to me by Martin Skaan, the owner of Chewton Glen. It is very Provençal, with hops wreathed around arches, and a French doll on every table. Claude Laage, the co-owner with fellow Frenchman Eric Nicolas, explained this is "instead of flowers, which you have to change every week". Very French, that. There was a very posh, large menu, as well as a blackboard menu headed "Pigs", with a picture of a pig on top. The wine list offered a substantial selection of half bottles, which is excellent and rare. My pastry basket with scallops in it was genuinely tasty, with a nice sauce. Vanessa's John Dory was not on the bone. Fish always tastes less interesting filleted, unless it's fried. Hers tasted of very little, and was accompanied by a sort of raspberry sauce. For dessert I had a *fondant au chocolat*, which was a very good hot chocolate mousse, runny on the inside, crisp on the surface, sitting in a sea of creamy custard.

Let me recommend **Lainston House** near Winchester: excellent food, beautifully decorated 17th-century house, with super-attentive staff.

I phoned Martin Roberts, the boss at the ivy-covered **Greyhound Inn** in the pretty Hertfordshire village of Aldbury. "We're coming to lunch," I said. "Six of us." Stating things as fact is a good way of getting what you want. Mr Roberts was unconcerned. "We're used to hundreds on Sunday," he said. That did not augur well. On arrival we were shown to a wooden table in a front room overlooking the village, with a bookcase and an old fireplace. The first thing I tasted was someone else's duck pâté. It was admirable. Nice texture. The bread was good, even though the butter was in foil. I had potato wedges with a chilli and garlic dip. The potatoes reminded me of World War II when food was food and not chemical twaddle. My lamb was the most generous portion I've ever seen, set around a large bone. It was every bit as good as the meat from my butcher, R Allen of Mount Street, or at Claridge's or The Dorchester. Home-made chips appeared for me, with some really old-fashioned, lovely cauliflower cheese and robust carrots and beans. Treacle tart was like schooldays: thick, not heavy on finesse, but tiptop. All this is pretty remarkable for a pub. "In high season we do 2,500 customers a week," said Martin. "We've pushed about 300 meals through today so far." It is rare that quantity and quality go hand in hand.

When I was at my Quaker boarding school in Letchworth, my parents would come down at weekends and drive me in the Rover to an excellent lunch at the **George and Dragon** hotel in Baldock, Hertfordshire. Baldock was a nice town with lovely old tearooms, a lot of good antique shops and a delightful 1930s cinema called the Astonia. I decided, some 47 years later, to visit it again. You now enter Baldock through horrid housing estates that I knew as green fields, the Astonia cinema has gone and there are no good antique shops. But the George and Dragon looked much the same, with wisteria still climbing up the front. Inside, the restaurant was full of ghastly, cheap little chairs and tables. Rock Muzak played constantly. We waited a very long time before menus arrived. There was a normal menu, a vegetarian menu and a vegan menu, lots of things to choose from. After another long wait came some of the worst bread I've ever seen. Vanessa's melon was okay, my soup was watery and undrinkable. Vanessa took one bite of her cashew nut paella, pulled a face and said, "Revolting". My 8oz fillet steak was edible, not good. I got the waiter back to clear the table by shouting "Thank you", otherwise we'd still be there. After another long wait, I got the worst chocolate fudge cake I have ever seen or tried to eat in my life, Vanessa a poor fruit salad. This was a memorably, absolutely horrific meal.
PS *This is now closed, and reopens soon under new management.*

Instead of driving to The Ivy for Saturday lunch, Vanessa redirected me to the **Alford Arms** in Frithsden. It was very pretty. White stucco, on the edge of a charming Hertfordshire village. Excellent countryside. Trestle tables outside were too communal and too uncomfortable for one in my delicate condition: I think the medical term is egomania. Inside I surveyed the menu. For a starter I chose roast ham, bubble-and-squeak hollandaise and poached egg. Then I had the fish cake, followed by bread-and-butter pudding, which was nice. The warm chocolate brownie was very good too, crisp outside and then runny in the middle. I would describe the food as robust to highly pleasant – good Middle England fodder.

I was awakened at 7.15am by loud moaning and groaning. Not a companion with food poisoning, but something in the pipes. There was whistling, then a rumble, a sound like an old tugboat motor dying, high wind noises. This was at the **Pendley Manor Hotel**, Tring, Hertfordshire, described in the brochure as "a setting which speaks of tranquillity". The peak of non-tranquillity continued until 7.50am, then subsided, but for the next hour strange noises came back, as if a monster, now caged, was trying to fight his way out. Forced to rise, I read the brochure further. The hotel (built in 1872) had been "transformed to its former glory, allowing guests to enjoy once more the distinguished elegance and beauty of the Victorian era". Breakfast was ordered at 9.09am and arrived at

9.14am. A world record for a cooked breakfast. I thought it was pretty good. Nine pats of unwrapped butter, a small but nice portion of egg, sausage, tomato and mushrooms, and orange juice they assured me was fresh. The general manager, Mr Michael Tadros, was charming and very apologetic about my being disturbed. Well, it wasn't his fault. Craydown Ltd, who own the hotel, obviously thought Victorian plumbing carried its own elegance.

In Manchester, on a tour to meet the people, I stayed at the **Meridien Victoria & Albert**. This is a delightfully froufrou, overdecorated oddity with rooms named after Granada TV series. My suite was the Wealth of the Windsors, which I was told had something to do with *Brideshead Revisited*. The shower curtain had great swags and curls on it, as if designed for a grand ballroom. I was particularly impressed with Simon Murphy, the deputy manager, who'd obviously been told to watch my every move. He was cheery and hospitable.

At **Yang Sing** in Manchester I thought the food was tasty, though it was all a bit gooey for Vanessa. I tried a roast pigeon, which appeared on my plate with a dummy white swan. Even the pigeon head was sitting there staring at me. With it was a mustard sauce and a spicy sauce. I had Peking-style dumplings, asparagus in a Sichuan sauce, bean curd with two sauces, prawns and scallops with a light saffron sauce, spicy nut dumplings, corn dumplings, spring onion in a pancake and more. This was one of my few dinners ever in Manchester – pleasing, I hope, for those who think I solely haunt the effete and overstylised south.

Liberty's in Teddington High Street, Middlesex, is owned by a movie art director, so it's done in pleasant brick with old photos and is very spacious. I ate a lot of bacon and cheese potato skins, a few hamburgers and some nice desserts. The staff were exceptionally pleasant.

Not many happy returns

I was in Teddington high street, in Middlesex, not one of Britain's architectural splendours. We had checked out a photographic studio for our film. It was lunchtime. "That's a very good Italian restaurant," said our location manager, Michael Harvey, pointing to the **Trattoria Sorrento** next door.

Michael is a splendid fellow, but food judgement is not one of his specialities.

"When I worked at Thames Television," he continued, "they brought people here who had been made redundant."

"Did they bring Benny Hill?" I asked as we walked in.

"I've been in this restaurant when Benny Hill was eating," said Michael.

That's not a recommendation. I was a Benny Hill fan. His "murder" in the name of political correctness was one of the most shameful idiocies of British show business. My friend, the film director Lewis Gilbert, once made a movie with Benny, and gave him a lift to work each morning. "What did you have for breakfast?" he asked.

"Soup," said Benny. "Why soup?" said Lewis. "I go to the super-market and buy cans that the labels have come off because they're cheaper," said Benny. "It's nearly always soup." He was extremely rich then, bless him.

Memories of Benny flooded back, intruded upon by a rather surly Italian waiter telling us we couldn't sit at a table for six as we were five people. It was next to an enormous layout for a birthday party, so I retired quietly to a table further away.

The Trattoria Sorrento is a downmarket cousin of the Trattoria Terrazza group that first made me aware of Italian restaurants in the early 1960s. Chianti bottles hung from the ceiling; there were deer antlers, pink tablecloths and, behind us, a mural. A waiter pointed: "There is Venice, there is Milan, there is Naples." "A montage of Italy," obliged my associate producer, Ron Purdie. "Set lunch is £7.95, children half-price," I announced. "Roll your trousers up, quick," Mr Purdie said to Michael Harvey.

On the menu were things you never see any more: egg mayonnaise, avocado vinegarette (sic) and prawn cocktail. There was a list of "To-day's specials" on the menu and another on a blackboard. They were both different.

My bread roll was disgusting. Vanessa said: "The olives are very well flavoured," but I don't like anything where you have to take a stone out – I am too delicate. My starter sardines were mediocre, tasteless and looked peculiar. The heads, almost parted from the body, seemed to be in agony. Vanessa couldn't find much taste in her asparagus, either.

In the old days, food wasn't over-preserved, chemicalised at birth, long frozen. Whether you ate in posh place or poor, the basic content was similar. Today there is the most enormous difference between "well-bred" veggies and animals and the mass-produced. A whole stratum of people exists that rarely, if ever, experiences what real food tastes like. This is sad.

Michael Harvey, the culinary optimist, interrupted my reverie. "This is excellent," he said, devouring his mushrooms in garlic butter. Then the birthday party came in, 16 of them, middle England to the core. I mean that as a compliment. They fitted in perfectly with the white pebble-dash walls, the two ship's life belts hanging from the ceiling (we were near the Thames), the stale, strung-up salami, and the lanterns, some with green bulbs, some with white.

My main-course trout came without lemon. It was perfectly cooked, but I didn't like it. The service was excellent. They quickly brought me a large tumbler of ice. Vanessa said her salmon wasn't bad, but I thought it odd that they served cold mayonnaise with hot salmon. The potatoes were all right, the mangetout very good.

The birthday party people had eaten their first course and, as wine flowed, the noise level became louder. Not out of order, but more laughter, raised voices. Men with ties and white shirts with spectacles in the pockets; women with pearls and carefully done hair, flowered, striped or blue dresses.

It was getting busy now, you had to fight for service. I'm good at that. I chose Italian trifle from the dessert trolley. It was pretty good except for the crust, which was sickly and horrible. Vanessa left her fruit salad, saying, "It's okay, but it has this liquor with it I'm not quite sure about."

The birthday party group had fallen silent as they ate their main course. There were two birthday ladies, Margaret and Sarah. I thought they all seemed very decent people. In the street, one of my group told me there was no lock on the gents' toilet door.

On my next visit to Teddington, I was surprised to see my review, much blown up, displayed on the window of the Trattoria Sorrento. On closer reading, I realised they'd altered the text. The headline, Not many happy returns, had been changed to Many happy returns. The article itself had been doctored to make it favourable. A letter to the local trading-standards officer had the piece down in seconds. But I have to admire their cheek. Nice to know they thought people would care what I'd written.

At the **Fishermen's Hut Organic Food Restaurant** in Twickenham, Middlesex, a printed note on the table announced that all the fish served was amazingly fresh and that everything other than the fish was organic. I had a feeling we'd struck lucky. We were given some sundried tomato and olive bread – scrumptious. While waiting for the food, I strolled round the restaurant checking out other customers' plates. A party of five children and four adults were just getting served. Two of the kids, aged five or so, acquired a portion of mixed grilled fish. I stuck my hand in and took two pieces. A lady said indignantly, "It's their lunch!" as well she might. I retired, wounded but not deterred. (To make up for it, I paid their entire bill, which, as it was grandma's birthday and they'd had champagne, came to £187.) My fish soup was all right, although it would have been better served hot. I thought my plaice was a tiny bit overdone. It was pleasant, not as juicy as the fish at Wilton's. But the whole meal was very good indeed for a quick stopover in Twickenham.

Fawsley Hall, managed by The Halcyon hotel in London, is bizarre. In the brochure, the photographs showed what appeared to be a historic house tastefully converted to hotel use. Photographs can be deceptive. But, ever adventurous, I drove there through delightfully unspoilt Northamptonshire countryside, down tracks that coated the Ferrari with mud. The brochure describes the house as a "panoply of styles". I'd say a fair old mess, aided and abetted by poor decoration and tarting up. The dining room was high-ceilinged with leaded windows, a tapestry, a fireplace regrettably not in use, and some stone walls and some plaster walls. My deep-fried salt cod with a garlic velouté was excellent. Vanessa had asparagus and herb risotto with a red wine sauce, which was "tasty". The service was very quick indeed. My main-course roast pigeon and braised savoy cabbage with foie gras and lentil sauce was good. The food's the best thing at Fawsley Hall. The chef is Tim Johnson, under the consultancy of Nico Ladenis.

"Excuse me!" I shouted downstairs to the receptionist. "There are two people in the lounge here without a drink. Can you tell me what year they arrived?" At this the manager, who had been having a long conversation about wine with a customer and ignoring me, came running. After that the service was good. I was at the **Langley Castle**, a tarted-up 14th-century pile in Langley-on-Tyne, Northumberland. The North is peopled by delightful residents, but the food is generally Langley Castle-style. Grandly described hors d'oeuvres were six bowls of dried-up sausage and tinned beans, followed, believe it or not, by a heavy sorbet. The duck was over-cooked strips, the apple tart so solid you needed a power drill to break the pastry. When the charming, efficient young waitress said, "I hope you enjoyed your meal, sir", I replied, honestly, "The service was excellent".

At **Jackies Tearooms** in Burford, Oxfordshire, "established in 1870", there was a large selection of cakes and pies on view. "Are these made here?" I asked the waitress. "Oh yes," she said proudly. I took a slice of four or five and went to my table to have them with the Earl Grey. The chocolate cake was poor. "I'd like to discuss things with the chef," I said. A pleasant chubby young man named Maurice Franklin wandered out. "This chocolate is cake mix," I volunteered. "Yes," said Maurice, his shame uncovered, "but all the others are mine." And very excellent the rest of them were. "What's in the Mars Bar cake?" I asked. "That's a secret," Maurice replied. So I went back and got a couple of Mars Bar cakes. "What do you think's in them?" I asked Vanessa. "Rice Krispies," she said. "Maurice," I said, "you have Rice Krispies in your Mars Bar cake!" Maurice smiled. He did not seem unduly concerned that his recipe was out and might now fall into the hands of Nico Ladenis. "And sultanas," he added, all secrecy abandoned.

Knight Club

It was on a Sunday film reconnaissance that my production designer suggested the **Sir Charles Napier** near Chinnor in Oxfordshire. I rang up. The owner, a nice lady called Julie Griffiths, said: "We'll squeeze you in. How many will you be?" "Six," I replied, thinking this would cause a problem. It did. Julie could only manage two. On a recent Sunday, years later, I booked with her daughter, the equally charming Caroline. I told my neighbour, the lyricist Don Black, that I was going. He said: "You won't like it. The tables are very close together." On the way I phoned again. "Are the tables close together?" I asked. "Not yours," said Caroline. "We're not that silly."

We arrived at a pebbly car park to find the flintstone and brick inn next to a tacky housing estate. Julie showed us to a nice table by the window, facing a paved terrace and guests' cars. I was introduced to Caroline's husband, Chris, who does the wines. Chris said he wouldn't offer me the normal wines by the glass, he'd bring a special bottle and finish it himself later as a treat. "I want you to try it," he said, "because it's quite an eclectic choice." "Don't give me a test, I'm useless," I pleaded. It was a very smooth Hamilton Russell, South African Pinot Noir 1998. Chris altered his description of it to "capricious".

I ordered casserole of snails à la catalane. Why, I don't know. You have to be a twit to order a typical Spanish dish at an English pub in the middle of Oxfordshire. To compound my silliness I ordered a main course of bouillabaisse with saffron potatoes. Why didn't I order English stuff like roast pork with crackling (which I love), or roast beef, or even braised oxtail? I soon wish I had. There was a very dead bit of toast stuck in the middle of my starter. The snails were small, rubbery and of no taste whatsoever. The surrounding chopped-up veggies were quite nice. The bouillabaisse was poor. The white fish was all right but uninteresting, the sauce or soup with it was of no taste I've ever associated with bouillabaisse. Dull in the extreme.

Miss Lid enjoyed (though was not crazy about) both her starter of timbale of crab with lemon juice and her main course of pan-fried scallops with celeriac and truffle ravioli. She also praised her fresh orange juice.

The desserts were very good indeed. Miss Lid had hot date cake with toffee sauce. I thought it was terrific. Not overfancy, solid, lovely taste and texture. My pithivier of almonds and dried fruit had good flaky pastry and was a pleasant experience. There were no silly red squiggle decorations around the plate. Just two excellent, solid desserts deserving top marks.

The other diners were very nice people. There was a good atmosphere. Guests are obviously deeply loyal to the Sir Charles Napier. They were concerned I should write well of it. I liked them all, even though I feel compelled to write as I find.

The oddest thing was the bill. I never look at bills. I just pay them. But one of the food guides noted a surcharge of £1 when a second starter was taken in place of a main course. Quite fair, I thought. Miss Lid had done that, so I checked the bill. First I found we'd been overcharged 75p on our two starters. Not a lot, but overcharging nevertheless. Julie apologised by fax. Then I noticed the scallops and the bouillabaisse came, as per the menu, to £24.25. But we'd been charged £31. When we queried it we were told £4.25 was added to the scallops to make them a main course. And a further £2.50 was for the vegetables. But vegetables were included without charge for all main courses. Miss Lid's starter had been upgraded to a main course by a surcharge of almost 50%. Surely that qualified it as a main course and for free veggies like everyone else. Well, it didn't. Thank goodness I don't look at bills very often. The mental turmoil would be too great. Even for me.

My mob visited the **Chequers Inn** at Fingest, in Oxfordshire, for Sunday lunch when on a location recce. It's a pretty place – the dining room is pink with oak beans, dried hops and wheelback chairs with padded seats. I chose the honeydew melon gondola, which had a 1950s look – sliced with a bit of orange bent over a stick topped by a glacé cherry. The soup was pea and mint, "like posh mushy peas". The beef and Yorkshire pud came swimming in gravy; the carrots and beans were overdone. It's a nice enough place – not a high rating on the Sunday lunch score, but not a disaster.

To the Manoir borne

We arrived at Raymond Blanc's **Le Manoir aux Quat'Saisons** in Great Milton, Oxfordshire, at 4.20pm. We were very well greeted. There were a lot of customers in every public room. It was absolutely crowded. "Who are these people?" I asked the lady showing us round. "They've stayed for lunch," she said. "They're making a day of it." Personally I like to see one old colonel asleep in the corner.

Our rooms were in a kind of unused stable block, except that it was purpose-built, adjacent to the 15th-century manor house, to accommodate new suites. Mine was called Opium. It was Japanese with huge, beige, suede sofa cushions on the floor, Japanese-style trellis work and, outside, a little walled garden with a pond and a Buddha. Rain was pouring down.

Vanessa said: "It's a sexy bed." "Deep red ceiling, wood with red lights, endless cushions on the bed," I dictated. The final touch was a bunch of twigs standing 6ft high against the wall. I'd ordered tea and sandwiches as soon as we arrived. Twenty-three minutes later, the tea arrived. Normally the tea and sandwiches come together, so I said, "Take the tea away and when the sandwiches are ready bring it again." An extremely snooty French waiter departed grumpily. At 4.55, I rang reception and said: "What's going on? We came here 35 minutes ago and we haven't got anything." At 4.59, tea and sandwiches arrived. A lady appeared and said: "I'm the duty manageress. We normally send the tea a few minutes before the sandwiches." I said: "This wasn't a few minutes before. The idea is you have the tea and the sandwiches together." I paused. "They meld," I added.

"That's a sandwich!" said Vanessa appreciatively as the management team departed. She was right. The sandwiches were as good as you could get. There were 32 of them on two plates, one vegetarian, one not vegetarian. They were totally fresh. They didn't have that frozen or slightly moist-from-a-cloth-feel that you get even at Claridge's. But Claridge's does boast a sensational four-piece girl orchestra at Sunday teatime. When I first heard them they were not all playing the same melody and, if they were, they were not all in tune. They have become immaculate, but not better. They are a great draw. The place was packed when I went. But Raymond Blanc's sandwiches beat theirs by far. If only he'd thrown in some twanging Japanese instruments plucked by costumed Orientals sitting on the floor.

There were no tissues in my bathroom and no shampoo. Hearing me dictate this, Vanessa looked at a sachet of "Bath Soak". On the back it said it was Body Wash and Bath Soak. It also said in tiny letters that it was "A mild moisturising shower gel for body and hair care". Which could mean it was a shampoo. In the old days shampoo was labelled shampoo and was better for it.

On this occasion we didn't have dinner at Le Manoir, although I have eaten many main meals there before. They were never less than good and, on occasion, historic. I particularly enjoyed the time Raymond had a crying baby removed for me and wheeled endlessly round the garden by a liveried waiter.

Breakfast was superb. Amazingly fresh and tasty croissants; brilliant eggs; sausages and mushrooms perfect; Vanessa's poached eggs excellent. Three delicious home-made jams in open bowls with spoons. Vanessa tried a chocolate croissant and thought it was wonderful. Beautiful crockery. This was legendary.

Later, as he was showing us his cookery school at Le Manoir, Raymond said: "You'd expect the French to understand breakfast." I failed to grasp that. The French are not famous for their cooked breakfasts. Raymond took us on a tour of the rooms. One, near ours, called Snow Queen, had tissues. "Not like in my bathroom," I said snottily. "There is no question your room has tissues," said Raymond and insisted on going in. "Oh no!" he said, finding none there.

The variety of rooms, all incredibly well done, is extraordinary. One had romantic murals with two baths facing each other like a love seat; others matched names on the doors. Raymond has, with great devotion and pride of ownership, turned Le Manoir into an extraordinary, really pleasant, eating and living experience.

As we went back to collect our bags, the rain still pouring down, I saw a row of umbrellas in motion on the other side of my little garden's brick wall. No people could be observed. Just umbrellas going right to left. As if invisible men were holding them. They'd have liked the breakfast too.

I had a call from my very dear friend, the wit and brilliant writer Laurence Marks. "I'd like you to have lunch with Maurice [Gran, his television writing partner] and me at Le Manoir aux Quat'Saisons," said Laurence, suggesting a Sunday many weeks ahead. "I'll ask Nigel Dempster." That was nice: I greatly like Nige. Apparently, Messrs Marks and Dempster met on a freebie hotel trip and hit it off splendidly. Marks and Gran are famous as two of television's most successful writers and producers.

Lunch was superb, the best I've ever eaten at Le Manoir. There were eight courses, including freebies, coffee and chocs. Watercress salad with pan-fried foie gras, baked Périgord truffle in a brioche, pan-fried sea bass with roasted langoustine, roast loin of venison... I could go on.

Fat of the land

The B4027 runs north off the M40, shortly before you reach a hideous roundabout on the outskirts of Oxford. It is the sort of road I always feel greatly relieved to come upon; it smacks of the past, when tracks wobbled about between fields and occasional little villages.

It was about 1pm – lunchtime. I had made no reservations. We passed a ramshackle farm: barns with corrugated-iron roofs, cracked concrete courtyards and a sign saying "**Royal Oak Farm**: Teas".

"It said light lunches, too," said Vanessa.

"Let's try it," I suggested.

"Go on and see if we can find something better," Vanessa replied.

But I was already backing the Ferrari to go and investigate. I crossed a courtyard beset with fountains and strange garden ornaments of girls sitting on poles, and walked into the farm shop. A sign announced vacancies for children in the Jan Weller playgroup. I ventured through an open door that led to a concrete path through a back-garden area full of animals, many with pens named after them. There were African pygmy goats: Baldrick, born in March 1995, Capricorn, and many more. A large number of ducks, cockerels, pigs and other animalia abounded.

At the end of the path was a hut. In it were four tables, with four chairs round each and, at the rear, an opening to a kitchen. Nobody was there, but one of the tables was full of home-made cakes and biscuits that looked highly attractive. I walked back into the shop and the farmer's wife, Nathalie Soames, appeared. She offered an enormous array of home-made soups. I checked that one, at least, had no meat stock, Vanessa being almost vegetarian, and established that there were various quiches and ploughman's lunch. Drooling over the cakes, I assured Vanessa it would be terrific.

Vanessa's lentil and thyme soup would have graced any Michelin-starred establishment, as would my leek and orange. Bethany, the chef's three-year-old daughter, established herself. She had already told us which table to sit at.

"I have tea the same as my daddy," she announced. "I don't have sugar, I only have milk."

I accepted this fact. "Are those scones?" I asked.

"Yes," said Bethany.

"Are those more scones?" I continued, pointing to brown and white bags on the table.

"No, those are goat and chicken food, because people buy them to feed the animals."

Bethany asked for apple juice and occasionally said loudly: "Where is my apple juice?" Then she went to a full yell, "Mummy, get my apple juice!" followed by: "Is it coming, mummy?" When it did, she bashed the table to show exactly where she wanted it. This kid could take over any time I have a week off.

I had chosen a tomato, cheese and onion quiche; Vanessa had a ploughman's lunch. Both came with fresh salad. Mrs Soames, who had frizzy hair and was wearing a Royal Oak Farm T-shirt, offered salad dressing of mustard and garlic, spicy herb, Californian tomato, roasted garlic and mayonnaise, or salad cream. Not bad for a hut off a B road. The quiche was terrific and the cakes amazing. I'd tried a lemon and lime cookie before lunch. Now I had a chocolate fudge slice, some coffee sponge and a chocolate-orange chip shortbread. I started on the chocolate fudge slice, which was hard to cut, but unbelievably delicious. They all were.

Bethany was having lettuce and ham. "And I want tea," she added. "I'll wait for my daddy to get it." Then, after a brief silence: "I've got a big shirt on today."

I walked through the garden, where they serve teas and lunches on less rainy days, to see five ducks ganging up on another duck. They held it down and pecked at its face. Death Wish in animal land. When I came back, Mrs Soames explained it was an attempt to mate, and told me the cockerels also think they're ducks, so they "tread" the ducks as well. Life on the land is riveting. They have 900 free-range chickens, and sell lamb and game off the farm, as well as wild boar and ostrich.

I was tempted to have meringue and clotted cream, with maybe a bit of pear and butterscotch flan, but narrowly chose against it.

This place is a real find. If you want a meal that tastes like food, and not like over-mucked-about plate decoration, get out your road map – the nearest town is Headington, Oxfordshire. And bring me back a chocolate fudge slice, will you?

The very posh **Lovell's**, in an old farmhouse in Old Minster Lovell, Oxfordshire, serves first-rate food. And what extraordinary value! A seven-course dinner for £27.50, ex service – although they did count the cheese beignets, which came in the bar with the drinks, as one of the courses. A nice bit of turbot, venison, which is usually rather difficult, done very well. And six cheeses preceded by an odd discourse from the owner's daughter, a pretty girl. She told us the exact order in which the cheeses should be eaten. I ignored it, of course, and went straight for the one I liked best, getting to some of the others in order of Winner-sight-appreciation.

Le Petit Blanc in Oxford is a cheerful, buzzy place. White ceilings with red walls, red chairs. But ghastly Muzak of some deranged idiot overblowing a wind instrument. Piped music should be banned. If it has to permeate, let it be classical piano only. I had a crab and lobster spring roll (very tasty), then an enormous Oxford sausage, apparently pork marinated in beer, with parsley crust potatoes. It was excellent. Vanessa had spiced potato cake with chick peas, tomato and coriander, which she said was extremely good. I finished with lemon tart.

Before my humorous and informative (!) lecture at the Oxford Union, I had the misfortune to dine in **Whites**, a local restaurant. This was a nightmare. We got there at 7.15pm, quite enough time to eat and be out by 8.40. Eventually the menus arrived, but then there was no one to take our orders. We had to wait a long time for the food. I would have liked dessert, but by then it was 8.30pm. So we ordered coffee and petits fours instead. Ten minutes later, we still had no coffee, no petits fours. In one hour and 25 minutes they'd struggled to serve two courses, appallingly. Food, service and restaurant atmosphere – totally diabolical.

Reading that I was going to the **Mason Arms** in South Leigh, as guest of my friend the television writer Laurence Marks, Robert Warner of Woodstock, Oxfordshire, wrote to me, saying: "You will either love it . . . or loathe it." I loathed it. It was the most extraordinary meal I've ever had. Not because of the food, but because of the bizarre behaviour of the "host", Gerry Stonhill, and his waiter, Roger Castel.

The pub itself is vastly, but not unpleasantly, overdecorated. There are photos, plates, prints, books, stuffed birds, carefully placed cigar boxes and, pretentiously laid out on a table, "every armagnac from 1919 to 1993", explained Marks.

The whole meal was ruined by constant, pathetic repartee from Gerry or Mr Castel. I came to have lunch with my friend Laurence Marks, a quiet-spoken gent who's always interesting. Not to participate in buffoon dialogue with the staff.

The problem with Gerry is someone obviously told him he was a character and he believed them. That was a mistake.

Country ways

They were kind enough to put a large white cross on the croquet lawn at **Ston Easton Park**, Somerset, so my helicopter pilot could see it and not deposit me at the wrong hotel. I took this transport (50 minutes instead of two-and-a-half-hours) because there was a rail strike and I assumed the roads would be packed. As it happens, they weren't, and I looked down on fast-moving traffic some £1,500 the poorer.

The manager, Mr Kevin Marchant, came to greet us with a member of staff. As the luggage was being taken upstairs I caught sight of tea laid out on a round table, circling a bowl of flowers, in the highly impressive Georgian lounge. This was too much for me. I immediately started eating. It was the best tea I have ever had. I am normally a pig, but on this occasion I excelled myself. There were egg mayonnaise and cucumber sandwiches, carrot cake and coffee cake, éclairs and meringues, fruit cake and ginger cake, scones and a great deal more. Every item was utterly exceptional in its quality. The Earl Grey was served in a splendid room in first-rate crockery. Dominating the lounge (other than me, of course) was a bust of Pitt the Younger by Nollekens. This is a splendid, supercilious figure, one that I see most days of my life because I bought an identical Pitt at the sale of the Londonderry House contents in Park Lane in the early 1960s. After I got it, the curator of Kenwood House told me he'd been instructed to buy it, and could he have it? I said no. The bust was, I am told, taken from Pitt's death mask by Nollekens, who had always been refused a sitting when the master was alive. Mine has a City of London's Police helmet, presented to me by the commissioner, sitting on it. Pitt, of course, was Chancellor of the Exchequer aged 23 and prime minister at 24. He made a taciturn tea companion.

Ston Easton is an architectural gem dating from the mid-18th century. When I had tea the next day with its admirably hands-on owners, Peter and Christine Smedley, they explained they'd bought it from Sir William Rees-Mogg. "Didn't know he had that sort of money," I muttered, stuffing down a bakewell tart. Apparently he got it in wrecked condition, sold it on to the Smedleys who lived there, then "as needs must" they opened it as a hotel in 1982. It is superbly decorated, in unison and with great taste, although my bathroom was terrible. Not only was it small, it looked like every item had come from a warehouse sale on a bad day. They've had a number of famous people to stay. "Terry Wogan and Larry Hagman," said Christine helpfully, "and Cary Grant." "Before he died, of course," added her husband, Peter.

Dinner, I'm sorry to say, was less impressive than the tea. We had home-made courgette and dill soup which was all right. But the Dover sole, oddly served with slices of hot grapefruit on it, had definitely died of exhaustion after being on a lengthy diet. However, I greatly enjoyed (or should I say endured!) the gems of conversation from other tables. "Was it under British mandate at the time?" "Oh yes, very peaceful, a lot of Palestinians and very few Jews." The lime sorbet was good and the room was elegant, but I'd call the food English-boring.

Given the Bird

A nice group met the helicopter as it landed on the lawn by **Dovecliff Hall**, a hotel outside Burton-on-Trent. They were the owners, Brian Moore and his wife Jeanne and their son Nick. "I never thought the day would come when Michael Winner came up here to Staffordshire to this hotel," said Jeanne. "I never thought it would happen." "All good things come to an end," I responded.

In the lobby, a delightful old lady was playing the piano. She looked as if she came from a 1950s movie with Joyce Grenfell and Alastair Sim. The whole place had that black-and-white atmosphere of times sadly gone by. Amazingly, Mary Green had not been brought in just to play for me. There was a wedding and she was the icing on the cake. Brian explained that after he'd spent 30 years in the family engineering business making taps and dies, his children fancied catering. Well, let's face it, taps and dies are not everybody's idea of a laugh. So he bought a couple of restaurants and then this pleasant country-house hotel.

"Sir Edward Mosley used to live down the road," said Jeanne proudly. "This is the best she can drag up for the area," I dictated into my tape. "And it's Oswald Mosley anyway." Jeanne changed the subject. "We only allow residents in for Saturday lunch," she said. How this squared with a golden wedding of 13 people in one room and a wedding of 40 in the other, all non-residents, I didn't like to ask.

Our room was very cheerful. Views of gardens and grounds, not over-tarted-up. They had the taps the wrong way round on the washbasin, hot on the right. To make it worse, the "label" had come off, so I nearly scalded myself. Lunch was in a conservatory. I chose "rillettes of pork-belly pork cooked in its own juices, shredded set and served with pickled vegetables." It took longer to read than to eat. It was fine. For my main course I had baked supreme of chicken carved on to an asparagus sauce. Vanessa thought her sea bass was very good. My chicken was all right but ordinary. The veg were excellent.

"The meat comes from an old-fashioned butcher in Alfreston with an abattoir at the back of the shop," the son, Nick, told us. "So he killed this chicken, did he?" I asked. "Ah no, the chicken, that's the only thing he doesn't do." "How would he kill a cow?" asked Vanessa, who doesn't eat red meat. "He definitely kills cows at the back of the shop," said Nick. "He kills the lamb, the pigs, the beef. He's got this large electrical abattoir." "That's enough!" said Vanessa. "What's he like as a person?" "Very religious," said Nick. The pastry chef, Mrs Samantha Dowie, came and told me how to make a chilled praline parfait served with a raspberry coulis. It was splendid to eat, but I never understand recipes. That's why we have chefs – to do the menial work.

We went for a walk by a river, not too strenuous, of course, and back for tea. Very fresh sandwiches, real old-English tea with scones, chocolate cake and strawberry tart. The large wedding group appeared and asked if I'd be photographed with the bride. The next day daughter Tania was there. She'd been off duty. "What's your function?" I asked. "Mum says I fill in for whoever hasn't turned up," Tania said. For some reason, Mary was still tinkling away. "Do you just play the piano?" I asked. "I have an electric organ as well," said Mary. It was extremely delightful, the whole thing. Another world, really. Went back to normal when I left.

At a snail's pace

The location reconnaissance is standard procedure in motion pictures. You go around looking for real places in which to make your movie. You drive along checking what a location manager has already found, or knocking on doors saying: "What a lovely house, I'd love to film here." You meet a marvellous variety of people

The best day for this is Sunday. There is less traffic to hold you up and people are more likely to be at home to answer the doorbell. An essential is lunch.

"Ah!" I hear you say, "I bet with Winner they get well fed."

Forget it – they don't. Lunch is a necessity, not a luxury: something to fortify you so you can carry on the job, spending as little time eating as possible. You can't book ahead as you know not where you may be; you just travel and at the appropriate time say, often desperately: "Where shall we stop for lunch?"

I have eaten more lousy food on location recces than anywhere else. Only rarely do you get lucky. On a recent occasion we had turned off the A3 and were cruising through Cobham, Surrey, on the way to points south. There was me, my associate producer, Ron Purdie, my assistant producer, John Blezard, and my location manager, Michael Harvey. We passed the **Snail** – no, not good enough. On the right was the Copper Chimney.

"That looks nice," said Mr Purdie, who was driving. But it had gone by. Facing us was the Vermont Exchange. We pulled into the parking area. It fell to me to check it out, rather like they sent canaries down the mines to see if there was air: if they came out dead, there was not; if they lived, it was safe for others to follow.

The Vermont Exchange did not take my fancy. Loud Muzak, interior neon signs. I got into the car and we headed back up the A245. We would have to make do with the Snail. Outside, it was rather pretty – fake Tudor with a lot of plant pots on the eaves; a wheelbarrow full of flowers up there, too.

"This definitely has a better class of parked cars," I observed as we pulled to a halt. Once again, I scouted the situation. Not posh, ghastly Muzak, but beggars can't be choosers.

"Table for four," I said to Pamela, a pretty dark-haired girl wearing glasses. She indicated a round one. "How about that?" I asked, pointing to a table for eight.

"That's all right," she replied. I went and beckoned my gang inside. We sat down and Pamela took our drinks order.

"Can we do the meal?" I asked. "We're in a rush."

"I'll be with you in a second," said Pamela.

"You mean you don't do the food?" I queried.

"Yes, but I need another pad," she said before returning with a blackboard menu.

"Is the soup made here?" I asked.

"It's fresh, sir, but it's not actually made here. It's made in Belgium."

That I couldn't figure at all. I chose the soup of the day – asparagus. If that was made in Belgium, it's a very good reason for leaving the European Union. Mr Blezard and Mr Harvey pronounced their Thai soup excellent. Mr Purdie was eating prawns "Slightly overcooked," he said. "Difficult to peel."

Another very pretty girl, a blonde, came over. Her name was Elizabeth.

"Are you the manageress?" I asked.

"I'm not old enough," she said

"How old are you?"

"Seventeen," was the reply.

One thing's for sure: the waitresses looked better than the food. They were highly efficient and charming, too.

My main course was fillet steak with sauce diane, medium rare, with vegetables, £12.95. The steak was just okay, the sauce unbelievably awful: brownish muck with funny mushrooms floating about. Mr Harvey had chosen fish mornay. He declared it tender and tasty. I'd also ordered some rabbit with prunes. The rabbit tasted of jelly, no firmness or substance, revolting. My roast potatoes had a rubbery skin – you chewed for ever and nothing much happened. Mr Purdie had duck.

"How is it?" I asked.

"It's cooked to exactly the right consistency," he said, then moved his hands in a circle over the plate as if he was going to levitate it. "Lacks flavour," he added.

None of us dared try dessert. The coffee was all right.

The real manageress asked: "Everything okay with your meals?" and wisely moved off before I could answer.

Quite honestly, if this is how the other half eats, I'd rather not know about it.

This has now changed hands and the new management assure me that standards have greatly improved.

Set on the grandeur of the South Circular Road in Richmond is a real find, **Crowthers**, with extraordinarily good food at bargain prices. It's run by two of the nicest people in catering, Shirley and Philip Crowther.

I had an excellent lunch at the **Thai Elephant** in Richmond. It was a set meal and the silence that came over us as we ate was a sign of the excellence of the food. Chicken satay, fish cakes, spring rolls and deep-fried prawns in pastry.

Shere is a picture-postcard village in Surrey. It has a small village green and a lovely church, with two rows of quaint houses and shops peeking at it. On the other wide of the triangle is a historic old builing called the **White Horse Inn**. Outside it are wooden benches, tables and some stocks where I once photographed Marlon Brando, his head through the centre, his hands in the holes left and right. Inside, we were placed by an old open fireplace. It took an extraordinarily long time for our food to arrive. My Thai-spiced chicken breast came with McCain-type chips, a salad and some hot red sauce. It was quite dreadful. We waited endlessly for desserts. I was all so slow we got the bill and fled without getting our desserts at all.

At **Prima Pasta** in Brighton, after eating a historically bad pizza, I waited so long for coffee that I went to the restaurant next door, got some and brought it back. This greatly amused Lia Williams, star of my film *Dirty Weekend*, but made the waiters glummer than before.

When I first stayed at the **Copthorne Hotel Newcastle**, I had a wonderful, memorably large room with an enormous, canopied bed and a window overlooking the river Tyne and a marvellous iron bridge. The next visit I found they'd divided things up into two smaller rooms with a worse view. There was very 1950s yellow diamond wallpaper and a tacky three-piece suite. It all looked gloomy. But in the morning a delicious, enormous fry-up English breakfast arrived 18 minutes after being ordered, which I thought was good. And we had a delicious lunch in a room called The Bar, decorated with oars and boating stuff. The fish was exceptionally fine and fresh, one of the nicest bits of fried fish I've every eaten. The batter was superb. The mushy peas were good, but tepid. I only ate one chip.

On my last visit to **21 Queen Street** in Newcastle-upon-Tyne, I'd described it as being like an airport lounge. They've since changed the decoration, and it is now warm and welcoming. The owner-chef Terry Laybourne still has a Michelin star. For our group of about 50, he prepared warm salad of seared scallops, cured salmon and aromatic vegetables – close to superb – followed by new season's lamb with veg, which was also very good. Then custard tart with nutmeg ice cream. That was fine. The organisation was spectacular. The entire three-course meal was effortlessly served in an hour.

Affairs of the Heart

As the English winter encompasses me in gloom, I have placed a further 17 spotlights in my garden, making 115 altogether. It looked like a film set. "They're doing coach trips now, instead of going to Blackpool," observed my builder, Mr Edwards. In bleak times, as the flames (real, not gas) provide warmth and colour to my bedroom, I recall the balmy month of August. I console myself that it will come again.

On such a day I drove down a leafy Wiltshire lane to the **White Hart Inn** at Ford. Kate Miller, the landlady, had reserved a table in the dining room. I promptly changed it for a larger, round table, then decided I didn't like it. So Kate and I checked the tables in front of the inn, then walked across the road to the river, beside which were tables with wooden benches. As I examined them, Kate's husband Peter drove by, recognised me, and shouted: "Are you all right?" He obviously thought I was dangerous. We walked back to the tables in front of the inn, on into the dining room, and then out the back where there were some more tables. But they overlooked a car park and an air-conditioning unit. So we looked at all the areas again. It was the biggest walkabout ever to choose a Winner table. And very tolerant of Kate.

I finally decided to eat by the river. Large flower baskets hung behind me from the hotel part of the building. "Is all this made here, Katie?" I asked, surveying the menu. "We don't buy anything in," she replied tartly. "And it's Kate without the e." "You mean with the e but without the i," I said precise as ever. I ordered spicy lamb curry with spinach and saffron, served with rice and dressed salad. Miss Lid (the real Lady in Danger) asked for braised chicken in white wine with garlic cream and sweet peppers, again served with rice and dressed salad. Shortly thereafter, Miss Lid, who is no pushover, said: "My chicken is perfect." Then, "Very good." Then, "Very well prepared." My lamb curry was excellent.

The concerned husband, Peter, came over. "Who does the desserts?" I asked, regarding a suspiciously large menu selection. "An 18-

year-old lad trained by the chef," Peter said. "They're all made here except for the treacle tart and apple and raspberry crumble. They're bought in." His wife had said nothing was bought in. I kept quiet. In the cause of exploration I had the banoffie pie and the lemon cheesecake. The pie was robust, nice taste, filled with bananas. The lemon cheesecake very liquid. Both good. Overall, a pleasant experience.

Lacock Abbey, Wiltshire, was due to open at 1pm. It opened at two-and-a-half minutes past. Two-and-a-half minutes can be a long time when you're waiting and don't know what may happen. Particularly when you're as impatient as I am. I strolled round accompanied by Miss Lid (Lady in Danger) the Third. We both enjoyed it. Contrary to the general view that I ponce about only in the richest and most elegant places, I like a balance. Occasional visits to the English countryside, rather twee and full of people whom I see only on television quiz shows or Countryside marches, can be quite refreshing.

When I came out of the abbey, it was past lunchtime. I eat on the dot of one. It was 1.40pm by the time I was in the pretty village street of Lacock, despoiled only by plebeian cars littered everywhere. Near the church was a little old stone-and-beamed house with a back garden serving refreshments. We sat under an apple tree. A bee was trapped in the sugar bowl. I ordered a pot of tea and a "warm cheese and olive round" for £4. It was like a savoury scone with a lot of nice, crisp salad and spicy home-made chutney. I also had teacakes, which were very large and as good as I've ever eaten, and a cup of tea. Miss Lid the Third had delicious fresh vegetable soup. The bill, ex gratuity, was £12.35. It included very fine lemonade. The service was excellent. I went into the kitchen to congratulate the owner, but Margaret M Vaughn was having an operation. The place is called "**King John's Hunting Lodge**. Tea rooms and guest house". It's a credit to the nation.

This Charming Manor

I didn't intend to visit **Lucknam Park** in Wiltshire. I was thumbing through my 1997 Egon Ronay Guide (the last year it came out) and there it was. I phoned at four o'clock on Friday. The general manager. Claire Randall, was apologetic. "We can only do a room in the courtyard," she said. "The best suites are in the main building."

"Ask someone there to leave," I suggested. "I can't do that," said Claire. "They're already in."

"Tell them it's a health hazard," I advised. "And I'd like to hire a car."

Later, Claire rang back. "All the car-hire places are fully booked," she said.

"Stand in your kitchen and say, 'Winner'll pay £300 for the loan of your car,'" I continued, trying to be helpful.

"Our staff are very well paid," responded Claire huffily.

"They'll still be glad of a few hundred quid extra," I said.

"I couldn't do that," replied Claire.

"It's 6.30pm on Friday," I said. "The helicopter lands 11am tomorrow. That's masses of time to get a proper suite and hire a car."

We glided along a few feet above the lawns, past a fine avenue of beech trees, to land in front of the lovely Georgian manor house. "We?" I hear you say. "Who exactly is we?" For the time being, no names, no pack drill (if you recall that old expression). I shall call my fortunate companion Miss Lid. That stands for Lady in Danger. Although I am far too decrepit to be dangerous. Waiting to greet us was Miss Randall and the managing director of Lucknam, Harry Murray. On entering the exceedingly elegant and welcoming hall I was surprised to see Jenner Harding, their restaurant manager. I'd last observed him getting my breakfast at the Sandy Lane Hotel, Barbados, on my final day there before they pulled it down. Jenner was the maître d'. There ensued interesting gossip about Sandy Lane's management. Shortly thereafter, I learnt that Lenner had moved on from Lucknam Park. Even when you use helicopters you can't keep up with staff turnaround in the catering world.

We were shown to a lovely suite in the main building. A gleaming hire car was waiting, proving everything is achievable when you try. Exhausted by the 40-minute flight, we sat on the terrace and Jenner provided coffee and biscuits, but no napkins – even though one of the biscuits was chocolate and sticky.

Apparently our suite had recently been inhabited by Barbra Streisand and her newish husband, James Brolin. I notice she didn't sign the room guest book. I wrote: "On balance a first-rate hotel. Thanks." This was possibly overcautious. I think Lucknam Park is a find. Tastefully decorated, elegant, very beautiful setting and nice countryside around it.

For dinner, I had terrine of baby leeks and langoustine, a boring, triangular slice. I asked for crispy duck but got pink sliced duck, which was actually very good; so was its own confit of puy lentils and a hermitage sauce. Miss Lid greatly praised her salmon. The poached peach was fine.

Breakfast was excellent. I particularly admired the way Mr Murray and Miss Randall worked the room that early in the morning. I asked Jenner if the kipper was fresh or deep-frozen. He thought about that for a while. "You've just said everything, haven't you?" I observed. "Every picture tells a story," said Jenner and giggled.

Bishopstrow House, Warminster in Wiltshire, is a pleasant, unspectacular ivy-covered thing built in 1817. In their **Temple Restaurant** the first thing I noticed was the plates were dirty. I showed this to the lady in charge, and the plates were taken away. There was no bread or butter, but I was told it was on its way. "From Alaska?" I thought as we waited. Vanessa's asparagus soup had far too much pepper in it. I had potted smoked Wylye trout with grilled Granary toast, which tasted of nothing, I left most of it. The service was interminably slow, even though there were only 10 people there. The roast beef and Yorkshire pudding were totally ghastly. Heavy, tough, horrible. Not much of anything was being eaten. For dessert I had warm treacle tart and vanilla ice cream. Very hard pastry, no taste of treacle. I left most of that, too. The cost of this fiasco was more than The Dorchester Grill, where everything is superb. I checked and was told Mr Suter was in the kitchen. He didn't come out. I don't blame him.

For atmosphere, it's hard to beat Guilian Alonzi's **Harbour Bar**, a 1950s American-style diner in Scarborough. The customers are local tear-aways and wonderful old ladies. The ice cream is the best I ever had.

There are times, if things do not go absolutely splendidly, when it is better to give people A for effort than severe castigation. Such a moment occurred when I visited, of all places, Sheffield. **The Old Vicarage** is, as one might guess from the name, the old (1846) residence of the Vicar of Ridgeway. It is done out in a diluted version of northern overkill with just too many colours and bits and pieces abounding. The first real surprise was finding a bowl of soft fruit in the lavatory – above the wash-basin, next to the pot-pourri, in a white china basket were raspberries, strawberries and gooseberries. I touched them to check they were real. I wondered if other people prodding them had done so before or after washing their hands, so I didn't eat any. The owner and chef of this much-cared-for establishment is Mrs Tessa Bramley. She was just genuinely and unbelievably *nice*. So were her handsome son, Andrew, and his lovely fiancée, Justine, who run the dining room. Oh dear, I thought, I shall feel awful if I write a word of criticism about this place. But then came the canapés. Dinner after that ranged from very good to adequate to awful. Things did look up a bit with an exceptional dessert of baked chocolate pudding with hot fudge sauce and English custard.

Greasey descent

When I was in Belfast on a meet-the-people tour, I heard the greatest joke session ever. I did *Any Questions?* for the BBC and afterwards we went back to the **Europa Hotel** with various BBC bigwigs. We sat in a bleak room with little chairs round the edges and the local people told jokes about "the Troubles". These were at their height, with mass killings, the IRA prisoners defecating and spreading it on their cell walls. As always in times of tension, humour is a great relief. The jokes they told were, by any standards, utterly sick. They made fun of the murders and all the other horrors of those days in Northern Ireland. But they were indescribably funny. It was a night I shall always remember.

On a recent visit I was in room 101, the President Clinton suite. It may sound grand, but it was tiny. A small sitting room with a yellow two-seater sofa, and then an opening, no door, to the bedroom. There are various presidential memorabilia. A signed photo of him and Hillary, a certificate of appreciation from a man in Presidential Communications called Dale Ellenberger and a framed letter from Hillary thanking someone for the beautifully engraved crystal ball. It's the least presidential suite I've ever stayed in, but perfectly comfortable in a boarding-house way.

Downstairs we dropped into the Brasserie for a snack. I dictated into my tape: "This is a seriously revolting room." It had blue balloons all over the place because the musical *Grease* was playing next door and the Brasserie was done up in sympathy. There was a very tired-looking salad bar. Vanessa asked what the soup of the day was and that sent the waitress into total frenzy. She came back and said it was vegetable broth. There were slices of dessert on view that looked as unappetising as anything I've seen in my life.

A lady came over with a badge saying Frenchy, who is a character in *Grease*. "I've just come to let you know things will be going smoothly from now on," she said. She was Mary Smith, Brasserie deputy manager. I noticed the table next to ours was served well before us; not my idea of things going smoothly. Eventually, Frenchy served Vanessa my Kenickies Kikin Chicken and gave me the nachos Vanessa had ordered. There was one soup too few, so Vanessa wasn't served any. After a brief taste she was pleased about that. The chicken was highly indifferent and the sauce much too hot. The baked potato was horrific. The soup was horrific. Even the tea tasted odd.

Highland fling

Vanessa wanted to see a tree. I don't know how the word Scotland got in, but suddenly it was a typical Winner excursion. "I'll think about the private jet – is £9,000 the best you can do?" "Take the helicopter from Inverness to **Inverlochy Castle** and back. £1,300! That's bloody high!" I had found Inverlochy Castle in a guide book; it said the room rate was £276 per night. On Thursday, I phoned. "Have you got a cancellation for the weekend?" A voice said: "Yes, as a matter of fact we have." It turned out to be Michael Leonard, the general manager. "I'll take it," I said. "What's the name?" said Mr Leonard. "Michael Winner." There was a pause. "The Michael Winner?" he asked. "Afraid so," I replied. Another pause. "Maybe I shouldn't have said we had a cancellation." "Too late now," I said cheerfully. "Ah well," said Mr Leonard, uncertainly, "we like a challenge."

I decided the jet, at £9,000 for two nights, was a bit over the top, so I ended up on the British Airways shuttle. Mistake, that. The helicopter was next to it when we landed on Saturday morning, and a dramatic flight ensued over Loch Ness through varied weather from bright sun, to rain, to light cloud, to black cloud. There were great mountains sweeping down to rivers and lakes. I'd never seen the Highlands before. We landed on the lawn a few feet from the Victorian pile that is Inverlochy. Not so much a castle, more a wonderful, 19th-century fantasy of Ye Olde Britain. Mr Leonard was there to show us up to a very large room (upgraded from a small room when I'd first phoned) that had a lovely three-window bay with views over lochs (lakes), bens (mountains) and glens (valleys), only slightly diminished by a paper mill in the distance standing up from the town of Fort William.

The shower was ridiculous. It was above the end of the bath that slopes down, and trying to stand under it was like climbing a slippery hill. At what turned out to be £600 a night, a proper shower would be reasonable. There was ample room to take the lobby outside the bathroom and ... oh, never mind. In the bedroom were prints; one, with the inscription Throat, showed two fighting cocks with one holding the other. The next, Death, showing the victor standing on the vanquished's dead body. Very jolly.

The hotel lounge was comfortably regal with a real log fire. The main hall was a period Disneyland with Venetian chandeliers, cherubs on the ceiling, old-style British chairs and a chess set laid out on a table. It all worked rather well. Mr Leonard came as I checked out the dining room. "I'll sit there!" I announced, showing him the table in the centre bay window. "I fear that's taken by a regular visitor," said Mr Leonard bravely. "We think this is the nicest table." He indicated one at the side bay window. "It has the best view." "Not for the person sitting looking at the wall," I remarked, dourly. I alternated tables. "King Haakon of Norway gave the tables and chairs to the present owner," advised Mr Leonard, going on to tell me that Charlie Chaplin, King Hussein and Mel Gibson were among those who had stayed.

The food, knocked up by a young Michelin-starred chef, Simon Haigh, was mostly extremely good. Ballotine of foie gras with smoked apple purée, very fresh salmon, later amazingly fresh and juicy lobsters, raspberry crème brûlée. Only two mini-disasters. I checked the vegetable soup (adequate) for Vanessa, who's vegetarian, and they said it had a meat stock. So we asked for a salad two hours in advance. When it arrived it was full of bacon! And the morning Loch Fyne kippers were very tired. Later, Simon took exception to my criticising them. "It's a Mallaig kipper and it came in Friday." "Mr Leonard said it came in Wednesday," I said. "What does he know, he doesn't order them!" said Simon. As Mr Leonard was standing next to him, I thought that rather brave. "I would not have called the kipper juicy," I continued. Mr Haigh defended his kipper to the death. Nice chap, though.

After that we turned to important matters, like how he finds girlfriends in this distant part of the Highlands. Bit of walking, bit of helicoptering around, all very pleasant. Hotel service was exemplary. Coming back Monday morning, we were late to Inverness airport. "Land beside the shuttle," I instructed the pilot. "Then it won't be able to take off and they'll have to let us on." He did. Nothing like private planes, really. They're great fun. Except when you get the bill.

We arrived at the **Malmaison** hotel in Glasgow around 11 o'clock at night. Although the people at the desk could see me coming, no attempt was made to get our luggage until I said: "Porters off duty, are they?" We were shown a duplex suite. It was a nightmare, 1950s decor gone seriously wrong. The bedroom, if you can call it that, was up a spiral staircase. It was a cramped ledge with just room for a bed, a tea-maker, a kettle and a cupboard. The bathroom and toilet were below and equally small. I measured the downstairs lounge area. It was about 12ft 2in by 11ft 8in. Outside the windows was a large office building, lit up and occupied at midnight. In the morning, I went to the dining room. The menu advertised "freshly squeezed orange and grapefruit juice". "Does that mean you cut the oranges in half here and squeeze them in the hotel?" I asked. "No," said the waitress. Eventually, after a lifetime of negotiation, they provided me with freshly squeezed orange juice, which they promised on the menu anyway. For lunch, I asked for a pizza romano with two fried eggs on it. "Seriously?" said the waitress as if this were the height of culinary ignorance. "Yes," I said. "No problem," she responded. (Orso's and Orsino's take note.) I had to ask three times for a cappuccino, eventually walking the few paces to the machine to help myself.

Yes, in Glasgow, is in a basement. People on the pavement above stare down at you. On the left of the dining area is a bar that's full of people who stare at you as well. So you're surrounded by gawkers. It's a noisy, yellow room with pictures on the walls and red and purple banquettes and chairs. We ate pithiviers of wild mushrooms, grilled asparagus and Madeira essence. The meal progressed to fillet of Shetland salmon and scallops with stuffed baby vegetables, lemon and dill. Very nice bit of salmon, the veg cooked perfectly. The restaurant had terrible Muzak, sort of discothèque music gone wrong. Then that stopped and a pianist turned up. He was extremely unmelodious. Thank goodness bitter dark chocolate tart with white chocolate ice cream and vanilla sauce appeared. The chocolate filling was very good, but the base was a bit how's-your-father.

Lochinver's Larder in Lochinver looked dreadful from the outside. Frozen fish fingers if we're lucky, I thought. I entered with a heavy heart. The first room had a counter on the right. It was full of pies. My spirits rose. "Do you make those here?" I asked. "Yes," said a nice girl. There were 16 different pies – from leek and mushroom to venison and cranberry to chicken curry. Above were rows of home-made cakes that looked amazing. We ate in a large room overlooking the loch, an old church, wonderful scenery. I had a steak and ale pie and a chicken, cheese and potato one. Both absolutely tiptop. Then I chose a chocolate fudge cake and a vanilla fudge cake. Totally, absolutely, incredibly historic. Touch of moisture, delicious icing, perfect. My only regret was that I couldn't go through the lemon cake, pineapple fruit tart, shortbread tarts, carrot cake, rhubarb and strawberry pie, banoffi pie and the home-made cherry cheesecake, to name but a few. I'd like to have eaten everything, but I'd done pretty well having two main courses, two desserts, a chocolate milkshake and coffee.

If I was the comedy version of an American tourist, I would call the **Old Station Restaurant** "cute". It is a genuine, working station: Spean Bridge, on the London Midland Scottish, now Scotrail, one stop before Fort William. It is everybody's idyllic picture-postcard station. Little overhanging, woodworked roof with flower baskets, lovely flowerbeds all around, a bridge to rolling fields and, on the other side, a village and majestic mountains. The tables are well spaced out, the murmur of Scots voices extremely pleasant. I started with honey and ginger soup, very tasty, real country stuff. Then I ate some duck breast with apricot and lemon sauce, very good. Carrots a bit overcooked, but they tasted of carrots; cabbage tiptop; nice roast potato with a crisp skin. Mashed potato with nutmeg, too! Mozart piped through as I had white chocolate cheesecake. If this restaurant was moved to Holland Park it would be a terrific local and I'd go there a lot.

The **Altnaharrie Inn**, which has two Michelin stars and three Ronay stars, is in the western Highlands over the water from Ullapool. It's a smallish house that takes only 16 people, and you have to get there by ferry. I landed in the back "garden" by helicopter. The owner, Fred, the husband of Gunn Eriksen who cooks, went into a serious frisson when he heard I was coming. "Er, we don't seek publicity," he said, and made it clear they didn't want to be reviewed. That's fair. It's their place, they can dictate the house rules. Later I phoned Gunn and said: "Do you want to take a chance?" She did not. So that's it – about the food, my lips are sealed.

David Smyrl got a bit worried when I rang him at the **Morefield Motel** in Ullapool. "We're only a fast-food fresh lobster place," he said. Chef's specials included half lobster grilled with garlic, and mussels served with a jacket potato and dressed salad. They were the best mussels I've ever eaten. Fat, juicy, not shrivelled like they usually are in London. Lobster good, potato very good. Vanessa had turbot. Fresh, excellent. As pleasant a meal as you could ask for.

Pilot error

I am a total moron. I am stupid beyond human belief. I let greed overcome common sense. I am pathetic. This will now doubtless be quoted out of context, so let me add that this is not my normal condition. It occurred recently when I accepted a free helicopter ride, usual price £4,500, which I can well afford, to **Henllys Hall Hotel** in Beaumaris, north Wales.

My helicopter pilot, Philip Amadeus, gets some of his machines from a nice chap, John Rodger. Through Philip, Mr Rodger offered me a return trip to his hotel. For everything else on my two-night visit, I would pay full price. I thought: "I've never seen Snowdonia, I liked central Wales, I'll go."

I should have listened to Philip. "It's not the sort of hotel you usually stay at," he cautioned. Mr Rodger should have listened to Philip: "I don't think asking Michael Winner is a good idea," he had said. Mr Rodger should have listened to me. "This may well be something you regret," I told him on the phone. "I shall write exactly as I feel." "I don't care what you say, I don't want no favours," was the reply, which I wrote down carefully in my diary.

So I joined Mr R on his helicopter, and an hour and 10 minutes later we landed at Henllys Hall, a splendid Victorian building with earlier foundations. We entered the lounge. A sense of foreboding engulfed me. The room had an awful, tacky bar in the corner in two shades of green with poorly painted pictures of medieval monks. The framed oils of noblemen could have come from the wall of a cheap pantomime set. Cold Earl Grey tea arrived. The triple-decker sandwiches and biscuits were okay.

We went to our room. My heart sank. It was dreary. There was a repro four-poster bed, a dressing table, a chipped chair, a wooden wardrobe and a single upright chair with arms. All seedy. The paintwork on the door was filthy with black fingermarks.

The bathroom was tiny, the composition floor looked like cork with sparkly bits in it. The sink was minuscule, the bath plastic, the wastebin full of rubbish left by the previous guest. The taps were the wrong way round – hot on the right, cold on the left. There were tiny slivers of cheap soap, no face flannels. The view wasn't bad. A lot of it was a recent golf course. I don't like golf courses at the best of times. This had tiny new trees which may look nice in 40 years but I won't be there. Then there were fields, then the Menai Strait and Snowdonia.

We retired downstairs to the dark olive-green leather sofas, surely from a sale at a furniture warehouse off the North Circular Road. The manager, Nick Brown, served us. "I find it extraordinary," I said: "You know I'm coming, you know I will write in detail about what happens, yet in the first half-hour the tea is cold, the door of the room is filthy and the bin in the bathroom is full of the detritus of the previous guest." "I know, it's disgusting," said Mr Brown. "When I heard I was disgusted." "What are you talking about?" I said. "You're not visiting from Mars. You're not passing through. You're the manager, you're responsible." Mr Brown exited glumly. "I wish I could talk to 'em like that," said John Rodger. "If I did, they'd walk out."

John explained the "Victorian" oil paintings in his Hampton Court Restaurant came from Taiwan. "One person does the hands, one person the clothes and so on. A lot of splash for a little cash. The Americans love 'em." Luckily, his American group of art experts was off duty that night. At least that was a blessing.

The freebie starter was scrambled egg. Nice. The white poppy-seed roll was fresh and warm. Then came the most amazing dish ever put before me. It was described as roast breast of wood pigeon, Savoy cabbage, bespoke bacon with a rich game sauce. John and I tried to cut it. It was impossible. It resembled a theatrical rubber fake. It gave a bit, but no knife would enter. "It's uneatable," said John. Before the waiter took it away, he tried again, like a man who couldn't believe what was happening. He's a tough chap, John, but he made no impression on this pigeon.

Over the weekend things stayed much the same. I could tell you of many more catastrophes, but I'm trying to expunge the whole visit from my memory. They say there's no such thing as a free lunch. There's also no such thing as a free helicopter ride.

PS This hotel has changed ownership, after this review John Rodger sold it!

Tempting fete

Betws-y-Coed is a quaint little town of grey stone houses with slate roofs, spread out along a single roadway, with a river running on one side with mountains behind. I parked the car and noticed across the road a **Women's Institute fête** at St Mary's Church. That's for me, I thought. There were some enormous evergreen trees with little stalls beneath them offering a bedside cabinet for £2, some Sainsbury's vacuum-cleaner bags and a 1955 road atlas of Great Britain.

Inside, the Church hall was full of marvellous things. A large table was stacked with home-made jams, cakes and pies. Nearby, Anne Knowles, wearing a red striped apron, stood by a hot griddle. Anne is famous for her Welsh cakes (two for 30p), her drop scones and jams. I tried the cakes and scones with her strawberry jam – £1.80, and the best I've ever eaten. The cakes were totally, beyond belief, historic. This was a serious taste experience. I added a cup of tea and read the notice board. The Morris Beachy Singers from Texas, USA, were an imminent attraction; also advertised was Weight Watchers and a ceilidh and barbecue at 8pm at Cwmlanerch Farm. The WI president, Moya Panting, explained this was pronounced cayley and meant a dance.

Looking for further sustenance, I bought an onion, cheese and tomato pasty from the trestle table and persuaded Anne to heat it for me on her griddle. I don't care if you think I'm unsophisticated, I have never eaten anything better in my life. These ladies have extraordinary skill. Simple it may be, but the result is pure heaven. I still have some of Anne's strawberry jam left at home and it beats anything in that line I've ever bought. A lady with short blonde hair, Charlotte Irley, came up and said was I there because I'd heard she'd played Sporty Spice in the local show. She made a fruit cake that was being raffled, iced with unbelievable skill by Elsie Oughton with beautiful flowers, leaves, sweetpeas, and a purple and pink ruff. A cake that would grace any shop in the world.

I proceeded to buy five tickets for a pound from a tombola stall run by Marion Betteney and won a greeny-blue face flannel and two large bars of soap.

We then wandered up the high street, where Vanessa decided to inspect a small bivouac-like tent erected on a little green. I bought some "Real ice cream made on the farm – Denbigh Farmhouse Ice Cream" from a van by some tables and chairs next to the river. It was at best reasonable. The ice cream seller didn't know the name of the river, so we both entered the Potteries factory shop, where everyone had a different opinion. We finally decided it was the Llugwy running into the river Conwy.

By this time Vanessa had entered the SiopTanderwen, a local health-food shop and bakery. She bought a tuna roll with cucumber and some sparkling Decantae Welsh mountain natural mineral water. I chose a brown cheese salad sandwich and we both had some "Gourmet, hand-cooked potato chips, probably the finest you'll ever taste", made by Kettle Foods of Barnard Road, Norwich.

We crossed a pretty stone bridge to sit on a wooden bench over-looking some little waterfalls and the river. There we ate our purchases. "This is better than lunch at The Ivy, isn't it?" said Vanessa. To which I replied very firmly "No", thinking nervously, "I do hope the Ivy and Le Caprice stay as brilliant as before Chris and Jeremy sold out to the Belgo group". My sandwich was fine, the chips were a bit heavy; Vanessa said her roll was good. The water was described as "bubbling through rocks and the beautiful Snowdonia foothills". As it was fizzy, I couldn't really taste it.

We walked back over the bridge and a man came up. "You won't get much good food here, pal," he said. Later, Vanessa was in a shop. A lady who'd been at the Women's Institute fête came over and remarked, "When I read Michael Winner I always thought he was full of his own self-importance. But he was absolutely lovely with those ladies." If only I could meet everybody. I'd be the most loved man in the world.

The **Nantyffin Cider Mill Inn**, at Crickhowell, has a big restaurant in a barn, but that was too smart for me. They'd reserved a table in the bar with the common folk, rightly assuming I'd prefer it. This bar had a gas stove in it, whereas in the adjacent bar, for people even more common, they have a proper log-burning one. Vanessa asked for orange, avocado and mint salad followed by whole, warm cracked Cornish crab served with new potatoes and salad. I chose grilled langoustines with a herb-crumb coating and garlic butter followed by roast leg of Welsh lamb with roast potatoes and mint sauce. To drink we ordered Hedges Red Mountain Reserve 1992, "probably the purest fruit we have ever tasted, a stunning array of flavours". It was all right. Give me a Lafite '61 any day. The bread was very good. The first two courses were excellent. We finished with a superb bread-and-butter pudding. The bill for two was £122.50. Must've been the wine. At early-evening dinner you get three courses for £11.95. This is the sort of place that gives Welsh food a good name.

The **Gwynn Arms** at Glyntawe, between the Black Mountains and the Brecon Beacons, is a pleasant-looking inn facing open fields and hills, little baskets of flowers and rambling roses outside. Inside it is predictable olde world pub decor, chairs with round back and spindles, a multicoloured carpet, fake oil lamps, cases with stuffed animals – an owl here, a badger there, a stuffed fox with a dead rabbit thrown in for good measure. Dark beams, white walls and Frank Sinatra singing 'Strangers in the Night'. A blackboard offered a selection of six starters and 27 main courses, including 18 types of curry. Absurd, I thought. I ordered "Caribbean curry – chilli and banana, very, very hot". That it was – so hot it made my eyes water. I was in pain, My fault really, they had warned me. I feel, though, that had it not been very hot it would have been terrible anyway. Vanessa had what appeared to be very tired fish covered in a horrid-looking sauce – uneatable. We left in haste.

Nino's, in Hay-on-Wye, is very much a bistro, with minuscule tables. My chair was on a massive slope. I was served cawl, described as "a traditional Welsh lamb broth". Rather like Irish stew, only weaker. Not bad. My "whole grilled lemon sole with coriander, chilli and garlic" was a tasteless mush. Curiosity, with a touch of piggishness, had me try the baked American vanilla cheesecake, which was marginally in the range of pleasant. It came surrounded by little dots of red sauce. The chef obviously took a correspondence course in plate decoration. Nino's is the place to come if you're on a heavy diet. If you don't eat, you aren't missing much.

In a sweet little antique shop in a cobbled street in Hay-on-Wye, a dear, white-haired Welsh lady sat behind a desk surrounded by bric-a-brac. My eye was caught by a piece of white paper hiding a picture in a wooden frame. "Do not lift this up if you are easily shocked," was written on it. I lifted it at once. I was shocked. There were two people, in an old print, caught *in flagrante*, and in considerable detail. A few inches away another such picture, then another. It was all too much for me. Vanessa, also obviously deeply traumatised, suggested a cup of tea to calm us down. Opposite was **Oscars Bistro**, with a large display of cakes, flapjacks, vegetable tart, beef in beer, chicken and leek pie, sausage in red wine gravy, and so on. I took some chocolate cake, carrot cake, and date and walnut cake. The second two were very good. I also grabbed a flapjack, the old-fashioned kind, moist, delicious. "Marvellous," I said, my mouth full. I felt better.

Cymru hither

I've always considered the Welsh to be marvellous. This is based on two people in my life. The first, Mrs Bawden, was, for a very long time, my cleaner. Mrs B was a small lady with dyed-blonde hair. Every year I automatically gave my staff a salary increase. Every year Mrs Bawden would come to me and say: "I don't know why you've given me a raise, I haven't done anything to earn it." She finally retired to a Welsh caravan park and then, assuredly, to heaven. The second was the wonderfully vibrant actor Stanley Baker, belatedly knighted as he lay dying of cancer. Stanley was a macho movie hero of immense wit and charm. At the premier of my film *The Games* in which he starred, Stanley appeared, immaculate as ever in a dinner suit, and said: "Well, what do you think?" "About what?" I asked. "Me," he said. "Look at me!" I did notice something, but it couldn't possibly be what he was referring to. "My toupee," he finally said. "How do you like my new toupee?"

Thus, I was particularly disappointed with the lack of warmth and wit at Llangoed Hall. But the chef, Ben Davies, did me a very good turn. He recommended a number of nearby restaurants. "The **Griffin Inn** in the village serves good local food," he said. I got the impression he meant "good local" as a slight put-down, as opposed to the "international" food that he served. I visited the Griffin Inn in Llyswen the next morning to check out the table situation.

There are places you enter that you feel at once are going to be good: something about the atmosphere, the owner, the position of every-thing around you. Seated by the fireplace were four ladies talking in the Welsh language. Heaven! What a wonderfully melodious, mellifluous sound it is. I'm all for the Welsh nationalists. Ban McDonald's and Marks & Spencer, get back to traditional Welsh names and shops. Let everyone speak in their native tongue. There's quite enough English spoken in England. I may not have quite got the nationalist platform spot-on, but who cares?

The landlord, Richard Stockton, showed me a nice corner table for that evening and we went on our day's excursion. That night, the Griffin had a warm, orderly feeling. A notice on the bar read: "Eat British lamb: 50,000 foxes can't be wrong." The menu described it as a 15th-century sporting inn – whatever that was. Flowers were on every table in the small, low-beamed dining room. We had an excellent fresh brown roll. I listened for some Welsh language, but the diners seemed to be speaking posh English. Pam Morgan was identified as the lady with the most refined voice. "She can speak Welsh," whispered Richard. "But she spent a lot of time in Hong Kong."

All the food was historic-plus. It was as good a dinner as I've ever eaten. Apparently, people drive from miles around to come here. I'm not surprised. I had hot smoked salmon to start, like a little filet. With *glanwye* sauce. Amazing! Then roast haunch of wild venison on a shallot ragout in red-wine sauce. Venison can be tricky. This was superb. Vanessa and I emptied our plates with total enjoyment. Service was smart and speedy, Richard's wife, Diana, helping out like a good 'un.

The best was left to last. The hot treacle tart had just the right thick, treacly taste, wonderfully moist texture, great pastry. Very fine crème anglaise with it. The lemon mousse was supreme. As I was on a diet I left some of the treacle tart. That pained me.

Wye bother

Sir Bernard Ashley, husband of the late Laura, owns **Llangoed Hall** in Llyswen, Wales. "It has always been my ambition," he writes in the brochure, "to find a country-house hotel that would successfully re-create the atmosphere of an Edwardian house party. Here, guests would arrive, tired from their travels and the workaday world, to be greeted and cared for by their hosts as if they were indeed guests and not people simply renting rooms and patronising the restaurant. When you arrive there is no reception desk, no-one demanding a hostage credit card, just friendly staff to take your coat and carry your bags." Boy, is that a joke.

My helicopter landed at the time I'd told the general manager, Andrew Brockett, I would arrive. One hotel porter represented the "friendly staff". He alone could not take all the luggage, so the pilot, Philip Amadeus, grabbed some and we trekked into the hotel. There, nobody else greeted us. The porter led us to the room and left. I can't think when I last entered a hotel without the manager, or at least the receptionist, welcoming me.

We went to the deserted lounge for tea. The same aged porter told us there were sandwiches and cakes. We ordered those, plus Earl Grey tea. After a while, cakes arrived and tea that was not Earl Grey. No sandwiches. I went into the hall and found an English lady, who said she'd deal with it. The staff are almost exclusively not Welsh. Warmth is not high on their list. A recently frozen éclair was poor; the fruit cake was okay but bland; a shortbread biscuit superb.

Another couple entered and a young man took their order. Our correct tea came with unexceptional sandwiches, which were also cold, as if the bread had been in the fridge. The new arrivals got tea with cakes, sandwiches and scones with home-made jam and cream. "I never got scones," I said, peering at theirs. "Well, you didn't ask for them," said the man. "Nor did you," I replied. "I heard you order. You asked for an assortment." The gentleman kindly offered me one of his scones. I took a bit of it. It was the best I've ever eaten.

Llangoed Hall has an attractive, faded elegance and excellent Edwardian oil paintings and drawings. Wild flowers grow through the cracks in the stone steps leading to the lawn. The view of fields, sheep and hills is first-rate. Walk outside and you hear the roar of the nearby A470. Go further and you hit the noise of engines dealing with the septic tanks. Only when you reach the river Wye and the rapids after a small waterfall does that noise drown out the sound of traffic.

The restaurant, an elegant, yellow room, has a Michelin star. I would describe the staff as snooty. An atmosphere so restrained nobody dared talk above a whisper. "Boring," said Vanessa.

My first course was salad of quail with sautéed scollop (sic), foie gras and balsamic dressing. You can have foie gras with quail or scallops. But quail and scallops – ugh! Individually, they were adequate. It was an enormous portion. Vanessa liked her three large pan-fried scallops. Next I had black Welsh beef and Vanessa had salmon. Both were all right, but the whole thing totally lacked finesse and imagination.

Dessert was stated to be strawberry millefeuille. Millefeuille is thin layers of puff pastry; it dates back to the late 19th century. This one dated back to June 1998. It had hard, sweet biscuits in two layers with strawberries and cream. It was awful. I left most of it.

Vanessa had some cotton trousers ironed, and I've never seen anything like it: great ridges and furrows – unwearable. The room was nice, the bathroom large, but the bath too small even for normal people.

At breakfast one of the two pots of home-made jam (very good) had a big blob of congealed, old jam on the side. I removed it with my finger and then had great difficulty dislodging it. Eventually, I rubbed it off under my chair. The service was very slow. Again, the atmosphere was frigid. If this is an Edwardian house party, thank God nobody asked me to any.

Andrew Brockett left me a letter saying: "If I or any of my colleagues can help, please let us know." Mr Brockett was only there for a fleeting moment on Sunday morning, having been absent on Friday and Saturday and again on Monday.

When I left, I passed Sir Bernard Ashley coming in. "You took my helicopter pad," he said, smiling pleasantly.

The **Ty'n Rhos Country House and Restaurant** is a rather grand name for a modest, but beautifully situated, domestic dwelling near the village of Seion in Gwynedd. A three-course Sunday lunch with coffee was £14.95 excluding service. Vanessa ordered a crispy pancake filled with a ragù of avocado, tomato and spring onion to start and fillet of salmon infused with lime and coriander with a white wine sauce to follow. They were excellent. My twice-baked goat's cheese soufflé was just right: properly crisp on the outside, not soggy on the inside. Then I had pot roast shoulder of lamb with an onion marmalade, herb dumplings and a minted red wine sauce. Plus superb veg. All the food was close to historic. The desserts were good too: summer pudding, vanilla baked cheesecake, home-grown gooseberry and elderflower cobbler with vanilla custard, and caramel ice cream. All this served in a pleasant domestic setting in the middle of nowhere. Bit of a triumph really.

WINNIE LEAVES LLANGOED HALL

In the **Beginish Restaurant** in Dingle, there was a peat fire, nice oil paintings of Irish scenery, a bar you could sit at and, above all, Irish voices, which should be imported into every restaurant because they manage to sound vital, melodic and not disturbing. The owner John Moore used to own the local cinema, but gave it up to front for his wife Pat's cooking – the restaurant is in what was their living room. The food would grace any London posh-place. Crab claws in beurre blanc sauce, oysters, grilled fillet of wild Irish salmon, Bailey's and sultana parfait with fruit coulis.

Since my visit to **Dick Mack's**, I am totally hooked on draught Guinness. I'm arranging for a draught Guinness apparatus in my house. Dick Mack's is a wondrous pub in Green Lane, Dingle, Co Kerry, where the left-hand bar is for shoe repairs and the one on the right for drinks. It's totally period, with little booths and a mêlée of old rooms at the back. Grandpa started it in 1899 and it must have looked just the same then.

Dingle, on Ireland's west coast, is where David Lean made *Ryan's Daughter*. There I stayed in **Milltown House**, a white Victorian house with a white picket fence and lawns leading down to the waterside, expertly looked after by the smiling red-haired owner, Angela Gill. It was the best value ever – for £42, not the sort of bill I'm used to, we got a charmingly decorated and well-cared-for room with a stunning view over Dingle, the estuary and the hills. The breakfast orange juice was genuinely fresh-squeezed, the jam and the bread were home-made, there was a newly baked apple cake, and everything else, from griddle pancakes with maple syrup to eggs to sausages to bacon, was as good as you could hope for. I had Ballyhea kippers! If you want a far-flung gem, this is it!
PS There is now a new owner. The old one probably retired rich because of me!

I was going to Dublin to address the Trinity College Philosophical Society on the subject I am most expert on: me. I'd asked them to book dinner somewhere not touristy, off the beaten track, and they chose **Gallagher's Boxty House and Shebeen**. (Shebeen means an illegal drinking club, which it wasn't.) We went through swing doors to find people sharing long tables in a pleasant room with a bookcase and a rustic quality. There was Irish music. It was full of American tourists. Boxties were widely listed on the menu, so I ordered a beef and Beamish one, Vanessa fish, someone else corned beef and cabbage. Boxty turned out to be a potato pancake with whatever in it, supported by cauliflower, turnip and salad. Mine was fine, but not historic. I followed with an extremely good bread and butter pudding with raisins. A perfectly pleasant meal, helped greatly by the company.

During the second world war, I would often go with my father to the Savoy Grill. In those days meat was rationed, and not much was available anyway. Whenever Dad ordered chicken, he would ask the head waiter, "It will be chicken, won't it? Not rabbit?", for it was not unknown to switch one for the other. Today at posh restaurants, the humble rabbit is enjoying its day. It comes dressed up in all sorts of guises. *Jambonette de lapin aux girolles* is how rabbit with wild mushrooms is presented at **Patrick Guilbaud**, a bit of French chic in Dublin. The lump of rounded rabbit tasted okay, but was not remotely memorable. The sliced potatoes that came with it were so hard on the outside that I had trouble cutting them, and gave up. Luckily, the bitter chocolate tart with pistachio ice cream was exceptional.

The **Shelbourne** in Dublin is a classy place I've always admired. It has a marvellous, old-fashioned Irish elegance. The communal rooms are as buzzy as anything, with guests and locals meeting for tea, drinks and whatever. The Princess Grace suite is exceedingly stylish with an air of faded grandeur that I greatly like. Here I went totally bananas. It isn't often that I scream and shout, but I made up for lost time on this occasion, because the laptop and printer I had asked for were not there, and then did not appear until the next morning. Also, breakfast was poor. A lot of detailed fuss was needed to get fresh orange juice. A horrid tin tray was dumped on the grand dining table and I was left to lay out the plates and cutlery myself. The toast was awful and there was no butter. So I had to send them Winner letter 23B complaining madly. They replied with a gracious apology – unlike those wobblers at Cliveden, who blow up over the target at the first sign of gunfire.

My suite at the **Park Hotel** in Kenmare was as elegant and old-fashioned a hotel space as I've ever seen. There was an 1882, dog-eared, limited edition of the works of Charles Dickens, very charming antique furniture and mirrors, some pleasing oil paintings and, above an enormous double bed, a set of seven saucy Edwardian pin-up pictures in an arts and crafts frame. I wondered if they'd heard of my age and decided I needed help. The view from the suite's bay windows was spectacular – palm trees, sloping lawns, a tidal estuary and rolling hills beyond. Guests were having tea on the lawn, so I joined them. It was the worst tea I have ever had in my life. The sandwiches were grossly indelicate, great lumps of white bread, with two sandwiches speared together with a toothpick! The cakes were unspeakable. Food at dinner was okay. They have a Michelin star, but the chef who got it for them has since left. To be fair, the hotel, in general, is definitely pleasant. I liked it. Put me in charge for a couple of weeks and maybe it would live up to its award.

Longueville House, in Mallow, is a beautiful 18th-century restaurant and hotel that's rather like someone's home: a bit faded, very tastefully furnished with lovely old mirrors and armchairs, a grey marble carved fireplace with a log fire, and beautiful views of rolling green hills from the tall Georgian windows. My friend Oliver Reed was a regular visitor here. For lunch we ordered vegetable broth made with vegetables from their garden, a pâté of spinach, pork polenta and tomato in a millefeuille. I also asked for smoked salmon with garden salad. The bread was excellent, the salmon outstanding. My dessert was biscuit glacé with strawberries. That was nice too.

Happy landings

The Concorde was late. Seventeen hours late, to be exact. We were half an hour from Heathrow at 9 o'clock when the dreaded announcement came. You could tell from the tone of the captain's voice, the second he started, that it was a downer. Apparently there were storms and landing in London was too dangerous. These storms were widespread and affected every airport in southern England. We would divert to Shannon.

In the lounge I was given a pint of draught Guinness by Michael Pemberton, who owns luxury hotels in Barbados. Our chauffeurs in London were being told the plane had landed because it had a faulty tyre. My Mr Fraser confirmed the wind had long died down and there were no storms. Someone else phoned and found London airport fully operational. Why, then, were a lot of very posh people in an airport lounge in Ireland?

Being highly sophisticated, I knew the answer. The storm had caused a backlog. Planes were having to circle Heathrow for an indefinite time. The Concorde had little fuel left after its trip from Barbados, so it would take on more. We were herded back to the plane and told we would leave at 10.30pm. Then the pilot returned with that disaster tone in his voice. The noise restriction at Heathrow came on at 11.30 and we weren't going to make it. "British Airways representatives got the head of the British Airports Authority out of bed, but he still refused to lift the noise restriction." Colouful I thought, but unlikely. I couldn't imagine some lower echelon executive dragging Sir John Egan from his rest to say: "Winner's on the plane. For heaven's sake let it land!"

We were to spend the night in Ireland. A very bright man named Anthony Buckingham was madly working his cellular phone. Mr B is in fascinating things such as oil and diamonds. He travels widely to strange African countries. He is a man of the world. Like me, he has the sense to travel only with carry-on luggage, so he was ready to disembark pronto. First, we tried for private jets to rescue us. "Count me in!" I said eagerly. But no, they could not guarantee getting back. Mr B's man in London then informed us that **Dromoland Castle** was the only place to stay. "I'll book us in," he said. "They're asking is it Michael Winner as in Michael Winner," he added.

Then he was besieged. "Book for me, please," said Lady Annabel Goldsmith in row 2 behind me. "And for us," said Lady Rayne from across the aisle. "Us, too!" called Lord Feldman from further back. Mr Buckingham obliged, and by the time he and I were hotfooting through the airport, all had been done.

If you have to be stuck somewhere, Ireland is the best place. The people seemed to know every word I'd ever written. A highly intelligent race. Pat Keogh, a wonderfully ruddy-faced taxi driver, took us to Dromoland Castle, an impressive historic building facing a large lake. There, the senior assistant manager, Niall Rochford, was all charm and efficiency. I was led up a grand staircase past enormous portraits, including William, 4th Earl of Inchquin in the robes of the Order of the Bath by Sir Godfrey Kneller. There was a distinct smell of smoke; I later learnt they'd had a fire. Luckily, my room was smell-free and very clean, with nice Tudor-style wall hangings and an old-fashioned bathroom that worked perfectly. My hot chocolate and biscuits arrived quickly and with lovely crockery, cutlery and terrific napkins.

The next morning, breakfast was superb. Quite the best kipper I've ever eaten. "Is it local?" I asked. "From Donegal," said the waiter. "Is that local?" I continued. "Quite local," he said. The dining room was very grand: four marvellous chandeliers, more oil paintings, a sensational view of the lake and the lovely Irish countryside beyond. This hotel I can recommend to anyone. I found no failings at all.

Aha, but when I had arrived Niall told me all the suites were occupied. Was he speaking with forked tongue? "Did you have a suite?" I asked Lady Rayne, opposite me on the plane. She dipped into her bag and gave me four Opal Fruits. "I didn't say sweets, I asked if you had a suite at the hotel," I said. "No," said Lady Rayne. I therefore confirm Dromoland Castle is a sensational place.

WINNIE DEPARTS FROM CONCORDE
(WHICH WE HOPE WILL RETURN)

ABROAD

WINNIE ENJOYS
A SWIM

WINNIE EATS
CHICKEN PIE
IN BRUGES
A) 2000

3

B E L G I U M

Breydel de Coninck, just off the market square in Bruges, was packed for Sunday lunch, so I prostrated myself before Caroline Janssens, a statuesque blonde at the counter. Her husband, Fernand, is chef and owner. She led us upstairs to a table for six by an open window facing whitewashed walls and flower baskets. "You may have to share," said Lieve, the waitress. I looked so shocked that she thought better of it. I got some really incredible white, very cold beer made in Bruges. Miss Lid had fried scampi that were very tasty. I had moules in cream sauce, one of 11 sauce options. They were good, but not south-of-France good. The chips were absolutely sensational. Home-made. You very seldom find that today. The grand finale was a superb apple pie with whipped cream and ice cream. An enormous portion. Totally historic.

Pie in the Sky

The 24-year-old American chef from the US ambassador's residence in Brussels declined to give an opinion on the three-star-Michelin food served at **De Karmeliet**. Timothy Byres sat there in a corner, with his wife Brianne. He wore no jacket, but a nice blue spotted tie. They were the only other lunchtime customers. He'd travelled to Bruges to sample the supposedly wonderful food. On the whole I found it awful. Marginally worse than the Waterside Inn at Bray – and that's saying something.

We started off with drinks in a lovely atrium overlooking a small garden. Bany Sonnavella, the maître d', was upset when I ordered chicken pie. "It's enormous, it's for two people," he said. "I'll pay for two people and leave some," I volunteered.

"It's not a question of paying," said Bany. "Can you take it home with you?"

"How can I take it home?" I replied. "I'm in a hotel."

"It's a whole chicken," persisted Bany.

"Well, let the staff eat half of it," I said.

The main restaurant was not so attractive. Yellow washed walls and paintings ranging from nice to awful. No cohesion. There was piped music coming from black loudspeakers hanging in the corners of the room. Disgusting. Bany recommended I get in early and order a dessert of pasta with cream in it.

I started with roast langoustine and bits and pieces. Miss Lid had coulis of eggplant, tartare tomato and slices of mozzarella with goose liver. "It doesn't mix, the taste, with the goose liver," she said. I took some goose liver. It was excellent, went very well with my langoustine. Miss Lid got a bit overexcited when they brought her Coca-Cola with lots of ice when she'd asked for none. She spilt it all on the table. They laid down a cloth backed with silver paper, which was odd. It rustled throughout the dinner.

Miss Lid enjoyed her risotto greatly, but my chicken pie was unspeakable. They served half of it. The chicken was very light and lacking in texture. I've never tasted anything like it. It resembled a mousse of man-made, or false, chicken. It tasted of nothing. Also, I don't think the chef, Geert Van Hecke, should expect you to eat salad with the same knife and fork you've been eating hot chicken with.

Miss Lid tasted my chicken and pronounced it, "Absolutely terrible: no flavour or taste." It was one of the worst dishes I've ever been served. Then they brought new napkins and put the side plates on the right. "I want to know why these side plates are on the right," I said to Miss Lid. "I've never had a side plate on the right."

"They want to annoy you," she replied. "They want you out of here as quickly as possible."

Some petits fours arrived before the dessert. I ate a small éclair that tasted as if it had been in the fridge. The recommended pasta and cream dessert was memorably terrible. The pasta was very overdone and chewy, particularly at the edges where it was sort of caramelised. You had to work very hard to pull a piece off to eat. Miss Lid found her banana greatly overcooked. I tried it and it was. The finale was partly saved by some historic honey bread cakes.

When our mint tea came it tasted ghastly. I'd asked for fresh mint, but it didn't seem like it. When I inspected, there was dried mint under the fresh mint. At another place I was told they put Earl Grey in the mint tea to add colour. All this goes to show that three Michelin stars don't always mean much.

De Snippe, a one-star Michelin restaurant in Bruges, is owned by Luc and Francine Huysentruyt. When I rang up it was full, so I explained the enormous importance of my persona: Hollywood movies, *The Sunday Times*, et al. "Can you prove it?" said Luc Huysentruyt. That's the oddest question I've ever been asked. There I am sitting on the phone in a Belgian hotel and this man wants me to prove who I am down the mouthpiece. "What shall I do, sing *My Yiddish Mamma* in Flemish?" I thought. "I'll prove it when I get there," I said.

Luc graciously decided to accept that I was me, and we got a lovely table by the fireplace. De Snippe is in an historic house, very elegant. High ceilings, decorative cornices, Venetian chandeliers. The freebie starter was a codfish curry soup. Then they had a young beer hop served either with langoustine tails or a poached egg. I had *pigeon de Bresse* done as... "It's a kind of stew," I observed. "It's not a stew – because of the shallots and Madeira wine," said Luc.

At some time or other we had baked oysters with sour cream and a tower of bitter chocolate, which was more like a bun with a layer of sauce in the middle. Miss Lid tried apple pancakes flambéed with Calvados. This was an excellent meal. Not historic, but very nice.

A printed sign on the table read: "Please Don't Smoke At The Table." I objected to a man smoking at the next table. Madame Francine said: "It's a request, it's not like a real thing because we put an ashtray there as well." Since the Don't Smoke table sign was in English, German, Flemish and French, it seemed fairly pointless if my chainsmoking neighbour had the approval of management. I'd have chucked him out. That's why I'd be disastrous running a restaurant.

Flemish Masters

It's always nice to stumble on something marvellous when you aren't expecting it. This particular stumble occurred in Bruges, which even out of season seemed to be full of English people. The restaurant has one Michelin star and is called **Den Gouden Harynck**. The owner, Philippe Serruys, found the name buried in the 17th-century house, indicating it was once a fishmonger's named The Golden Herring.

Driving around Bruges is a nightmare unless you're prepared to disobey all rules, something I'm extremely good at. It's full of one-way streets. I was advised to go out of the town, on to some ghastly motorway, and come back in across one of the canals to get to the restaurant.

I broke my first traffic rule by mistake. Cyclists are allowed to go the wrong way up one-way streets. I followed one – and there I was sailing along in the direction I wanted to go but against the legal traffic. Nobody seemed to mind, the Belgians being very polite. They also, I was told, obey all traffic rules and thus drive very slowly. This greatly assisted me in driving, throughout my stay, up one-way streets the wrong way.

The Golden Herring is exceptionally attractive. Large tables, well spaced, very quietly speaking diners, a real log fire, a tiled floor, white walls. Marike, Mrs Serruys, wafts between the tables in a grey silk coat. It's all extremely civilised. Wish there was somewhere like it in London. Butter was not wrapped; a large square of it rested on the table. Real orange juice came quickly with a little carafe for me to mix it with champagne. I did and it frothed on to the tablecloth. Scallops marinated with truffle were a freebie. The Belgian water was called Spa. "It's a little weak," I said. "I'd say bitter," added Miss Lid, determined that her views be known. "I'm trying to be helpful," she explained.

I started with excellent langoustine grilled with basil and mozzarella, and then we had roast lobster in butter with a curry sauce. Everything was sensational. They gave me a bib for the lobster, which is useful, as hardly a meal passes without me spilling some of it on my shirt. I should have taken my bib home.

The couscous with raisins was particularly tasty and I had more of it when they brought some extra curry sauce. To finish, I had *millefeuille* with gingerbread ice cream: Miss Lid had ice cream, hot chocolate sauce and cream.

They didn't make the mint tea with fresh mint, which was the only downer. Otherwise, this was all very memorable. Philippe even drove back to the hotel so that I could follow his car. Thus I took my only legal journey through Bruges in my entire stay.

It's always wise to ask the best restaurateurs where they eat on their days off. Phillipe Serruys, owner-chef of Den Gouden Harynck (one Michelin star) said, "Try **Heer Halewyn**. It's where the in-crowd of Bruges go." Later he left a panic message at the hotel that I should take cash because they didn't accept credit cards. The Heer Halewyn is a small bistro-like room featuring brick walls with maps on them and a charcoal grill in front of a roaring log fire. Two old ladies sitting close to it were going redder and redder. I'd eaten a lot of rich food, so the tasty grilled steak with jacket potato was most welcome. Miss Lid had an extremely good kebab. I started with a fine salad with cheese and walnuts and ended with vanilla ice cream with chocolate sauce. All very nice. The in-crowd of

Bruges didn't look much like the group you see at San Lorenzo in London, which sports more plastic surgery per square foot than anywhere in the world. And superb, much under-rated food. But they were a wholesome lot.

I don't often take risks. I go regularly to the same places. So when I recently decided to spend a weekend away, the question was – where? I decided on Bruges. I'd last been there in 1956 when I made my first ever movie, a documentary entitled *This Is Belgium*. It rained a lot that summer, so it was finished off in East Grinstead. It made it into the *Guinness Book of Records*, as the only film about Belgium ever shot in Sussex.

My first problem was that there's no legendary hotel in Bruges. In the *Michelin Guide* it has one three-star restaurant and two one-stars, but the highest-rated hotel had two black towers (three is top) and was modern. I hate modern. Among one-tower hotels listed, two were coloured red. For those who understand the *Michelin Guide* (and I've never met anyone who does) red means *Hôtels agréables*. Neither place could offer much, but the **Relais Oud Huis Amsterdam** came up with a junior suite.

Bruges is easy to get to. You take a private Learjet from RAF Northolt and it's a half-hour flight to Ostend. The hotel was a 40-minute drive. It's a lovely 18th-century house on one of the beautiful canals. The junior suite was an attic with a high, pointed ceiling and four tiny windows looking on to rooftops; very gloomy, not much furniture. I phoned downstairs to an immensely charming 22-year-old girl, the only person in charge. "Ilse, this is the worst room I've ever been given!" I said, trusting the message would get through. Ilse appeared, quite unworried, with a bunch of keys and showed us six other rooms, all of which were worse. The next day someone failed to turn up, so we moved to a real suite, pleasantly furnished with three large windows overlooking the canal.

WINNIE WITH
A BIB AT
THE GOLDEN
HERRING

M 2000

WINNIE BY
THE SEA

4

C A R I B B E A N

Carambola sits on a commanding cliff top in Barbados. There the grilled fillet of swordfish with bajan pepper sauce mayonnaise, served with apple, tomato and blackeye pea salad, is a delight.

I think most people would place **The Cliff** at, or near the top of, their list of favourite restaurants in Barbados. It sits overlooking the sea. It is owned by Brian Ward, whose family once had Treasure Beach hotel. You'll find it hard to beat their Caribbean shrimp with green curry sauce.

Coral Reef, the best Barbadian hotel of the old days, is still nice. But I always notice how the beach there has diminished. Indeed the ravenous removal of the coral reef to sell in little pieces to tourists has played havoc with the yellow sands.

Inland in Barbados, when driving your Mini Moke, almost as soon as you left the coast road you used to go through banana plantations and little wooden villages. Now you journey through acres of posh housing estates on your way to the Atlantic side of the island, windswept and severe but comparatively untouched, for a lobster lunch at the **Kingsley Club** or a stroll round the Andromeda Botanical Gardens.

At **La Maison**, Barbados, you sit inches from the sea at beach level. I had an excellent meal there, hosted by Robert Earl of Planet Hollywood fame.

Star in His Eyes

It was called the Lone Star Garage and Motel when it opened a couple of years ago as a boutique hotel on Barbados's St James's coast. It was quite awful. I had two of the worst, most tediously served meals I've ever eaten and had to put up with a ghastly charity-night speech from a third-rate comedian who has a small flat next door. So it was with some nervousness, even though it was recommended by that excellent photographer Terry O'Neill, that I booked myself two rooms. I was so nervous that I covered myself with a four-room, three-bathroom house at the nearby Royal Pavilion. I became even more neurotic when an English lord inspected it and said that an open sewer ran through the beach and the food was indifferent.

The place is now called the **Lone Star Hotel and Restaurant** because the word "motel" put people off. It is quite exceptional. I mean that nicely. There are only four rooms. I was on the raised ground floor in two adjoining rooms with large balconies facing the Caribbean Sea. It was hotel accommodation of extreme elegance. Modern, but tastefully designed by one of the hotel's owners, Steve Cox. He also has restaurants in Richmond, Surrey. The beach is uncomfortably small, but no sewer runs through it: it's a storm drain from the coast road.

The Lone Star Restaurant, also beautifully designed, is right on the sea and has improved greatly since its opening. I was in Barbados for six dinners and six lunches. I ate all of them, bar two dinners, at the Lone Star. It's also the most "buzzy" place on the island. Everyone seems to pass through: from Jodie Kidd to Cilla Black (admittedly with me); from Robert Sangster to Frankie Dettori. Even Vinnie Jones booked a table for 10, but I exited before they arrived. I had heard they could be noisy.

The Lone Star's excellent chef, Andy Whiffen, comes from Poole in Dorset. He produced some memorable fresh lobsters, some superb crab cakes, a very good white- and dark-chocolate mousse, nice chicken tikka and one of the worst, most overdone plates of spaghetti ever. The service is very good. When I noted there were no cotton buds or slippers in the rooms, they were there the next day. So it would be churlish of me to mention that one of the bedside tables had only been half-dusted, the dirty half being so thick I doubt it had been touched since the place was built.

They should also have a weighing machine in the bathroom, even though I wouldn't use it for fear of becoming depressed. They sported piped music in the restaurant, but it was quiet and consisted of 1950s hits. I'm prepared to drop all objections to piped music if it's Dean Martin singing *Volare*, or any other tune for that matter.

Christian Roberts, a former actor, is a co-owner, and Rory Rodger the general manager. They are both immensely charming. You even get 125g of beluga caviare as a freebie at your first meal. So it seems churlish (yet again) to mention one of the most diabolically inept moments I've ever suffered in a restaurant. I had chosen, with Rory, a table "by the rail", as the Americans say. I told him if I wasn't coming I'd be sure to phone. One night I particularly told him I'd be there with very dear friends from England. I entered the restaurant and, as my guests hadn't arrived, I sat down with Frankie Dettori and his manager. When my friends showed up, they joined us for a moment. Then – a sight I shall never forget – Rory was leading a party of four to my table. They sat down. I shot up. "What on earth are you doing, Rory?" I demanded. "You've given away my table."

"We had a phone call from the Royal Pavilion cancelling for you," he said.

"Nonsense," I replied. "You can see I'm here. Clear my table at once."

Rory, nervously, got the people off. Not unnaturally, they made a derogatory comment about me as they passed by. I felt guilty, even though I was totally innocent.

We later found the Royal Pavilion had cancelled a table for Mr and Mrs Ogden. Only in Barbados does that sound like "Winner".

As the meal progressed, I called Rory over. "Go to those four people," I said. "Apologise again. Make sure they know it's your fault and tell them the meal is on me." On the way out, the displaced, freebie group stopped to thank me. They even invited me to a cocktail party a couple of days later. Rory, you will be glad to hear, is forgiven. Because I am so incredibly kind. But you know that already.

A Pavilion Too Far

Barbados has become a goyish Golders Green. In case you're not *au fait* with Yiddish-New York dialogue, this means Barbados has become a suburban housing estate largely inhabited by non-Jews. My friend Lord Glenconner says it's "like the Costa Brava blown up bigger. Not prettier, just larger". I used to travel from the airport through lovely sugar plantations, past coloured-hut villages, old stone sugar mills and on to the sparkling Caribbean Sea. Now you sit in endless traffic jams on tacky motorways, looking out at car showrooms and supermarkets. What are laughingly called villas stretch back from the coast, annihilating the landscape that attracted people to the island in the first place.

The St James's coastal area is still pretty. The Sandy Lane hotel, predicted, with pathetic optimism by the managing director, Richard Williams, to open in October 2000, will surely not. It might be finished by October 2001, two years over schedule. I wouldn't even put money on that. So I reserved a house with three bedrooms, a large sitting room, terraces and a garden in the grounds of the **Royal Pavilion**. And two further rooms at the chic little Lone Star hotel nearby. I chose which hotel to sleep in each night.

I unpacked first at the Royal Pavilion, locally nicknamed the Pink Pavilion. This is the second grandest hotel in Barbados, set in beautiful grounds. Unfortunately, it suffers from a design fault, irreversible unless it's knocked down. They destroyed the wrong hotel with Sandy Lane. They could have rebuilt the Royal Pavilion further from the sea. Now it's so close to the beach that an 8ft sea wall stands in front of the ground-floor suites, giving the residents nil view. The beach is a thin strip backed by a boring residential block. But it does expand at one end and that's where I sat.

Not before drama with my rooms. Both the new general manager, a nice young Dutchman called Jan Schöningh, and the deputy general manager, an immensely likeable, charming local chap, Alpha Jackman, agreed that a suite only needed one locked door – the entrance to the living room.

When we returned that night the side door for maid service had been left open – so why lock the front? And my bedroom was locked. I had to call security to get in. After managerial apologies, the following night my bedroom and another one were locked. I became agitated. For £1,500 a night you should be able to go to bed.

Service at the Royal Pavilion seemed diabolical. It took me 44 minutes in boiling sun to get a Sprite. Jan Schöningh was apologetic. "I can assure you, Mr Winner," he said, "that I intend to spruce the place up. If you come back in three months, you won't have to wait 44 minutes for a Sprite." "I won't be here in three months, Jan," I said. "What about tomorrow?"

Thereafter, room availability and beach service improved immensely. Sometimes there were five beach attendants asking if I wanted anything – and then there'd be none. But they were all nice people, particularly Egbert, who traversed the paved walkways throwing an iced bucket nonchalantly in the air and catching it behind him. Until it fell and dented, as we all knew it would. I left Egbert my hotel freebies: a bottle of champagne and a strange glass ornament of hands doing something odd.

Dinner at the Royal Pavilion is famous for being terrible. The hotel itself is actually pleasant. But I never saw more than six people eating dinner. Even regular and devoted guests told me it was abysmal. They wouldn't eat there, so I didn't. Breakfast was extremely good and well-organised, in a pleasing room on the beach. I got genuine, freshly squeezed orange juice without much trouble. The staff were all a delight; the bacon was excellent. They even started bringing ice lollies round the beach, compliments of the management. The Royal Pavilion is run by Fairmont Hotels and the Canadian Pacific group, and it's well worth a visit. If you eat dinner there, tell me about it. I'm sure it will improve.

The sweet taste of power

I still have some niggles about the **Sandy Lane Hotel**, Barbados. I wouldn't be me if I didn't tell you. But I have never seen such improvement in a hotel within a one-year period as at this beautiful place, which has been my Christmas/New Year home for the past 15 years. Two years ago I rather tore into the Sandy Lane. While overall it was a great experience, I politely pointed out the food in its main Sandy Bay restaurant was dire. In the Italian eatery below, it was gloomy and, at best, adequate. The dress code was daft beyond belief, and so on. Some guests, who spent their time on the beach saying much the same thing, wrote crawling letters of hotel-support, perhaps to ingratiate themselves with management? But those in command listened to MW and smartened things up no end.

Last year they had a new chef, a new under-chef, a new food and beverage manager; they'd redecorated part of the gloomy downstairs room and generally perked up immensely. This year the changes have come to near-total fruition. The food is fine, the downstairs dump is now totally renovated. New tables and chairs have been put in, lovely, jolly undersea murals added and the buffet-serving area transformed. "Entirely due to you," the current chef, Hans Schweitzer, said, as we admired it. The staff was always great, except for the only Italian with no charm I have ever met. He head-waitered the downstairs Italian place and he's gone. Mino, a warm, nice chap from Rome, has replaced him. Who says it's a dis-advantage having Winner on the loose?

Herr Schweitzer even gave me some truly memorable food. Although it did vary! His cold grapefruit and guava soup was delicious. Deep-fried shrimps with vegetable chips and three sauces – sweet and sour, tartare and tomato – were superb. In the downstairs Italian, Max the chef served some of the best spaghetti and tomato sauce ever. I felt confident enough to have my friend Owen Arthur to lunch – and he's prime minister of Barbados!

What then do I have to grumble about? First the hostesses. Last year I complained about Miss Verbal Muzak. This year she has been replaced with two! They were wisely kept away from me, but the word on the beach was dire. "Why," I asked the manager, Richard Williams, "have them at all?" Lord A (it's very posh at Sandy Lane come Christmas) was going to his table when one hostess said: "I see you know where your table is." "I should do," replied Lord A tartly. "I've been going to it for 20 years!" And as he was leaving at 10pm came the brilliant remark: "Enjoy the rest of the day!" Another distinguished aristocrat was appalled at having these ladies continually interrupt his dinner with: "You are enjoying your meal?"

The dress code is still a mess. First, denim of any kind was not allowed in the evening, even in the casual downstairs restaurant. But much nastier, cheaper material was. Then, just jeans were not tolerated. "This year," I said to Mr Williams, "I have studied the guest reference book and your daily newsletters. I cannot find the word jeans!" Mr Williams looked glum, even though I meant it as praise. Later, the distinguished aristocrat's two extremely elegant sons appeared in the lower, casual place. An under-head waiter said: "I won't serve you, you're not well-dressed enough!" They wore nice trousers, not jeans, designer T-shirts and waistcoats. Too good, I would have thought. The lady-wife of the distinguished aristocrat came roaring down. She is one of my favourite people, but not someone to cross. "We don't serve guests in T-shirts," explained the under-head waiter. Lady-wife checked the room. "You're serving five of them already!" she said. Mr Williams was duly called and lady-wife gave her views most clearly. Next day on the beach, the distinguished aristocrat, who brings a large family each year, was heard to mutter: "Any more of this and I'll go somewhere else."

When, last year, Sir Rocco Forte left his own hotel on New Year's Eve to attend my private party in a restaurant, a newspaper later asked him why. "Because I don't go to the Caribbean to dress up," he replied, sensibly.

Mr Williams should stand on his sweeping beach, face a wondrous Caribbean sunset and repeat: "I must fire the hostesses and revise the dress code." Then he can think on how well he has done overall.

The re-building of Sandy Lane continues. To no-one's surprise, except hotel boss Richard Williams, we Sandy Laners face a third Christmas without our normal base. The hotel was closed in May 1998 with Mr Williams seriously announcing it would be back for clients in October 1999, having been totally demolished and then re-built! But I have the highest regard for its Irish owners, Dermot Desmond and J P McManus, and wish them well. Realistically, their hotel looks like re-opening in May 2001. Exactly when I prophesied it would! They have a new General Manager, a Frenchman, Jean-Luc Naret, who was at La Residence in Mauritius. Announcements on their website suggest the coming of a super-totally efficient wonderland.

The outstanding ex-manager of Sandy Lane, Pierre Vacher, said to me recently: "The great thing about Sandy Lane was you knew every day something would go wrong. That was its charm." I've no doubt thus it will remain. I greatly look forward to its rebirth.

Isle be damned

My January experience of Barbados hotel life was dire. I chose what used to be a good little place, **Treasure Beach**. Their only supersuite, for a period out of peak season, cost £1,200 a night, accommodation only.

Marilil Troulan in reservations wrote: "We'll arrange for a taxi to meet Mr Winner at the airport." My Mr Fraser replied snottily: "At those prices a limousine is usually provided free of charge." The manager, Trevor Ramsay, said they'd send one, explaining: "We are a very small property, no pomp or grandeur." For well over £1,200 a night all-in, a bit of grandeur would be quite acceptable. When we arrived at one o'clock in the afternoon the suite wasn't ready. It had not been occupied the previous night. We waited glumly in the tiny lobby. Finally, I walked into the suite and sat on the balcony as they cleaned up.

The second night no service was provided at all. We came back from dinner to find the same mess as when we'd departed. I went bananas. Mr Ramsay apologised profusely. The fourth night the same thing happened again. Unbelievable! Mr Ramsay deducted one day's charge. I don't go for discounts, I go for service. It took 40 minutes to get tea and biscuits, and their biscuits were dry cheese crackers. It was all basically horrendous. Room service even sent paper napkins.

The restaurant wasn't bad. The excellent maitre d', John Douglin, looked, talked and laughed exactly like Frank Bruno. "All the English guests say to me, 'You know what I mean, Harry?'" said John. "I don't even know who Harry is." I had three lunches there. Pan-fried dolphinfish was good. So was the chef Jeffrey Hyland's bajan chicken; the seasoning was memorable. Vanessa liked her catch of the day, kingfish, with herbs and spices. She said: "They should have proper, smarter ketchup here. The ketchup is horrible."

I called "Hello!" loudly to get attention. A smiley, chubby Welsh lady at the next table, wearing a pink cruise-ship cap with Oriana on it, cried "Hello" back. Her husband hated his Caesar salad. He said: "It was just lettuce, very dull. Thank God for breakfast." I had no sympathy at all. They weren't paying £1,200 a night, plus food and extras, for poor service and scant hotel facilities. But then, they were Welsh. They had more sense.

Peace of Caicos

It was like something out of a Fellini movie. There were these luxury beach huts facing white sand and the most turquoise blue sea you could imagine. Then staff erected a series of open-sided tents, placed long tables in them, and more servants filed down from the hotel carrying food on silver trays. Ensconced in this little area, which common folk like me could only gaze at from the wooden walkway that led to the beach, was Donatella Versace, her daughter, bodyguards in assorted colours, and selected friends, relatives and who knows what.

Thus was the scene at **Parrot Cay** in the Turks & Caicos Islands, where the sun beat down from a blue sky onto the recently planted palm trees and other flora, as Robert Earl, of Planet Hollywood fame, struggled to perfect his hotel in time for my arrival. Possibly he also took into account the other guests, none of whom Signora Versace deigned to move among. She stayed in her manor, we crawled over the hotel – although Vanessa nearly got to see her close-up in the gym, stopped only by a large black bodyguard, who said: "Why are you carrying a camera?"

I had to be content with the sighting of a blonde lady accompanied by burly minders, walking in the distance from sea to hut-suites. Still, there was the very jolly and excellent New York playwright Wendy Wasserstein, currently working on the screenplay of the musical *Chicago*, and a beautiful American blonde, Amber Valletta, whom I was assured was the most famous model in the world. I'd never heard of her, but the last model I knew anything about was Jean Shrimpton. So call me stupid, I don't care.

In this part of the Caribbean, Cay means island and Parrot was changed from Pirate, possibly to stop guests at this highly posh resort thinking they were heading for Disneyland. It's an elegant place, set on a 1,000-acre private island some 20 minutes by pleasing boat ride from the main island of Providenciales, which you get to from England via Miami. The 56-room hotel is co-owned with Earl by Christina and V S Ong, who also have the superb Metropolitan and Halkin hotels in London.

We arrived to be picked up by golf buggies at the small pier, taken to an excellent colonial-style suite with a large balcony and thence poolside, with the sand and sea only a few yards away.

I'd like to tell you what I had for lunch, but as I started dictating into my tape recorder, which has taken over all natural functions of memory, Mr Earl snapped (very unlike him, he's usually super-cheerful): "We're not going to have to listen to you talking into that at every meal, are we?" Never one to offend, I turned it off, and it never saw the sunlight again, poor thing. I did manage to sneak a few hand-written notes when Robert wasn't looking. They recall the food was very good. In particular a strawberry sorbet that was majorly historic, some lovely Thai beef curry, a delicious papillote of lobster tail with spiced balsamic rice, and a memorable supreme of duckling with poached pear in spiced red wine and honey.

As the place was new, I was given a mercifully short document from Alison Marshall Public Relations of New York, whomever she might be. It provided me with the names of the French chef, Franck Aubert, who got a Michelin star in St Maxime, and the general manager, Michel Neutelings. I was very impressed with him. He pitched in and did things. He'd been at the K Club in Barbuda, much visited by Princess Di. My press release told me: "His interests include scuba diving, boating and reading." That's rather like listening to Miss World contestants telling you they want to help the poor. I've always wanted to read a press release saying someone terribly significant is "interested in picking his nose, ironmongery and farting", but then I'm extremely childish and I don't suppose I ever will.

I can definitely recommend Parrot Cay. The plan is to build many houses on what is now virgin land, so get there before all that. There's a nearby place you go to by boat called Iguana Island, which has 4,000 iguanas on it, and that's all. It's fascinating, just like a midget version of Jurassic Park. My only problem at Parrot Cay was when I walked into the lovely, warm sea. And walked. And walked. About quarter of a mile later the water was still only up to my waist. Vanessa was able to swim under those conditions. But my athletic skills are not yet that well developed. Nor will they ever be.

Glenconner

"Memories," as the wonderful Dean Martin sang, "are made of this." But made of what? Wives – not in my case. Girlfriends – I'll say "yes" to that. Magical views – possibly. Food – definitely!

I wish to recall one of the most memorable meals ever which I devoured last New Year's Eve. It was prepared by Lord Glenconner, aka Colin Tennant, the subject of a recent TV portrait *The Man Who Bought Mustique*. This captured Colin in all his glory, wandering around in flowing robes, castigating whites and blacks alike, hitting the TV soundmen, and generally acting like Basil Fawlty on speed. In fact he's the kindest of men, utterly positive and forward looking in spite of having lost two sons to AIDS and another crippled in a motorcycle crash. On top of that a load of moronic ingrates living in luxury on the island estate he created for them, turned on him and turfed him out of Mustique. I will not dwell on the whys and wherefores. I prefer to see, in my mind's eye, Colin on December 31st 1999 in his small restaurant and bar in St Lucia offering Georgina and me this staggering meal.

After the Mustique debacle Colin acquired a rain forest between the mighty Pitons (large hills or small mountains according to how you look at it) on a beautiful undeveloped coastal area of St Lucia. One third of this land is now the Jalousie Hilton. The rest belongs to Colin who is selling it off as building plots, undoubtedly some of the best available in the world.

Returning to the end of last year: it was tropical downpour time with highly energised rain. Intermittently, it stopped only to start again. Colin's marvellous little complex, **Bang Between The Pitons**, had been demolished by a hurricane a short time before. But he'd re-built, doubtless spurred on by the knowledge I would be turning up. The restaurant offers a row of booths covered with an awning, lovely lanterns, some transplanted, old Caribbean houses, a gift shop, a small bar, a dance floor, a bandstand, and in the centre four poles holding a roof over the best table. There we watched the rain beat down around us. The only other diners were a British party of airline hostesses with men who did whatever men do on airlines. The ladies were marvellously overdressed in sequins and high heels. The group all entered with streamers and blowing whistles. They were a delight and danced vigorously during such moments as they could without getting drowned.

We started with grilled coconut slices. Delicious beyond belief. Sometimes Colin offers local fish or fishcakes. On this occasion there was christophine gratinée. Then came the main triumph, crayfish picked that very morning from the rain forest rivers high up in the mountains. This was a taste to remember forever. We also had stir-fried okra, a salad and Chinese potatoes. To drink there was fresh mandarin juice, always softer and less acidic than orange. Knowing my fondness for jelly Colin had prepared a lime jelly with tangerine slices in it served with superb coconut ice cream from the local firm Ferrands.

A band played. Staff scurried through the rain. Around ten o'clock I got in my jeep and drove back to the adjacent Jalousie Hilton to sit with concert pianist and conductor Vladimir Ashkenazy and his family and later with some people I'd previously met at La Samanna in St Martin. It's my intention to return to both Jalousie and Colin for the 105-day away New Year's Eve.

Friends in High Places

I was chatting to Michael Edward, superboss of Caribbean Connections, about where to go after La Samanna in St Martin was hurricaned. "How about Coral Reef, Barbados?" he said. "That's not a first-class hotel," I responded. "I'll try the **Jalousie Hilton**, St Lucia." "That's certainly not a first-class hotel," said Mr Edwards with such scorn the phone wilted in my hand. Mr Edwards is right. The Jalousie Hilton Hotel and Spa is certainly not a first-class hotel. But I went there, extended my stay to 16 nights and declare it one of the most pleasant holiday experiences ever.

I was for many years in real estate – an absurd business where any moron can make a fortune and then preen around as if they'd done something clever. There's a golden rule about buying property. You need three things: location, location and location. In this respect Jalousie is unparalleled. It's the most stunning hotel location I've ever seen. A beautiful tropical rain forest set between two 2,700ft-high mountains – the Pitons, clad in luxuriant tropical growth – was cleared by an Iranian prince, then working with Lord Glenconner. A plantation-style hotel appeared. I saw it being built. I went there when the prince ran it. I saw it go into semi-liquidation and close, until, two years ago, Hilton took over. They added a marvellous white sandy beach and run it to their own standards, which are okay, but nowhere near the class of the Orient Express Group or the Amman people. This is a pity, because Jalousie, notched up, could be one of the best hotels in the world.

My trip started badly. I took Concorde to Barbados and then a 40-minute flight by an excellent private airline, SVG of St Vincent, to St Lucia. Rui Domingues, the general manager of Jalousie, had assured me a helicopter would be waiting. There was nothing and nobody to greet me. "Well, Rui," I said after a 45-minute bumpy taxi ride on potholed roads past stunning scenery, "you're at rock bottom now. You can only go up." Rui promptly left for 12 days in Canada. "How bizarre," I thought, "for a manager to go on holiday during the peak Christmas season." "I'll be looking after you," said his No 2, a pleasant young Englishman called Jeremy Mutton. He said it with confidence. "Doesn't know what he's in for," I thought. Things went pretty well, except for horrific trench warfare on the beach (see below). We had a small house overlooking the sweeping gardens and the bay. Two bedrooms, two bathrooms and a sizeable roof terrace.

The first irritation was tacky piped music blaring away at breakfast. It showed management's view of the place and customers – the most ghastly lot I've been in a hotel with, mostly there, it seemed, on Hilton points collected from using other hotels. "We're sitting here with a wonderful view, with the sound of the sea, tropical birds, the wind in the palm trees, and there's this horrific music," I said. Eventually they got rid of it. It was the same at the Bayside beach restaurant. "Most of our guests request background music," said the boss there, Alan Pierre. "Absolute nonsense," I said. "Let's you and me go round all the tables right now and ask if they want this appalling, cheap din." Mr Pierre, wisely, didn't fancy his chances. The music was turned off.

The food is below par even for the Caribbean. But I learnt to make do. I had English muffins with fried eggs for breakfast, plus excellent fresh orange juice, specially squeezed. Mr Mutton had tried to put me off. "It's very pale," he said, obviously preferring me to have the mass-produced muck. In fact, it had a marvellous taste. For lunch I made do with a mini-steak, charcoal-grilled, or hamburger and caesar salad. They let us sit on the breakfast terrace for dinner, Miss Lid and I, solitary, with a waiter. The soups were fine. Later, their storm-damaged Pier restaurant buffet opened. I scoffed the kiddies' menu of meatballs, spaghetti and baked beans.

Lord Glenconner, who has a restaurant complex next door, always came for breakfast. One morning, exceptional piano playing wafted down from the terrace above. "It's Vladimir Ashkenazy," I said. "No, it's an automatic piano," his lordship replied. It turned out to be Ashkenazy, who'd bought two hotel cottages. He played every morning. Breakfast with a witty lord and the world's greatest concert pianist is quite bearable. You could go to Jalousie for £2,168 per person for two weeks for a standard room, no food, including air fare. Vladimir will have gone. With luck, the piped music won't have fought its way back.

I promised to tell you about my harrowing times on the supremely beautiful beach of the Jalousie Hilton, St Lucia. As with many resort hotels, beach management was appalling. Guests of extraordinary vulgarity nick your chairs. Nobody protected the regulars. In well-run hotels, residents have a spot and it's kept for them. When the hotel-provided nanny of a highly volatile American sat on one of my chairs, I objected and he started screaming. Nearly hit me. It took a day before my charm won him over. We both yelled abuse at a large yacht vomiting smoke. "You can be in my team any time, pal," he said, honouring me with an energetic handshake.

Another time, after lunch, two English girls were prostrate on my loungers with a garage sale of clothes spread around. I asked them to go.

A few moments later their grandmother appeared. "My granddaughters are very nice girls. You were rude to them," she snapped.

"They're not nice, they're chair grabbers," I responded.

"You should have left possessions," replied enraged granny.

"We did. An umbrella, a bowl of fruit and newspapers," I said indignantly.

"That's not enough," she retorted. "I shall report you."

"Who to?" I asked.

"The gift shop."

Lovely place, the Jalousie Hilton; I did like it. But if you go, take barbed wire and landmines to protect your space.

The **Fish Pot** in Grand Case, St Martin, is run by Kristal from Macedonia with husband Jean-Marc from Normandy. Lovely salmon and cheese tartlet. The French onion soup was good. Snapper and mahi-mahi were excellent, with a real, French-tasting sauce. Desserts reasonable, but profiteroles, always tricky, were poor.

It seemed you couldn't just phone up and book **Mario's**, a much-praised restaurant in St Martin: it was full for ever. I decided to visit and apply my legendary charm. Mario's is in a hut on a canal overlooking a junkyard. Martyne Audet, the wife of chef Mario Tardis, sat at her computer fending off would-be eaters. After a bit of chat, Martyne agreed I could come that evening. At night the place looked very nice. Candles on shiny wood tables, the ripple of light on the water, sunflowers everywhere. Martyne had not succumbed to greed and packed people in. Tables were well spaced. She was a superb hostess and order-taker. The service was like lightning. I tasted Vanessa's black bean soup. It was totally brilliant. But I could smell, with great clarity, my Maine steamed mussels in a tomato, Parmesan and fines herbes broth. They weren't nice. I had chosen the main course "signature" dish of half duck, honey-garlic glazed and crisply roasted, served with caramelised onion, mashed potato and sweet-and-sour sauce. The duck was shiny white. I've never seen anything like it. The texture and taste were poor. Vanessa had grilled tuna accompanied by gnocchi in tomato sauce and blue cheese that was smeared over everything. It was an extraordinary dish. Dessert was crispy profiteroles with ice cream and chocolate sauce. Nice and gooey, rather like they served on TWA in the 1970s.

Saints be praised

I was apprehensive going to La Samanna for Christmas on the half-Dutch half-French island of St Martin in the Caribbean. I'd been to Sandy Lane for 15 years, and while I greatly admire the Orient Express people who own La Samanna, I'd had a dreadful time at their hotel in Madeira. I was met at the airport by two managers, Bernard de Villèle, who was leaving two days later, and the new American chap, from the ski resort Vail in Colorado, John Volponi. "Managers normally leave after I've been there," I said to Mr de Villèle, "not before."

The suite was terrific. Nicely furnished in "modern French rustic". Great view of a large bay unspoilt by any rubbish, the balcony wrapping round to the front of the hotel. Our first lunch, by the pool, was horrid. My salade niçoise was disgusting. The tuna looked like slices of steak and tasted nasty. It had green and red peppers, which I've never seen before in a niçoise; many of the regular ingredients were missing. Vanessa's Caesar salad included tomato and had a sharp, unpleasant taste.

As it was five hours later for us because of the time change, I ordered room-service dinner. "Is the orange juice fresh?" I asked. "Yes, definitely," said the room-service voice. "Let's get clear what I mean by fresh," I continued. "It means an orange has been cut in half in this hotel and squeezed, quite recently." "All our orange juice is fresh," replied room service snottily.

My order arrived. The two fried eggs I'd asked for on my hamburger weren't there. The so-called fresh orange juice definitely wasn't. It tasted deeply unpleasant. I telephoned again. "Are you seriously telling me this orange juice is fresh?" I said. "Yes, it is," came the reply. When the room-service waiter came to take the tray, I repeated everything. He, too, assured me the orange juice was fresh. It was now 9pm – two in the morning my time. I rang for Mr Volponi, having kept one glass of orange muck, which I was quite prepared to carry to England and have analysed in a laboratory. Mr Volponi was sorting out a problem with a guest, so I rang the chef, a nice young man named Alix Thierry. "Is all your orange juice fresh?" I asked. There was a pause that spoke volumes. "Would you like some?" volunteered Alix. "Thank you," I replied.

Alix, with his fresh orange juice, arrived at the same time as Mr Volponi. The original stuff, not dividing as real orange juice does, sat on a ledge next to the new juice. They were not related. Move the glass with the real one and bits stayed on the side, the other left nothing. I asked, could I please not be treated as an idiot. "Or, to use a first-rate American expression," I said to Mr Volponi, "I did not fall off a turnip truck".

Life after that was very nice. Including the orange juice. The staff at **La Samanna** are basically superb. It's a very well-run, excellent, beautiful hotel. The food, for the Caribbean, where fresh supplies are rare, was good.

Security at the hotel entrance gate was slack, but I put a stop to that. Cruise-ship people and any wanderer with a rucksack seemed to get in, sit on guest beach loungers and generally bring down the tone. They reckoned without Winner the beach vigilante, this time superbly abetted by Mrs Martin Bandier, he the head of EMI in New York, she a hotel regular who told of the days when the manageress, Lynn Webber, would patrol the sands like a storm trooper, removing intruders. That's my kinda gal. The guests were great too. There was an English computer genius who's the chairman of Psion, and a host of highly robust New York music-business people headed by the renowned lawyer Allen Grubman. In his home town Mr Grubman has dishes named after him in posh restaurants. That's the American equivalent of a peerage.

From the hotel super-staff I hereby anoint the marvellous food and beverage manager, Nathalie Senez, who threw herself in wherever needed. She never walked, always ran. And the waitress whose smile made my lunchtimes, Edna Joseph. With Edna serving, a hot dog and chips became two-star Michelin fare. Maybe even three.

I booked dinner at **La Santal**, in St Martin, a poshed-up hut overlooking the sea, tented in pink- and cream-striped, pleated silk. The lady at the desk was extremely snooty, and with the Muzak going the place felt like a Jewish wedding. I ordered a Carton Charlemagne Grand Cru. Then suddenly thought: "I don't think the wine list showed the year of any vintage." I went to the desk and looked. "We don't put the vintage because the stock always changes," said the snooty woman. "So the price stays the same whether it's a good year or bad!" I exclaimed. Nobody cared. The head waiter assured me ours was 1994. The bread was terrible. I felt I was chewing gum. When the wine came it was 1991, not 1994. The gazpacho was like nothing I've ever tasted: it could have been tomato soup with HP sauce added. I ordered chicken casserole and got roast chicken with a sauce. It tasted of absolutely nothing. It was like chicken at a bar mitzvah for thousands of people. The soufflé ordered for dessert was sickly. I am the most sweet-toothed person in the world, but I couldn't eat that one. This was a grossly mediocre dinner.

WINNIE AT LA SANTAL

WINNIE ENJOYS A BELLY DANCER

M2000

5

E G Y P T

Entranced by the rule of tum

Okay, we haven't had a quiz yet. What time do you think Miss Lucy, the belly dancer at the Nice Hilton, started her two-hour act the Friday I was in Cairo? Go on, guess. The answer is 4.30 in the morning! In Cairo nobody goes to sleep and the big stars are the belly dancers. Some people support Fifi Abdou at the Sheraton, some Miss Lucy, some Mona Said at the Meridien. We opted for dinner with Mona on the 15th floor at the oddly named **La Belle Epoque**, sporting a red menu with black silhouettes of a lady dancing with a monocled gent to a horn gramophone.

Mona was coming on early that night, 1.30am I was told. So I had a sleep, got up, and we presented ourselves in this enormous barn with a tired three-piece orchestra playing on a large stage. Some 20 people were lost in a room that seated 200. We got a table for six with a Japanese party of four on our right. It looked desperately sad. I ordered a glass of wine, but a bottle appeared. It was Omar Kayyam from the Egyptian Vineyards Company. Rather sweet, no great taste, but quite harmless. We had the inevitable and good general mix, with mezze to start. By the time we got to the sea bass, a few more people had come in. The traditional bread and butter pudding, *om aly*, was gone, and it was still like sitting in an aircraft hangar at the function that time forgot.

Then at 1am things started to move. The three weary musicians left the stage and a rather grand 15-piece orchestra appeared in black trousers and flowered shirts. An Egyptian singer, looking like a mafioso Tony

Bennett (mind you, Tony Bennett looks like a mafioso Tony Bennett), started to sing 'Autumn Leaves'. An Egyptian wedding group clapped as the bride danced well and the groom danced nervously on the stage. Then the singer started on upbeat numbers. Lots more people came in, and it all began to get lively.

The singer exited to great applause. The room had filled up. It was a quarter to two. The belly dancer's own 43-piece orchestra came on with six singers! Suddenly it was all happening. To a cacophony of rhythm, yelling and clapping, the very ample Mona Said appeared, making a triumphal entrance through the tables, accompanied by six male dancers in long grey smocks waving sticks above their heads. This was it! The star had arrived! The act was extraordinary. Bit of large-belly movement, many bespangled costume changes from a Liz Hurley safety-pin outfit to yellow sequins galore. A lot of finger pointing at the audience accompanied by small, sexy moves. The whole thing a cross between a jolly auntie and a massively voluptuous siren. "I bet you'd be scared if you were alone with her," Vanessa volunteered. "She'd envelop you." "I'd be terrified," I admitted.

A few seconds later I was welcomed as the famous English film director, a microphone was thrust in my hand and I had to say a few words. Arabs who got up and danced at their tables as Mona tripped the heavy fantastic, grinned and waved at me. A second bottle of Egyptian wine came and went. Around 4.15 Mona finished to a tumultuous roar of appreciation. The box of tissues which she'd dipped into for two hours to wipe away the sweat was discreetly taken from the side of the stage. We went back to our hotel through the X-ray check, past the soldiers on guard and up to sleep. Gosh, I thought, as I nodded off – I wish they had events like that in London.

Enjoying the Nile rushes

"Don't eat anything," I was told. "If you must eat, then only oranges or eggs because they're covered with peel or shell. Take stomach pills, take antibiotics." I had been asked to Egypt for the Cairo Film Festival. They were paying a tribute to Oliver Stone, Ismail Merchant, Nicolas Cage, Marsha Mason and me. A motley crew. If I was not to be shot by terrorists, it seemed I was to be food poisoned. We arrived at Cairo airport at one in the morning and a bank official tried to swindle me on the exchange rate. The motorway into town had raised sentry boxes every so often, with soldiers armed with machine guns looking down on us. More soldiers round the hotel and massive security. What, I wondered, am I doing here?

After a few hours of nervousness, I ate everything and anything. It was mostly terrific, none of it gave me tummy trouble. I saw no terrorists, no mugging, no violence, just fascinating places and jolly nice people. So much for over-caution.

I went to the **Cairo Sheraton** for my first Egyptian meal in the city. A staple starter here is one of my all-time favourites, mezze. It's lots of things in bowls with a thick, plate-shaped bread to dip in. There's samboussek with spinach, shrimps, deep-fried brain, chicken wings, hummus, babaghanough, stuffed vine leaves, tabouleh, kobeba and more. I have no idea which bowl was which (well, I could just identify a shrimp), but it was all excellent. The main course was beef and veal with sauce and veg. Far better, I thought, than mass catering in England. There was an amazing cabaret of whirling dervishes, men with tambourines and castanets dressed in skirts. They they eventually peel off over their heads in layers while going round and round at an amazing speed. An orchestra of many strange instruments goes barmy in the background. Most diverting.

I can recommend **El Mashrabia** in a part of Cairo tourists don't normally go. A jolly starter of grape leaves with calf's trotter and an excellent follow-up of stuffed pigeon.

The **Gezira Sheraton** is not the sort of place I'm used to. Okay for normal people and commercial travellers. But there are no posh hotels in the centre of Cairo. It was efficient, with sweeping views over the Nile and the ugly high-rises that dominate the city. And on our one smog-free day we saw the pyramids from our balcony, nestling by the suburbs between a closer view of two other Sheraton hotels.

The **Mena House Oberoi Hotel** in Cairo, near the pyramids, is the only real luxury hotel Cairo has. It was built in 1869, and has since had more gilt added than even The Dorchester. But it's simply terrific. The rooms, the pool and the restaurants all have a spectacular view of the pyramids. I ate by the pool. Good tahina and an "Arab mixed grill'" with four singers and a band playing. The Mena House is where the first peace talks between Egypt and Israel took place. In 1943 it hosted a conference with Roosevelt, Churchill and Chiang Kai-Shek. "They sat in the sun and decided not to decide anything," said Hussein Marzouk, one of the philosophical managers, as he showed me round suites and rooms of unbelievable opulence.

The **Windsor Hotel** in Alfi Bey Street, Cairo, used to be a biggie, but the area got burned down in 1951 and it remains a total time warp in a city overtaken by ghastly modernity. Luxurious it isn't, but atmosphere it has in spades. I had a drink with the owner, Wafik Doss, who's had it since 1964. Wooden tub chairs, wooden stools at the bar, just like you imagine Egypt was when upper-class British were going beserk nicking everything they could from the pharaohs' tombs. In the old-fashioned lounge there were two English people reading the *Guardian*. They looked unbelievably miserable.

WA'DYA MEAN DIDN'T WIN!
I PUT THREE CHOCOLATE
CAKES ON
NUMBER
EIGHT!

M 2000

6

F R A N C E (including MONACO)

Brasserie Bofinger in La Bastille, in Paris, is a great art deco place where Monsieur Bofinger himself drew the first draught beer ever served in Paris in 1864. Very bustling, tall pillars, artistic marquetry. Wonderful onion soup and pot au feu of fish.

Le Corset restaurant in Paris, which has nicely printed cards offering "Drag queen service'" is not everyone's *tasse de café*. Vanessa and I were there at the opening, which was being filmed for Channel 4's *Eurotrash*. Le Corset is a small place near Les Halles with a yellow top bit with a bar and some rather strange cellar rooms downstairs. The decor is almost nonexistent, so it has to rely on the drag queens and the customers for the atmosphere I am positive it will achieve. Three drag queens served us dinner with suitably elaborate gestures and facial expressions. There was excellent sliced salmon and sauce, okay steak and chips, and some splendid crème brûlée. The drag queens were chirpy and charming.

There is something about a really dopey cabaret, seen in comfort and with a reasonable meal that is quite enchanting. The **Lido** in Paris has attracted everybody from Hemingway to the Duke and Duchess of Windsor and on through Cary Grant, Brigitte Bardot, Laurel and Hardy, Danny Kaye, even Presidents Nixon and Reagan. The menus vary from "Touristique" at £80 to "Passion" at £122, including half a bottle of champagne. The show is thrown in. It is a whopping spectacle, changed every four years. I was delighted to catch it near the end of the run because it exuded a sense of dated chauvinism which I rather enjoyed. I have to admit that after what seemed the hundredth lot of girls with pink ribbons flowing, or feathers flying, or pineapples coming out of their heads, waving to and fro, I welcomed the Chinese juggler and the swarthy acrobats. As the fourth horse galloped on and chandeliers edged down and a fountain came up, my mind wandered to thinking how good the air-conditioning was and whether anyone else was drinking Louis Roederer Cristal.

The **Napoli Bar Restaurant Pizzeria** in St Ouen, a northern suburb of Paris, hides beneath one of those endlessly efficient raised autoroutes. This is in the Marché aux Puces, the greatest antiques/flea market ever, which boasts everything from rubbish to vastly expensive antiques. The Napoli, my most favourite caff in the world, has very small tables. It's so busy even I at my most demanding stood no chance of getting two of us alone on a table for four. The waiters ran to and fro, sweating. A mound of steaming rigatoni here, steak and chips there, some incredible pizzas, a hand raised to help the next-door diners get their spaghetti *frutti di mare*. Cheap, cheerful and marvellous.

I am beginning to think going to the **Plaza Athénée** in Paris is a bad habit. Like picking your nose or biting your fingernails. Recently I asked for a suite I'd had before, with a nice balcony overlooking the garden. When I got there I was shown into something different. I settled for a gloomy suite on the fifth. Actually, trouble had started earlier. "Could I have a convertible rental car when I arrive at 8.30pm?" I asked Mr Cailotto of guest relations. "No," he said. It is relevant that my modest suite and the car together cost £1200 *a day*! For that you might reasonably expect service! "Why can't I have the car at 8.30pm?" I asked Mr Cailotto. "Because the Hertz office shuts at seven," he said. Did I find anything good about the Plaza Athénée? Yes. The building's elegant. I only ate there once, then in the Relais Plaza, the snackier bit. It was good, even if Vanessa didn't get what she ordered. There was no waste basket in the bedroom and the TV handset didn't work. But it does have the Winner World Record for room service. The breakfast arrived 2 minutes and 51 seconds after I put the phone down from ordering it.

The **Ritz** isn't perfect (well, nothing is other than me), but I am prepared to make a definitive statement. Anybody who can afford it and stays anywhere else in Paris is mad. There are very few hotels in the world where you are enveloped in an aura of timeless super-excellence. The Ritz is one of them. I was shown to a lovely sloping-roofed suite overlooking the Eiffel Tower. We had a good snack lunch in the downstairs bar. I had goujons of sole and Vanessa had some sort of Ritz special sandwich that was historic. I couldn't stay for dinner, but I walked round the unbelievably opulent halls and corridors in my old jeans and falling-apart shoes and entered the main restaurant and the Ritz Club just long enough to see how the rich live. I well recall Christmas lunch at the Ritz some 20 years ago. A string orchestra played while old women sat alone or with lady companions and waiters hovered with white gloves. Like a Fellini movie. It's even better now.

It's the place to be Seine

The photo I most regret not taking was at **Tour d'Argent** in Paris in 1980. I was by the window, with the incredible view of Notre Dame, and the island it sits on and the River Seine. At a centre table, eating his lunch, was Salvador Dali with a dark-haired woman. I only had a Polaroid with me, but to photograph Dali! I remember him, his fingers shaking a bit, as he studied and pointed at the dessert trolley. Whenever I go into Tour d'Argent I see Dali sitting there. Of course, the middle of the room is not the best table. There is only one place perfect for that staggering view and that is on the bend of the window. At night the tourist boats glide by, lighting up the cathedral and the lovely old buildings either side of the Seine.

I always get the best table, not because of my incredible charm, but because I invariably go to Tour d'Argent with my girlfriend (who doesn't help get the table at all) and a wonderful old man called Thomas Quinn Curtiss, who does. Tom has lived in Paris for years. He first came there in 1922. He's an American, a writer about films and plays for the *Herald Tribune*, and a great raconteur. He saw Sarah Bernhardt on the stage in *Glory* in Paris when she had a wooden leg and played her role in a chair; he's seen John Barrymore's *Hamlet* in New York; and he lives in an apartment just underneath the restaurant, crammed with books and cats. He is a friend of the owner, Claude Terrail.

Claude looms over the restaurant like an elegant Jacques Tati, watching the ducks, all numbered, disappear into the mouths of his wealthy clientele. It has three Michelin stars and five red crossed forks, which is as high as you can get. It's a bit posh for me, because I'm a country boy at heart, but I always find it most agreeable. The menu is silver and the print is small, but if you've got 20-20 vision and can read in very low light you will make out *caneton* Tour d'Argent, *caneton* Marco Polo, *quenelles de brochet* André Terrail, *crêpes Belle Epoque* and other delights. I recently had some lobster bisque (superb), sea bass with red wine sauce (lovely), nicked a bit of somebody else's *salade languoustine* (a taste experience) and ended up with a *soufflé Valtesse* (major). I watched the wine waiter, a nice lad from Sutton named David Ridgway, glide around with the skill of a chubby surgeon. He told me my 1982 Château Lafite, which sits in my hall at home in crates, is best drunk in the year 2000, but he's started to drink it already!

My only disappointment was that the downstairs bar, normally most elegant, has been visually demented by some new, gaudy yellow covering on the sofas and new tables that look as if they come from a do-it-yourself kit. The downstairs area was attacked by a left-wing mob in 1981 when Miterrand got in. If Monsieur Terrail had those awful yellow sofas then, the mob would have run out screaming. But the place survived as one of the world's most legendary eating places. What's more, even I like it.

PS This now has two Michelin stars. It is still great.

A place that's changed unbelievably since the 1950s, when it was considered the best restaurant in the south of France, is **La Bonne Auberge** near Antibes. Under Joseph Rostang, its pink stucco front with crinkly tiles, overlooking the railway line, the Route Nationale 7 and the sea, was a mecca for highly sophisticated food-lovers. Then, one year, I looked in the Michelin Guide and it wasn't even there! "Gone to pot, son took over," people told me. Driving back from Joan Collins in St Tropez, I stopped off at La Bonne Auberge for an early dinner. A nice, fresh-faced young man came out of the kitchen and secured a good table for me when I became difficult. This was Joseph's son Philippe. The whole atmosphere of old-money posh is out the window. But here is quality of a different sort. Only French people came in, as opposed to mainly tourists before. A great deal of *bonsoir*-ing and smiling from the locals. Philippe and his young wife, Delphine, have made the place their own. The lobster ravioli – great. *Soufflé de quenelle Jo Rostang*, a tribute to Philippe's legendary dad – delicious. Snail casserole – remarkable. Pétafine dauphinoise, a creamy, soft cheese – exquisite. The millefeuille Bonne Auberge – great, in an all-custard and flaky French way. Evening turned to night and, outside, trains passed to and fro. Silenced by the thick glass, soundless cars whizzed along the N7. Around me, cosseted, was a piece of French theatre. Old ladies here, a family there, a tiny dog everywhere. How wonderful to see that not all "modernisation" is a disaster.

No such thing as a free lunch

The bridge at Avignon only goes two-thirds of the way across the river Rhône and it crosses a four-lane highway. Perhaps it should be Sur le Pier d'Avignon, but it doesn't have the same ring. It costs £3.57 per person to go on it. I was taking two days in Provence on the recommendation of Mrs Helen Hamlyn, wife of Paul.

Helen put me on to Martin Stein, who runs, with his parents, the **Hôtel de la Mirande** in Avignon. This looks on to cobbled streets and the Pope's Palace, an impressive, fortress-like building, knocked up in the 14th century. It is, indeed, a gem. A transformed 600-year-old town house that once belonged to a cardinal. It has 20 rooms. The Michelin describes it as *"Ancien hôtel particulier, beau mobilier"*; the restaurant gets one star. It's decorated in wonderful provençal taste: tapestries here, old jars there. The rooms are not large, but of an exceptional standard. All the staff are discreetly excellent, including a dear girl who came as a trainee from a Manchester school. I wondered if being a trainee meant she wasn't paid. Either way, she seemed remarkably cheerful.

We got there at two o'clock, so lunch was just a thick pumpkin soup, lovely taste, with croutons and bacon. The tables are very well spaced. Mine was 5ft from the nearest guest chair.

I went speedily to tea on wicker chairs in a glass-topped inner courtyard. The little madeleine cakes that Proust wrote about in his book *Remembrance of Things Past* were historic. So were the fig cake and some other sliced thing. At dinner, the candle-lit high-ceilinged dining room with its log fire was a discreet setting for me to eat *rouget barbet en céléri rémoulade*. Then *éminence de cuisse de biche, sauce poivrade*. This was deer. I noticed how hot the plates were. Food was good, too.

Breakfast was the best ever display of croissants and the rest – home-made jams, honey, freebie stewed apple thrown in. Only thing wrong: they served hot milk with the Earl Grey. The second night I was a bit put out. The restaurant manager is efficient, but he won't win the charm-school prize. I was placed at a different table, not quite as good, I thought. Slightly put me off my *filet de loup à la vapeur de mélisse* and an interesting vegetable called *topinambour* (Jerusalem artichoke to you).

Martin Stein had the misfortune to wander over. "I was told your table was reserved tonight," he said. "Nobody reserves my table, Martin," I explained. "Anywhere." When I left not only was "my" table unoccupied, there had been nobody else in the restaurant at all! A mild black mark, but La Mirande remains one of the all-time great hotels. Cared for, well run and that largely because the family Stein is there caressing it.

Barbizon, an extraordinarily well-preserved village about 45 minutes from Paris, is one of my "finds" in France which I'm really not very keen to tell people about. The **Bas-Bréau** is a small hotel with a large dining room that has that feel of goodwill and personal welcome.

I have always had incredible meals there and wonderful service. The food is historic. There's a lovely garden you eat in in summer and a large, very nice dining room for non-summer. We knocked back a *salade de cèpes d'été*, some *grosses langoustines de Loctudy rôties* (very juicy), *blanc de gros turbot braisé sur l'arête* with caviar, *canard sauvage Colvert rôti* and I really don't know what else! One particularly wonderful thing they do is a cheese called Fontainebleau, named after the nearby forest. It's rather like candy-floss or a cold cheese soufflé made with cream and sugar. Light and whipped, it is one of the great tastes of the world.

In Beaulieu-sur-Mer we were attracted to a charming little six-piece band playing adjacent to the lovely 1930s casino in the restaurant **Petite Fleur**. The band was at one end of a flowered and paved garden, softly lit by old-style globe lights on decorative wrought-iron poles. I expected Gene Kelly to appear and dance. We sat down. "This'll be pleasant," I thought, looking past the palm trees to the moonlit beach and the sea. Then came my ham and melon. You could have chewed the ham for a century and a half and still you couldn't have swallowed it. Vanessa's mozzarella with pesto was old and horrible.

"Let's go before it gets worse," I said, calling to the waiter and asking what I owed them. He beckoned to a senior waiter, who asked why I wanted to leave, and finally said grumpily, "No pay, no pay." We fled, only to be pursued down the road by the first waiter. "The manager wants to see you." Wearily, I turned back, to be confronted by a very officious man. I told him of the awful food and offered to pay again. He asked me to repeat my views of the food. Finally he looked at me and said: "Well, you can't expect to leave without paying!" "But I've offered to pay *four* times!" I said. I reached for my money. "You don't have to pay," he said. "I'll pay myself." And off he went in a huff.

Cagnes-sur-Mer is one of the least attractive towns on the coast, and **Charlot Ier** on the Boulevard de la Plage is the sort of place you whiz by on the way from Nice airport to anywhere west. But it is an undiscovered gem, a great fish restaurant. I went there with Roger Moore and composer Leslie Bricusse, both locals. It's a very non-touristy place and price-wise far below those restaurants, good as they are, that cater for visitors. It's owned by brother and sister Gilbert and Michelle Bottier. They run it, serve and generally do a great deal of everything.

Reading that **Josy-Jo**, a restaurant on the edge of the medieval quarter of Cagnes, had been annointed with a Michelin star, I went there for dinner. I was offered a tiny corner table that I ungraciously declined. This left Josy Bandecchi confused. I don't think she was used to tourists being difficult. She found me a round table for six, looking to the door of the farmhouse-style room. On the right was a large bar, behind which was a charcoal grill with a man continually grilling. A Jane Fonda from Barbarella lookalike, circa 1966, entered with high boots, a very short miniskirt and deep cleavage. She was accompanied by what looked like a pit bull terrier. They went to a small square table. We'd just been given our freebie starter – excellent fried zucchini flower – when a fairly elegant group of three came in with an enormous boxer dog and pink dog mat. They sat at the table next to us and encouraged the dog to reside under their table. We had a not unpleasant meal, but why they get a Michelin star for grilling I do not know.

Lost in France

Clécy appeared on no maps. Not even a very big one of Normandy. I set out to find it, nevertheless. It had been recommended most highly by Gérard Feuillie, the excellent chief concierge at the Hôtel Normandy. It was, he assured me, a village of particular charm set in the Suisse Normande, an area that resembled Switzerland. Odd that, because Normandy, like Norfolk, is very flat.

I did have a photocopy of a map, given to me by M Feuillie. On it he had written in his own hand, somewhere in the ocean, the word "Clécy". On the map itself he had pencilled a largish blob south of Falaise and north of Pont Ecrepin. I pride myself on being one of the great place-finders of all time, so my limited paperwork didn't worry me. It was a day when many weathers appear in quick succession: rain, cloud, bright sun – and then they all rotate again. The Normandy countryside is fine, the architecture olde-worlde and nice, but the trip needed the boost of discovering Switzerland off the beaten track.

Things were not made easier when my rented Renault Safrane kept talking to me. As it only spoke French, I wasn't sure what it was saying, but lights flashed and a female voice of grave urgency reduced me to terror. It was particularly annoying that, when the fuel tank nudged into the final quarter of emptiness, the voice went hysterical.

"Get petrol at once!" she instructed, and the little petrol pumps flashed all over the place.

But we should have miles and miles to go, I thought, if the petrol gauge is accurate. Who do I believe: it, or this madwoman trapped somewhere under the bonnet?

It was 12.50pm, we were on the road and at the spot where there should have been a sign on the left to Clécy there was none. No looming Swiss mountains – if anything, it was flatter than ever. It is rare for me to get depressed, but a teeny-weeny bit of it was trying to get in. Vanessa then spotted a bedraggled wooden sign that read **Château du Tertre**, with an arrow and the word *"Ouvert"*.

I turned off right, and soon we were in a very pretty stone village. We followed the signs to the château and suddenly, there like the gold at the end of the rainbow, was this marvellous, un-mucked-out château set in fields and gardens that had not been overcivilised. It didn't look *ouvert*. Only one car, no sign of life – except, as we drove up, a small tubby man appeared at the top of a flight of stone steps and welcomed us in French. When I said: "Good morning", he replied in English, which well he might, as his name was Roger Vickery and he came from Somerset.

He showed us inside to a magnificent, beautifully done-out mansion. He had come to France at 14, because Taunton was twinned with nearby Lisieux, and thus had ended up with a French wife in an apartment in Paris, and this place as a dream hobby.

"Separated?" I asked in discreet fashion.

"Not yet," said Roger. "I'm just going to Paris to see."

A few moments later, he decided to deal with me himself and delay his trip. Quite right, too.

Let me say clearly: make a note of this place. It is only an hour from Le Havre, half an hour from Caen. It is an important find. Up a well-worn marble staircase with its original wrought-iron balustrade are nine rooms, all decorated exquisitely in 18th-century style and with stunning views. The Suisse Normande, with great hills and gorges and beautiful villages, is adjacent. This is turning-the-clock-back time. The food is absolutely spectacular, the dining room elegant and comfortable, with the most excellent hand-carved wood that looks like fine plasterwork, but isn't. Only two other customers, which suited me fine.

We had breast of chicken, with slivers of black truffle under the skin, cooked in fresh Normandy cream with white wine, leeks, onions and carrots and served with spring vegetables. Good as you could hope for. So were my langoustines and scallops. So was the chocolate tart and apple tart with honey ice cream and crystallised lavender from the garden.

Then Roger took us on the scenic tour. He must be a genius because he knew Clécy well. As we entered, I saw white plastic tables, plastic boats and a lot of cars parked everywhere. A nice waterfall and an old mill house. Well, it was a Sunday, and it's a much-sought-after village. Bit like the Cotswolds – but I'm yet to find anywhere there as good as the Château du Tertre.

We enjoyed a marvellous dinner at the **Brasserie Miocque** in Deauville. There is something about a French brasserie at full pelt that is a wonder to behold. The sheer activity, like a co-ordinated ballet, the good cheer. I had first-rate langoustines. Vanessa had a historic onion soup. Then I had nice tagliatelle with butter and Vanessa the same, with salmon added.

Normandy invasion

I have a golden rule. Never book anywhere unless you are sure it is good. You are lucky, you have me to guide you. I have me, too, but occasionally I let myself down. It was a bank holiday weekend; I wanted to go away, but not too far. Should I try the old favourites – Portofino, Venice, Florence, South of France – or somewhere new? I decided new.

Mumsie, who did in most of our £6m at casinos in Cannes, made occasional sorties to Deauville. I recalled it was a place of class and elegance. I had meant to go before, but no aeroplanes seemed to make the trip. Now I was into private jets. I made a reservation for the best available suite at the **Hôtel Normandy**. It had the highest rating in the Michelin Guide, "luxury in the traditional style" – the same as another hotel in the Lucien Barrière group, the excellent Majestic in Cannes.

I arrived at Deauville airport to be met by the Normandy's chief concierge, an extremely efficient chap named Gérard Feuillie. The self-drive Renault Safrane was at the steps of the plane, and he drove us to the hotel.

The moment I entered, I knew I had made a terrible mistake. It was dreadful. Run-down, tacky, funny guests. I asked the general manager, Marco Zuccolin, to assure me I had a wonderful suite. "It is very beautiful," he said.

It was diabolical. The sitting room had two hard, just padded, upright wooden chairs and a matching sofa against one wall. In the middle of the room was a central table covered in dust. On the opposite wall, a commode with a marble top, also dusty. The bedroom matched in awfulness, so did the bathroom. There were small windows overlooking an inner courtyard. If I'm at the seaside I like to see sea.

I called the front desk. An assistant manager showed me a nasty room that overlooked the sea, and another horrid suite that didn't. I returned to tell Vanessa I had failed in room improvement. I looked out of the window at the central courtyard with some people, dressed even worse than me, eating off cheap plastic chairs and tables.

But what was that? Balconies. I phoned downstairs again. The assistant manager had vanished, as had the general manager; each room trip was guided by some staff member further down the totem pole. A young lady showed me a bright room with French windows onto a large terrace with a table, chairs and two sun loungers. Unfortunately, it was on the raised ground floor and looked onto the main road and tennis courts covered with advertising. Somewhere behind them and further buildings was the sea. Next door was another terrace. I decided they should clear that room of beds and turn it into a sitting room. Thus I would have a two-terrace suite – the best I could do before total exhaustion set in.

The suite faced west and had become extremely overheated by the sun. Vanessa laughed. "I can't believe you're here," she said. "It's like a cheap hotel chain." I was too busy looking for air conditioning, which didn't exist, to see the joke.

In the morning, we had the worst breakfast ever. The orange juice that we'd asked for newly squeezed was bizarre. Vanessa tried a croissant and said: "These are very unfresh." I took a bit of chocolate brioche – awful – and gave up.

"I cannot stay in this room a moment longer," I announced. "I will throw myself on the mercy of a French farmer, offer to drive his tractor to blockade English lorries – anything to get out."

Cottage Industry

Menus are a bore. I can't bear it when everyone studies them and starts asking questions about the food. Then people order, then they change their minds. Then the waiter brings the wrong stuff anyway. The whole thing is an utterly tedious ritual. I'd like to see many more restaurants in our new century offering a set menu. If you don't like it, go to another restaurant with a different set menu. I'd like to see courtesy and welcome and comfortable restaurants with a noise level low enough for you to hear other people at your table. And I'd like to see more restaurants owned by people who turn up and run the place, not enormous enterprises run by committees and employees who don't give a damn and make it quite obvious.

I don't think the British are good at hospitality. They're either too po-faced or too concerned with loss of dignity if they do a "service" job.

There is a restaurant on La Grande Corniche above Eze-sur-Mer in the south of France that personifies the sort of place I like. In an area full of wonderful but rich cooking, with menus so long you need a library card to read them, **La Chaumière** is homespun simplicity personified. It's a rustic farmhouse – chaumière means cottage – run by the Coppini family: Sylvie, Nando and Marie. The only thing you can order, and that must be in advance, is a chicken. Otherwise your main-course choice is totally superb lamb or beef, charcoal-grilled in front of you, the chickens turning above an open log fire.

There's a big wooden table where Nando attacks the meat with a cleaver, cooks it and passes it on to his family to distribute. It's unbelievably popular and rightly so. Starters are a salad with an enormous bowl of crudités. Excellent carrots, cauliflower, radishes, and so on. Great mayonnaise. I went a while back with Miss Lid the First, who was the national kick-boxing champion of an eastern European country. She had a delightful colour photo of herself in boxing gloves, one leg dangerously raised in attack position and with long, blonde flowing hair. She said that in her country they had radishes on bread for breakfast, certainly not for dinner.

You also get a historic home-made pâté: pork, chicken liver and juniper. Then baked potatoes and green salad with the chicken, beef or lamb. Luckily, Chris Rea was there and he'd ordered an extra chicken, so Miss Lid was able to scoff it. Dessert was apple tart, crème caramel or chocolate mousse. An enormous bowl of crème fraîche turns up for good measure. The mousse and the apple tart were as good as I've ever eaten.

La Chaumière is a real, family-owned place. They knew who I was, so there was a lot of kissing in the kitchen, embracing and smiling. If you go to the south of France, try and get in. It's very special.

Eze is an exceptionally pretty village, with its cobbled high-sloped streets of medieval houses leading down to a wonderful cactus garden. **Le Château Eza** is set on a hill high above Eze. The views down to the sea are spectacular. Absolutely everything I've ever eaten here has been superlative beyond belief. The place also does rooms with a view so you can stay if you like.

Old film directors never die, they open hotels in the South of France. So I visited my old friend Wolf Rilla and his wife Shirley at **Le Moulin de la Camandoule** near the unspoiled town of Fayence, some 45 minutes northwest of Cannes. Wolf was most famous for directing *The Village of the Damned*, a classic horror story about staring children, possessed. Not bad training, as it turned out, for running the old mill house dating back to the 15th century. Early on, one of their helpers tried to poison Mrs Rilla by putting something extremely nasty in the drinking water she kept in the kitchen fridge. Another attempted to burn the place down, but ended up setting fire to himself! Well, we all have staff problems. Things have now settled, and the 13 acres of orchard, grass, river, Roman aqueduct, swimming pool, assorted flowers and terrace make it one of the most delightful places in the area. We sat in the sun eating a *petite tarte de tomate et basilic*, and then *marmite de pêcheurs*, which was Mediterranean fish in a saffron soup with boiled potatoes. At the moment the locality is still enchanting, but there are plans for housing developments and golf courses, so nastiness will one day engulf it.

I had been recommended **Le Cep** (also known as Auberge du Cep) in the village of Fleurie. It has two Michelin stars. When I arrived the place was totally empty. I like empty restaurants, you get much better service. Le Cep is simply furnished with wooden, cane-bottomed chairs, flowered cushions and neatly laid tables. An extremely attractive lady, Hélène Chagny, the daughter of the owner, turned up as the hostess, and utterly brilliant she was. She recommended the champagne with freshly squeezed blackberry juice (lovely). I ordered frog's legs (unspeakably delicious), which came after a freebie starter of a zucchini flower with truffle butter and were followed by a main course of chicken with home-made croutons, a sauce with Fleurie (the local wine) and a fresh pasta. I nicked some of Vanessa's snails and then ate more desserts than I should. If only I could find restaurants as good as this in England without having to get poshed up as if you're going to some temple of taste.

In Golfe-Juan, a delightful, smallish port that I have known well for nearly 50 years, you can find the **Bistrot du Port**. It has an old restaurant on the seafront and a wooden platform area right on the sea opposite. We sat there. The house is shuttered, one up one down, and is one of the many remaining old-time buildings. I had some nice marinated salmon and a rather odd local sausage with a sort of aubergine stew with cheese; Vanessa ate a first-class grilled *loup de mer*. It is owned by Colette and Jean-Claude Druffen, a nice, jolly couple always in attendance.

The walled, 16th-century village of Haut-de-Cagnes houses one of the many legendary restaurants of the area, the superb **Le Cagnard**. It is set in an old stone building on the ramparts. The painted ceiling panels slide back to let in the sun and reveal the blue sky. We had sea urchins with their outside spikes still moving! And some oysters and a *loup de mer* so fresh it tasted unlike any other I have ever eaten. Roger Moore calls it the best seafood restaurant in France, and he's no pushover. I can also report the millefeuille was major! There's a laurel wreath on the menu and under it "*Grand Prix de la Gastronomique de la Foire de Paris – Toutes Catégories*". I have no idea what it means, but I agree.

Stormin' Normandy

I had escaped from the Hôtel Normandy, Deauville and was heading for Honfleur. I knew not what to expect, but after the Normandy, Wormwood Scrubs would have been a relief. I turned from the coast into a tree-lined lane and there it was: a very attractive Edwardian house with grey tiles and carved fretwork – the **Ferme Saint Siméon**. Would this save my weekend?

We were shown into a suite which, surprisingly, I liked. It had violently coloured wallpaper with large pink and red flowers, two white leather sofas, and the door frames and beading picked out in pink to match the carpet. Not like my ultra-conservative decor at home, but proof that privately owned French hotels can hold their own with their over-fussed English cousins. A balcony looked on to a lawn on which sat a helicopter, backed by an old barn and lovely trees. A French window led to its own garden with two deckchairs.

Soon came the moment to test Denis Le Cadre, the Michelin-starred chef. Lunch was served in a pretty orchard at the back of the hotel. Xavier Parent, the concierge and general aide, showed us to a table. He was charmingly good, even though when I said "Xavier Cougat" he had no idea what I was talking about. In case you haven't either, Xavier C was a famous Latin American bandleader who appeared in many of the great MGM musicals. I tried to explain that Señor Cougat had a highly renowned, buxom young singer-wife, but I don't think Xavier P was interested in buxom young women – he was far too busy – so I concentrated on lunch.

I was glad to see that, unlike in England, the wine list had a lot of half bottles. It was a pretty good list, the most expensive item being a Château Pétrus 1993 at £550. I had asparagus in a puff-pastry case with sauce mousseline, Vanessa, a terrific salad – only the French can make salad interesting. I had mackerel as a main course, which was fine.

Vanessa ordered cheese. Three tiny bits arrived. Even British Airways offers a wider selection. I did a little number – time they knew I was not easy. "Where is the cheese trolley?" I asked. They produced a large wicker tray, which had four local cheeses on it, and that was that.

Service was leisurely to very slow. The desserts ordered at one o'clock still hadn't arrived by 2.30pm. At 2.31pm we got an *avant dessert* (first time for me), which was cherries in custard. Then came hot apple pie and a chocolate sponge thing, which were excellent. We finished them at 2.50pm – luckily nobody was in a hurry.

Xavier said we should look at the old town of Honfleur, a short distance from the hotel. Honfleur is a masterpiece. I can absolutely recommend it to you. If you go to Le Havre it's moments away, and you could do far worse than stay at the Ferme Saint Siméon. I recall Henry V or some similar bombast was always attacking Honfleur. It hasn't changed much since. Beautiful old cobbled streets. The port of perfect proportions resembles a particularly attractive stage set.

We had three dinners at Saint Siméon. It's run by the family Boelen. Mother, Michèle, has all the severity of a headmistress high on discipline. Full of warmth and welcome she isn't. She kept a strict eye on everything, but in spite of a No Smoking notice on the table, a lady sitting next to us lit up on arrival. When I told the waiter I found that offensive, he did nothing. Madame's sons Bruno and Jean-Marie help manage the place and the chef is married to her daughter Marie-Pier. None of them speak English. But then the French are too arrogant to learn English and the English are too stupid to learn French.

The food was largely brilliant. Best ever filet of pigeon with an onion sauce and little potato pancakes. Spectacular lemon sorbet. Disappointments included thin slices of fried potatoes with lobster, which was rather sickly.

But don't let minor criticisms put you off. Honfleur is historic. The Ferme is good and Normandy is well worth a visit.

After a highly dramatic drive in the rain through the incredible autumn colours of the Provençal countryside, with towering white rocks and vineyards aglow with yellow leaves, I had lunch in an antique-filled town, l'Isle-sur-la-Sorgue, in **Le Jardin des Quais**, near the railway station. Nice garden, very unpretentious, French dogs barking and that. Excellent meal.

Club Class

"The point about this meal," I dictated into my tape recorder recently, "is that it's totally unique. What I've eaten today I could only eat at this restaurant. I can't eat it anywhere else in the world." I was talking about one of the great meals of all time, a meal that's amazingly consistent. The restaurant has been run by the same family since 1920. I first came in 1947. The hut on the Mediterranean where you eat has been poshed up a bit over the years. The little fishing port of Golfe-Juan has become overbuilt and overharboured, so it's a gigantic yacht park like nearly every other seaside place in the south of France. The roads leading to it, which were narrow, tree-lined delights, have become proper highways although the actual coast road the place is on remains much the same.

The restaurant is called **Tétou**. It was highly fashionable when I watched King Farouk of Egypt playing chemin-de-fer at the old Cannes

Casino, and long before that.

I hadn't been to Tétou for four years, but as I entered and was greeted by members of the Marquise, Prins, Morlet and Gay families who have run Tétou for ever, I knew everything was fine. I always eat the same thing because it's top-of-the-league historic. First, I have bouillabaisse, which has lobster, dorade, rascasse, St Pierre and rouget. You get the lobster first, gently placed in the yellow soup, to which you add croutons and garlic. You also get yellow boiled potatoes. The taste of the soup is beyond-belief superb. The lobster and all the white fish are fresh and cooked to perfection. "Huge spoons," said Georgina, using one of them to feed herself. The room is highly attractive. On my right was the beach and the sea. Ahead and around white tablecloths and striped chair covers. The service is unbeatable.

The crowning glory is the dessert. I've never seen it anywhere else. Deep-fried beignets come with enormous jars of home-made jam, sugar and whipped cream. The jams include marmalade with whole slices of orange, cherry, peach, grapefruit, tomato, apricot, melon, lemon and fig. Nine in all, each totally delicious. I remember lunching here one Christmas with a very famous film producer for whom I'd made some movies. "Ah Michael," and he named one of my films, "we did very well with that, we made $20m." I was on 15% of the profit. His reports to me showed the film losing! I didn't even bother to say anything. If I did he'd just have said he'd made a mistake, was thinking of another film. "What a funny business," I thought. "Here's a man who's just admitted swindling me out of $3m and I'm discussing with him where to go for dinner!"

Put out to grass

If there is such a thing as a great national scandal regarding the giving of knighthoods, it is that my friend Paul Hamlyn does not have one. I am not being partisan in this, he has quite simply performed services for the nation far beyond those of most dimwits who get knighted when they should get knotted. It was he who, almost single-handedly, popularised publishing in this century by printing books ever so cheaply and getting them into places they had never been before, like Marks & Spencer *et al*. He sold out his publishing enterprises a number of times for ever and ever more millions, and poured masses of those millions into a variety of charitable causes, running today a substantial charity organisation. He is also a very nice chap with two splendid restaurants.

One of these is Bibendum in his Michelin building in Fulham Road, where he has two partners. The other is in the **Château de Bagnols**, a rambling castle of incredible beauty dating from the 13th century, set among the Beaujolais countryside in south-eastern France, near Lyons. It is perhaps because Paul is a socialist that he never got what he deserved, but he does have a private jet for 10 people and in this we flew recently to the Château. It is a creation of art undertaken largely by Paul's wife Helen, who was at school with me and survived. Paul was, by coincidence, at the same school, but much earlier than Helen and I. Considering the school was vegetarian and during the war served grass from the cricket pitch to help the war effort, it is surprising any of us lived, let alone to own or write about restaurants. The grass, of course, was vastly indigestible. As children we all got ill, but we produced the best milk in Hertfordshire.

But back to the Château de Bagnols, which Helen rescued from a ruin and spent four years and many millions (how many they will not reveal) restoring brilliantly, uncovering wall-paintings from the 15th to the 18th century and generally doing such a remarkable job that at least she got a title, being awarded the Chevalier of the Order of Arts and Letters by the French government.

The château has eight suites and 12 rooms, each one a museum masterpiece. Mine was quite the finest hotel accommodation I have ever been in, an enormous sitting room with 17th-century wall-paintings and a poetic, yellow-silk-hung four-poster in the bedroom, set off by grisaille wall-paintings. Nearly everything in the place is designed by Helen, from plates and cutlery to towels, to brass lights and excellent, strange floor-uplights which look like they come from King Arthur. I immediately bought 25, all of which came back in the private plane! Mrs Hamlyn is delightfully eccentric, because when I dared to ask why there were no cotton-buds or sewing kits in the bathroom, she said: "I don't like the look of them. If you need something, the ladies will do it." I thought of ringing the staff to clean out my ears, but then decided, narrowly, against.

The view from the château is over vineyards to the Monts de Beaujolais, with the odd *pigeonnier* dotted about in old stone. As the sun sets on this, guests repair to eat under the lime trees by candlelight, which is like something out of a Fellini movie. The chef is Philipe Lechat and, as you would expect, with the unbelievable care that is taken with everything else in the place, the food is good, too. I had cold marinated vegetables with local crayfish, then I nicked a bit of Sir Norman Foster's foie gras with pear marmalade, thinking, as I did so, what's a supra-modern architect doing in an old dump like this? Then I had pigeon with rice and mushrooms, but awfully good, and finished off with so many desserts it's a miracle I could stand up.

The public rooms of the château are not quite Versailles, but not far off either, although mostly of an earlier period. Thank goodness there are still loving husbands left prepared to indulge their wives in such extraordinary enterprises. It's surprisingly cheap, considering! About £400 to £600 a day should see you in and out for two, for everything. It's only open from end March to mid-November. It may not be profitable for the Hamlyns, but for me it was a gas!

A real super-luxury hotel with massive grounds, hidden in the heart of St Jean-Cap-Ferrat and by the sea, is the **Grand Hôtel du Cap Ferrat**. This has a Michelin star for its food. I at there once overlooking the flowers and the Mediterranean. A wonderful spot, a haven for the "rich and famous"!

I think the **Hôtel Royal Riviera**, on the Beaulieu-Cap Ferrat border, is startlingly good value. It's an excellent place greatly loved by my friend, the beautiful Felicity Kendal. She stays there frequently. The Riviera is owned by Willy de Bruyn, the only entertaining Belgian in the world. The superb gardens overlook their own beach and pool. I toddled on to the terrace for lunch, and had some extremely good shrimp canapés, a very fresh John Dory and a wild raspberry soufflé. Vanessa had a lemon soufflé that was historic. No wonder the locals support chef Yves Merville and come to eat here!

Le Provençal, a restaurant near the harbour in St-Jean-Cap-Ferrat, is one of Andrew Lloyd Webber's favourite locals. There's a little outside area covered by a yellow awning, a larger area inside and exterior tables set amid trees and flowers. We had an excellent *papillon de pomme de terre aux anchois frais cebettes du pays jus d'olive* – potatoes and anchovies to you. Then a bit of *langouste*, *fromage de chevre* and a selection of desserts. The charming but not untemperamental chef is named Jean-Jacques Jouteux.

We can't all be perfect

When Vanessa and I returned from dinner recently at **La Réserve de Beaulieu**, the room had not been made up! I thought of storming out, but where to? Instead, I rang the normally impeccable general manager, M Gilbert Hirondelle, and let my feelings be known. Ladies duly appeared, saying: "We're just two to do the rooms, we don't have time." "I came back at 11.30," I said. "What time do I have to stay out 'til, three in the morning?"

La Réserve de Beaulieu, situated in one of the last unspoiled coastal villages on the Côte d'Azur, has always been a favourite. But after an incident like that you tend to notice everything. Why was the bath mat not replaced one morning? Why was I told, on walking towards the paved gardens where people were already eating, "Breakfast is over there", the waiter pointing to a different area that I didn't want to go to. Why was a dirty plate not cleared from the suite? Why was the man at the pool so rude-as-usual? Why was the bathroom so inadequately stocked?

The Réserve bathroom had shampoo, bath oil, soap and that was about all. The check list for every hotel is provided by the Mount Nelson, Cape Town: cotton buds, tissues, shoe horn, shoeshine things, dental kit, vanity kit, cotton wool, sewing kit, nail file, razor, shaving cream, loofah, soap, bath salts, shampoo cap, hair dryer, two vases of flowers in the bathroom, two bathrooms, phone in each and a weighing machine. On that basis, La Réserve gets three out of ten.

But there are a great many good things about La Réserve and I shall certainly go back. It is one of the last really elegant, old-style hotels, like an ocean liner, right on the water, with a staggering view of a sweeping bay from the pool and the rooms. The gardens are full of pink geraniums, roses, beautifully laid-out flower beds. The guest book has quotes from Humphrey Bogart, Rita Hayworth, Yul Brynner, David Niven, Princess Grace and dozens more. A parade of bygone elegance and real stardom.

The dining room is one of the most beautiful in the world, a throw-back to the 1930s. Barthélemy Lanteri, the greatest maitre d' ever, recently retired. After replacing him briefly with a strange young man, they now have a fine chap, Roger Heyd. The wine waiter, Jean-Louis Valla, looks like Mr Bumble in *Oliver Twist*, a latter-day Francis L Sullivan (that's one for the movie buffs) and very good at his job, too. The food is superb, even though people warned me it wouldn't be! I'll list some of it, so I look professional. *Poêlée de langoustines aux raviolis de fenouil et crème de petits onions confits, rougets du Cap en vinaigrette vierge, quelques purées de légumes*, and so on. La Réserve de Beaulieu is a gem.

Two years after this visit I learned that Gilbert Hirondelle, who had become my least favourite hotel manager, had been let go by La Réserve and that the place has been bought by Jean-Claude Delion, who owns the renowned St Tropez hotel, La Pinède. I nipped in for lunch shortly after the purchase and everything was improving like mad, so I returned recently for a stay.

La Réserve now has a Michelin star through a new chef, Christophe Cussac, who had two stars at his previous place. The atmosphere is back to the highly civilised aura it used to be, the guests are more buzzy and interesting, the pool has been done over, although it still sports the most surly pool attendant I've come across. I thought I'd really try, so I gave him a jovial good morning. All I got in return was a grunt. I suppose I was lucky to get that. But the setting of the pool is so great – mountains one side, the sea facing you and the bay of Beaulieu and St-Jean-Cap-Ferrat the other – that my equanimity remained intact.

My first night in what has to be as elegant a dining room as exists – and with no tie required – I ordered a fine *blanquette de chevreau*. Goat! I last had that on the beach in Jamaica when the locals gave me curried goat. It was memorably marvellous. On this occasion, when they whipped off the silver cover it revealed sard fish. A wrong order. But I got some goat later. It has a lovely taste and soft texture. All the food at La Réserve was exceptional.

The breakfast came in nine minutes. The quality of rolls, croissants, that sort of thing, was as good as I've ever tasted. It's all back to its gem-like state, once tarnished by M Hirondelle's extraordinary management style. Now M Delion is owner, general manager and manager. And it shows.

M Delion has reframed, beautifully, the wonderful signed photos of stars who stayed at La Réserve. On the second landing are Laurence Olivier and Vivien Leigh; in the bar, my friend Lauren Bacall and her then hubby Humphrey Bogart. Elizabeth Taylor wrote: "It's still as wonderful as ever; May 1993." In the lobby my (yes, you guessed it) late friend Rita Hayworth and Yul Brynner and ... I love movie memorabilia. I wish M Delion would remove the architectural watercolours that make up the other half of the decoration and bring out more of the star photos I remember from the old days. I could even provide him with a wondrous 10 x 8 of me. Perhaps not. The place is back on top. No need to take risks.

There is one task M Delion could undertake. Beaulieu and St-Jean-Cap-Ferrat are spotless. Time has passed them by. No litter, everything so well kept, the flower beds, the grass – except for the sea. This shows floating muck in abundance. When I wrote about the area before, a reader who lives there wrote to me that at one hotel (not La Réserve or the Royal Riviera), if you went to the lavatory and rushed to the window you could observe in the sea a few moments later ... No, I will not go on, you are too sensitive. But it is a downer in an otherwise idyllic setting.

I've now made friends with the pool attendant, Gérard Lucas. And on my last visit the food was so good at the hotel I ate in quite a lot (the restaurant now has two Michelin stars).

Jean-Claude Delion has appointed a marvellous lady manager: Estelle Wicky is blonde and smiles a lot. Recently Miss Wicky led me to the landing before the first floor. There, on the wall, beautifully framed and signed, was a photo of me. If you go to La Réserve, which I strongly recommend, you can always avert your eyes if you walk up the stairs. Or, better still, take the elevator. That's what I do.

Andrew and Madeleine Lloyd Webber took me to **Sloop**, one of dozens of small restaurants dotted along the harbour at St-Jean-Cap-Ferrat. Look at them as a novice and there's no way to know if one is better than the other. But the locals know. Andrew's a local and one of the great bon viveurs.

In St-Jean-Cap-Ferrat, home of the most wonderful period villas, **La Voile d'Or** looks over the harbour and the tiny waterfront village. It's immaculately run by the Lorenzi family, father Jean, after 30 years, handing over some of the job to daughter Isabelle. I've had some extremely good meals there in the garden.

Family favourite

At the Colombe d'Or in St-Paul-de-Vence there was no telephone in the bedroom of my suite, nor a television, the beds creaked and sank in the middle, and if you ask for your car to be brought up from the distant car park you may spend a vast amount of time waiting. It might surprise you that I was there at all. In fact the **Colombe d'Or** is one of my favourite places in the world.

It was opened in 1931 by Paul and Baptistine Roux as a Provençale inn near the entrance to the old walled town of St-Paul-de-Vence where they ran a cafe. I remember St-Paul-de-Vence when it was a lived-in town; now its cobbled streets are full of extraordinarily good-class shops which have edged the residents back a bit. It is still enchanting. The Colombe d'Or looks down on the valleys and hills, which, when I first went there, had a few old farmhouses scattered about. Sadly, fashionable villas are springing up relentlessly and the dreaded sight of cranes building more looms over the vista.

Paul Roux became a friend of many of the great French artists of the period and the place is alive with excellent paintings by Braque, Miro, Picasso, Matisse and others. Not the sort of thing you find on most hotel walls! The poolside mobile is by Calder, there is a mosaic dove by Braque, a finger-sculpture on the dining terrace by César and a tiled wall-mural by Léger. Rumour has it that these were donated in return for food and drink. The terrace of the Colombe d'Or is still one of the greatest places in the world to eat. The food is not Michelin-rated, but excellent nevertheless, the speciality being an hors d'oeuvre that puts every other one on offer anywhere to shame. The sight of the little bowls coming towards me creates an excitement hard to understand!

The hotel is now run by Paul's son Francis, his son François and François' wife Daniele. The French have a habit of viewing all hotel guests as a nuisance. They are, of course, quite right. Guests are a nuisance, particularly me. Ask Daniele for something as she stands behind the wood-grilled reception area and a look of slight disbelief is followed by consider-able but brief irritation. A sort of internal "tut-tut" comes, if you are lucky, before a smile. That is an absolutely proper way to behave, and I wouldn't have her any other way. Her husband François is rather jolly, and his father Francis works so quietly and efficiently that I never realised until recently that he was the boss.

There is something about the *loup de mer* with an accompanying yellow sauce ("How dare he not know the name of the sauce?" you rightly say) that places it apart from all other fish offerings. The famous people who have been attracted to the Colombe d'Or are too many even for me to mention. It remains an unchanging gem in a world of non-progress and increasing ugliness.

St-Rémy-de-Provence is where Van Gogh lived for a year, and the surrounding countryside is full of those mad, thinnish, dark green trees. St Rémy itself is delightful, a substantial old town in its middle. **L'Assiette de Marie**, a very quaint little restaurant, was my destination. The place was Provençal picturesque (I mean that nicely). All three rooms were stuffed with old hats hanging on mirrors, old gramophones, photos, advertising signs, antique clocks, an accordion on the wall there, an old coffee machine behind the bar. It was the opposite of minimalism. Maximalism. I greatly liked it. The waitress turned out to be Marie, the chef and co-owner with her husband Max Ricco. Marie recommended fish soup. It was superb. Then they dished up some amazing cannelloni and a whopping great plate of lasagne. The cannelloni was apparently a speciality of Corsica, that being where they come from. It was the best I've ever had, a wonderful sauce with it. For dessert I was given cake *châtaigne*, special to Corsica, also a tiramisù and a crème brûlée. Word must have reached them I was a pig. After a large soup and two main courses, I could only sample each of them, all brilliant.

Auberge de la Môle is not a highly known restaurant. I was there because Joan Collins, who lives in nearby St Tropez, had told me it was one of the best restaurants on the coast. Joan can be fussy, so it was essential to try it out. It's a homely place next to a painted church, quite large, with very good old travel and other 1900-ish posters on the walls. The food was extraordinarily good. We started with various terrines including (for £16 extra) the best foie gras I've ever had. Then I had some frogs' legs and after that the special – goat with pasta. It was delicious. I don't remember what the dessert was, but we got there at 1.30 and the meal didn't finish until 5.30! If you can ever find a map with Môle on it (which isn't easy), go there.

In St Tropez, I often eat at **Byblos**, for years the most fasnionable hotel, set well back from the sea, with a nice pool to relax by.

Côte tales

I've never quite understood St Tropez. I visit it from time to time, usually driving through Cannes and then along the winding coast road where the rocks turn red and the architecture becomes less interesting, until eventually you hit the harbour of St Tropez. It's pleasant enough, without being spectacular, and surrounded by a warren of lanes stuffed with boutiques, remarkably offering shirts large enough for me to get into.

I was told about **Résidence de la Pinède** by Jean-Claude Delion, owner of the hotel and La Réserve de Beaulieu, when I was staying. Madame Nicole Delion runs La Pinède, leaving her husband miles away in Beaulieu. What effect did such parting have on their marriage, I wondered, before accepting it was absolutely none of my business. M Delion suggested I visit La Pinède. I discovered you could park a helicopter only a few feet from La Réserve de Beaulieu, although you needed permission from the mayor's office as it took two police officers to ensure tourists didn't get chopped to pieces by the rotor blades. You could also land in St Tropez, some 20 minutes away, very close by La Pinède. I decided a day trip would not be out of the question.

Résidence de la Pinède was built in 1952, with more of it added in 1970, in Provençal style. It has a beach, a pool and overlooks the harbour of St Tropez. It's very luxurious in a modern way. We were taken to a suite with a view of the courtyard and the sea. A television showed pictures of the hotel set to Muzak. One was of the front desk, where two male staff looked into each other's eyes. Vanessa recognised one of them as the receptionist we'd just left behind in Beaulieu. Then there was a photo of a blonde looking lovingly into the eyes of a man in a suit and one of a lady making the bed.

We went downstairs for lunch, admiring a 400-year-old cypress tree, a number of pine trees (*pinède* means pine) and a bit of the hotel that is an 18th-century windmill, much tarted up. There's a large, stone terrace with white plastic chairs and yellow-striped cushions, a lawn, red geraniums, palm trees and, on two sides, stands the hotel with lots of balconies and those crinkly terracotta tiles.

I walked towards the table with the best view of St Tropez. The waiter said, "There's a nice table over there," pointing to one with no view at all. "If you want to eat there, please do," I said. "I shall sit here." "I wonder if pine cones fall on your head," said Vanessa looking up.

The Pinède has a Michelin star. We both ordered salade niçoise, then, for Vanessa, spaghetti with tomato sauce and, for me, tagliatelle à la carbonara. The freebie starter was a rosette of salmon and crayfish. We were hardly testing the chef, but it was all very good. We also had an excellent pre-dessert, a sun of chocolate with three wild strawberries decorating the rim. It was like a frozen chocolate truffle. Some time later, I recommended the place to a highly significant newspaper editor. He went to dinner there with a party of three and thought it totally superb.

I noticed that when they brought the cutlery, the spoons and forks were placed face down on the table, not with the prongs pointing upwards as usual. I'm sure that is unbelievably chic, but I couldn't be bothered to ask why.

Madame Delion told me she and her husband came there on holiday in 1985, liked it and bought the place. She was very elegant in a light blue blazer and dark blue trousers – or were they black?

I can highly recommend La Pinède, it's less formal than the excellent La Réserve de Beaulieu. Madame Delion told me there were only 5,000 permanent residents of St Tropez, but in the summer there were 100,000. She added that the main nationality of her guests was Belgian. This is something you may have to put up with.

Jean Ducloux's **Restaurant Greuze** in Tournus is a slightly poshed up family place, comfortable in every way and with food so good I wish it was located round the corner from me in Holland Park. I had champagne with fresh raspberry juice in it. Ask in London and see how often, if ever, you get fresh juice added to champagne other than orange juice! The food was described as "traditional", whatever that means. They offered cheese set in a brioche so light it flew. On the continent they often start with an absolutely extraordinary bread offering, so good it sets you off wonderfully. In London you get eight sorts of drying-up rubbish and it takes half an hour while you're told what each one is, which doesn't matter anyway because it's all dull, whether it's with carrots, caraway seeds or whatever. Anyway, Monsieur Ducloux produced a totally historic meal, and if I could read my notes on the menu I'd tell you what it was! I can just make out "sorta game pie, beyond belief" and "langoustines, delicious sauce" and "Mr Ducloux is 74 and his lovely wife is Paulette". If that's any use, terrific. If not, go there yourself.

A little pizza place I discovered in the town of Vence is **Chez Guy**, Guy presumably being the aproned chap who throws the pizzas in the air, catches them after they've had a good twirl, and then puts them into a log-fired oven to bake. Everyone in the place was local except for us. We sat on rush chairs at check-table-clothed tables in a white stucco room with old beams above and windows looking out on to period buildings. The pizzas had built-in fried eggs in the middle (Orso's please note). Quite delicious, unbelievably cheap, and no-nonsense waitress service.

Roger Moore took me to an excellent restaurant in Monte Carlo, called **Chez Gianni**. It had a nice little garden at the back, although it was still heavily overlooked by high-rise flats. But the food was extremely good.

Full Monte

Paul Firmin picked me up at the swimming pool of Le Réserve de Beaulieu. He was a nice chap, so I didn't object. I even acceded when he asked me to dinner. It's the first time I've permitted a civilian (that's what we call someone outside show business) to get me to go out with him while on holiday. In case you're getting the right impression, let me add there's a Mrs Fermin, a pretty lady named Melinda, and Vanessa was also party to this foursome. Mr Firmin (he's in property and trucking) had made a reservation at his favourite restaurant, the **Grill of the Hôtel de Paris** in Monte Carlo. "It's where we had our honeymoon," said Melinda. "I went there for my 50th birthday," added Paul. "And you risk going with me! Brave man!" I said.

Paul checked the dress code. Luckily I had packed a 1950s black, interwoven pattern tie bought from Cyril Castle, with the phone number Whitehall 3751 on the back and another label telling me it was by Guy Laroche of Paris. The main square of Monte Carlo, with the casino, the gardens and the Hôtel de Paris, is about all that's left of the old splendour. The rest is high-rise half flats for tax evaders. The hotel has four marvellously naked, rampant women sculpted on the front, with flowers and ribbons above them. The casino nudes were carrying spears. Melinda assured me they were mermaids, but as they had nothing to do with fish tails whatsoever and no water of any kind around them, I think she must have been mistaken.

The Hôtel de Paris has a very grand lobby, but the people in it looked as if they'd come off a tourist bus. On your right is the three-star Michelin Louis XV room. Very heavy on gilt. I entered and looked around before being snootily asked to leave. I thought this was rather rude. On my way out, I went in to get names so I could tell them off in print. Once again, I was pounced on. A lady said: "There's some clients, it's not possible to see." "Are these people eating all from the secret service?" I asked. "That lot can see those people there." But a man joined the "Throw out Winner" group, explaining if I wasn't going to eat I couldn't stay.

On reflection, I think they were right. It's a very exclusive place and they don't need gawpers, even if it's me. My friend Maurizio Saccani, manager of the historically good Hotel Splendido in Portofino, should learn from this. You can't mix visiting cruise-ship sightseers with genuine guests who pay top whack for exclusivity.

Thus put in my place, we took the elevator to the eighth-floor one-star Michelin Restaurant Panoramique, Le Grill.

Cavorting over the bar were two naked mermaids, which pleased Mrs Firmin. We walked through a fairly dull room to some outer area. "That'll teach me to dine with civilians," I thought. "They're giving us a lousy table." But no. We were shown to a large terrace with very few tables, and the principal one in the centre was ours. There was a lovely view of the harbour, the royal palace, the oceanographic museum and the sea.

There were very cheerful plates with naked ladies draped in peacock feathers painted on them, and the menu had a nude lady on the back. Obviously political correctness has no place in Monte Carlo. The food was admirable, too. My *soupe de poissons* was excellent, Vanessa's melon was fine; my main course prawns and sauce were pleasant, Vanessa said "Mmmm, very good" about her fish. Mr Firmin said his chicken was "superb" and then "lovely".

The strawberry soufflé was as good as I've ever had; they poured cream in the middle and spooned it onto a nice hot plate. The accompanying strawberries were almost jammy. I noticed they'd removed the spoon from my ice bucket, so I now had to scoop out the ice cubes with my fingers.

Mr Firmin pointed out the cup and saucer for the tea were both hot, so hot that Vanessa's had cracked and all her tea poured into the saucer. The petits fours were very posh; a chocolate one had the words Grill Room written on it in white script. I had noticed an elegant elderly lady eating alone on the terrace behind us. What was her story, I wondered. Briefly. Then, even though I'd been the guest, I paid the bill. We Scorpios like doing that, we hate to be indebted to anyone. Mr Firmin took care of the taxi back to La Réserve. I thought he and his wife were extraordinarily nice people. For civilians.

The Guy Who Loves Me

I'd rather live in Balham and pay British taxes than live in Monte Carlo and pay none. The south of France I grew up in has become vastly overbuilt. And nowhere worse than Monaco, consumed by tacky high-rises that sprout like weeds. They've annihilated the lovely old villas and Victorian apartment blocks. When I arrive at Nice airport, I see the towering modern buildings between the terminal and the hills where once I saw Provençal farms with crinkly roof tile and vineyards.

The only unspoilt parts of the French Riviera are Beaulieu-sur-Mer and St-Jean-Cap-Ferrat. There, even in the height of the season, you're in the France of the 1950s. Walk out of the elegant Réserve de Beaulieu, turn left and you stroll along by the sea with tall palms, lovely flower gardens and hardly any people.

Monte Carlo is another story. **La Piazza** is set between towering "council flat" blocks, with roads, tunnels and underpasses all around it. It's a pleasant, tiled restaurant with pink tablecloths and murals of old Italy on the walls. Our group was me, Roger Moore, his lady friend, Kristina Tholstrup, her daughter, Christina Knudsen, a sparkling girl who finds properties and does interior decoration, and her jolly banker boyfriend, Nikolaj Albinus. There was also Miss Lid the First.

We started with some excellent crostini – tomatoes on toast to you. This was followed by babajuan, little pancakes of ricotta cheese and spinach in a pastry shell. "You only get them in Monaco," said Kristina. I find ordering extremely tiring. "What am I having, Rog?" I asked. "You're having seafood salad, then you're having loup de mer, branzino, sea bass," said Roger, enunciating very clearly in case I didn't understand. This was the only time ever I had a jacket on and Rog didn't.

Very rudely for one so soigné, I said to Kristina: "Can I taste a bit of that, please?" But I'd taken her ham with my fingers before she could answer. It was very good. My main course was fine. Later Christina, the daughter, said: "I'll have some of your crème brûlée." I said: "You can have it all because I should really not be ordering it." When I got the crème brûlée, I scoffed it down. "My goodness, I've eaten it," I said, realising it was a bit late. "You ate so quickly I didn't like to interrupt you," said Christina.

Roger Moore is a rare creation: a generous actor. He took me to **Rampoldi** in Monte Carlo, which is near the casino in a street called Avenue des Spélugues. It has a crowded cafe feel about it. Indeed, most of the tables were so close together that I said a silent prayer of thanks I was with a movie star so we got, at least, the most separated spot. Rampoldi is owned by an Italian named Luciano di Saro who's had it for 15 years; before that he worked with nightclub queen Regine. It was terribly chic and the food was the very best.

WINNIE AT THE COLOMBE d'OR

WINNIE EATS A GERMAN SAUSAGE

7

G E R M A N Y

Movable feast

Dinkelsbühl is a staggeringly preserved medieval town on the "Romantic Road", with cobbled streets, richly decorated step gabling, wonderfully ornamented half-timbered façades and so on, et cetera and the rest. Never mind all that, it was lunchtime. We had booked into the **Hotel Restaurant Eisenkrug**, a beautiful building in the old wine market. It looked fine, except it was totally deserted. It was exactly 1pm, which is when I said I'd arrive. Nobody anywhere. Like the wreck of the *Marie Celeste*, but not even a half-eaten sandwich. A man eventually came up from the basement in a white uniform. I asked if he was Martin Scharff, the chef-owner. He said something about being his brother and was highly offish, so we left.

A bit down the road was the **Café Extrablatt,** set in another exquisite old house with exterior dining in the autumn sun. I went inside and found a lady in Bavarian costume, and told her that I was sitting outside, I was terribly hungry and I wanted amazing service. It worked a treat. Everyone became terribly efficient and jovial. I had excellent Bavarian white sausage with pretzel and mustard; Vanessa had noodles with cheese.

Then a worried man in a chef's uniform walked by. It was Martin Scharff, looking for me. He had no idea who the rude man had been in his hotel. He had no brother. We'd finished our main courses, so Martin went back to his hotel to make the most incredible desserts, which he brought to the Café Extrablatt (they didn't mind – they're all pals in Dinkelsbühl).

Vanessa's pud was strudel leaves filled with white chocolate mousse, strawberries and Franconian riesling ice; mine was cold plum soup with cottage cheese dumplings and white chocolate ginger ice cream.

Then Martin went to a friend who had a cart which seated 16 tourists and was drawn by two lovely horses. He negotiated for Vanessa and me to trot round town on it alone. You think that's naff? Good luck to you. I found it a delightful jaunt through an amazingly historical place. But then I'm unsophisticated. We're much nicer people.

Romance in the air

The Romantic Road – "Germany's best-known holiday route" – runs from Würzburg to Füssen. To which I hear you saying, loudly and in unison: "So what?" I, too, never considered Germany high on the romance calendar. But when I arrived at the **Gasthaus Schwarzer Adler** in Kraftshof, near Nuremberg, in the company of Mr and Mrs J Cleese and Miss V Perry, a whiff of amour stirred in some strange part of my body. And Kraftshof is not even on the "Romantic Road" – only adjacent to it.

The Schwarzer Adler is an old inn with a Michelin star, situated in a pretty Bavarian village. Vastly comfortable, lots of room, posh without being overbearing, pleasing oil paintings, wattle walls. "Nice big chairs," said John, making the point that "nine out of ten restaurant chairs in London are too small for anyone over six foot". "And me," I chipped in.

We were given an aperitif of raspberries, blackberries, blueberries, a little bit of cassis and port, home-made raspberry schnapps, topped up with Franconian sparkling wine. Almost equal in excellence to the bellinis at Harry's Bar in Venice.

The food is quite simply amazing. If you happen to be in Nuremberg – and I'm sure you drop by regularly – it's on offer about 20 minutes from the centre. I had mushrooms in herb sauce with dumplings to start. Brilliant. We considered three pork dishes, including saddle of piglet with smoked beer sauce and potato dumplings. "Germany is not a good place to be a pig," Mr Cleese mused. I had venison on savoy cabbage with a cassis sauce, Vanessa had skate, Alyce, lamb... Oh, it doesn't matter – it was all absolutely exquisite. The boss, Gunther Hertel, was "on a journey", said his daughter, Tanya. So she and the others took charge. Waiters of great charm; daughter ditto.

They served a millefeuille of chocolate, and apple fritters with rum sauce. Mrs Cleese had cheese with little grapes from the waiter's garden. "I'll tell you what they are," said John. "Put this down on your recorder. They are very small grapes. They are so small that they only consist of grape seed and the skin around it. There is no room for any grape." "And they look pretty," said Alyce. "He has tried to sell them elsewhere," added John. Anyway, we all agreed it was a spectacular meal.

In the picturesque Tiergärtnertorplatz in Nuremberg, John Cleese and I inspected and chose the exterior eating area of the **Belm Schlenkeria**. Nice red-checked tablecloths. I had ogled the enormous shoulders of pork people seemed to eat at every turn, enough to feed a family of six, but served for one person. I ordered that. Historic. John had chicken soup with dumplings, which I tried and it was excellent. He said: "What we don't have in England now is a tradition of English regional cooking. This is what they would have served us here in the 1920s."

The **Gasthaus Rottner**, run by Claudia Rottner, is a lovely German inn, 300 years old, much bedecked with hanging lanterns, deer heads and antlers. The Rottner family, who've been there since 1812, produced a superb meal. The wild duck was exceptional, very non-fatty. We declared it the best ever.

Bavarian high

My friend Mr J Cleese, Weston-super-Mare's favourite plenipotentiary, decided to take to the water with his lady wife, Alyce Faye, the Texas belle. The water was the River Rhine. I decided to call Marwan and grab the Learjet to join Mr and Mrs C in Nuremberg, where they had a two-day stopover.

Nuremberg may not sound like everyone's idea of fun, but it, and the exquisitely preserved surrounding towns, provided a terrific experience and some marvellous food. I started out totally ignorant. My Michelin Guide showed two hotels in Nuremberg with two black "castles". Not the best hotel rating. Which should I take, the Grand or the Maritim? I phoned a lower-down-the-list hotel, Lowe's Merkur, and requested the general manager. Brigitte Kaltenecker came on line. She seemed vastly unamused when I asked her which was the best of the two. She eventually recommended the Grand and laughed in amazement that I'd picked her with a pin, as it were, to be my guide.

The Grand is a solid, turn-of-the-century Meridien hotel opposite the railway station. Mr and Mrs Cleese booked in for a night to join us. Horst Berl, the general manager, assured me that the small, dark suite I was ushered into was their very best. Mmmm. In general, it was efficient. I even grew to like it, although my first impression was of a hotel for upper-class travelling salesmen. The breakfast room was very well run by David Stern. I definitely love Bavarian sausage, and if you sat by the window you had an uninterrupted view of the old town, an awful lot of which someone had bombed.

We settled at little tables outside the **Hotel Meistertrunk** in Rothenburg. I showed the owner one of my Winner multilanguage mini brochures printed for film festivals. It was its greatest and only failure. The owner looked positively hostile. Still, we sat in the medieval street in hot, late-autumn sun and got by on my renowned charm.

VERY SMALL DRIVER →

WINNIE GOES ON A CART-RIDE IN DINKELSBÜHL

WINNIE
EATS A SMALL
PORTION
OF
SPAGHETTI
A 2000

8

I T A L Y

In most countries, including our own, concierges do not recommend the best restaurants. They point you to ones that give them the most commission. An exception is the superb concierge of the Hotel Quisiana in Capri, Leone Manzi, who put me on to some nice places. My favourite was **La Capannina**, which could have been done out by a 1950s MGM set decorator. It's a typical family-owned place, tiled floor, wooden chairs with flowers painted on the back, flowers on the table. The owner is Antonio de Angelis, who looks like a professor from a minor university. He's helped by his American wife, Aurelia, who met him on vacation aged 16. Although it's full of Italians and very unpretentious, the signatures in the guest book include many glitterati. Vanessa and I shared sea bream covered in a light potato crust, which was excellent. I also had ravioli and grilled scampi. When I went again I had baby calamari filled with cheese, courgette flowers from Antonio's garden and chips, which were cut by hand in the kitchen: rare these days. Although La Capannina has low ceilings and hard walls and was full, you could hear conversation quite easily. In London, with our overhyped screamers, it would have been a noise nightmare.

Feraglioni in Capri is in a lovely open area overlooking a field of yellow flowers (please check a horticultural calendar; they may not be out on your visit). There's a view of staggering bougainvillea and a lilac tree wrapping itself round the outside. Juliano Tortiello is the owner. English is not spoken. The pasta and veal were good, and they served Coca-Cola in an exemplary way: in a tall glass, not a namby-pamby thing, with large ice cubes right down to the bottom and a healthy half-slice of lemon. The Coca-Cola in Capri was a little thinner and sharper than in the UK. (There are very few writers who'd go to Capri and do a dissertation on Coca-Cola. More's the pity.)

Da Gemma, near the market square in Capri, was bustling: a straw or bamboo ceiling; pink; a large antipasti buffet in the middle. I had linguine with lobster, which was terrific. Before that, they plonked an enormous bowl of soup on the buffet. It was called a *pasta fajolie*, made with pasta and clams. It was highly memorable. I also tried an excellent pizza. For dessert, I got a superb lemon profiterole, then some limoncella, a marvellous Italian liqueur tasting like lemon. I keep some in the fridge at home.

Insect aside

The ants walked with great precision in an immaculately straight line. The distance between each ant and another was identical. They came from a corner on the south-east side of the suite. On reaching a reproduction antique commode, they climbed up a back leg nearest the wall. When they got to the marble top they walked around only the right-hand side; the one nearest the roof terrace looking down onto the blue sea and the two famous rocks, the Faraglioni, that rise out of it as Capri's trademark.

I was hypnotised by this endless flow of animal life. Would they, I wondered, take over the entire room? Would I be writhing in bed at night, fighting off an increasing horde of insects as if starring in a horror movie? At this point I started squashing them. I felt extremely guilty. But it was them or me.

I had flown, courtesy of Marwan Khalek, in a rented LearJet from London. I declined the pilot's offer to hear, on his radio, voices of American pilots and their instructors as they screeched in to rocket Serbia. I arrived at the **Quisisana**, a highly rated hotel, following on foot a small porter-driven electric cart that transported my luggage from the area where taxis had to stop. As I walked onto the veranda in front of the hotel the doorman said: "Welcome, Mr Winner." I had never been there before. Had they displayed my photo on the notice board below stairs? It can't have been a flattering picture: they recognised me.

Dr Gianfranco Morgano, the owner, showed us to a lovely suite with a roof terrace facing unparalleled views of wooded mountains, the old rooftops of Capri, the sea, the aforementioned dramatic Faraglioni rocks and the hotel gardens. This terrace saved us. Because the alternative to sunbathing there would have been to sit by a rather naff swimming pool, with a modern fountain with the words "I" and "Quisi" with a drawn heart between them. There was no view from the pool and it was constricted in area and ambience. The adjoining restaurant, the Colombaia Grill, offered a half-hour wait for a pizza because the ovens were never heated up, a salade niçoise served once without tuna, and no sorbet because the fridge had broken down.

Breakfast was particularly disastrous. There were tiny plastic containers of Lurpak butter, disgraceful for a supposedly top-class hotel. The fruit salad was tinned. Beyond belief! There was a limited supply of croissants and jams, there were tea bags instead of proper tea with a strainer and the crockery was uninteresting. The sugar was wrapped when it should have been in a bowl.

All this is a pity, because in many ways the Quisisana is extremely likeable. You could not find better staff. The chief concierge, Leone Manzo, operated Winner-management superbly and with immense charm. He's one of the greats of his profession. Dr Morgano was also impeccably hospitable.

The main dining room is garishly bright in the evening. They really must dim the lights and get some candles on the tables. The maitre d, Giuseppe Esposito, was fine at our first dinner, but on the second ignored us completely. And Vanessa looked particularly fetching in a new dress. She said of her salad: "The tomatoes are not ripe." She was displeased because her sea bass came with mussels and she wasn't expecting that. My veal was excellent. But the triumph was a historic rum baba with custard. Rum babas used to be common in England. They have, sadly, gone into decline.

On our second dinner the bellini was memorably ghastly, my ravioli was uninteresting, but my local fish, *la pezzogna*, was as good as I've ever eaten. Apparently this fish lives 120 metres down and is caught one at a time. I had it baked in salt.

The next day the ants didn't appear until noon, when I saw one on my diary. By one o'clock ant activity had increased considerably. Vanessa asked me not to mention it because she didn't want the room to smell of insect spray. But I couldn't keep it a secret. Dr Morgano assured us he'd manage without using a spray. When we came back the pong of disinfectant was overpowering. The ants had gone, and who can blame them. We opened the sliding doors to the balcony and stuck it out. Which is just as well. Because, in spite of some disappointments, I greatly enjoyed the Quisisana. Capri was nice, too. It's the only place where I've seen convertible six-seater taxis. It's overcrowded, though. Full of Italians and others on day trips. The streets display endlesss famous-name boutiques. I think I arrived at least 20 years too late.

A charming restaurant in Cernobbio is **Trattoria del Vapore**. I had a nice bean and pasta soup, some decent small macaroni with tomato and basil, and a terrific zabaglione.

At the highly exclusive and expensive **Villa d'Este** hotel in Cernobbio on Lake Como, our suite had the most awful bilious green carpet and a bathroom so small it would have been demi-monde in a council flat. When I went down to breakfast the first morning and asked if the orange juice was fresh, I was told it wasn't! This at a bed and breakfast rate of £375 a night! They squeezed some when I insisted. The room service breakfasts arrived speedily, but they were the worst. A heavy croissant; butter in those tiny, ludicrous plastic and silver paper cartons that you get on British Airways; and the tea was not hot. The face flannels were not replaced two nights out of four. On the plus side, the chief concierge, Romano Scotti, is superb. The grounds and views are spectacular, and the hotel has an attractive old grandeur. We had dinner there as guests of the manager, a very nice chap called Marco Sorbellini. I had one of the best spaghetti dishes ever, with *bottarga* of mullet roe and fresh tomato. Okay mixed grilled fish, very good raspberry soufflé with a peach sauce. But one good dinner does not a hotel make.

If you're adventurous, find **Restaurant La Vigne** set among vineyards at Radda in Chianti. I once sent a Scotland Yard commissioner of police there and he got lost!

I used to like the terrace of **Villa Sangiovese** at Panzano in Chianti, but the owner, an Austrian named Herr Bleuler, shouted at me when I tried to show it to Vanessa. Can you imagine somebody shouting at *me*? Now that's a turnaround situation if ever there was one!

Scoop of the day

My introduction to Benvenuto Puricelli did not go smoothly. I was walking out of his restaurant **Locanda dell 'Isola Comacina**, when he followed me onto the terrace. This is on the only island in Lake Como, opposite the exquisite village of Sala Comacina. It's ugly, rebuilt in 1963 like an East Grinstead roadhouse. A barn of a place divided into two. The good bit faces the lake, the back bit faces the front bit.

When we arrived from Bellagio on our rented speedboat we saw the dreaded Villa d'Este tourist boat moored. We had seen it leave in the morning full of d'Este-ites, who waved and smiled up at Vanessa at the balcony window of our suite. As well they might. She was stark naked at the time. There they were again, now inhabiting the front room of the Locanda. I surveyed the table offered in the back, turned and did the Winner-walk-out. Benvenuto took it well. "I'll lay a table up on the terrace for you," he suggested. I considered the matter. The terrace was far the best place to be. A lovely view of the lake, but was it warm enough? It was early October.

The sun came out, so I decided to stay. There is a set menu, unchanged since 1948. They do exactly the same for lunch and dinner every day. Weddings, receptions ... all get the same menu. "Suits me," I said to Vanessa. "They must have got it right by now." That was an understatement. It was superb plus.

First you get seven dishes of veg and fruit as hors d'oeuvre plus some incredible bresaola and ham. The baked onions were memorable. The ham is fragrant, cooked, baked and slightly smoked. Benvenuto puts olive oil and lemon on the bresaola. The white wine was Soave 1985 Paesaggi. Very pleasant. Then you get salmon trout, fresh as anything, delicious. Benvenuto scoops rough salt from a dish, flicking it out with a spoon, then he pours lemon, olive oil and pepper over the fish. "Can I have a knife?" I asked. "You have the bread," ordered Benvenuto. So I scooped up the sauce with the bread and he was quite right. He's a tall, thin man, wearing a tartan waistcoat, black trousers, a white shirt. He worked in the Penthouse Club in London and in Chigwell, Essex, and the Palace in St Moritz.

The fried chicken that followed was brilliant, with a lettuce salad delightfully flavoured with some dressing or other. There's a technical description for you! Then he produces this enormous Parmesan and cuts a bit off. After that, ice cream with pears and banana liqueur.

I think Ben has a terrific idea. I'm fed up with seeing enormous menus none of which I understand. I'm bored to death with waiting while everyone orders, then changes their mind and orders again. I hugely like the idea of each restaurant perfecting its own menu and serving nothing else. Then we could all move from place to place, depending on what we feel like at the time. I doubt it will catch on. People like to delude themselves they are capable of choosing correctly. They aren't and they're exceptionally tedious as they try.

The San Villa Michele manager recommended a magical little lunch place near the Piazza Della Signoria called **Cantinetta Verrazzano**. They refused to serve Coca-Cola, but everything else was brilliant. No space left to tell you more – just note the name and go there. That's if you can push your way through the human throng in Florence's jam-packed streets.

The matchless San Michele

The Villa San Michele, in a little town called Fiesole above Florence, is quite simply one of the best hotels in the world. It is owned by Mr and Mrs James Sherwood of the Orient-Express group and well run by a very jovial chap named Maurizio Saccani, who also manages the Hotel Splendido in Portofino and drives between the two at great speed. The **Villa San Michele** was a monastery and a church, its façade attributed to Michelangelo. It dates from the 15th century and still has that feel about it.

The hills of Fiesole are covered with cypress, olive and ilexes sloping down to the city and the Arno. The dining room is approached through an internal courtyard with the stone crest of the Davanzatis family, who endowed the monastery. With wide arches overlooking Florence (sadly now often blighted by smog), it is one of the nicest places to eat. The food is exceptional. I had more truly first-rate meals in a row at the Villa San M than I've had anywhere.

We ate rosemary-flavoured pumpkin risotto, home-made ravioli with chickpea filling and herb sauce, baked fillets of turbot with mustard, scampi stunningly plump and tender, fresh fruit tart, millefeuille of raspberries – all beyond belief good. No bad meal, except for one made a bit dodgy by a young couple looking into each other's eyes at the next table through a haze of their own cigarette smoke. They smoked before the meal, during each course, after each course…totally revolting. How they tasted the quality of the food I can't imagine. At least when I smoked cigars I waited until the end.

Can't find *anything* to criticise at the Villa San Michele? Let me think. Well, the restaurant service did go off a bit when Vittorio Dalle, the restaurant manager, wasn't there, but it was never bad. And with Attilio Di Fabrizio in the kitchen, who cared?

I was recently in Florence. Unbelievable. New housing estates going up everywhere. Endless tourists taking every inch of the Piazza Della Signoria. A mile-long queue for the Uffizi gallery. So I advise you to stay away from the mob.

There's nowhere better to do this than Fiesole, a charming, uncluttered little hill town from which the Villa San Michele looks down on Florence. On this visit they kindly offered me the Jim Sherwood suite, but it was away from the main hotel. I like to be in the centre of things. So I repaired to my usual very large room with high-up windows and an enormous bed on a dais.

The food is exceptionally good. For lunch I had grilled scampi and then Florentine grilled steak. The chocolate cake was seriously brilliant and the lemon sorbet was terrific. I'm amazed this place hasn't got a Michelin star.

Highly important people stay, ranging from Kofi Annan to Barbra Streisand. Barbra's been everywhere I go recently, in England and abroad. This is highly adventurous of her. She likes her grub, does Barb. When she was making a movie in England, she so adored my cook's fairy cakes that we delivered them to her house every day for a week. Then we got bored and gave up.

For dinner Mr Saccani suggested Chianina beef, which comes from Tuscany, south of Siena. This was totally historic. It's hung for 21 days and was marinated for a couple of hours in oil and herbs. The hotel staff even got me into the Uffizi gallery without queuing. I was so impressed that I almost decided not to mention their breakfast display was rather poor.

> At the "wrong" end of the Ponte Vecchio is a lovely little restaurant called **Bibo**, in Santa Felicita. Pink tablecloths, black hooped chairs. It was extremely efficient in a refreshing, non-fussy way. They behaved most properly and gave me a table for four. A quietly well-dressed Italian in a grey suit supervised all and shook my hand. He was the owner. Everything was excellent and inexpensive. The ravioli with ricotta cheese and spinach inside with a tomato, basil and cream sauce was tip-top. The lemon sorbet was soft, historic and the best ever. If you go to Florence, find it.

Faded glory

I have come to a highly important conclusion. I was not put on this earth to unwrap butter. I considered this as I looked at a number of small, silver-wrapped butter pats in my £700-a-night suite at the **Grand Hotel Villa Cora** in Florence. For that money, I expect the butter to be in nice little ringlets on a bowl, the bowl itself set in a larger bowl with ice in it. I also do not wish to unwrap sugar from paper sachets which give the appearance of British Rail, nor do I expect to see four large black chips in one of the cheap-looking plastic baths. It would be nice if the television were positioned facing the bed, and not the only two small chairs in the most enormous ballroom-like bedroom.

We got there by accident. It has the same Michelin rating as the Villa San Michele near Florence, and I couldn't get in that for two nights. The Grand Hotel Villa Cora *is* grand. Built by Baron Oppenheim in 1865, later lived in by the Empress Eugénie, widow of Napoleon III, its pure neo-classical style includes a great deal of rococo gilt and pillars, ceiling paintings (cherubs and doves doing odd things above my bed) and ornate rooms that look rather different from the brochure. The main lounge, beautifully furnished in the coloured pictures, had hardly any furniture in it at all. "It lets in more light," explained a hotel manager helpfully.

The dining room is ugly and in a windowless basement. It also smelled musty so I never ate there. The swimming pool is tacky-modern with, thrown in for bad measure, five little islands with poles on them and the flags of Japan, Europe, America, Germany and France. Since I was not attending a convention of the United Nations I didn't use the pool, either.

The breakfast orange juice was so bitter we couldn't drink it and the croissants were chewy. The staff were rather nice. The whole thing has great possibility but hardly any actuality.

You can sit in a "best view" position at the **Rivoire Pasticceria** in the Piazza della Signoria in Florence, facing the old tower and statues including a copy of Michelangelo's David. Snacky, good quality, old-fashioned but at speed.

Worth the fuss

It was Fausto Allegri, the concierge at the Hotel Splendido, Portofino, who produced hand-drawn squiggles on a small piece of paper and said: "This is where you will go to lunch, Mr Winner. **Cà Peo** in Leivi." Fausto has always directed me superbly. "It looks a long way," I said nervously. "Forty-five minutes," replied Fausto dismissively.

An hour later we were still twirling along the Ligurian coast road with no sign of Chiavari, where we had to execute a complicated left turn into the mountains. Same the world over, I thought. Everyone exaggerates the ease of getting from one place to another. "I'm 20 minutes from central London," say people in north Hampstead. Oh yes. Sixty minutes in the rush hour, if you're lucky. The three miles from Piccadilly to my house in Holland Park can take 45 minutes on a bad day, and that's with a chauffeur picking me up on the doorstep. So I cut my journey to the office to 15 seconds, the time it takes to walk down 14 steps from bedroom to study.

Fausto had failed to draw any details of Chiavari on his artistic map, so we got lost. Eventually, more by luck than judgement, we found ourselves rising ever higher, through tiny villages, until we arrived at the farmhouse with its stunning view.

I always like to get to new restaurants early to sort out the table. A scholastic-looking young lady in rimmed glasses with swept-back hair, a dark suit and a white shirt appeared to be in charge. In case Fausto had not done the full monty on how unbelievably important I was, I carried with me the *pièce de résistance*: a small pocket-sized brochure, originally produced for film festivals, on stiff shiny paper, with a fetching photo of me with my director's chair on the cover and a potted biography in French, German and Italian on the following pages. "I wonder if you could be so kind…" I said to Nicoletta Solari, the owner's daughter, indicating that some furniture-moving would be appreciated.

"I've been all morning getting the tables in position," said Nicoletta. "Well, nothing is impossible, dear. Let's put four chairs there and two by the window there and change this table to go…" You'll be glad to hear all this was achieved splendidly, leaving me with a nice, large table in the main window bay, neatly laid for two.

Thus with everything shipshape, Vanessa and I took a walk along the narrow village road, admiring the local church, strolled back and settled to look out at the view of olive trees and old farmhouses down to Chiavari and the sea. A nice, airy room, I thought. Nicoletta had kindly given me an article from the *New York Times* which stated that "Franco and Melly Solari never serve fewer than 10 courses". Obviously in the three years since the article was written Melly, who does the cooking, had decided to slow down a bit. We were offered a mere eight courses for lunch.

We had Solari wine, from the vineyard 500 metres away on the hillside. A very nice, soft taste. I have a note saying: "This radicchio flan, whatever it is, is absolutely sensational." It may not mean much, but it denotes pleasure. The dishes were all described in Italian: *ravioli di triglia*, *lattughe ripiene in brodo*, *bianco di branzino*, a sorbet, some lamb. Desserts included a historic strawberry mousse and some sweet bread with orange and lemon in it called *golopa*. It was all sensationally good. Lunch took four hours and I never complained or tried to rush anyone.

Service, please!

"You see what I mean," said our driver. "One of the most horrible sections of Milan, human-being containers." We are passing working-class flats on our way from Lake Como to Milan's highest-rated Michelin restaurant, the two-starred **Aimo e Nadia**. We'd been told to be there no later than 1.30pm. We arrived at one, rang the bell of a nice door in an ugly block and were buzzed in.

A man in a dark grey suit, white shirt, grey and black striped bow tie and glasses showed us to a back room with two other people in it. A larger front room to the right was empty and better. I walked into the front room, the bow-tied one indicated a good table and we sat. Then we sat some more. It was the start of the worst 15 minutes I have ever spent in a restaurant. We were totally ignored. Occasionally a chef could be seen walking in the distance. Occasionally, Mr Bow Tie walked in the distance. After seven minutes, I asked Bow Tie to come over.

"Excuse me," I said. "Is the maitre d' here?" "Maitre d!" said Bow Tie as if I'd got off a tourist bus and was using a word of horror that he failed to understand. "The restaurant manager then?" I continued. "Restaurant manager?!" sneered BT and he walked off. Another four minutes went by. BT returned. "The restaurant manager will be here in an hour," he announced. Off he went yet again. I had seen enough of the beige rag-rolled walls, the black up-lights, a few trees and ferns, some nice pictures. When I spotted BT again, I called him over.

"This may be a surprise to you," I said, "but it is normal when entering a restaurant to be asked whether you want a drink, given a menu and then given some bread. It is not normal to be left sitting for 15 minutes." A bit later he reappeared with some sparkling white wine "I don't want that," I said. A wine waiter in a red coat joined him. "What do you want?" asked Bow Tie. "Two mineral waters, one still, one fizzy," I said. Let them know the big spenders have arrived. He went off and soon thereafter returned.

"The general manager and owner," he introduced the chef I had seen in the distance, now with another, younger chef. Both wore tall, white hats. The boss was Aimo Morani. "You're a chef, too, are you?" I asked the younger one. "No," he said in an American accent. "I'm a photographer." "Then why are you dressed as a chef?" I enquired. It transpired that his name was Conrad Firestein, from New York. He married into the family and was helping out.

"Tell Aimo this is the most horrible time I have ever known in a restaurant," I requested. I listed my complaints. They then sought the villain. They explained that Aimo's daughter Stefania was the manageress, but she was at the bank.

"It must have been Fabio," said Conrad. "He doesn't understand greeting, he's the wine waiter." "Then why didn't he offer me a drink?" I asked. Fabio was brought in. "It's not him," I said. Fabio grabbed my arm. "Thank you," he breathed.

"It's the man in the dark suit. I'm going to murder him," I announced. "Don't do that, he's my brother-in-law," said Conrad. He turned to Aimo and mentioned the name Marco. "I don't care if he's in the family or not," I said. "He's a total disaster." Having made my point, we settled down to one of the best meals I have ever eaten.

Aimo, endearingly helpful, was now all attention. He showed us mushrooms, suggested this and that. His daughter, Stefania, wife of the dreaded Marco, turned up looking like Liza Minnelli and with the same forthright charm. I liked her. We were given red Barbaresco 1993, a pleasant wine. I had what I thought Aimo said was Hotten Hen in a sauce of raspberry vinegar marinated with sweet peppers. Sensational. Vanessa had fresh goat's cheese with a salad sprout and mushrooms. Then she had green lasagnette with nettles, watercress, tomatoes, ricotta cheese and basil. I had Italian lamb cooked in sweet grape juice with chickpeas and thyme pie. All was absolutely, totally brilliant. A crab hors d'oeuvre figured somewhere, bresaola – old cured beef in oil, a chestnut flower tart with pears, chocolate with cinnamon cream, some cheese from Val D'Aosta. Vanessa had hazelnut biscuits filled with whatever. It was superb.

Then Aimo's jolly wife, Nadia, appeared. They started the place 35 years ago after moving from Tuscany. This restaurant is absolutely great. Seek it out when you are in Milan. If you see Marco the son-in-law, tell him Winner thinks he's... Oh well, better not.

Italian Ruins

When I decided to show Miss Lid the Leaning Tower of Pisa, we decided to have lunch at **Il Bottaccio** in nearby Montignoso. On a scale of 1 to 10, this was a weak 3 – in spite of having had in residence luminaries ranging from Barbra Streisand to Eric Clapton. The immensely charming host and chef, Nino Mosca, exhibits photos of himself with them to prove it.

The dining room itself is a disaster. To sit among the beauties of Italy in what is no more than an enlarged garage or small aircraft hangar is a total waste of time. Five hideous, brown air-conditioning vents faced me. A large stage took up about a third of the room, covered in dirty grey material with a piano and a guitar. Four plant holders full of shopping-arcade flora faced a pool. Some dreadful modern sculpture added to the visual cacophony. There was what looked like a copy of a Kandinsky gone wrong on one wall and something equally horrid on another. Nino assured me that they were all of artistic magnitude and valuable. Not to me they weren't.

There was one unisex toilet for a restaurant that holds 60 people. That's odd. Even odder is that the lock didn't work and the taps produced no water. Apparently there was a pump underneath the sink that you had to work with your foot. The hotel is owned by a Mr d'Anna, who has a restaurant in Grosvenor Place, London, called Il Cenacolo. I know of nobody who has been there.

At Il Bottaccio there was a very large menu and very few people were lunching. "This can't all be fresh," I said. "Eighty per cent of it is," replied Nino.

I started with four shrimps and a small portion of black rice. Quite nice. The piped music was Addams Family at its gloomiest. Miss Lid greatly liked her salad of greens and vegetables. There was then a long delay before my main course arrived. "It's like a kind of nightmare sitting here," I observed to Miss Lid. "You're a menace," she replied. We were probably both right.

My main course of lamb with a sauce and stuffed with spinach and kidneys surrounded by veggies looked nice. But the plate was cold and the appearance of the food was better than its taste. Miss Lid's *penne con scampi* with tomato sauce didn't go down too well. "The edges of the pasta are cold," she said. "Because they put it on the plate and ponce about for half an hour before they bring it here." That's esoteric food reviewing at its best. She added that the shrimps hadn't been shelled, so by the time you finished doing that all the pasta was cold anyway.

For dessert, I had what Nino assured me was his speciality, chocolate cake in the form of a triangle, standing upright. It was impossible to use your fork without laying it down. "You've destroyed my *piramide*, my pyramid!" Nino expostulated. It was more like mousse on a vague pastry base and it tasted of coffee not chocolate. "Mushy and very oversweet," I dictated in order to inform the world. Miss Lid thought her sorbet and fruit salad very good.

As I left, I was asked to check the toilet door. It had been fixed and you could now lock it. The final note onto my tape was "There's no question this is a terrible place, but made pleasant because of Nino, his attitude and personality." Unfortunately that isn't enough.

Heaven preserve us

Luigi Miroli (aka Puny) is a key player in Portofino. Mr Big. Vastly energised. When all the restaurants and shops shut down "on strike" one Saturday last summer in protest against the government declaring the Ligurian coast a preservation area, it was Puny I saw leading a crisis debate with his group in the almost deserted village square.

It's an interesting battle and one with the outcome still in doubt. The Ligurian coast is one of the most unspoilt in the world. But I've noticed an increase in enormous private yachts dwarfing Portofino's little multi-coloured houses. Even worse are the cruise ships anchored just out to sea, spilling hordes of tourists into the tiny town and even breaching the Splendido for itinerary events. It's a nightmare. The effluence and pollution from the ships is horrendous, the sight of them ghastly. To see these billionaires sitting high upon their decks, drinking cocktails and looking down on us peasants is enough for a rerun of the French revolution.

Personally, I'd shoot the lot of them, drag their horrid ships out to sea and burn them at night. That would look pretty. Although I'm not sure this is official Italian Green Party policy.

The shopkeepers and restaurateurs of Portofino hold another view, and their protest forced a delay in the enforcement of the government's edict to preserve the beauty and dignity of Portofino and the surrounding area. I suppose natural beauty is irrelevant if it hits you too hard in the pocket.

Puny's restaurant is set back from the waterside. It's generally considered to offer the best food in Portofino. I agree with that. From the front tables in **Puny** you get a great view of the cobbled square, the boats, the bay and the hill with a large *pino marittimo* growing out of the castle courtyard on top.

When I first went to Puny we had some terrific sea bass in salt. There was so much salt over the fish and the baked potatoes that when the waiter bashed it, everything rattled and Puny came to save the day. It tasted memorably good. On another visit, I had sea bass with bay leaves and black olives from Genoa. There's a romantic guitarist wandering about singing 'I Found My Love in Portofino'. Not one of the most melodious ballads I've ever heard. I made a note on my tape that "Puny wins the award for the best flower display in the toilet".

He also does terrific pasta. His pappardelle with basil and tomato is an old recipe from Genoa; his gnocchi with shrimp sauce and green peas is totally historic. Portofino is an experience at any time of year. Puny is its senior food server. But I shall be absolutely furious if he wins his battle with the government and lets those dreadful monster boats and monster people roam freely over one of the last great preserved – not full of high-rise – areas in Europe.

I'd even be prepared to pay three times as much for my pasta. Come to think of it, I can't see why Puny cares: his place has always been totally full when I've been there. Perhaps the billionaire yacht people are bigger spenders? Shoot 'em anyway, I say.

The **Ristorante Delfino** is right on the waterfront in the lovely old harbour of Portofino. You sit facing one of the great views of the world. The totally preserved, tiny harbour, the multi-coloured houses with washing hanging from them, bobbing boats, fishermen unloading their catch, a hill, a castle, a church. It is just like an old Sophia Loren movie. Carmelo Carluzzo is the 34-year-old chef-owner here, and his beautiful wife Palma fronts the show. He knocked up a wondrous *trofietto al pesto*, sort of spaghetti and potatoes, all green and very good. Then a mixed grill of langoustine, lobster, sea bass and swordfish with courgettes, aubergines, seconi and onions. The fish was so fresh that you realise with great force the difference in flavour and texture of fish just from the sea as opposed to the London "days-later" variety. I finished off with lemon sorbet and espresso. All miraculously good. One of the most pleasant meals ever.

A religious experience

Something unique happened to me. It was dinner time on the terrace of the hotel Spendido in Portofino, where the view by night is staggering. The floodlit castle floats on a dark, wooded hill, two large pine trees growing out of its upper courtyard. It's called, rather boringly, Castle Brown, after a 19th-century British consular official who lived there. Below it, the lights of the boats rocking in the harbour ripple on the water. What happened was that Giorgio Tognazzi, one of my dream team and the maitre d', had kept both the unfinished bottles of mineral water (fizzy and still) and the bottle of white wine left over from lunch and offered them up. Surprisingly, the wine tasted just as good. I hate to think, pricewise, what I leave on the table in wine and water each year.

The **Splendido** is set on a cul-de-sac, narrow coastal road. You can drive into Portofino, but to get out you have to return by the same route. This covers a number of fantastic little towns before it meets up with any alternative roadway. The whole area has been remarkably preserved. No cranes loom on the hillside to signify overbuilding.

The food at the Splendido has gone from good to very good. Tagglialini with porcello mushrooms, scampi baked in the oven with a light lemon sauce, ravioli with potatoes, anchovy and fresh tomato and so on. Everything deeply memorable. Apart from a ghastly moment when a dessert, which I had been told would be with vanilla ice cream, turned out to have sickly British-Rail-type soft meringue on top, then dreary ice cream and then the most awful chocolate cake ever. It tasted as if it had spent a long life in the deep freeze before suffocating. I didn't bother to mention this to Giorgio because he'd been so good at recommending the local wines. Thus I met Vermentino Vigna u' Munte 1994, Pigato lo Petrai (date forgotten) and a couple of others. All terrific.

Slightly beating the general manager, Maurizio Saccani, who is extremely funny and laughs a great deal, to be the star of the Splendido is the chief concierge, Fausto Allegri. It was Fausto who was dispatched to the swimming pool when I went berserk because the attendant had walked off leaving chaos and confusion and, most importantly, my loungers "stolen" by someone else! I made such a fuss that Mr Saccani, who'd just reached the Villa San Michele in Florence, drove all the way back to stay until I departed. Fausto has an answer for everything. I rang him one day and said, "Fausto, this pool is full of people reading English newspapers. Why don't I have any?" "Mr Winner," said Fausto, as if explaining to an idiot child, "they are yesterday's papers." "As they're the only ones we're ever going to get," I replied, "do you think I could have some, too?"

Fausto's greatest moment came in the manager's office when I was complaining about the wrapped butter served at room-service breakfast. Mr Saccani was doing a number about the heat and all the guests being violently ill from rancid butter if he sent it unwrapped (although he did send mine unwrapped for the next couple of days and I survived). Then I went on about the sugar also being wrapped. Mr Saccani went to a filing cabinet and proudly produced a sugar bowl with the double sea horse emblem of the hotel. It was, he said, not quite right yet, but would soon be adored by guests when on display each morning. To divert me he produced an album of photos of a speedboat in various choice coastal locations. "Why don't you take the boat tomorrow, Mr Winner," he said. "Sometimes it works, sometimes it doesn't. When it doesn't work we have two telephones so you can call for help. That's if they work." And he roared with laughter. "Go to lunch at the abbey of San Fruttuoso and then on to swim in a lovely cove. It's a marvellous day out." He wants to get rid of me, I thought.

"Okay," I said. "We'll do that." Fausto Allegri was brought in and told to arrange it.

"Ah, Mr Winner," he said, "you don't want to go to the abbey for lunch. It's far too crowded. You want the boat at three o'clock when it's quieter." "Actually I do want to go there for lunch, Fausto," I said. "No, I promise you, you don't Mr Winner. You want to go later," was the reply. "Why?" I asked. "Because another guest, Mr Mann, has the boat booked each day from 11 to 3," said Fausto.

It's unassailable logic like that which I find totally disarming.

PS The maitre d' is now Carlo Lazzeri, the marvellous chef Corrodo Corti, and the food is superb.

There has been a dramatic change at the excellent Hotel Splendido in Portofino. Fausto Allegri has been given the job of guest relations manager. This means Fausto is no longer uniformed and behind the reception desk. Instead, he wanders around the hotel in a variety of clothing that can generously be described as eccentric. One day he may be in short trousers and a red shirt; who knows what the next. Fausto will suddenly appear like a demented violinist in search of an orchestra, peering through the railings around the pool.

He is in terrific form, full of marvellous suggestions – and even found me a helicopter pad in a nearby field when I decided to move on to the south of France. A mere 40-minute flight. As we drove to the landing site, Fausto ruminated on his change of role. "Nobody in Italy knows what a guest relations manager is," he said. "They think I am a tailor." "Not with the clothes you wear, not with those short trousers they don't," I replied.

Lo Stella is next door to the Delfino on the waterfront in Portofino, with the same incredible view. Vanessa had *pansotti* with nut sauce (ravioli filled with veg) and then langoustines. I had a salad and then fish ravioli, the house speciality, which they only do for two people. So I paid – and ate – a bit more! Finally, a very creamy tiramisù. During all this, a man with a guitar sang 'I Found My Love in Portofino', the old Dean Martin hit 'Volare' and a lot more.

Santa Margherita, near Portofino, is a town where the clock has stood still. Grandly designed 19th-century hotels look out over the sea, their windows surrounded with shutters and ornately painted decorations. There's a delightful bistro called **Skipper** overlooking the port, where you sit in white directors' chairs and get marvellous local shrimp, mussels, cuttlefish and whatever. I assume it comes from the old-fashioned marble-slab-ridden market nearby, where the fishermen unload their catch and it's displayed for locals to buy. I had memorable mussel soup with white wine, tomato sauce, olive oil and pepper, and an excellent tart.

Climb the steep hill that rises behind Santa Margherita and you'll eventually reach **La Stalla**, which has dramatic views overlooking the bay. You sit on the terrace. We had risotto with mushrooms, and "Daddy fruit cake", which was like a sausage roll with fruit in it. The sorbet was more like a fruit frappé, rather liquid and in a tall wine glass.

I had a very good lunch at **Il Campo** in the Piazza del Campo in Siena. One of the great views of the world is the main square, the 14th-century tower and the well-preserved medieval buildings. Lovely spaghetti with truffles, good prawns and assorted Siena cakes, which range from nougat to orange-tasting things. Totally exceptional.

Al Frati in Murano, the glass-blowing Venetian island, is in an old building with a deck overlooking the canal and the crumbling Palazzo da Mula. The view is wonderful, and Gi-Gi, real name Luigi Camozzo, who owns it, a totally charming host. I had fried scampi and *granzella*, which is spider crab. I then tried spaghetti with clams, and Vanessa had a mixed fish grill – the sort of thing they do particularly well around Venice. It's a place to go for lunch, and I thoroughly recommend it.

I liked **La Caravella** in Venice even though it resembles a roadhouse in East Grinstead. Dark with silly nautical stuff on the walls. We booked for 8pm and out of courtesy I called to say we'd be there at 8.15. "Come at nine," said the maître d'. "No, no," I replied patiently. "I was booked for eight but shall be 15 minutes late." "Rather have you at nine," he said in the great customer-service style now affecting restaurants everywhere. I came at 8.15 determined to hate it, but only the bread was awful. The calamari risotto, the carpaccio with spider crab, the drink of Titziano – fresh orange, strawberry and sparkling wine – all were good. So much as I wanted to, I didn't complain. Now *that's* something.

Venetian class

I do not go to restaurants, I go to tables. I do not go to hotels, I go to suites. Suite 225 at the Cipriani in Venice has always been one of my favourites. It is enormous, with six windows looking out over the church of St Giorgio Maggiore, the tree-filled island behind it and the lagoon; two more look to the beautifully flowered gardens at the front of the hotel and three more to the swimming pool and to Venice proper. The hotel is on the island of Giudecca, a four-minute boat ride from St Mark's Square and the Doges' Palace. The trip on the hotel launch is one of the most beautiful little excursions you can take – you get a water view of one of the greatest architectural sights in the world as you approach the piazzetta.

The food at the **Cipriani** is good, although not historic. On one visit I was disappointed that service was rather slow, so they got the Winner-napkin-wave on its outside-the-UK debut. As I was waving my napkin slowly over my head, an American lady at the next table asked: "Are you surrendering?" I feared I might be hitting her: "I hope I'm not disturbing you." But no, she was delighted with the whole performance. The maitre d' was rather snooty. He eventually turned up and asked dryly, "Did you want something?" I refrained from making a smart remark and just said: "I'd like to order dessert, please."

I can report now, though, that under the highly distinguished Dr Natale Rusconi, a much admired doyen of hotel managers with a serious suit and a wry smile, that the food has much improved and the staff are all excellent. And the views to the lagoon and the piazzetta are as staggering as ever.

The Cipriani is still far and away the best hotel in Venice. On my birthday, at the end of October, I dined there with Miss Lid No 3.

I had Adriatic fish soup with home-made noodles; Miss Lid had mixed salad with scallops and deep-fried porcini mushrooms seasoned with balsamic vinegar. The standard was excellent. The fried scampi with rice that followed were impeccable. Then for dessert, a sort of plum cake with nuts, a lovely, old-fashioned cassata and… oh dear, a young Englishman at the next table heard me dictating and interrupted: "Can I say something? Is that allowed?"

I felt like uttering a grossly vulgar dismissal, but he carried on. "I thought the beef was very good," he said, speedily changing it to "pretty good". He added that the onion soup was "passable". This is what I have to put up with. I met the chef, who has really spruced things up, a nice local chap called Renato Picolotto.

Da Ivo is a small place clinging to a canal in Venice. I bumped into my friend Lauren Bacall (Betty to me!) coming out. She liked it, but I found it claustrophobic and horrid. Tiny tables and an appalling group of tourists being slowly served. I got up and fled to the Cipriani pool.

Lapping up the water music

Orchestras used to be everywhere when I was younger. A pianist and single violinist played in the teashop in Letchworth, just to the left of the mural of a stone balcony wall with flower gardens beyond. At the Criterion in Piccadilly, I remember at least eight men in evening dress, with a conductor, playing at lunchtime. Now the only regular place I visit with musicians is Claridge's.

Somewhere I visit less regularly, which has musicians galore, is Venice. In the Piazzetta, the bit you walk through to get to St Mark's, there's the Gran Caffè Chioggia, which advertises hot dogs and boasts a rather jazzy trombonist with a pianist and double-bass player, all too modern for my liking. But pass through into St Mark's itself, always a place of magic, and you are met with triple-stereophonic orchestras from three caffès – the Florian, the Quadri and the Lavena – which vie to attract passers-by on to the display of chairs and tables that face them.

My favourite has always been the **Florian**, which boasts, for most of the day and night at least, six musicians playing their hearts out with a selection of light classical and show tunes. Vanessa thought her vegetarian club sandwich was very good, my regular one was delicate and not bad, the wine was disgusting. But the service is exemplary, and to sit with a coffee or a *citron pressé*, listen to the music and look at the greatest architecture in the world is still a wonder. At night they floodlight the cathedral, the *campanile* (bell tower to you) and the two sides of the square, hung with lanterns, and called the Procuratie Vecchie and the Procuratie Nuove, dating back to the 15th century.

If it rains, the orchestra turns to face inside the cloistered archway and the restaurant beyond. You can sit in the glass-painted Caffè Florian and imagine you are in the 18th century when it was built, and even for a total realist like me it is the most romantic place ever. Guardi, Canova, Byron and Proust sat in the Florian while the **Quadri** opposite boasts the patronage of Alexandre Dumas and Wagner. There the band is dressed in rather bilious green and puts on more of a music-hall act. The clarinettist holds a note for ever and other musicians stare and mime surprise. The violinist twirls his violin before striking it dramatically with the bow to start the session. They get the crowd clapping with them in jolly, seaside fashion. Inside, paintings by Ponga of 18th-century Venetian life are modelled on those done in the Florian.

The **Lavena** seems to have a musician or so less than the others and the caffè itself is fronted with ice-cream cones and Venetian chandeliers. They speak of Franz Liszt and Rostropovich as their coffee-drinkers. At night, individually lit little stalls appear selling paintings and handbags and various twaddle, but quite like you see in Canaletto or Guardi paintings of centuries gone by.

It has been raining and a cold wind now runs through the square. The white tables are tipped up, most of the chairs are empty. It is 11 o'clock and the band turns, optimistically, from playing to inside to outside. A couple waltz through the puddles to Lehar's *The Merry Widow*. I have stayed in Venice at Christmas when nobody else did (sadly it's now fashionable); then, mists swirled along the canals and the lights spilled from church doors into the alleyways as the choir sang. It really is the best place.

The best bar none

Harry's Bar in Venice is the best restaurant in the world. Not slightly, not marginally, not by a hair's breadth or whatever, but firmly, absolutely. It overlooks the start of the Grand Canal, but the windows are so small it doesn't matter. It was founded in 1931 by Giuseppe Cipriani, is now owned by his son Arrigio and has been a hang-out for Hemingway, Cole Porter, Joan

Crawford and me – not in that order of importance, I might add. It doesn't look much. A bar downstairs with some tables and a posher bit upstairs, both levels quite small. The Italians eat downstairs; tourists mingle with locals six-deep around the bar. The tables are so close together you need to be a contortionist to get in. Through it all, the white-clad waiters weave with dexterity. The room is genuinely chic, even though it has a linoleum floor and décor so plain I couldn't describe it. But it's a spirited place, noisy and cheerful. And it typifies the sort of food I like. Brilliant, natural ingredients, not over-fussed in the cooking or presentation, just *direct*.

Harry's Bar is famous for their bellinis, a serious frothy combination of Italian champagne and white peach juice squeezed by hand and put through a sieve. Giovanni Cipriani invented the bellini in 1948, and the barman, Claudio Ponzio, has been making them meticulously for over 25 years. The taste is unbelievable. One day at the bar I knocked back three of them, some croque-monsieurs, shrimp sandwiches and chicken patties. All were beyond belief superb – not like they sound, but in another stratosphere. On other visits for lunch or dinner I've had tagliolini with white truffles, with ham and with wild mushrooms, a scampi and zucchini risotto, a risotto with baby artichokes, ravioli with asparagus and with spinach and cheese, an osso bucco and liver Venetian-style. Liver and onions may not sound much, but their way it is. Each meal was quite simply perfect. And desserts? Unbelievable! A chocolate cake that is definitely far and away the best I have ever tasted, and I consider myself the number-one world expert on chocolate cake! Lemon meringue pie, apple cake, zabaglione cake, vanilla meringue cake, vanilla yoghurt ice-cream with biscuits and three home-made jams – strawberry, prune and redcurrant, crêpes with lemon custard cream. Mind-blowing! Even their bread is special.

As I was coming back on the hotel launch to the Cipriani, an American woman gushed: "I read your column every week." Her elderly male companion said: "I'm told you're a famous food writer. Can you recommend me a restaurant?" "Harry's Bar," I replied. "Eurrgghh!" he said, as if I were an idiot. They want you to recommend some little place in a smelly back street, Harry's Bar deserves my Best in the World Award. I checked it out on that trip and again a few weeks later. For one of my advanced years, I have been unduly active.

Lady Rose Lauritzen, whose husband Peter is the world-renowned Venice expert, recommended the **Hotel Monaco** as the best food in Venice. She's a local, so we tried it. A fading, Frinton-on-Sea dining room with everything ordinary, from the watery fish soup to the zabaglione cheese cake.

The island of Torcello has 25 inhabitants, three restaurants, two churches and a museum. One of the restaurants is the **Locanda Cipriani**, owned by Carla, sister of Arrigo of Harry's Bar in Venice, and run by her son. There's a rose garden, an arbour and then the beautiful old church of Santa Fosca with the larger Santa Maria dell'Assunta behind it. The bellinis almost equal Harry's Bar, the spaghetti with peas is historic, the apple sorbet and meringue cake tip-top. Not expensive, either.

The *New York Times* once named the **Osteria Da Fiore** in Venice among the five best restaurants in the world, so I decided to try it. It is in a claustrophobic room with regency-stripe wallpaper, a low ceiling and no windows. The menu was all fish except for Parma ham. The freebie starter was baby shrimps, white polenta and zucchini. Polenta is the most over-rated stuff in the world. My main course was baked scallops with olive oil and thyme. I found it quite ordinary – I've had better scallops in my local Chinese. How this restaurant ever got into anyone's top five in the world I can't imagine.

San Pietro in Volta is an out-of-the-way Venetian island. At first you see only decrepit churches with a few boatyards thrown in, and you have a feeling of being lost. But it grows on you in a big way. The **Restaurant Nani** faces the old cathedral and the cobbled seaside square. It's a family business, legendary for its fish. As we entered, four of the family were preparing fresh lobsters and other fish at a table. Upstairs on the balcony, Joseph, son of Nani, looked after us superbly. Nice crusty bread, and then the most marvellous mix of lobster, crab meat, different types of shrimps, sea eels, everything. This was the best cold seafood starter I've ever had. I went on to noodles with fish, then a sort of mixed fish grill. We watched a man come from a shop and put some scraps on a plate on the dockside by a boat, then three cats walked over to eat them. It was so calm, the lagoon lapping on our left. At weekends, it's packed with locals who come from all over, but it's never touristy – except for me. And, if you're clever, for you as well.

The islands surrounding Venice have an individual atmosphere of their own. Burano specialises in lace and is full of mini canals and small houses painted in different, bright colours – green, deep orange, pink, blue, red … every colour you can think of. The church tower leans alarmingly and has grass growing out of the top. In Burano, the **Trattoria da Romano** offers quite the most wonderful food and in a lovely setting. In good weather you sit outside with a view of the houses and their wavy terracotta-tile roofs. Orazio Barbaro, the owner of da Romano, names some of his famous guests on the menu, ranging from Charles Chaplin to Matisse and Mel Brooks. I started with a mix of octopus, escargot, lobster and shrimp. All totally historic plus. Then I had *grand fritto* Romano, sole off the bone, eels, shrimps, squid. I finished with strawberries and ice cream. For those concerned about cost, our river taxi was £60, one way, from the Rialto bridge. After lunch, there were no taxis, so we returned on an enormous full-of-public ferry boat. It took for ever, wandering hither and thither, but was exceedingly jolly.

The **Trattoria San Marco** is a Venetian restaurant you'd never take a second look at. The street in which it resides, Frezzeria, near St Mark's Square, is anonymous, a street you walk through on your way to somewhere else, and the San Marco looks like a cafe. I would never have gone there without being taken by Giles Shepherd, former boss of the Savoy Group and now chief of The Ritz hotel. It is run by the four Fiorin sisters who have had the place since 1954. It has stood still in looks and atmosphere. Pictures on the wall, wood panelling up to a dado rail, terrazzo-type floor, wooden chairs with rush seats and white tablecloths. The food is terrific – we had tiny shrimps with oil, fried scampi, then ice cream with something brown in the middle called *tartufo*. It's a little-known gem, and I've been back many times since.

Cinque Terre means five lands – incredible bypassed towns, one perched on the cliff tops, old houses, churches, tiny, spectacularly beautiful. Vernazza has a small harbour, behind it a little square with a church. Very few tourists, and most of those Italian. Here I found the **Trattoria Bar Gianni**, a Winner special. There's a bar, an enormous open kitchen and a room of very old stone and brick walls with great wooden beams. I let Gianni recommend. "Appetiser is many styles of anchovies, is very good, is small fish. Can you take maybe one pasta? Small macaroni with scampi. Then we'll see," he said. Onto the immaculate white tablecloth was placed the local wine, Cinque Terre 1995 Cantina de Molo. Delicious. Little plates of starters surrounded us. Anchovies like this and like that. Cheese puffs. Some of the dishes hot, some cold. Sweet tomato and herring slices. Octopus, calamari. Just when I thought I'd had everything, some stuffed mussels arrived. This was the best starter I have ever eaten. Fresh, tasted of something. Incredible. The macaroni with scampi, brilliant. Don't tell me food in England has got good. Go to some village, population 700 or so, and see if you can get a meal like this. No chance. I finished off with chocolate mousse. This is where Lord and Lady Rogers (her ladyship owns and runs the River Café) go two or three times a year to get a few tips. They stay in Gianni's adjacent hotel, which has very small rooms and lots of stairs. Not for me. I like to sit looking at one of the greatest restaurant views ever. And eat. Those are my specialities. Sitting and eating.

9

LUXEMBOURG

When I went to Luxembourg to play a role for Steven Berkoff in the film of his riveting stage play, *Decadence*, I enjoyed dinner at a restaurant called **Saint-Michel**. It's in an extremely lovely setting, a 16th-century castle, and the food was more than excellent. We stuffed ourselves on lobster salad with mango and avocado, a fine *foie gras d'oie maison*, an exceptional ravioli of langoustines, pigeon stuffed with foie gras, a turbot with fine sliced potatoes and *sauce persillée*, a very good wine and tip-top desserts. If you feel an urge to rush off to Luxembourg, you should definitely visit the Saint-Michel.

WINNIE ACTS FOR MR BERKOFF

HAPPY PORTUGESE PEOPLE
SING TO WINNIE IN ARSÉNIO'S

1 0

M A D E I R A

Net gains

We drove through the utterly uninteresting streets of Funchal, turned left after a car park, passing some tacky-looking open-air cafes, all fairly empty, and then between them to what is laughingly called the old section of town. This sports indeterminate, small-scale hacienda-type architecture. But there stirred a feeling of optimism as we walked toward **Arsénio's**. The first sight is of an open-air grill, a large display of fresh fish and a moustached man in a chef's hat with rimless glasses on the end of his nose. This is Arsénio, a restaurateur who cooks and works on the premises. We squeezed past the grill into a large, dim interior space with beams above the windows, arches, real cobwebs on the pillars and red tablecloths. It looked old, a very nice room.

At the back, a man played a Yamaha keyboard. The menu offered an enormous variety of fish. Arsénio brought some over to show us. I chose prawns with garlic, Vanessa melon with ham, but she only wanted the melon. To follow: mixed swordfish, tuna fish and squid fish on the skewer (sic).

The man left the Yamaha and turned down the lights. Two men arrived, one with a guitar and one with a mandolin. Then a lady in black joined them and started singing. She got a good round of applause. The music was local, called fado. My Coca-Cola arrived. It tasted nothing like English Coca-Cola, but Coke can taste very different as you progress around the world if they mix it on the premises. The local water used with the syrup makes a difference, too.

Then a man with a moustache appeared in a bright red jacket and a black polo-neck sweater. He walked round the tables as he sang. It was very pleasant. He shook hands with two people at the next table.

My prawns and garlic sauce arrived. Totally delicious. Memorable. Never mind that there wasn't some souped-up chef poncing about in the kitchen with Michelin stars in his eyes, this was a terrific first course.

Then a woman with grey hair and a black shawl sang and two men joined in from the back of the room, one a new chap in a blazer and jeans and a white shirt. He went round the tables as everyone clapped. There was stereophonic live singing from all round the place as the various entertainers joined in. A delightful atmosphere.

My fish on the skewer was as good as you could ask for, genuinely fresh, not the so-called fresh you get in most British restaurants. A woman brought a plate of beans, potatoes and carrots, and some butter sauce. Outside, Arsénio was engulfed in a mass of smoke. Inside, the singer in the red jacket was selling signed cassettes of his performance to other diners.

My dessert was flambéed bananas with vanilla ice cream. Superb. Local bananas, very good quality, excellent texture. Wonderful syrup with it all. This was a memorably first-class meal.

Oh Madeira!

I decided to visit the revered Reid's Hotel in Madeira for a long weekend. It's difficult to get there, so I took a private jet at £18,000 return. Within five minutes of leaving the airport in Madeira I had that sinking feeling. Nothing looked interesting. I drove through Funchal, the capital city: boring beyond belief. I passed a group of hideous modern hotels. Then we turned into the small driveway of Reid's.

The key to buying property, and the same applies to hotels, is you need three things. Location, location and location. **Reid's Hotel** is set in a row of horrid modern hotels that loom over it. You look out of the windows of the suite, and that's what you see. Sit by the pool, that's what you see.

The public rooms had the faded desolation of a Bournemouth hotel on its uppers. It meant nothing to me they were to be redecorated. The suite was small with that awful hotel view. I asked to see something else. The general manager, Anton Küng, escorted us to a larger suite which didn't face the ghastly hotel cluster. I was considering it when I noticed a large air conditioning vent, in it some fibrous white material crumbling and exposed. That'll shoot rubbish into the room, I thought. Vanessa called me to the bathroom. The bath had a dirty watermark, the surround had been filled in with Polyfilla, a black line of dirt ran along the top and bottom of it. We decided to stay put.

We went down for the famous Reid's tea. I had received a severe letter from Mr Küng instructing me not to wear jeans, T-shirts or track shoes in any part of the hotel. I counted five T-shirts in seconds. I have never seen a worse-dressed group of people in my life. They wore shoes as if bought at a reject store in the poorest part of an American city. "They're mostly locals," advised Luis Pinheiro, the genial manager. He's recently arrived from the excellent Mount Nelson in Cape Town. The sandwiches were adequate, the scones good, the cakes utterly dreadful.

For dinner in the main restaurant, Mr Küng had informed me, in writing, the dress code was suit and tie; on the phone he said dark suit and most people wore evening dress. I started counting. There's a man in a light brown sports jacket, there another in a pink jacket and grey trousers, there... I gave up. Mr Küng should learn that if he has a dress code, keep to it. Don't write telling people you have to dress a certain way when clearly you do not.

The wine waiter poured hot water into the decanter before decanting the wine. I found that odd. Not as odd as the wine list, which gave no date for any of the named wines. "Have you ever seen this?" I asked Vanessa. "Yes," she said, "in Pizza Express." My tartare of tuna was bland and tasteless. Vanessa's smoked salmon tired – she left most of it. My soup was wishy-washy, Vanessa's okay. Of her John Dory fish she said: "I don't think this is very fresh." It clearly wasn't. I had ham, which I was told was a locally reared item. The chocolate cake dessert was even worse than the one at tea. The brown bread for Vanessa's smoked salmon stayed on the table until halfway through the dessert course when I asked for it to be removed.

At breakfast the next day, we ordered Earl Grey tea and got some undrinkable slush. They changed it for Earl Grey. Vanessa ordered mixed stewed fruits. Prunes arrived. The orange juice was the worst I have ever tasted. "Is this squeezed here?" I asked Room Service. The man said: "It's fresh, I'll squeeze you some." What he brought was of a different colour, texture and taste to the nonsense I had been given. It was all a nightmare. The brochure refers to: "Attentive but discreet service, an unspoilt coastline, the last word in luxury and civilised elegance."

The last word it is. But not a word I care to mention in polite society.

M O R O C C O

Let the show begin

Being a poor boy from Willesden, I'm always greatly impressed by aristocracy. So when a marchioness at the Mamounia pool recommended some Marrakesh restaurants, I gratefully doffed my peaked Yankees' cap. The marchioness even sent a handwritten card to my suite confirming her choices, the card topped by embossed black letters giving her full title and a Belgravia address. I was all a-quiver. Top of the list was Chez Ali, which was 'great fun'. When the aristocracy say something is great fun they could be referring to a public hanging, a day out in Harrods, or pulling a Christmas cracker.

Chez Ali is a spectacular, enormous Moroccan restaurant and show palace. There are rows of Arab horsemen either side of a fake castle entrance. Once inside, hundreds of Arabs in different Moroccan tribal costumes blow some instruments and bang others. It's highly labour-intensive. There are camels, tents everywhere with people eating in them, a large, outdoor sawdust ring, more fake castles. It is the human row of extras that impresses. As you pass they come to life, dancing and playing music until you move to the next tribe and the old group relaxes waiting for new guests.

You recline luxuriously on rich cushions, dining off specialities described as harira, pastilla, tagine, mechoui, couscous, pastries, mint tea. An endless supply of tribespeople enter the tent bashing, blowing and dancing. Some of the Moroccan guests get up and jiggle around with them.

266

It took some while before we were served a beef broth with beans and rice. Then an enormous plate of lamb with beef on skewers. The lamb was very good. After dinner, in the arena, the show started with a great display of stunt horsemen, guns going off and general pageant-type things. A bit later a man on a flying carpet appeared above one end of the arena, and all the stuntmen, camel-riders, horsemen and varied assorted tribes came forward and waved. The show was over.

As we headed back to Marrakesh, our guide Mustapha said: "Once in a lifetime, everyone comes to Chez Ali. All the Moroccans." "Very nice for them too," I said. And I meant it.

A good restaurant in Marrakesh is **Dar Marjana**, where the owner-host, Chaouqui Dhaier, walks around in a green robe with a hood, and has a marvellously chiselled face. It offered the best service I've encountered anywhere, a miraculous pigeon pie and a group of Swedes somewhat overjoyed after drinking the local wine.

The restaurant **Diaffa** in Marrakesh, owned by Brahim Rmili, was recommended by my guide, Mustapha Hussaine. Mustapha is the superb greeter for the Casino at La Mamounia, owned by my friend Willy de Bruyn, the only amusing Belgian in the world. We sat at a large round table, soon joined by the chief of police of Marrakesh, who spoke in confidential tones to Mr Rmili. It was like a scene out of *Casablanca*: the movie, not the town. I expected the police chief's eyes to flicker and I'd find Peter Lorre and Sydney Greenstreet eating sheep's eyes in the corner. Diaffa does a set six-course meal, which is superb. Moroccan salad, savoury pastries, lamb tagine with prunes and almonds. Marrakesh tangia meat stewed in a rich sauce... in the meantime, two musicians play and do a tap dance. Oh, I've got another main course now, meat and chicken done in herbs. Then the musicians changed and one of them, in red, dances round the room as if stoned. Finally, in comes the belly dancer and a good time is had by all.

A place in the sun

The grounds of La Mamounia, in Marrakesh, are full of olives trees, orange trees and grapefruit trees. There are massive rose bushes. My two sun loungers rest at the garden end of the pool, so I face all this and the Atlas Mountains. On my left, a few blocks from the gardens, is the old souk of Marrakesh. The sound of the muezzin calling the faithful to prayer echoes over the chit-chat of those lingering poolside. The pool itself has the most enormous palm trees growing from an island in the centre; other great palms, flowering bushes and flowers abound. The buffet includes astoundingly good chocolate and coffee éclairs and as superb a millefeuille as I've ever tasted. No wonder Churchill spent the winters here, paintbrush in one hand, éclair in the other. Well, that's my version. On this occasion I had to settle for a sighting of United Nations Secretary-General Kofi Annan, Charlotte Rampling, Lord Carrington and a chat in the lounge with local resident Yves Saint Laurent.

The pool restaurant also does a good, though not outstanding, Moroccan salad and very reasonable grilled fish and meats. For some reason on this trip I became a great fan of the Fanta orange drink.

A three-piece orchestra plays on Sundays. That's when Robert Bergé, the small, dapper manager of **La Mamounia**, strolls, dressed all in white, greeting guests with the air of a man who had a wonderful supporting role in *Casablanca*, which, sadly, ended up on the cutting-room floor. "I must go and see my countess," he says, his eyes misting over. Or, on another occasion, secretively: "If you walk in the gardens you may see the prince playing squash." By contrast, Mohammed Chaab, his excellent local assistant, is large and his brother, Mustapha, owns a Moroccan restaurant in Windsor.

I enjoyed La Mamounia one Easter three years ago. Visiting again last November I liked it even more. At both times of year you can sunbathe or enjoy the architectural splendours of Marrakesh, or simply stroll through the Arab markets wondering if those small, shrivelled animal parts on sale for use in witchcraft ceremonies really work – and, if so, which should I buy: a dried-up toad, the leg of a rabbit, the iguana skin or the skull of what looks suspiciously like a dog?

The Moroccan restaurant at La Mamounia, as opposed to the various others on offer, is a bit bright, but provides food as good as you will get anywhere in Morocco. And be certain that the food there is excellent. I sat on a pink banquette having lamb maghdour-style with eggs; Vanessa tried sea bream in tagine, Fez-style. Then I had a major taste experience: puff pastry stuffed with pigeon and almonds. The pastry is rather sweet, but that suits me. The 12 bowls of salads which preceded all this included two with meat, veal brains and veal liver with onions. The sweet tomato, almost puréed, is extraordinary. Although it was three years since they'd seen me, they remembered my still water, ice and lemon. The dessert is an enormous pie-like offering of thin, crisp, flaky pastry with custard cream between the layers, which the waiter smashes to pieces in front of your eyes. There is an Arab orchestra and the mandatory jolly belly dancer.

Marrakesh is only three hours from London. You can go by scheduled planes and thus not be insulted by Chauffair, which charged many – and I mean many – thousands of pounds for my LearJet journey while providing paper plates with plastic spoons. The food was dire too. But boss Nick Probett is capable of better, and on the flight back it was very good.

I had a marvellous experience sitting on the terrace for breakfast one morning. I found an empty table with coffee, milk and sugar laid on it. "That's a good idea," I thought. I poured the coffee. Then an elderly couple turned up with food from the buffet. They obviously wanted to join our table, so I decided, "I'll be gracious, I shall let them sit with us".

I beckoned them to the two empty seats. They looked extremely angry. "This is my table and you're drinking my coffee," said the man. German, of course. He indicated a chair tucked right under the table, and I noticed it had an expensive camera on it. I felt like staying. As the saying goes: "I've started, so I'll finish." The English lady with him spoke frostily, repeating, "You've taken our table." "Oh well," I thought. And I rose. "Why don't you take my coffee with you?" said the German. So I did. It's amazing how unsociable some people are when they're on holiday.

In the autumn you should think about Morocco. In Marrakesh you could lounge by the pool of the hotel La Mamounia, facing the orange and grapefruit groves. Before I get to the nitty-gritty, which would be a change because I've never got to it before, I wish to protest about the Fanta orange drink. I became extremely attached to it, poolside, at La Mamounia. Recently I decided to relive those sunshine moments and dispatched a staff member to buy some in Kensington High Street. The can came back labelled "Fanta orange" with pictures of open-cut oranges. The ingredients were listed in French and other foreign languages but not English. I poured it, high with expectation. It was dreadful, nothing like the drink I'd had in La Mamounia. It didn't even look like it. The Marrakesh version was a proper orange colour, the UK crippled sister was akin to liquid I wouldn't mention in the pages of a sophisticated newspaper.

I have written to Mr Doug N Daft, the chairman and chief executive officer of The Coca-Cola Company in Atlanta, Georgia, asking him about this: Did his predecessor, Mr M Douglas Ivester, have a secret hatred of the British? Did he have a Moroccan wife, lover or some other connection with that fine country that led him to ensure they had a superb product and we got something so inferior? How could two products, supposedly the same, be offered to customers when they are so different? I can no longer keep my concerns to myself.

I await his response.

Le Tobsil is undoubtedly the best restaurant in Marrakesh. It's owned by a French lady named Christine Rio. She walks round her candlelit mansion in the old city in a black frock coat and trousers. The restaurant is the balconied inner courtyard, where a roof has now been added. The tables are large and placed well apart, with rose petals on the white tablecloths. It's truly romantic.

There's a log fire and two musicians chanting and playing stringed instruments. I had more than one meal there with Miss Lid the Third. We both loved the Moroccan salad of sweetbreads, puré of aubergine, sweet tomatoes, and more. Then there's spinach pie in crisp flaky pastry, pigeon without bones served with a magical sauce, lamb with tangerine, vegetable couscous and, for dessert, pear and oranges with grapes and almonds in a sauce, or almond tart – and, to finish, remarkable mint tea. Very fresh and real.

When you leave, you go down alleys that have remained unchanged for centuries. There are barefoot kids, cats scattering as you walk. Chanting of the Koran can be heard from an ornately carved doorway. It's real Arabian Nights stuff.

Honoured by the consul

Yacout is quite the most beautiful restaurant ever and owned by the British honorary consul in Marrakesh. To get there, you drive down tiny alleys with potholes in the road, little shops lit up at night with wooden slats leaning from them and old men in skull caps at the side of the road gesticulating as they talk. On past a fountain with multidecorated tiles until a man in a red fez with a black tassle and in flowing white robes opens the car doors for you.

He takes you to an ancient wooden door, which leads to a real Arab garden with a pool, lanterns, trees and palm trees round it. You are then shown up steep stone steps to the top of a tower and given a lovely view of the old city of Marrakesh. Sometimes drinks are served on the flat roof, but on our night it was a bit nippy. So we went down to an old hall, which had once been the central courtyard of an elegant villa. Big pillars above, a balcony round it with more arches, large, ornate carved lanterns on the floor with candles in them, candles in the hanging chandelier, and an enormous stone bowl in the middle of the room full of multicoloured rose petals floating on water. A two-piece band sing and play stringed and drum instruments. Our consul, Mr Mohammed Zkhiri, turns up. "When the British looked at me, they liked my face and said we'd like you as the honorary consul." He is a very smartly dressed Moroccan. Nine years ago, he opened Yacout as a restaurant.

Always keen to know where I stand, I asked: "So, if I lose my passport, you open the drawer, take one out, stamp it, and I'm okay?"

"No," said Mohammed, "I pass the details on to Casablanca." Mustn't lose my passport, I thought.

Moroccan meals are superb, but have a certain sameness about them. We had the Moroccan salad, many bowls – aubergine, carrots mixed with cinnamon and sugar, tomatoes and paprika hot and minced. No knives or forks: you're meant to scoop it out of the dishes with the bread. For wine a Moroccan Cabernet Medaillon 1990: mild, pleasant, but Bordeaux needn't panic. Then lamb and prune in puff pastry, and couscous with chicken and lemon. They even changed the water glasses for the second course. Then they served a whole chicken for me alone. You don't starve in Morocco! Then tiers of pâtisserie.

At 10.15pm, a man in a red fez put down a rug and two more musicians came and sat on green cushions with old-fashioned instruments and chanted in a rhythmic, stoned way. It was very good. I must get this as background music at home, I thought. The one with castanets spins his fez and the black tassle twirls round like a propeller. This is an experience I enjoyed.

I'm concerned about Marrakesh. Hundreds of bed-and-breakfast joints and new hotels are springing up. These are signs of terminal decay. I shall return, but nervously. The food there is sensational. The most romantic dining room ever is at Yacout. When I first went I saw a lovely Arab garden with a pool, lanterns, palm trees and exotic bushes around it. That's now tarted up to make another restaurant. The romantic room had been taken over by American tourists, so I was shown a small table in the now-phoney garden. The table was changed, the setting remained. On the roof of Yacout they serve pre-dinner drinks, degraded by the sight of American tourists photographing each other against the dim lights of the old-town background, none of which will come out when the photos are developed.

Gold standard

There are celebrated hotels in the world about which the cognoscenti speak in hushed tones. None is more regarded than Le Gazelle d'Or in Taroudannt, a small, unspoilt Moroccan town. Here, it is said, President Jacques Chirac spends every Christmas. Michael Portillo has been recumbent by the pool. A Saatchi, I know not which, definitely attended. It's where I met my childhood heroine, Valerie Hobson. We discussed her role in The King and I. Her husband, John Profumo, was charm itself.

I reach **La Gazelle d'Or** from Marrakesh, courtesy of Vincent Ducro, a tall thin angular pilot who looks like Harrison Ford. He flies a single-engined, old propeller plane with struts supporting the wings. The views over the Atlas Mountains are spectacular. After sheep have been chased from the runway, we land at a little-used airstrip. Adam Stevenson, manager of La Gazelle d'Or, meets us in a chauffeured Mercedes. We go to the Berber market in Taroudannt where a scarred man sells dead bats, dried lizards and other delights including amber, which I buy in bulk.

La Gazelle d'Or is owned by Mrs Rita Bennis, who spends much time at her flat in Notting Hill. The hotel was built in 1956 by a French baron; Mrs Bennis got it in 1981. It now consists of cottages set in large, beautiful and restful gardens. Wonderful flowers and shrubs vie with eucalyptus and jacaranda trees. Meals are served in the main house and by an idyllic pool. It is a magical world, very peaceful, near mountains, deserts and palm groves. The king of this domain is Stevenson, a slim Englishman who was barman and pianist at the Colony Club in Soho. This was also known as Muriel's Club because of the celebrated owner, Muriel Belcher. A 1971 magazine shows him there with Francis Bacon, Lucian Freud, Annie Ross and Tom Driberg. The 1970s live on in Adam's persona and demeanour.

Life by the pool is serene. Under olive trees and bougainvillea, guests bask on sun loungers while attentive staff in white flowing robes and white fezzes deal with everything, including a superb buffet lunch. Breakfast on the terrace outside the main building with a musical accompaniment of rare bird noises is spectacular. Rasping voices from north London are balanced by a delightful group of elderly Irishmen, one of whom, a bookseller from Sligo, speaks about dinner. "You don''t come here for the food," he says. It falls silent until a cat walks by, clomping madly. Or thus it seemed, so utterly peaceful were the surroundings.

Adam asked me to wear a tie for dinner. You sit for drinks in a domed room with Moroccan pillars and an open fireplace, looking onto a terrace with candles and lanterns on the ground and the tables. There is the sound of crickets. It's very romantic.

In the dining room ties were in the minority. "Tie, no tie," I dictated, looking around. "Man taking his jacket off, no tie and tartan trousers; man with sweater round open-necked shirt." Oh well, I'd done as asked. It was extremely posh. Everyone was very quiet. Vanessa had artichoke hearts and thought they tasted peculiar. I had *le magret de canard aux apricots* and a *purée de pommes de terre douces*. Feeble. But a beautiful setting and excellent service. Vanessa continued with vegetable couscous with a side order of onions and raisins, which "cheered the thing up no end". This was not a meal to die for. The millefeuille dessert was okay.

Adam was playing the piano. Brilliantly. Superbly arranged. From the heart. Melodies ranged from 'The Lambeth Walk' to Rachmaninov's *Piano Concerto No 2*. We adjourned to an outer room, where Adam sat at the grand piano. An old man with a white beard and a turban squatted in front of a bowl of mint. He broke up the mint sticks, put them in a teapot, and added sugar and hot water from a charcoal stove. Robed servants handed it round.

Adam looked neither to right nor left. Was he back in Muriel's Club? Was he in some hidden place of his own design? I would never know. There was no animation in the body or the face. But the playing was soulful. It transformed the atmosphere. He ended with Gershwin's 'Rhapsody in Blue'. I clapped. If Adam heard the scattered applause, he made no acknowledgement. He stood stiffly, turned and walked away. As if another secret communion with who knows what had come to an end.

We went back to the suite and lit the log fire in the bedroom. There are few places left in the world like La Gazelle d'Or. Dinner may not have been three-star Michelin, or even one. Who cares.

WINNIE DRESSES UP FOR
LA GAZELLE d'OR

WINNIE GOES ON SAFARI

FOR HEAVEN'S SAKE STAND STILL!

M 2000

1 2

S O U T H   A F R I C A

It's very rare I go anywhere ahead of anyone else. So it's a miracle that I have recently been to the new "in" place, Constantia and its surrounding areas, including Cape Town, in South Africa. There are leafy roads, pompous houses with flashy grounds, burglar-alarm displays and guard-dog shows. I was so impressed that when the actor Christopher Lee took me to **The Cellars**, a lovely country house hotel with "breathtaking views across Constantia to False Bay", I couldn't remember anything I ate for dinner! This is not good for someone meant to be giving an opinion of the food! I vaguely recall it was pleasant, but unexceptional. Table Mountain looked impressive.

Not tonight, Rita

I'm not actually saying Rita Hayworth tried to seduce me, but I think she did. This came to mind as I sat recently in the **Grill Room of the Mount Nelson Hotel** in Cape Town. It's very 1950s, with banquettes of black and red-striped cloth, with jockey-and-horse prints on the wall and the plates. It was the girl singer warbling with a pianist and guitarist who reminded me of Rita. She wasn't much like her really, but in the dim lighting and with her old-fashioned attitude, it made me recall a night at Chasen's restaurant in Beverly Hills many years ago. Chasen's was the famous red-couched habitat of the heavyweights of Los Angeles. They were famous for their chilli con carne and their New York cut steak. One night I was there with Rita, sadly well on the decline. The phones had stopped ringing for her. People gave her a left-handed handshake and looked over her shoulder to see if there was anyone more important in the room. For my goddess when I was young, this was hard to take and Rita had gone somewhat to the bottle.

With us was my agent, who was considering representing her, and his wife. They were very old, conservative Angelenos. Rita was a bit drunk. She kept insulting my agent's wife, so the atmosphere was chilly. Eventually we got up to leave. I had found her frail but charming. Nobody else had. As we waited outside for the valet parker to bring the car, Rita stood momentarily under a street light. She wore a belted raincoat. It is a moment I shall never forget. For that brief flash of time, she was the girl I ogled in the local Palace cinema in Letchworth. The light hit her goldish hair, the stance was film star, she was still thin and in the night atmosphere she was really Rita Hayworth. We drove her home in stony silence, my agent's wife fuming. We got to her house. "Will you come in for a coffee, Michael?" she asked seductively. It was late. "Not tonight Rita," I said. And I kissed her goodbye.

That was the last time I saw her. Me, the poor boy from Willesden, turned down a nightcap, maybe more, with Rita Hayworth! Later she came to London and started a film, but couldn't cope and was replaced. Russell Harty flew her in for a TV talk show and she was totally incoherent. Thus does the wonder of show business destroy its heroines. The not-so-Rita lookalike was now singing "killing me softly with his love". I was about to have another memorable moment, but of a very different kind. The jovial, bearded chef-in-chief of the Mount Nelson had prepared bobotie for me and Vanessa. I'd asked him what was a typical South African dish and here it came. Javanese-style minced lamb, bay leaves, cumin and other spices, washed with egg on the top and baked in the oven. A butternut and pumpkin bobotie for Vanessa. It was totally sensational. A tiny bit like cottage pie, but better. And I love cottage pie. Garth Stroebel, the head chef, gets my award for one of the best dishes ever. The Grill Room is a time warp with some customers in formal dress, others in open-necked shirts. The restaurant manager, Arthur Claasen, was exemplary. On another night, Vanessa even gave their chicken second-best only to Claridge's, and she is the chief chicken critic of the world.

The Mount Nelson is a pink, white-balconied hotel of the old school. It is owned by the Orient Express Group and that's about as good a recommendation as you can get. It looks out on to Table Mountain and villas. Soon the villas will be high-rises and Cape Town will be destroyed. But now it's beautiful.

Constantia Uitsig is a spectacular wine farm on the slopes of Constantiaberg, the first wine-producing area of South Africa. The bearded, bespectacled and cheerful chef, Frank Swainston, is from England. We had good local lobsters, and I greatly enjoyed the penne with olive oil, garlic and parsley. Frank did a classically good, creamy bread-and-butter pudding to finish.

Just outside Franschhoek we turned left at the Huguenot Memorial to find the restaurant, **La Petite Ferme**, with amazing gardens of roses and other flowers, lawns sloping down to a wooden-railed fence and then valleys with pine trees and, in the background, the mountains. The hot peppered mackerel was memorable. The "Hunter's Choice" was springbok. Not as good as impala, but okay. The brandy tartlet was spongy and exquisite. The views are breathtaking, but all I could think was: "Give it three years and this will be housing estates." I've seen it happen to the south of France; in fact, I've seen it happen to the world.

Impala with everything

At **Mala Mala**, the most famous safari camp in South Africa, they understand things. The first-class visitors have nice little huts with bedrooms and suites overlooking the jungle, and a dignified dining room with a balcony near a flower-surrounded swimming pool. Opposite the main entrance is a separate area for the others. (I personally visited the plebeian side, walked among the diners and exchanged many jovial pleasantries. No snob, I.) But back to the "select", and a fairly ropey lot they were. Aged Americans talking about Medicare and a South African cleric to whom the disappearance of apartheid was obviously a disappointment. Luckily, I was not asked to mix. You are given your very own white hunter. Mine, Jeremy Brooker, was a delightful fellow, so he, Vanessa and I ate on our own in the thatched room. There is an exterior compound with a camp fire where you usually eat, but the weather wasn't good enough.

At our first lunch, Jeremy showed us the terrace and said: "Do you want to sit out in the wind?" "We're English, we're used to that," I replied, seeing tables were moved to the exact spot I wanted. Thus we settled on the wide, wooden veranda for the first of many excellent meals where I had least expected to find them. Lunch was impala, a lovely deer that leaps all around. It was delicate, not heavy like most venison. For dinner we had venison steak (impala to you). The next day we had venison curry (impala too!) and, later, deboned leg of venison with marula jelly, which was –

surprise – more impala! Since it is unlikely to turn up on the menu at The Ivy, this didn't worry me.

The rest of the food was good, time-warp stuff, which is just what I like. Before cooking got too clever. There was red pepper soup, a brandy-snap basket with peach ice cream and, for Vanessa, who's almost vegetarian, delicious stuffed button-up courgettes with tomatoes, onions and mixed herbs. On the wall was a stuffed sable antelope; I searched the menu but he wasn't on it. Cheese and wine soup, very jolly; nutty baked bananas, ice cream and chocolate fudge sauce – to die for. Marvellous hazelnut and chocolate meringues, superb chicken pie and then cold sliced impala with salad and, on the final night, impala served with an oyster and mushroom sauce! Thus impala-d, I was served by Teddy Moodley, the superb bar steward, and Belinda van den Berg, who was called the Sable (our bit of the "hotel") hostess. The only hostess I've met who wasn't cringe-making.

A private plane later and I was at **Ngala safari camp**, about an hour away. This was more nouveau, but still immensely pleasant. Our suite at Mala Mala had been, for one of my intolerably ludicrous demands, fairly basic. The one at Ngala was sensational. An enormous stilted house with wide balconies, a very large living room, a sizeable bedroom, everything but a telephone! So if you wanted something, you couldn't ask for it! The bottle of champagne that greeted us with profuse messages of welcome was removed while we had dinner. So when we felt like drinking, it wasn't there! And I behaved so well! The open-air dining room overlooked a river with reeds, trees and bushes. We'd missed sitting next to Oprah Winfrey and Michael Palin, but the almond tart, hard to cut, was totally historic, even though the turkey stir-fry didn't have enough gravy. The cauliflower soup was nice, but not hot enough. The guinea fowl, moderate. The fried camembert, excellent.

Mala Mala wins the food stakes. Ngala wins the shop prize – a store full of good safari gear and animal-embroidered shirts that even I could get into. The clothes were so comfy I went back and had a second portion of lemon tart.

Ah, the thrills of the jungle life under canvas! The hard sleeping bag on parched earth. The mosquitoes. The red water discoloured by sand. Thank goodness I never got any of that. It was enough that the hair dryer broke down for five minutes.

Soweto's finest

If you're ever in Soweto, I've got a terrific place for you. "Why should we go to Soweto?" I hear you say. Well, I did. If you don't, it's your loss.

Soweto is not as seen on TV. My memory was people burning each other with rubber tyres. African tribes slogging it out with guns and machetes, white Afrikaner police looking decidedly nervous crouching by their armoured vehicles. I met a peaceful community, cheerful, decent, with housing ranging from posh to squatter camp. A spirit of genuine goodwill everywhere.

"Don't wear your gold pince-nez and chain," cautioned Vanessa. "If they want it, let 'em have it," I said. "They deserve it more than me." Thus we got into a nice Mercedes driven by Edward Mtembu. Just in case, we took a charming security chap, Lovemore Mabena, with dark glasses, a black striped shirt, a black bow tie and smart black trousers with black braces. I'm glad he came because he was delightful. As security, we didn't need him. The South Western Townships of Johannesburg house 5m black people. "They say three and a half," volunteers Ed. "But they did the census from a plane and it's growing all the time." It has 23 registered millionaires and a few more whose activities are such they're not keen on registration. We saw some of their houses, then Zulu hostels, fine schools with children in outfits far neater than their English equivalents and then into what was supposedly the danger zone. I never thought it would be, and it wasn't.

At Winnie Mandela's house, tough-looking guards sported a sign on their truck: Guns Not Peace. They were ever so jolly, shook hands and loved being photographed. I had my fortune told by a faith healer in a tin hut, saw where Nelson Mandela used to live and was arrested, and a lady carrying a cake said it was nice to see people like Vanessa and me in their area.

Wandie's Place, I was told, is Soweto's only restaurant. A sign on stilts also advertising Castle Lager tells you you're there. You go in through a wooden door to a tiny stone courtyard and on into a peaceful eating area with red and yellow tablecloths, two rooms interconnecting and a sign, "No person under 21 allowed". There's a good buzz and a Victorian print of a little girl writing and a cat pawing what she has written. Wandie Ndala comes over and recommends *pap* (maize) and stewed martin (lamb) with a salad. "We can sit 60 people comfortably, sometimes 100 uncomfortably," says Wandie and laughs. When he hears I directed *Death Wish*, the whole room falls into appreciative silence. I'm led to Wandie's wall of fame, where signatures include Pierre Cardin, Edsel Ford (grandson of Henry) and the Cuban ambassador, among other diminishing dignitaries. I am asked to sign in the middle.

Then we all sat and tucked in. Me, Ed, Lovemore and Vanessa. Wandie did the cooking, then joined us. The lamb fell apart as you touched it, tender and terrific. There was a pleasant, spicy sauce, some sliced bananas and the maize. The atmosphere was rather like a suburban rotary club. The only moment of tension was provided by me. I used their wall phone to call some awful white woman who had sent her ghastly husband to bring me from Sun City to a "Disneyland" dump called Gold Reef City. The drive took three and a half hours when they'd said it was two. They'd wanted me to stay for hours in Gold Reef City. I said I wanted Ed and Lovemore to take me back to my hotel after Soweto. She thought that would not be nice. So I let her have it, somewhat loudly. She hastily agreed. When I came off the phone everyone was looking at me. "Just a gag," I said, patting some diners on the shoulder. They smiled and went back to their meals.

They were very impressed I'd been flown to South Africa to judge Miss World. "Give me one of your cards," I said to Wandie. "I'll wave it about when I'm introduced: 1.8 billion people will see this flash of red!" Wandie went to his office. "He's gone to make a large card," said Lovemore, but he came back with a normal one, and I waved it like mad when they announced us judges on TV. Well, it was a jolly meal and it was the least I could do. I don't suppose I'll go back, although Ed and I have corresponded a bit. There are days in your life you remember vividly. They mean something in a superb sort of way. They stand out. This was one of them.

Sun stroke

I have made two big mistakes in the past decade. One was taking financial advice from Adam Faith. The other was going to Sun City. Sun City is a complex in the South African veld, surrounded by nothing, about two hours' drive from Johannesburg. It consists of at least two hotels and a so-called entertainment centre, all of increasing ugliness. The supposedly class hotel in this bizarre setting is the **Palace**. It's a lost city, early MGM gone wrong, with a touch of Indiana Jones's Temple of Doom. Great towers belch forth from an infrastructure with domes and quasi-minarets. At the top of the main tower four antelopes appear as if leaping from the windows. Doubtless they went mad waiting for room service.

It is, if nothing else – and believe me there isn't much else – on a grand scale. Not staggeringly grand like Las Vegas, but big enough. Vast high-ceilinged lobbies and restaurants look out on to fake rocks and waterfalls, with some quite nice trees and plants and African birds mixed with fake alligators. It is all fake, and clumsily so. When we got to the suite there was no hot water. So a man came and said he was going to "check the satellite heater station". The water was erratic in its hot-potential there-after. They kindly gave me a typewriter, but nobody knew how to work it – the lady who did was away and had left the instruction book locked in her drawer. After two nice ladies spent an hour and a half diffidently attacking it like it was a nuclear power plant, eventually someone came who got it right. A hotel messenger came to the door with a letter and said: "I've been all over, they told me you were there," indicating a distant wing. A letter I sent by hotel hand to Bruce Forsythe (thank God he was there, he's very funny) never got to him because the hotel got his room number wrong. It was endless.

I have never eaten such terrible food for seven consecutive days – and I lived through rationing and the second world war, when we had powdered eggs! It is not a place for me, but some seemed to like it. The Crystal Court, the main centre of the hotel, has a fountain with six elephants in green holding it, a glass-balustraded double staircase and groups of tourists from other areas wandering through in short trousers and with rucksacks, videoing you as you eat.

There's a fake lagoon by the secondary pool, Egyptian-lunatic except that the surface around it is so hot you cannot walk without great pain. The lagoon produces a large wave every three minutes, and wending their way up a steep hill are dozens of ant-like tourists with large blue rubber tyres. I never saw them reappear. There was obviously a high cliff the other side over which they threw themselves in despair. But you have to admire Sol Kerzner for building it at all – in a strange way when you leave, you miss it. Senior management were all over me, but when I left, signing my bill as always without looking, I sat in my private plane (show-off!) and found I'd been massively overcharged. First of all, they'd put all meals, laundry and other things on, when I was their guest to judge Miss World. Second, the difference between a junior suite and a luxury room (I'd said I'd pay for the suite increase) was down as being £2,303; when my office rang their English rep we learned it should have been £215.18!

After I threatened to sue Sun City, Sun International, Miss World, the Pope, Mickey Mouse and any passing tramp who would accept service of a writ, they apologised, knocked off the £215 room increase and finally reimbursed me £2,308 out of the bill of £3,340. A 62% overcharge! I should offer this to the *Guinness Book of Records*. It's what you call adding insult to injury.

WINNIE GOES ON SAFARI

WHERE'S THE SNOW?! I'M READY!

1 3

S W I T Z E R L A N D

I bet you've never been to Cully. It's a little town nestling by Lake Léman in Switzerland. Time has passed it by (always an advantage). There I found **Le Raisin**, a small hotel and restaurant, through checking the Michelin Guide, which is invariably reliable. Le Raisin has beautiful old wooden doors with a cast-iron display of grapes and vines above. It faces a small square with an ancient stone fountain. The restaurant is extremely spacious and comfortable with large, wooden-backed chairs and sizable tables, well apart, and a view of the lake – posh but peasant-style, period provincial in the best sense of the word. The guests were locals on a Sunday-lunch outing. They didn't know who I was, my resounding fame not having spread to Cully, so I made myself known, as they say, to the owner/chef, Herr Adolf Blokbergen. The food is exceptional. Between us we had scallops on couscous with curry sauce, red mullet with soya sauce, lobster risotto and some very good local wines. It's the sort of restaurant you're delighted to find. Everything's good and you have a terrific time. If you have a moment, go there.

The village of Feurtesoey consists of a few chalets, one called the **Gasthaus Rossli**. It's owned by Hubert Reichenbach and, each night, like all the little Swiss places around Gstaad, has customers of astonishing wealth trying to look like locals. Which they are in a way, as Gstaad is second home to the rich and famous masquerading as ordinary folk. On the first floor of the Rossli is a very old-fashioned bowling alley with genuine locals drinking beer and playing bowls. Downstairs in the restaurant we were joined by the famous advertising boss of bosses, Frank Lowe. He represents Coca-Cola among other clients, but I decided not to bring up the matter of my letter to his super-boss about the different colour and taste of Fanta in Morocco compared to the UK.

I was sorry to see the old-fashioned inn-like dining room offering wrapped butter. It reminded me of a moment in the Palazzo Vendramin, an extremely posh outhouse of the Hotel Cipriani in Venice. At breakfast, Miss Lid the Second was reading the *Herald-Tribune*. "There are so many terrible things going on in the world," she sighed. "Yes," I responded, "one of them in this room: wrapped butter."

I was dictating that Frank's charming wife, Dawn, takes echinacea, which she says prevents flu, when my enormous double portion of *truite bleu* arrived. Miss Lid the Third was having shrimps with saffron rice. Frank Lowe had *truite japonaise*. "It's absolutely delicious," he said. "Bits of leek and a lot of ginger." "Onions?" I asked, noticing a vegetable I could actually recognise. "Yup," said Frank, "onions, ginger and then green mustard." Dieter was having cheese fondue and then putting fondued beef into chicken broth. For dessert we all liked the apple pie and ice cream.

The glitterati of Gstaad have adopted **The Chesery**, an old-style chalet with a roaring log fire. *Loup de mer* was served in a vast shell of white, apparently the salt and whites of eggs in which it was baked. So large was the fish, they served us the top half first and then offered the second, which there was no room for. There followed a brie stuffed with mascarpone and truffles.

The Olden in Gstaad is a lovely and genuine old chalet hotel. The first-class **Le Cave** restaurant there looks like something out of *The Sound of Music*, with alpine flowers painted on china in frames all over the place, and Swiss music playing.

Tough at the top

It costs £10,600 to join the Eagle Club. It looks like a war-time bunker, sitting on top of Mount Wasserngrad, near Gstaad. Thereafter, the carefully selected members give an annual donation of their own choice, which the club announces on its notice board. I observed that most people gave £211, although Mr Sackler and Mr Wolff stretched to £245.

The purpose of the **Eagle Club** is to provide rest and succour to the glitterati, so they don't have to mix with tourists at a similar-looking restaurant a few yards below. People often ask, when I go to ski resorts, "Do you ski?" To which I reply: "No, I eat." I always enjoy going up and down in the ski lifts. You get a nice view of the snow, pine trees, mountains and villages. Occasionally over-virile skiers enter and pass a few bons mots. It's a thoroughly pleasant experience.

On the two occasions I have been taken to the Eagle Club – once by Roger Moore and recently by a German nobleman, Knautschi von Meister – it has been incredibly crowded. The trestle tables on the terrace look as if a contest is on, with a prize for the most-crammed-together bench seat. I was offered the best view, close to the rail, looking thousands of feet down the sheer icy drop below. Members' kids on a lower-level terrace threw plastic bottle tops into the ravine, which shows that vandals are the same whatever their class.

After waiting for ever at a door while overdressed skiers kissed each other and blocked it, we got to the terrace, where Januaria, Knautschi's friend, looked around. "Very disappointing," she said. "I don't see one single royalty today. Victor Emmanual of Savoy, he's often here; Maria Gabriella of Savoy, Gonzalo de Bourbon, he's the first cousin of Juan Carlos, king of Spain. Farah Diba was here two days ago; she was the wife of the Shah of Iran...." She peered intensely and gave up.

"And King Constantine with his mobile phone," added Dieter Abt, a successful fiction writer, once owner of the British caterers who did royal garden parties until things collapsed rather dramatically. Dear Dieter was accused of fraud on various counts. I always liked him: he once invited me to the Wimbledon finals. I knew he was too stupid to commit fraud and, indeed, on the few counts the judge didn't throw out, the jury found him not guilty with alacrity. He is now a key member of the Gstaad set.

Not only was it a bad day for royalty, it was a terrible day for food. Bipo, one of the few waiters, had an impossible task. Someone ordered spaghetti. "Once you get the order in, it comes very quickly," said Dieter. Over an hour later he looked pretty silly.

I fought my way to the buffet, which was like a Granada service station. What little there was left looked tinned and unpleasant. I did get some nice mackerel and filled my plate anyway, because I sensed food would not rush towards me.

After an hour and a quarter, the pasta, now cold, and some roesti arrived. "The pasta wasn't good, was it?" observed Januaria. Even the roesti, a national food of Switzerland, was described by someone at my table as "too greasy and not crunchy".

Still, it was a pleasant setting, and there's something endearing about seeing the super-rich putting up with conditions that would appal a coach party from Warrington.

"I'll just say 10 coffees," Januaria muttered as Bipo arrived again. "That's how they make money," said Dieter. "You have to order 10 coffees to get one." He looked around at the chaos. "The wine's flowing like glue," he observed.

I nipped back to the buffet and got the last of the meringues, all eight of them. They were excellent. After that, everyone complained there weren't any left. By the time the coffee arrived, I'd decided, all in all, the Eagle Club was a terrific place. Bizarre, yes, a time warp, yes, but I liked it.

Apparently, there's a problem. The Wasserngrad ski lift runs at a loss. "Three years ago it ran out of money, so the local people and the government put in money to save it," said Dieter. "It may not last much longer."

That would be terrible. The Eagle Club would be deserted, high in the mountains. Like the *Titanic* on ice. Where would Victor Emmanuel of Savoy go then? How would Gonzalo de Bourbon fill his days? Would King Constantine have to bring a picnic? Farah Diba, poor thing, would be inconsolable. So would I. It's too terrible to think about.

Swiss roles

The toilet seat was the most awful I have come across. It was of a very cheap, grey plastic. It didn't match anything in the bathroom. On top of it was an advertising plaque for Swiss Clean Anti-Germ Solution. This was red and green with the Swiss national emblem in the middle.

I was disappointed to see this in my suite at the **Palace Hotel**, Gstaad, because this is a very classy place. It was like being given frozen fish fingers at Claridge's – unexpected. Other than that, and the fact that no porters appeared to take our luggage when we arrived, until found and shepherded, everything was good to very good. I did miss Victor Ferrari, who used to be the reception manager. I was told he had gone into pharmaceuticals. There were rather severe girls in red uniforms in his place.

The Palace sits on a small hill looking down on the chalets of the unspoilt little Swiss town. It has four turrets that spring out of each corner, a typical Victorian folly-type of architecture, which I greatly like.

If you walk through the large, leather-chaired lounge with its open log fire and sweeping view of the mountains, you come onto the rear terrace, facing snow and high peaks, with a hot sun that gives you a tan. Greeting you is Gildo Bocchini, the maitre d'. Gildo has been there 30 years and the chef, Peter Wyss, for 24 years. They are both superb. The terrace is one of the great locations of the world. The Swiss love roesti, basically hash brown potatoes with an egg on top. Not posh, but very nice.

Is there any other hotel where people dress up each night for dinner in fully-jewelled regalia? Ladies in ball gowns intertwined with gold, men in suits and ties. It is from another world that has passed to be replaced by horrid, noisy, mass-customered restaurants that dare to think they are "in". If they represent the best of Cool Britannia, God help the world.

A man with slicked-back hair sat alone at a table on my right. Ahead, also alone, a lady in a silver, patterned dress looked at her diamond ring, then tucked into coconut ice cream with chocolate sauce, with a plate of fruit salad on the side.

A small orchestra – piano, violin, double bass – played melodies grossly alien to Noel or Liam Gallagher. I had a small potato with some caviare, then an escalope of veal that looked like meat – it was not disguised as some "artistic" nothing. Vanessa had rainbow trout and vegetables. All the food is exceptionally good.

There was one problem. Gildo recommended apple pie, which was not on the menu, so I asked for some. It did not arrive. Vanessa's camomile tea came. I had nothing. I called a waiter over and told him, quietly, that I was waiting for my apple pie and that it was customary for the dessert to appear before the tea or coffee. He scurried off and came back with a large plate of sliced pineapple. I pointed out, with extreme tolerance and gentle demeanour, that this did not look like apple pie to me. Eventually, the pie appeared. Jolly good it was too.

I knew I was in professional hands when Vanessa ordered apple juice for breakfast and got both bottled and fresh. The butter was in little pots and not wrapped. Other than the disgusting toilet seat, the bathroom had almost everything, including Dead Sea salts, but, surprisingly, no cotton buds.

The Palace is great in winter, with snow over everything, or summer, with its enormous swimming pool, the mountains alive with flowers and the chalets groaning under the red carnations lining every window. You expect to see Julie Andrews swinging about with a bucket and strange children.

The Palace has the splendid individuality of a place run by owners on the premises, in this case Ernst Andrea Scherz, numbers one and two. Number two is junior, who's being groomed to take over.

But I was disturbed on a recent visit. Although the service and the food were as good as ever, the guests seemed a bit degraded. Gildo Bocchini came over to chastise me as if it were my fault. "Can't you get your fellow Englishmen to put their jackets on?" he asked, referring to a group from which two men had come to greet me, even though I didn't know them. They sat in shirtsleeves; mercifully they wore ties. I was relieved when four Frenchmen entered without jackets or ties. My responsibility for the worst-dressed was over.

The Palace suites maintain the hotel's charming oddity. Strange blue sofas had been added to my usual area, but the rest looked like a pine shop on a moderate day. It was so not like a normal hotel that I loved it. The view down on to the chalets and the mountains beyond the village was stunning as ever.

I only register one complaint to Messr Scherz and Scherz. On a number of occasions the lounge, the jewel in the crown of the Palace, was not available. It had been let out for a wedding or other function. That ain't fair! The guests, in paying for their accommodation, also pay for the use of public rooms. To deny them the only large space on the ground floor is equivalent to renting it out twice. I can understand the lure of the Swiss franc, but the Scherzes run such a great place that they should resist the temptation to bar their guests from the most important part of it.

Mile-high club

"People are deserting the Palace and going now to the Park Hotel, Gstaad," my occasionally omnipotent Swiss friend Dieter Abt told me. "I'll book you a table." There are moments when you arrive for an evening out and know it will be a disaster. But something propels you onward. A voice says, "Run, get out!", but a second voice, which you know is stupidity incarnate, says: "Don't be silly, you've made a booking. Stay, it'll be all right."

That conversation ran in my head as I walked through the appalling lobby of the highly rated **Park Hotel**. It's a modern version of an overblown Swiss chalet gone madly wrong, full of unsuccessful attempts to retain Swiss charm in an ersatz, airport-anywhere interior.

In the restaurant we were given a table facing the door, near a central log fire largely blocked by two serving trolleys. Why not pile a few crates of Coca-Cola there as well, I thought. I went to look at their other restaurant featuring a cruise-liner buffet, which was horrible. Foolishly, I soldiered on.

The waiter objected to me saying I wanted to write on the menu. When I told him, rather tartly, that hotels from the Paris Ritz to the Splendido in Portofino and all places in between and around were delighted when I wrote on their menus, he changed and said: "We're very happy for you to write on the menu." "No you're not," I said. "You made that very clear."

There was a little terrine of cheese as a freebie starter. Vanessa pulled a face and left hers. I thought it bland. The maitre d' came over. "Did you make your choice, gentlemen?" he asked. I pointed out that one of the two people facing him was a lady. The Swiss are usually good at dignified, old-style service: this proved there are exceptions. The foie gras and the pigeon were both tasteless and odd, the atmosphere sterile. Vanessa's turbot had no texture; it had obviously been in the deep freeze far too long. "Did you enjoy your meal?" asked the maitre d'. "No, the fish was definitely old," I said. "It's fresh," said the maitre d'. "No, it's not fresh, it's frozen and it has been frozen for a very long time," I replied. It's rare that I am less than gracious, but this place brought out the worst in me. They said they had a wonderful selection of cheeses and produced a trolley with eight – all uninteresting. About the dessert, I wrote: "No special taste anywhere."

The other diners were seriously anonymous. Some absurd pretend windows of chalet design gave it a basement air, even though we were on the first floor. If I had not been knocking back a bottle of Lafite-Rothschild 1985, I might have considered suicide. When I got the bill, I noticed they didn't charge for Vanessa's fish. "Is the service on?" I asked. The maitre d' said: "The service is on, but the tip is up to you." I've got a tip for them. Close the place down.

Roger Moore and his lovely wife Luisa took us to **The Saanenhof**, one of those outwardly simple Swiss chalet-type restaurants with wooden walls and ceilings, hard wood chairs and long tables, which mask a remarkable standard of cooking and a major international clientele. It was the sort of place where, if you didn't have a title on the way in, you got one at the door. At our table was the King of Spain's cousin and the nightclub owner and now one-woman show singer, Régine. The food was terrific. Only the Swiss could make a carrot and orange salad taste historic. I was recommended the *saucisse de veau* with *rösti*, better than I'd ever tasted. A jolly lunch with the international set that live in the lovely chalets around Gstaad.

Unfortunately the new owners have discontinued the carrot and orange salad and the *saucisse de veau*. Now the food is unspectacular, but the view makes up for it.

In an old part of Montreux is the **Brasserie College**, a distinctly picturesque but downmarket caff in one of those lovely French-style buildings with shutters and wrought-iron balconies. I went in and loved the look of it. This was the "real thing"! Wooden tables, old advertising signs, a juke box, a pinball machine, net curtains and an owner-server. There were newspapers for the customers to read. The food was ghastly beyond belief! Vanessa got tinned beans and one tomato cut in half. I got nasty boiled potatoes and a selection of sausages and gammon, all boiled and all revolting. I, too, had tinned beans. That'll teach me to leave my Swiss Michelin Guide at home.

14

THAILAND / BURMA

At Ayutthaya, a Thai capital of old (they kept being attacked by the Burmese and burnt down, so new capitals abounded), there are incredibly preserved temples and royal palaces and, even better, hardly any visitors. The **Krungsri River Hotel** reminded me of a canteen in old Czechoslovakia. There was no sign of a river, but a glorious, totally uninterrupted view of the motorway. The dining room was large and busy. All orientals. Our guide, Sirirat Norseeda, ate Thai noodles, braised cabbage, hard-boiled egg, flying fish, chicken curry with sauce and rice, and veg. I followed her lead. All perfectly tasty. For dessert there was pineapple and watermelon on display, but – goody, goody – four different Thai jellies too. A green one, a black one, a red one and a strange wispy one in coconut cream, all topped with spoonfuls of sugary syrup. The jelly was in little strips, not rabbit-moulded as in my youth, but scrumptious none the less.

Thai to die for

When referring to the **Oriental Hotel Bangkok**, people say to me: "The service is so good you never get to press the elevator button!" Even though this is true, it is not a great hotel achievement. Pressing elevator buttons is one of the few things I can do myself. My first sight of the hotel was in an old book: small, colonial architecture, gardens leading down to the Chao Phraya river. Then I saw modern photographs showing two ghastly tower blocks like those East End council flats we see blown up because they are such a blot on public life. When I arrived, my first thought was, this is a seriously big hotel. The marble lobby is from the grand-airport school of design. It looks out onto a swimming pool, flowering bushes and horrible enormous buildings across the river.

I had been advised to take one of the authors' suites in the old building, named after visitors such as Somerset Maugham, Joseph Conrad and others. Melvin J J Robson, the English manager (Kurt Wachtveitl, the famed general manager, had the sense to be on holiday), led me to the Presidential Suite atop the large tower. "You asked for a view," he explained. "The authors' suites don't have one." I later discovered the "old" hotel is attached, Siamese twinlike, to the smaller block. The original lobby is used for tea with cane chairs, two musicians in evening dress on flute and guitar – and shops off it staffed by the rudest assistants I have ever found, which is surprising as most Thais are immensely lovely and charming.

The Presidential Suite had a huge living room, two large bedrooms, a dining room for 12, a kitchen, an enormous hall, two bathrooms, various lavatories and washrooms, and a cupboard full of electrical things where our floor butler pressed endless knobs in an unsuccessful attempt to stop the air conditioning from being deepfreeze level. There were terraces all around, with impressive views over an ugly, overbuilt, high-rise city.

My first meal was in Lord Jim's restaurant, one of seven places to eat provided by the hotel. Piped music everywhere – the Thais are very fond of that. They even blast it from loudspeakers attached to trees as you walk around their old palaces. There was a nice view of the river terrace, food certainly good, a high-class buffet, service remarkable. You could not sit down without staff holding your chair for you. The moment you neared the end of a Coca-Cola they asked if you wanted another. Good curry, excellent sushi bar, lovely apple flan. I wish there was something like it in London.

My favourite turned out to be their Thai restaurant, the Sala Rim Naam, to which you are ferried on the other side of the river. At night, the terrace, flower-bedecked and looking over to the hotel, is a terrific place to eat. There are trees with fairy lights and, inside an adjacent room, a costumed Thai dance troupe. We peeked in to admire, not wishing to join 200 people sitting on the floor. The prawn soup with coconut milk, chicken with lemon grass and steamed sea bass were all very good. On the terrace over the water is an Italian restaurant and a sort of grand carvery.

The hotel is too large to be my all-time favourite, but it works superbly well. It's just that when I see tour groups in the lobby, I feel queasy.

The Oriental has been voted the Best in the World many times by serious magazines. "Best" is a non-word. I prefer boutique hotels, small and exclusive. But as large ones go, you'd be hard-pressed to beat the Oriental.

My stay was made particularly pleasant through the immense charm and expertise of Melvin J J Robson, who even guided us into town, at my request, to see things I would not even hint at in the *Sunday Times*. He also provided me with a list of visitors who had inhabited the Presidential Suite: Richard Nixon, Pierre Cardin, Sean Connery, Michael Jackson, the Duke of Edinburgh, the Prince and Princess of Wales and George Bush, to name but a few. Just as well I stayed there. They could do with someone important.

> The **Sinvana** resort in Phitsanulok, the 13th-century capital city, is a beautifully gardened Thai-style complex outside Bangkok. Nobody else there. Stir-fried Thai water mimosa, a sort of fried water spinach, very nice. Fried fish with garlic and pepper, stir-fried Thai watercress, both jolly. The waitresses watched cartoons on the telly.

The new boat people

There's no doubt about it, I am the guest from hell. I don't want to be invited, I don't want to have to worry about being endlessly pleasant, about keeping to times and events planned by my host. I want to order what I want when I want it, not to have to eat what is served at times not of my choosing.

I care not what it costs to avoid all this. A good hotel nearby is fine. A bedroom in someone else's house is ugh. So I looked hard at the beautifully embossed card which read "James and Shirley Sherwood request the pleasure of the company of Michael Winner aboard the *Road to Mandalay* from Pagan to Mandalay Burma".

The "Road" is not an old Bob Hope–Bing Crosby movie but an elegant vessel that once glided up the Rhine. Now poshed up no end, it is a terrific Orient-Express adventure that goes up and down the Irrawaddy river. While I was considering my position, a letter arrived signed by James B Sherwood, super-chief of one of my all-time favourite hotel groups, with a tick on a little box at the bottom denoting "this is a personal letter". With it, a list of 88 other guests, a highly exclusive group of international importants, ambassadors, titled folk – you name them, they had them. Vanessa looked worried as she checked the names. "Well, basically, darling," she said, "you're going to have to be very well behaved." This is not something I am good at.

They must have been nervous, because when I arrived in Rangoon (now Yangon) all the others were booked for one night into a ghastly Russian-built thing called the Inya Lake hotel, whereas I, alone, was put in the Strand hotel, a lovely old colonial spot run by the excellent Amman group. The next day we flew to Pagan (now Bagan) – one of the most beautiful sights ever. A biblical landscape dotted with endless Buddhist temples and pagodas. Oxen drew carts along dusty streets, life unchanged by supposed progress.

The Orient-Express buses took us to the wide Irrawaddy river where was moored the elegant boat. I sought out the only brilliant PR lady I know, Nadia Stancioff. "I do not wish, ever again, to go on your buses!" I said cheerfully. Nadia's smile wavered just a touch. "I'd like, please, my own car, my own driver and my own guide. Where the others go in the morning, I will go in the afternoon. I wish to relish these sights undisturbed. On one day I hear we are to go by smaller boat, I would like my own boat." "They'll come off their buses, see you and gnash their teeth," said Nadia. "I don't give a damn," I replied.

Let me be absolutely clear, the Road to Mandalay is one of the great excursions of the world. Even if you go on the bus (and you'll be overjoyed to hear I got my car!), see it before it vanishes. Burma is hardly touristed at all, the people are beautiful, the atmosphere serene, the architecture old and breathtaking. But there are nasty signs. A big hotel starting here, posters encouraging visitors there. To cruise up the Irrawaddy seeing bamboo rafts floating by, canoes, bamboo tents, wooden huts, life being lived as it has for centuries, is mind-blowing. The food on the boat was excellent, mostly European and prepared by a Welsh chef! It was all tasty, from fish soufflés to English tea. The cabins are small but nice. The few staterooms bigger and nicer. Mine had satellite television and telephone. The service was all-over superb. James Sherwood, in peaked cap, looking like the manager of a successful baseball team, drank endless cups of black coffee and hosted guests like mad. His wife, Shirley, dark, petite and full of energy, is everyone's favourite aunt. She bustled about making sure we'd all seen everything.

Only problem was the sun loungers grouped around the deck pool. There were 14 of them for 90 guests. "Do I get an alarm call for 3am and put my paperback and towel on those two?!" I said to Carl Henderson, charming boat boss. "Or can you suggest..." "I'll do my best, Mr Winner," he said. "That strikes terror into me," I responded ungraciously. "I've only just met you, I don't know what your best is. I'll have the alarm call. Outdo the Germans!" "It won't be necessary," said Carl, and he pulled it off.

I have previously written of James Sherwood as my hotel hero. I've had more wonderful times at his places, from the Splendido, Portofino, to the Cipriani, Venice, to the Mount Nelson, Cape Town, than anywhere else. He is now my boat hero, too. Nothing else left for him to achieve really, is there?

WINNIE IN BURMA (MYANMAR)

TRAVEL

WINNIE MAKES AMENDS

15

PLANES AND
TRAINS

Taking liberties

There is nothing more sanctimonious than a reformed smoker. Except a reformed thief. I am both. I stopped smoking 14 Monte Cristo Number One cigars a day in 1994 when my cardiologists said: "If you keep going there's no point in us putting in new arteries." This saved me £25,000 a year and meant I could run up stairs without getting out of breath on step three. I stopped stealing when I was 17 and went to Cambridge. This was not the expectation of the joys of academia, it just happened that way. Now, although I frequently take towels, soap, cutlery etc from hotels, restaurants and airplanes, I always ask permission first!

It was food – believe it or not – that set me on the road to larceny. At my Quaker school, during the war, sweets were rationed. The government issued coupons to be exchanged for a limited amount of sweets and chocolates. Needless to say, the official quota fell far short of the demands of young Winner. Thus I needed extra coupons and extra cash. To get this I would go round the boys' discarded clothing during the games period and nick money from their pockets. It was always a great disappointment to me when I found another boy had beaten me to it. With the money thus disgracefully gathered, I would buy my fellow students' sweets coupons and then more sweets. When even that wasn't enough, we would buy fish and meat paste from the corner post office and scoop it out of the little glass jars with our fingers!

My thieving worried me greatly in later life. A few years ago, remembering I had nicked 10 shillings (50p now) from a boy called Clotworthy, I found his number and phoned him up. I expressed my great sorrow and told him I would send him a cheque for 50p plus compound interest since 1950; and this I did. I also invited him and his wife, at my expense, to come to London for three days and attend one of my film premiers; and this they did. But he was appalled to receive my cheque! He didn't remember the event at all and sent it back saying he hoped the money had in some small way helped in my success. I returned the cheque begging him to keep it, and at last he obliged. This was reported in a national newspaper, where I offered to give money to any boy who was at St Christopher School, Letchworth, with me. It says something (good or bad) about the boys of St Chris's that none came forward.

Nearly all of us take something or other from hotel rooms. Soap, used or unused, towels, bottles of this or that, even cutlery. I have a terrific collection of airline and hotel cutlery. There's nearly a complete set from the Pierre Hotel, New York. As I'm leaving I always say: "Got two forks and a spoon in my bags, OK?" Nobody has ever said "No". And at a thousand quid a night for a decent suite, what's 20p worth of second-hand cutlery? Especially to a charming, regular guest! There was a lovely old man named Mr Durcos on reception at the Pierre when it was managed by Forte – and incidentally far better managed than it is now by the Four Seasons Group – who saw me on a New York talk show going on about my set of Concorde cutlery, and that I needed six knives to complete my Pierre Hotel set. When he next gave me my room key, six knives were handed over with it!

Concorde used to have its own special cutlery, then it changed to the British Airways regular with a C on it. Now it's not distinctive at all. I've got a lot of that through all its periods. I use it for the staff. Only last week coming back from Nice I admired the new Air France cutlery, which has plastic handles with a nice blue and white stripe. I cautiously put aside a fork and spoon. "I'd like to take these," I said to the steward. "Let me get you some clean ones, sir," he replied. Mine were clean, but anyway he went to an unused tray and gave me a whole set!

Sadly, few hotels use their names on ashtrays now. But I have some rare, old Beverly Hills Hotel and Beverly Wilshire ones. Or rather, did have. On checking recently, I found a lot of my "donated" cutlery, ashtrays and the like have been genuinely nicked from my house! Unbelievable! Nobody ever asked my permission as they were leaving.

British Rail has never been my favourite place to dine. Recently I ventured on a train with the excruciatingly beautiful Miss Elisabeth Dermot-Walsh and headed for York. The dining car itself had First Class written on everything from seats to menus and of course wasn't. But it was expensive. I started with nachos, guacamole and *salsa picante*. This resembled a modest dip at a bring-your-own-bottle party. Following this, the lamb was shrivelled, the vegetables (courgettes, beans and potatoes) quite good. The whole thing forgettable. I finished off with black cherry and apple strudel. Ghastly.

At Nice I forewarned **British Midland** I was on heat and they whisked me onto the plane smoothly. Once there, however, *oh dear*. Those nasty, narrow little seats, same in Diamond Class as Economy. And the tray of dinner, beyond belief. A hot bowl with a tinny cover when unpeeled left me confused. "What is this?" I asked the hostess. "Fish," she said, "salmon, I believe." It didn't look like salmon to me, and it smelt not nice. There were some odd potatoes and stringy spinach, a rubbery bread roll and a chocolate egg with sickly-goo stuff in the middle. All in all these were the worst tastes ever to insult my persona. The cutlery was so awful I didn't even bother to ask if I could take some..

My excitement knew no bounds. There, in front of me, on the **Concorde** to Barbados, was a sight as rare as the bony-crested red-winged eagle: caviare on a British Airways flight. Old men tell their grandsons of the time they last saw caviare in such circumstances, but there it was. Not much of it, nestling in a small pastry shell, but caviare none the less. And at breakfast, too. On the way back from Barbados, we had – wait for it – a *jar* of caviare. Not large, but a jar nevertheless. It was Osetrova Caspian. I managed to wheedle two portions out of them. They gave us little plastic spoons to eat the caviare with. I was surprised to see a very distinguished member of the House of Lords opposite me wrapping two of them up and putting them in his briefcase. "They're mother of pearl," he announced. The hostess gave him permission for this. I had to make do with a teaspoon and fork for my collection.

I had to lunch with some Canadian film people in Paris, so I decided to take the **Eurostar** train. Door-to-door from my house, it would probably be an hour longer than flying, but it might be an adventure. And I could eat breakfast on the way.

The food was totally beyond human belief. It made British Airways look like Nico Ladenis (my favourite of the three-star British cooks). The croissant was cold and rubbery;

there were harmless cornflakes in a plastic container; the cutlery was a new low and I nicked a fork to remind myself of this later. Then I tried a rubbery chocolate brioche thing, followed by what the menu called a "traditional hot breakfast (scrambled eggs with smoked salmon, hash browns, button mushrooms and tomato)". When I say unbelievable, I mean *unbelievable*! I cannot remember anything worse ever being placed before me in my entire life. Tasteless, horrid, strange texture, a mad knife murderer disguised as food. On the plus side, the three girls serving were exemplary. They were elegant, charming, professional and lovely.

The food on **Thai Airways** was pretty normal airline fodder. Vegetable spring roll, not crisp, gooey. Prawn cracker, very bad indeed. Chicken consommé where the bits of chicken, even immersed in liquid, managed to be dry. Fish curry appeared in some leaves, swimming in sauce. But I forgive them everything for there, in a *large* tin, was Sevruga caviare. Such a sight has not been seen on British Airways in living memory. You could have seconds, thirds, even fourths. I know, because I did. After that, the dodgy ice cream gateau didn't matter. And when I told the stewardess I collected cutlery, she said: "Can I get you a bag to put it in?" "No thanks," I responded, "I've got two forks and a spoon in my briefcase."

WINNIE IN THE AIR

H O T E L S A N D

R E S T A U R A N T S

LONDON

Alounak, 44 Westbourne Grove, W2 5SH ☎ 020 7229 4158
ASK Pizza e Pasta, Kensington, 222 High Street Kensington W8 7RG ☎ 020 7937 5540
Assaggi, 39 Chepstow Place, W2 4TS ☎ 020 7792 5501
Au Jardin des Gourmets, 5 Greek Street, W1V 6NA ☎ 020 7437 1816
Aubergine, 11 Park Walk, SW10 0AJ ☎ 020 7352 3449
Avenue, The, 7-9 St. James Street, SW1A 1EE ☎ 020 7321 2111
Balans, 187 Kensington High Street, W8 6SH ☎ 020 7376 0115
Belvedere, Holland Park, off Abbotsbury Road, W8 6LU ☎ 020 7602 1238
Biagio, 15-17 Villiers St. WC2N 6ND ☎ 020 7839 3633 or
   30 Upper Berkeley Street, W1H 7PG ☎ 020 7723 0394
Bibendum, Michelin House, 81 Fulham Road, SW3 6RD ☎ 020 7581 5817
Bistrot 190, 190 Queensgate, SW7 5EU ☎ 020 7581 5666
Blooms, 7 Montague Street, WC1B 5BP ☎ 020 7323 1717
Bombay Brasserie, The, Courtfield Road, SW7 4UH ☎ 020 7370 4040
Brilliant, The, 381 High Road, Wembley, HA9 ☎ 020 8900 0510
   72-74 Western Road, Southall UB2 ☎ 020 8574 1927/0276
Café Fish, 39 Panton Street, SW1Y 5EA ☎ 020 7930 3999
Cafe Le Jardin, Kensington High Street. Closed 26.9.99
Cafe Pasta, Kensington High Street, 229 Kensington High Street W8 6SA ☎ 020 7937 6314
Canteen, The, Harbour Yard, Chelsea Harbour SW10 0XD ☎ 020 7351 7330
Caprice, The, Arlington House, Arlington St, SW1A 1RT ☎ 020 7629 2239
Hyatt Carlton Tower Rib Room, 2 Cadogan Place, SW1X 9PY ☎ 020 7824 7053
Cassia Oriental, 12 Berkley Square, W1X 5HG ☎ 020 7629 8886
Cecconi's, 5A Burlington Gardens, W1X 1LE ☎ 020 7434 1509
Chez Moi, 1 Addison Ave. Holland Park, W11 4QS ☎ 020 7603 8267
Chez Nico, 90 Park Lane, W1A 3AA ☎ 020 7409 1290
Chinon, 23 Richmond Way, W14 0AS ☎ 020 7602 5968
Chiswick, The, 131 Chiswick High Road, W4 2ED ☎ 020 8994 6887
Christopher's, 18 Wellington Street, WC2E 7DD ☎ 020 7240 4222
Claridge's, Brook Street, W1A 2JQ ☎ 020 7629 8860
Clarke's, 124 Kensington Church Street, W8 4BH ☎ 020 7221 9225
Coast, 26b Albemarle Street, W1X 3FA ☎ 020 7495 5999

Collection, The, 264 Brompton Road, SW3 2AS ☎ 020 7225 1212
Connaught, The, Carlos Place, W1Y 6AL ☎ 020 7499 7070
Conservatory, The, at The Lanesborough, Hyde Park Corner, SW1X 7TA ☎ 020 7259 5599
Criterion Brasserie, 224 Piccadilly, W1V 9LB ☎ 020 7930 0488
Daphne's, 112 Draycott Avenue, SW3 3AE ☎ 020 7589 4257
Dorchester Grill, The, Park Lane, W1A 2HJ ☎ 020 7629 8888
Durrants Hotel, 26-32 George Street, W1H 6BJ ☎ 020 7935 8131
Fifth Floor Restaurant, Harvey Nichols, Knightsbridge SW1X 7RJ ☎ 020 7235 5250
Fortnum's Fountain, 181 Piccadilly, W1 9DA ☎ 020 7734 8040
Fortnum & Mason, St. James's Restaurant, 181 Piccadilly, W1 9DA ☎ 020 7734 8040
Four Seasons, The Inn on the Park, Hamilton Place, W1A 1AZ ☎ 020 7499 0888
Frank's Sandwich Bar, 175a North End Road, W14 9NL ☎ 020 7385 8352
Frederick's, Camden Passage, N1 8EG ☎ 020 7359 2888
Goolies, 21 Abingdon Road, W8 6AH ☎ 020 7938 1122
Gordon Ramsey, 68 Royal Hospital Road, SW3 4HP ☎ 020 7352 4441
Greenhouse, The, 27a Hays Mews, W1X 7RJ ☎ 020 7499 3331
Grill Room Cafe Royal, 68 Regent Street, W1R 6EL ☎ 020 7437 1177
Halkin Hotel Restaurant, 5 Halkin Street, SW1X 7DJ ☎ 020 7333 1000
Harbour Restaurant, 302 Upper Street, Islington, N1 2TU ☎ 020 7354 2260
Harrods' Georgian Restaurant, Harrods, Knightsbridge, SW1X 7XL ☎ 020 7730 1234
Harry Morgan Restaurant, 31 St. John's Wood High Street, NW8 7NH ☎ 020 7722 1869
Hilton National London Olympia, 380 Kensington High Street, W14 8NL ☎ 020 7603 3333
Hiroko in the London Kensington Hilton, 179-199 Holland Park Avenue, W11 4UL
    ☎ 020 7603 3355
Holland Park Cafeteria, Ilchester Place, W14 8AA ☎ 020 7602 2216
Hush, 8 Lancashire Court, W1S 1EY ☎ 020 7659 1500
Il Portico, 277 Kensington High Street, W8 6NA ☎ 020 7602 6262
Intercontinental Hotel Coffee House, Hyde Park Corner ☎ 020 7495 2500
Ivy, The, 1 West Street, WC2H 9NE ☎ 020 7836 4751 ☎ 020 8495 2500
Julie's, 135 Portland Road, W11 4LW ☎ 020 7229 8331
Kai Mayfair, 65 South Audley Street, W1Y 5FD ☎ 020 7493 8988
Kartouche, 329-331 Fulham Road, SW10 9QL ☎ 020 7823 3515
Kaspia, 18-18A Bruton Place, W1X 7AH ☎ 020 7408 1627
Kensington Place, 201 Kensington Church Street, W8 7LX ☎ 020 7727 3184
La Brasserie, 272 Brompton Road, SW3 2AW ☎ 020 7584 1668
La Gaffe, 109 Heath Street, NW3 1DR ☎ 020 7435 4941
Langan's Brasserie, Stratton Street, W1X 5FD ☎ 020 7491 8822
Langan's Coq d'Or, 254-260 Old Brompton Road, SW5 9HR ☎ 020 7259 2599
Lowizanka, 246 King Street, W6 ☎ 020 8741 3225
Maison Novelli, 29 Clerkenwell Green, EC1R 0DU ☎ 020 7251 6606
Malabar, 27 Uxbridge Street, W8 7TQ ☎ 020 7727 8800
Memories of China Kensington, 353 Kensington High Street, W8 6NW ☎ 020 7603 6951
Michel's Brasserie, 6-8 Elliott Road, Chiswick W4 1PE ☎ 020 8742 1485
Mirabelle, 56 Curzon Street, W1Y 8AL ☎ 020 7499 4636
Muffin Man, The, 12 Wrights Lane, W8 6TA ☎ 020 7937 6652
Mosimann's, 11b West Halkin Street, SW1 8JL ☎ 020 7235 9625
National Theatre: Terrace Cafe, Royal National Theatre, South Bank, SE1 9GY
    ☎ 020 7401 8361
Nobu, Old Park Lane, W1 ☎ 020 7447 4747

Novelli W8, 122 Palace Gardens Terrace, W8 4RT ☎ 020 7229 4024

The Oak Room, Meridien Hotel Piccadilly, 21 Piccadilly, W1V 0PH ☎ 020 7437 0202

Orsino's, 119 Portland Road, W11 4LN ☎ 020 7221 3299

Orso's, 27 Wellington Street, WC2E 7DA ☎ 020 7240 5269

Oxo Tower 8th Floor, Oxo Tower Wharf, Bargehouse Street, SE1 9EH ☎ 020 7803 3888

Park Lane Hotel, Piccadilly, W1Y 8BX ☎ 020 7499 6321

Patio, 16c Curzon Street, London WIY 7FF ☎ 020 7409 1791

Pharmacy, 150 Notting Hill Gate, W11 3QG ☎ 020 7221 2442

Poissonnerie de l'Avenue, 82 Sloane Avenue, SW3 3DZ ☎ 020 7589 2457

Pont de la Tour, Le, 36d Shad Thames, Butlers Wharf, SE1 2YE ☎ 020 7403 8403

Quo Vadis, 26-29 Dean Street, W1A 6LL ☎ 020 7437 9585

Restaurant, The, Hyde Park Hotel, 66 Knightsbridge, SW1X 7LA ☎ 020 7259 5380

Richoux Restaurant, 86 Brompton Road, SW3 1ER ☎ 020 7584 8300

Ritz Palm Court, 150 Piccadilly, W1V 9DG ☎ 020 7493 8181

Ritz, The, 150 Piccadilly, W1V 9DG ☎ 020 7493 8181

River Café, Thames Wharf Studios, Rainville Rd. W6 9HA ☎ 020 7381 8824

Room at the Halycon, The, 81 Holland Park, W11 3RZ ☎ 020 7727 7288

Room Service Deliveries: Luna Nuova, Covent Garden ☎ 020 8840 3555

San Lorenzo, 22 Beauchamp Place, SW3 1NH ☎ 020 7584 1074

Savoy River Restaurant, Strand, WC2R 0EU ☎ 020 7836 4343

Scalini, 1 Walton Street, SW3 2JD ☎ 020 7823 9720

Scotts, 20 Mount Street, W1Y 6HE ☎ 020 7629 5248

Sheekey's, 28-32 St. Martin's Court, WC2N 4AL ☎ 020 7240 2565

Sheraton Park Tower, Restaurant 101, 101 Knightsbridge, SW1X 7RN ☎ 020 7235 8050

Shogun, Britannia Hotel, Adams Row, W1Y 5DE ☎ 020 7493 1255

Snows on the Green, 166 Shepherd's Bush Road, W6 7PB ☎ 020 7603 2142

Soho Soho, 11-13 Frith Street, W1V 5TS ☎ 020 7494 3491

Southeby's Café, 34–35 New Bond Street, W1A 2AA ☎ 020 7293 5000

Sound Republic, Swiss Centre, Leicester Square, W1V 3HG. ☎ 020 7287 1010

Square, The, 6–10 Bruton Street, Mayfair, W1X 7AE ☎ 020 7495 7100

Sticky Fingers, 1a Phillimore Gardens, W8 7QB ☎ 020 7938 5338

Sugar Club, The, 21 Warwick Street, W1R 5RB ☎ 020 7437 7776

Sugar Reef, 42–44 Great Windmill Street, Soho, W1V 7PA ☎ 020 7851 0800

Suntory, 72-73 St. James Street, SW1A 1PH ☎ 020 7409 0201

Tamarind, 20 Queen Street, W1X 7PJ ☎ 020 7629 3561

Tante Claire, La, Wilton Place, SW1X 7RL ☎ 020 7823 2003

Teatro, 93-107 Shaftesbury Avenue, W1V 8BT ☎ 020 7494 3040

The Tenth, Royal Garden Hotel, 2-24 Kensington High Street, W8 4PT ☎ 020 7361 1910

Titanic, 81 Brewer Street, W1R 3FH ☎ 020 7437 1912

Toto, Walton House, Walton St. SW3 2JH ☎ 020 7589 0075

Tramp, 40 Jermyn Street, SW1Y 6DN ☎ 020 7734 0565

Village Bistro, 38 Highgate High Street, N6 5JG ☎ 020 8340 5165/0257

Vong, Wilton Place, SW1X 7RL ☎ 020 7235 1010

Wesbury Hotel, Conduit Street, London W1A 4UH ☎ 020 7629 7755

Willie Gunn Winebar, 422 Garratt Lane, SW18 4HN ☎ 020 8946 7773

Wiltons, 55 Jermyn Street, SW1Y 6LX ☎ 020 7629 9955

Windmill Whole Food Restaurant, 486 Fulham Road, SW6 1HJ ☎ 020 7381 2372

Wine Factory, 294 Westbourne Grove, W11 2PS ☎ 020 7229 1877

Yatra, 44 Dover Street, Mayfair, W1X 3RA ☎ 020 7493 0200

Zafferano, 15 Lowndes Street, SW1X 9EY ☎ 020 7235 5800
Zamoyski Wine Bar, 85b Fleet Road, NW32QY ☎ 020 7794 4794
Zaika, 257 Fulham Road, SW3 5HY ☎ 020 7351 7823
Zen Central, 20 Queen Street, Mayfair, W1X 7PJ ☎ 020 7629 8089/8103
Zia Teresa, 6 Hans Road, SW3 1RX ☎ 020 7589 7634

ENGLAND

Avon: Bath: Hole in the Wall, 16 George Street, Bath, BA1 2EH ☎ 01225 425 242
    Ston Easton Park, Ston Easton, Nr. Bath, BA3 4DF ☎ 01761 241 631
  Bristol: Hunstrete House, Hunstrete, Bristol, BS19 4NS ☎ 01761 490 490
Bedfordshire: Flitwick Manor, Church Road, Flitwick, MK45 1AE ☎ 01525 712 242
Berkshire: Bray: Fat Duck, Bray on Thames High Street, SL6 2AQ ☎ 01628 580 333
    Waterside Inn, Ferry Road, Bray, SL6 2AT ☎ 01628 620 691
  Newbury: Hollington House, Woolton Hill, Newbury, RG20 9XA ☎ 01635 255 100
  Shinfield: L'Ortolan, The Old Vicarage, Church Lane, Shinfield, RG2 9BY ☎ 01734 883 783
  Sonning: French Horn Hotel, Sonning on Thames, RG4 0TN ☎ 0118 969 2204
Buckinghamshire: Amersham: Gilbey's,1 Market Square, HP7 0DF ☎ 01494 727 242
  Aston Clinton: Bell Inn, London Road, Aston Clinton, HP22 5HP ☎ 01296 630 252
  Great Brickhill: The Old Red Lion Inn, Ivy Lane, Great Brickhill, MK17 9AH
    ☎ 01525 261 715
  Taplow: Cliveden, Nr. Slough, SL6 0JF ☎ 01628 668 561
Cambridgeshire: Cambridge: Garden House Moat Hotel, Granta Place off Mill Lane,
    Cambridge, CB2 1RT ☎ 01223 259 988
  Midsummer House, Midsummer Common, Cambridge, CB4 1HA ☎ 01223 369 299
Devon: Chagford: Gidleigh Park, Chagford, Devon, TQ13 8HH ☎ 01647 432225
  Hallsands: Hallsands Hotel, North Hallsands, Kingsbridge, South Devon, TQ7 2EY
    ☎ 01548 511264
Dorset: Bournemouth: Oscar's, Royal Bath Hotel, Bath Road, Bournemouth, BH1 2EW
    ☎ 01202 555 555
  Gillingham: Stock Hill House, Stock Hill, Gillingham, SP8 5NR ☎ 01747 823626
  Highcliffe: Bertie's Fish & Chips, 331 Lymington Road, Highcliffe ☎ 01425 274727
    Fredericks, 251 Lymington Road, Highcliffe ☎ 01425 277035
Gloucestershire: Buckland Manor, Buckland, Broadway, WR12 7LY ☎ 01386 582626
  Paxford: Churchill Arms, Paxford, Chipping Campden, GL55 6SH ☎ 01386 594000
  Upper Slaughter: Lords of the Manor, Upper Slaughter, Nr. Bourton on the Water,
    GL54 2JD ☎ 01451 820243
  Stow-on-the-Wold: Wyck Hill House, Stow-on-the-Wold, GL54 1HY ☎ 01451 831936
Hampshire: Brockenhurst: Thatched Cottage, 16 Brookley Road, Brockenhurst, SO42 7RR
    ☎ 01590 623090
  Longstock: Peat Spade Inn, Longstock, SO20 6DR ☎ 01264 810612
  Lymington: Peelers Bistro, Gosport Street, Lymington, SO41 9B ☎ 01590 676165
    Provence, Gordleton Mill Hotel, Silver Street, Hordle, Lymington SO41 6DJ
    ☎ 01590 682219
  New Milton: Chewton Glen, Christchurch Road, New Milton, BH25 6QS ☎ 01425 275341
  Winchester: Lainston House, Sparsholt, Winchester SO21 2LT ☎ 01962 863588
Hertfordshire: Aldbury: Greyhound Inn, 19 Stocks Road, Aldbury, HP23 5RT
    ☎ 01442 851228
  Baldock, George and Dragon, High Street, Watton at Stone SG14 3TA ☎ 01920 830285

Frithsden: Alford Arms, Frithsden, Nr. Hemel Hempstead HP1 3DD ☎ 01442 864480

Tring: Pendley Manor Hotel, Cow Lane, Tring, HP23 5QY ☎ 01442 891891

Manchester: Meridien Victoria & Albert, Water Street, Manchester M3 4JQ ☎ 0161 832 1188

Yang Sin, 34 Princess Street, Manchester M1 4JY ☎ 0161 263 2200

Middlesex: Teddington: Liberty's, 114 High Street, Teddington, TW11 8JB
☎ 0181 943 1325

Trattoria Sorrento, 132 High Street, Teddington, TW11 8JB ☎ 0181 977 4757

Twickenham: Fishermen's Hut Organic Food Restaurant, The Nelson Public House, 175
Hampton Road, Twickenham, ☎ 0181 255 6222

Northamptonshire: Fawsley Hall, Fawsley, Daventry, NN1 3BA ☎ 01327 892000

Northumberland: Langley Castle, Langley-on-Tyne, Hexham, NE47 5LV ☎ 01434 688888

Oxfordshire: Chinnor: Sir Charles Napier, Spriggs Alley, Chinnor, Oxon, OX9 4BX
☎ 01494 483011

Fingest: Chequers Inn, Fingest, Henley-on-Thames, RG9 6QD ☎ 01491 638335

Great Milton: Le Manoir aux Quat' Saisons, Church Road, Great Milton,
Nr. Oxford, OX44 7PD ☎ 01844 278881

Headington: Royal Oak Farm Shop, Royal Oak Farm, Beckley, Oxford, OX3 9TY
☎ 01865 351246

Oxford: Le Petit Blanc, 71-72 Walton Street, Oxford, OX2 6AG ☎ 01865 510999

South Leigh: Mason Arms, South Leigh, Witney, Oxon, OX8 6XN ☎ 01993 702485

Staffordshire: Burton-upon-Trent: Dovecliff Hall, Stretton, Burton-upon-Trent, DE13 0DJ
☎ 01283 531818

Surrey: Cobham: Snail, 17 Portsmouth Road, Cobham, ☎ 01932 862409

Richmond: Crowthers, 481 Upper Richmond Road West, SW14 7PU ☎ 0181 876 6372

Thai Elephant, 1 Wakefield Road, Richmond, ☎ 0181 940 5114

Shere: White Horse Inn, Middle Street, Shere, Guildford, GU5 9HS ☎ 01483 202518

Tyne and Wear: Newcastle-upon-Tyne: Copthorne Hotel, The Close, Quayside, Newcastle
upon Tyne NE1 3RT ☎ 0191 222 0333

21 Queen Street, Quayside, Newcastle upon Tyne, NE 3UG ☎ 0191 222 0755

Wiltshire: Ford: White Hart Inn, Ford, New Chippenham, Wiltshire, SN14 8RT ☎ 01249
782213

Lacock: King John's Hunting Lodge, Tea rooms and guest house, Lacock, Wiltshire
☎ 01249 730313

Lucknam Park, Colerne, Wiltshire, SN14 8AZ ☎ 01225 742777

Nomansland: Les Mirabelles, Forest Edge Road, Nomansland, SP5 2BN ☎ 01794 390205

Warminster: Temple Restaurant, Bishopstrow House, Warminster, BA12 9HH
☎ 01985 212312

Yorkshire: Scarborough: Harbour Bar, 1-2 Sandside, Forshaw Road, YO11 1PE
☎ 017723 373 662

Sheffield: Old Vicarage, Ridgeway Moor, Marsh Lane Road, Sheffield S12 3XW
☎ 0114 247 5814

NORTHERN IRELAND

Belfast: Europa Hotel, Great Victoria Street, Belfast, BT2 7AP ☎ 02890 327000

SCOTLAND

Fort William: Inverlochy Castle, Torlundy, Fort William, PH33 6SN ☎ 01397 702 177
Glasgow: Malmaison, 278 West George Street, Glasgow, G2 4LL ☎ 0141 572 1000
  Yes, 22 West Nile Street, Glasgow, G1 4LL ☎ 0141 221 8044
Lochinver: Lochinver's Larder, Main Street, Lochinver, IV27 4JY ☎ 01571 844 356
Spean Bridge, near Fort William: Old Station Restaurant, Station Road, PH34 4EP
    ☎ 01397 712 535
Ullapool: Altanaharrie Inn, Ullapool, IV26 2SS ☎ 01854 633 230
  Morefield Motel, North Road, Ullapool, Rosshire, IV26 2TQ ☎ 01854 612 161

WALES

Beaumaris: Henllys Hall Hotel,Beaumaris, Isle of Anglesy, LO58 8HV ☎ 01248 810 412
Crickhowell: Nantyffin Cider Mill Inn, Crickhowell, ☎ 01873 810 775
Glyntawe: Gwynn Arms
Hay on Wye: Nino's ☎ 01497 821 932
  Oscars Bistro, Oscars High Town, Hay-on-Wye, HR3 5AE ☎ 01497 821 193
Llyswen: Griffin Inn, Llyswen, Powys, LD3 0YP ☎ 01874 754 241
  Llangoed Hall, Llyswen, Powys, LD3 0YP ☎ 01874 754 525
Seion, Gwynedd: Ty'n Rhos Country House and Restaurant, Llanddeiniolen, Seion,
    Caernarfon, LL55 3AE ☎ 01248 670 489

IRELAND

Dingle, Co. Kerry: Beginish Restaurant, Green Street, Dingle. Co Kerry ☎ 00353 66915 1588
  Dick Mack's, Green Street, Dingle ☎ 00353 66915 1960
  Milltown House, Dingle, Co. Kerry. by Slea Head Drive ☎ 00353 66915 1372
Dublin: Gallagher's Boxty House and Shebeen, 83 Middle Abbey Street, Dublin 1
    ☎ 003531 8729861
  Patrick Guildbaud, 21 Upper Merrion Street, Dublin D2 ☎ 00353 1676 4192
  Shelbourne Hotel, St. Stephen's Green, Dublin ☎ 00353 1766 471
Kenmare: Park Hotel, Kenmare, Co. Kerry ☎ 00353 64412 00
Mallow, Co. Cork: Longueville House, Mallow, Co. Cork. ☎ 00353 2247 156
Dromoland Castle, Newmarket on Fergus, Co. Clare ☎ 00353 613 8144

BELGIUM

Bruges: Breydel de Coninck ☎ 0032 5033 97 46
  De Karmeliet ☎ 0032 5033 82 59
  De Snippe ☎ 0032 5033 70 70
  Den Gouden Harynck ☎ 0032 5033 76 37
  Heer Halewyn ☎ 0032 5033 92 61/5033 92 20
  Relais Oud Huis Amsterdam ☎ 0032 5034 18 10

CARIBBEAN

Barbados: Carambola ☎ 00 1 246 432 0832
   The Cliff ☎ 00 1 246 432 1922
   Coral Reef ☎ 00 1 246 422 2372
   Kingsley Club Closed
   La Maison ☎ 00 1 246 432 1156
   Lone Start Hotel & Restaurant
   Royal Pavilion
   Sandy Lane Hotel reopening in 2000
   Treasure Beach ☎ 00 1 246 432 1346
Parrot Cay ☎ 00 1 649 946 7788
St Lucia: Bang Between the Pitons ☎ 00 1 758 459 7864
   Jalousie Plantation Resort and Spa ☎ 00 1 758 459 7666
St Martin: Fish Pot ☎ 00590 875 088
   Mario's ☎ 00590 870 636
   La Samanna ☎ 00590 876 400
   La Santal ☎ 00590 857 348

EGYPT

Cairo: La Belle Epoque, Nile Hilton ☎ 00 20 2 578 0444
   Cairo Sheraton ☎ 00 20 2 336 9800
   Gezira Sheraton ☎ 00 20 2 341 1333
   Mena House Oberoi Hotel ☎ 00 20 2 383 3222
   Windsor Hotel ☎ 00 20 2 591 5277

FRANCE

Paris: Brasserie Bofinger ☎ 0033 1 42 72 87 82
   Lido ☎ 0033 1 42 66 27 37
   Napoli Bar Restaurant Pizzeria ☎ 0033 1 40 11 15 00
   Plaza Athénée ☎ 0033 1 53 67 66 65
   Ritz ☎ 0033 1 43 16 30 30
   Tour d'Argent ☎ 0033 1 43 54 23 31
Antibes: La Bonne Auberge ☎ 0033 4 93 33 36 35
Avignon: Hôtel de la Mirande ☎ 0033 4 90 85 93 93
Barbizon: Bas-Bréau ☎ 0033 1 60 66 40 05
Cagnes-sur-Mer: Charlot ler ☎ 0033 4 93 31 00 07
   Josy-Jo ☎ 0033 4 93 20 68 76
Deauville: Brasserie Miocque ☎ 0033 2 31 98 66 22
   Hôtel Normandy ☎ 0033 2 31 98 66 22
   La Grande Corniche: La Chaumiere ☎ 00 33 493 017 768
Eze: Le Château Eza ☎ 0033 4 93 41 12 24
Falaize: Château du Tertre ☎ 0033 2 31 90 01 04
Fayence: La Moulin de la Camandoule ☎ 0033 4 94 76 00 84
Fleurie: Le Cep ☎ 0033 4 74 04 10 77
Golfe-Juan: Bistrot du Port ☎ 0033 4 93 63 71 16/63 76 82
   Tétou ☎ 0033 4 93 63 71 16/63 76 82

Haut-de-Cagnes: Le Cagnard ☎ 0033 4 93 20 73 21
Honfleur: Ferme Saint Siméon ☎ 0033 2 31 81 78 00
La Mole: Byblos ☎ 0033 4 94 56 68 00
　　Résidence de la Pinede ☎ 0033 4 94 33 91 00
L'Isle-sur-la-Sorgue: Le Jardin des Quais ☎ 0033 4 90 38 56 17
Lyon: Château de Bagnols ☎ 0033 4 74 71 40 00
St-Jean-Cap-Ferrat: Grand Hôtel du Cap Ferrat ☎ 0033 4 93 76 50 50
　　Hôtel Royal Riviera ☎ 0033 4 93 76 31 00
　　Le Provençal ☎ 0033 4 93 76 03 97
　　La Réserve de Beaulieu ☎ 0033 4 93 01 00 01
　　Sloop ☎ 0033 4 93 76 03 39
　　La Voile d'Or ☎ 0033 4 93 01 13 13
St-Paul-de-Vence: Colombe d'Or ☎ 0033 4 93 32 80 02
St-Rémy-de-Provence: L'Assiette de Marie ☎ 0033 4 90 92 32 14
St Tropez: Auberge de la Môle ☎ 0033 4 94 49 57 01
Tournus: Restaurant Greuze ☎ 0033 3 85 51 13 52
Vence: Chez Guy ☎ 0033 4 93 58 25 82

MONACO

Monte Carlo: Chez Gianni ☎ 00 377 93 30 46 33
　　Grill of the Hôtel de Paris ☎ 00 379 92 16 29 66
　　La Piazza ☎ 00 377 93 50 47 00
　　Rampoldi ☎ 00 377 93 50 43 84

GERMANY

Dinkelsbühl: Hotel Restaurant Eisenkrug ☎ 0049 9851 577 00
　　Café Extrablatt ☎ 0049 9851
Kraftshof near Nuremberg: Gasthaus Schwarzer Adler ☎ 0049 911 34 56 91
Nuremberg: Belm Schlenkeria
　　Gasthaus Rottner ☎ 0049 911 612 20 32
　　The Grand ☎ 0049 911 232 20
Rothenburg: Hotel Meistertrunk ☎ 0049 98 61 60 77

ITALY

Capri: La Capannina ☎ 0039 081 83 70 732
　　Feraglioni ☎ 0039 081 83 70 320
　　Da Gemma ☎ 0039 081 83 70 461
　　Quisiana ☎ 0039 081 83 70 788
Cernobbio: Trattoria del Vapore ☎ 0039 031 51 03 08
　　Villa d'Este ☎ 0039 031 34 81
Chianti: Restaurant La Vigne (Radda) ☎ 0039 0377 73 86 40
　　Villa Sangiovese (Panzzano) ☎ 0039 055 85 24 61
Comacina, Lake Como: Locanda dell'Isola Comacina ☎ 0039 0344 55 083
Fiesole: Villa San Michele ☎ 0039 055 59 451
Florence: Bibo ☎ 0039 055 23 98 554
　　Cantinetta Verrazzano ☎ 0039 055 26 85 90

Grand Hotel Villa Cora ☎ 0039 055 22 98 451
Rivoire Pasticceria ☎ 0039 055 21 13 02/21 44 12
Leivi: Cà Peo ☎ 0039 0185 31 90 96
Montignoso/Pisa: Il Bottaccio ☎ 0039 0585 34 00 31
Milan: Aimo e Nadia ☎ 0039 0185 26 9037
Ristorante Delfino ☎ 0039 4185 26 90 81
Portifino: Hotel Splendido ☎ 0039 0185 26 95 51
Lo Stella ☎ 0039 0185 26 90 07
Santa Margherita, near Portofino: Skipper ☎ 0039 0185 28 99 50
La Stalla ☎ 0039 0185 28 94 47
Siena: Il Campo ☎ 0039 0377 28 07 25
Venice: Al Frati (Murano) ☎ 0039 041 73 664
La Caravella ☎ 0039 041 52 08 901
Cipriani ☎ 0039 041 52 07 744
Da Ivo ☎ 0039 041 52 05 889
Florian, Quadri and Lavena ☎ 0039 041 52 05 641
Harry's Bar ☎ 0039 041 52 85 777
Hotel Monaco ☎ 0039 041 52 00 211
Locanda Cipriani (Torcello) ☎ 0039 041 73 01 50
Osteria Da Fiore ☎ 0039 041 72 13 08
Restaurant Nani (San Pietro, Volta) ☎ 0039 041 52 79 100
Trattoria da Romano ☎ 0039 041 73 00 30
Trattoria San Marco ☎ 00309 041 52 85 242
Vernazzza: Trattoria Bar Gianni ☎ 0039 0187 81 22 28

LUXEMBOURG

Saint-Michel ☎ 00352 22 32 15

MADEIRA

Arsénio's ☎ 00 351 91 22 40 07
Reid's Hotel ☎ 00 351 91 76 30 04

MOROCCO

Marrakesh: Chez Ali ☎ 00 212 4 30 77 30
Dar Marjana ☎ 00 212 4 44 11 10
Diaffa ☎ 00 212 4 42 6898
La Mamounia ☎ 00 212 4 44 89 81
Le Tobsil ☎ 00 212 4 44 49 52
Yacout ☎ 00 212 4 38 29 29
Taroudannt: Gazelle d'Or ☎ 00 212 8 85 20 39/85 20 48

SOUTH AFRICA

Cape Town: The Cellars ☎ 0027 21 194 2137
Mount Nelson Hotel Grill Room
Constantiaberg: Constantia Uitsig ☎ 0027 21 794 6500

Franschhoek: La Petite Ferme ☎ 0029 21 876 3016
Mala Mala and Ngala safari camps ☎ 0029 110784 6832
Sun City: Palace ☎ 0027 14 557 10 00

SWITZERLAND

Cully: Le Raisin ☎ 00 41 28 79 92 131
Feurtesoey: Gasthaus Rossli ☎ 00 41 33 75 51 012
Gstaad: The Chesery ☎ 00 41 33 74 42 45
  Le Cave at The Olden ☎ 00 41 33 74 43 444
  Eagle Club ☎ 00 41 33 74 43 670
  Palace Hotel ☎ 00 41 33 74 85 050
  Park Hotel ☎ 00 41 33 74 89 800
  The Saanenhof ☎ 00 41 33 74 41 515

THAILAND/BURMA

Bangkok: Oriental Hotel ☎ 00 64 2 23 60 400
Road to Mandalay ☎ 020 7805 5100

TRAVEL

British Rail: National Rail Enquiries ☎ 0345 484 950
British Midland: Heathrow ☎ 0181 745 7321
Concorde: Linkline ☎ 0345 222 100
Eurostar ☎ 0345 303030
Thai Airways, 41 Albemarle Street, W1 ☎ 020 7491 7953

INDEX